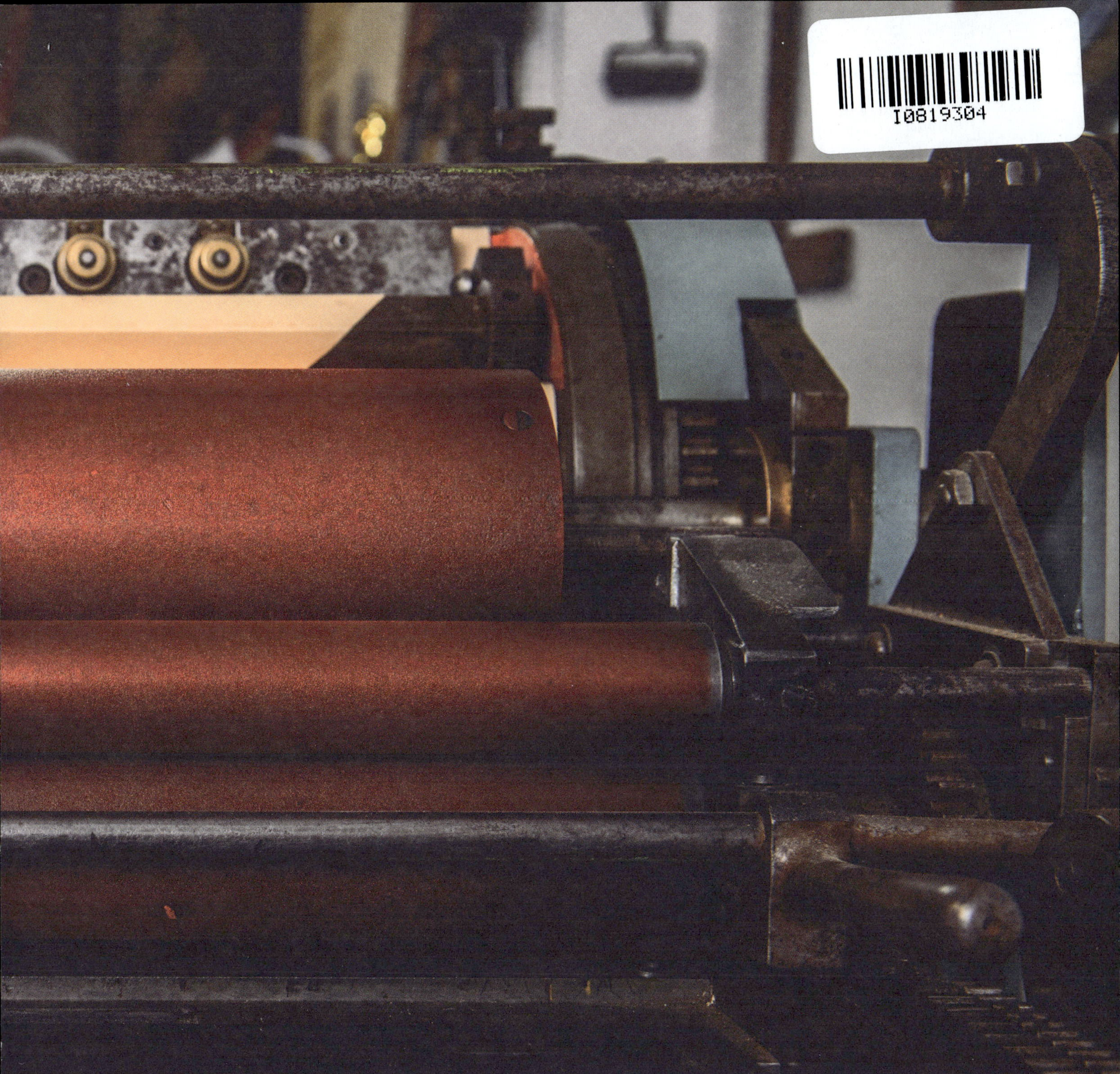
I0819304

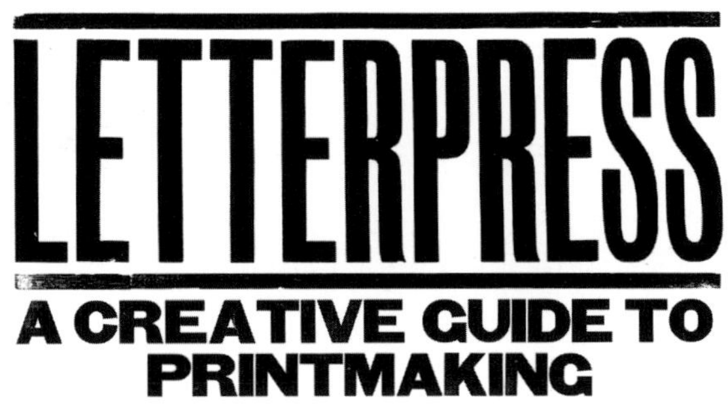
LETTERPRESS
A CREATIVE GUIDE TO
PRINTMAKING

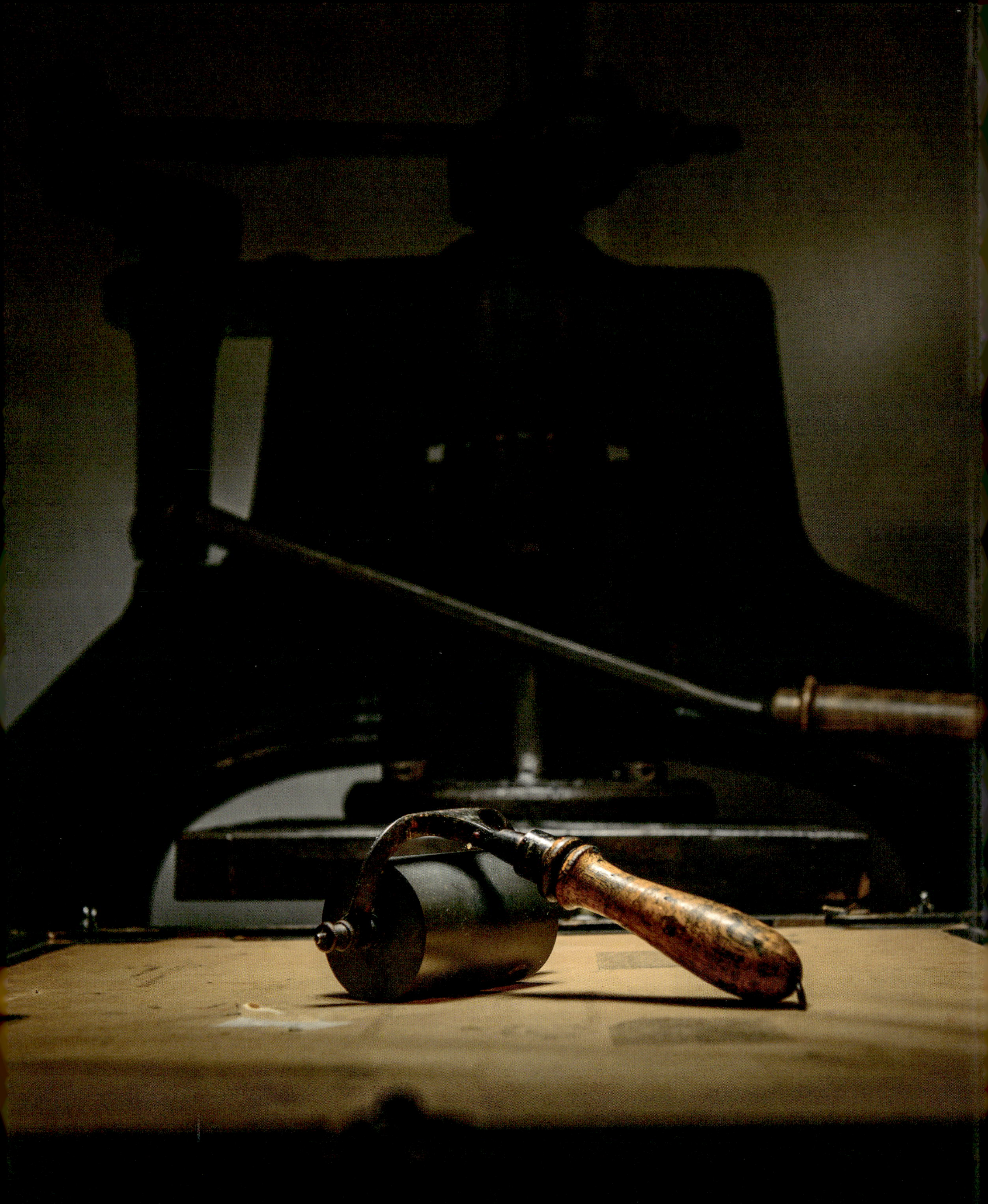

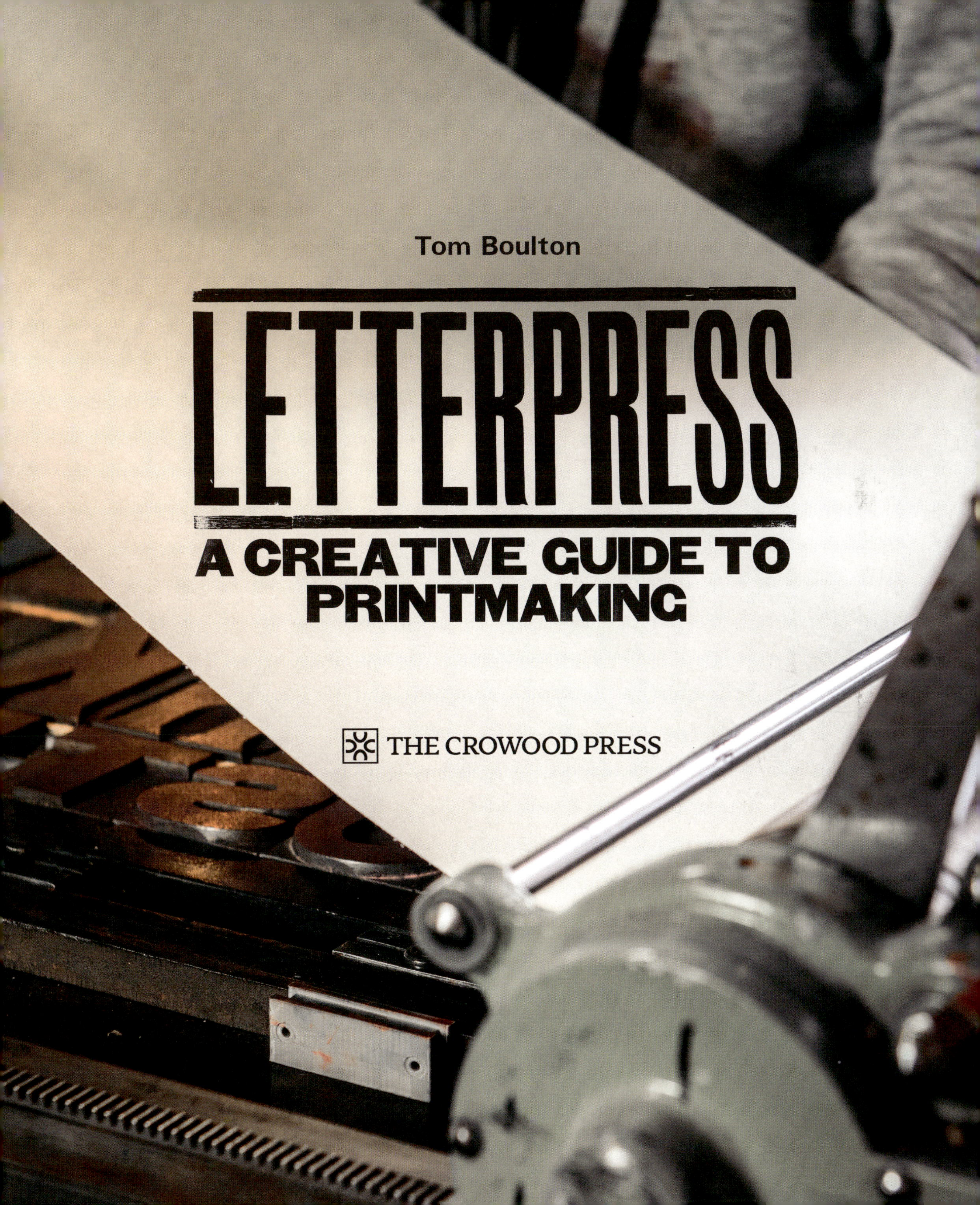

Tom Boulton

LETTERPRESS

A CREATIVE GUIDE TO PRINTMAKING

THE CROWOOD PRESS

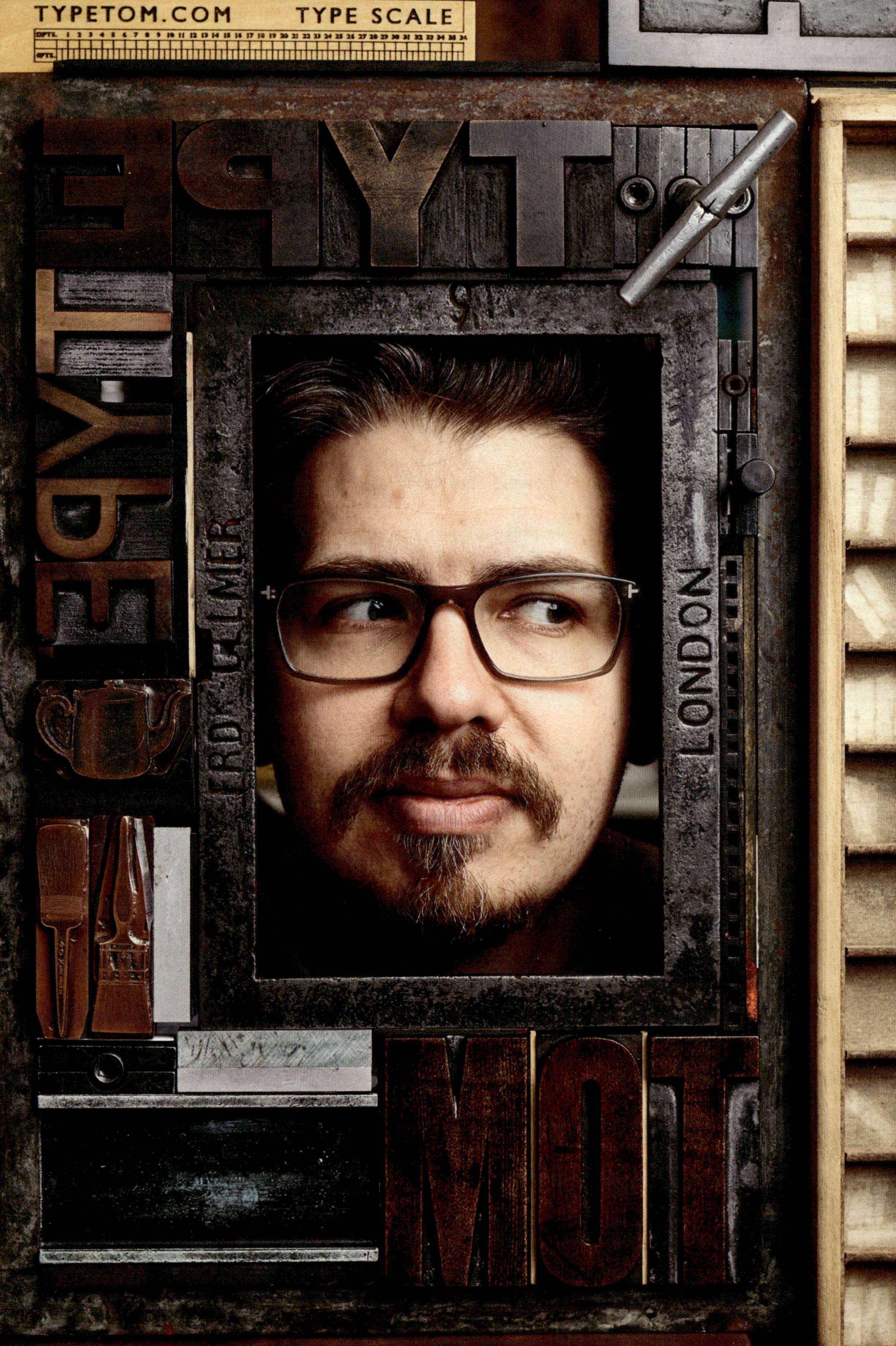

TYPETOM.COM
TYPE SCALE
LONDON

CONTENTS

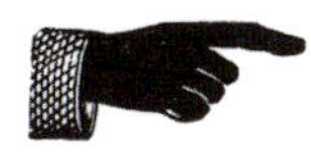

Introduction

The foundation blocks of letterpress printing were laid all the way back in the fifteenth century, when Johannes Gutenberg created the first wooden press. Fast forward over several hundred years, through the creation of metal cast iron presses, movable cast lead type, beautiful wood type and all manner of new ideas on how to print faster and cheaper, printed matter became available for the masses.

The high-paced development of technology that ensued during the industrial revolution meant printing took its place in history and helped to shape the modern world. The creation of this massive industry allowed the printing of books, tickets, newspapers, advertising, and more. Whilst letterpress is, and always will be, a key part of the history of the development of the modern world as we know it, it has stood the test of time and has gone through many periods of re-incarnation.

Some of these periods have been kinder to letterpress than others, with the value of what this process has to offer, including equipment, tools, type and a love for a craft and industry being seen differently by evolving generations, giving this unique process a true sense of working in the past, surviving in the present and evolving into the future.

At its core, letterpress printing is a very simple form of relief printing. A very smooth and flat surface has a layer of ink applied, then paper is placed on top and through the application of pressure the printing block is squeezed into the paper, transferring the ink to it from the block, creating a print that mirrors the original block. This logic applies to all forms of letterpress printing whether printing with a collection of ancient wood type, moveable lead type, vintage picture blocks or some lovingly hand-cut lino. As a craft that draws on skill and experience, letterpress can be complicated and daunting at times, sometimes feeling more difficult than it actually is.

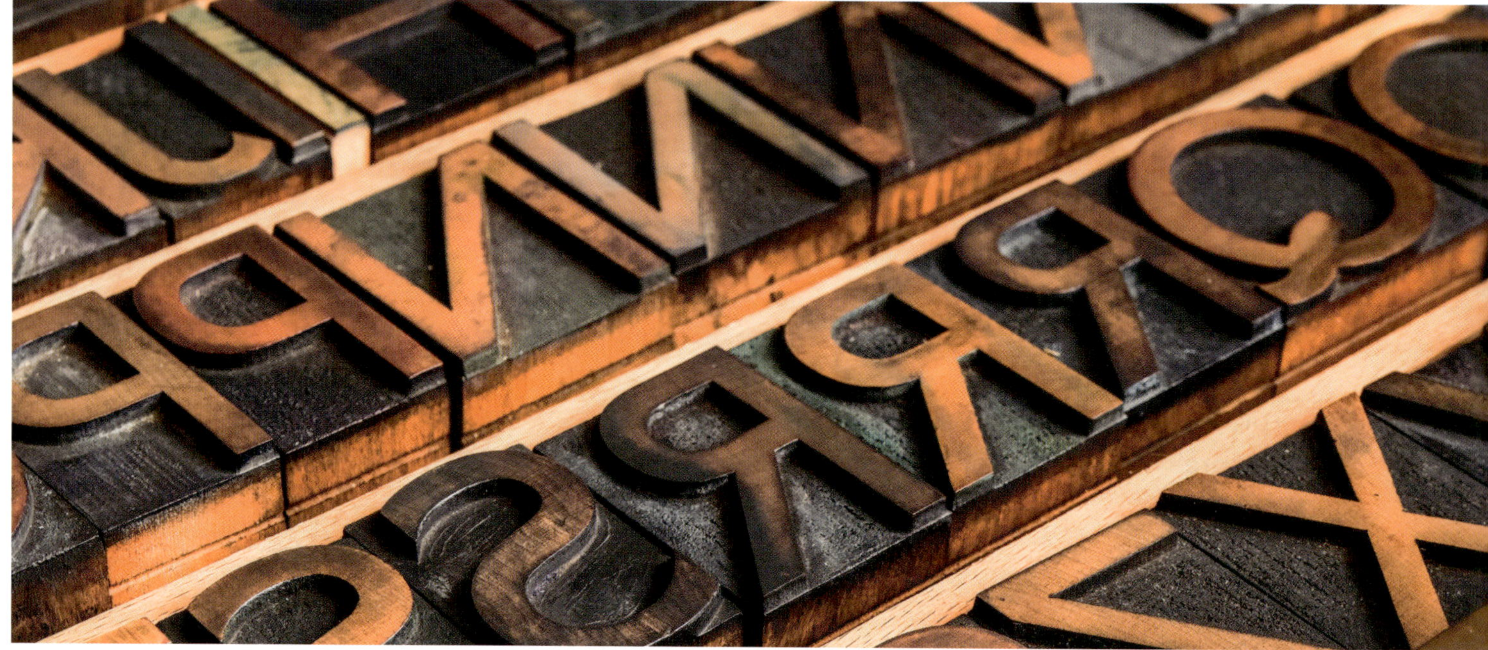

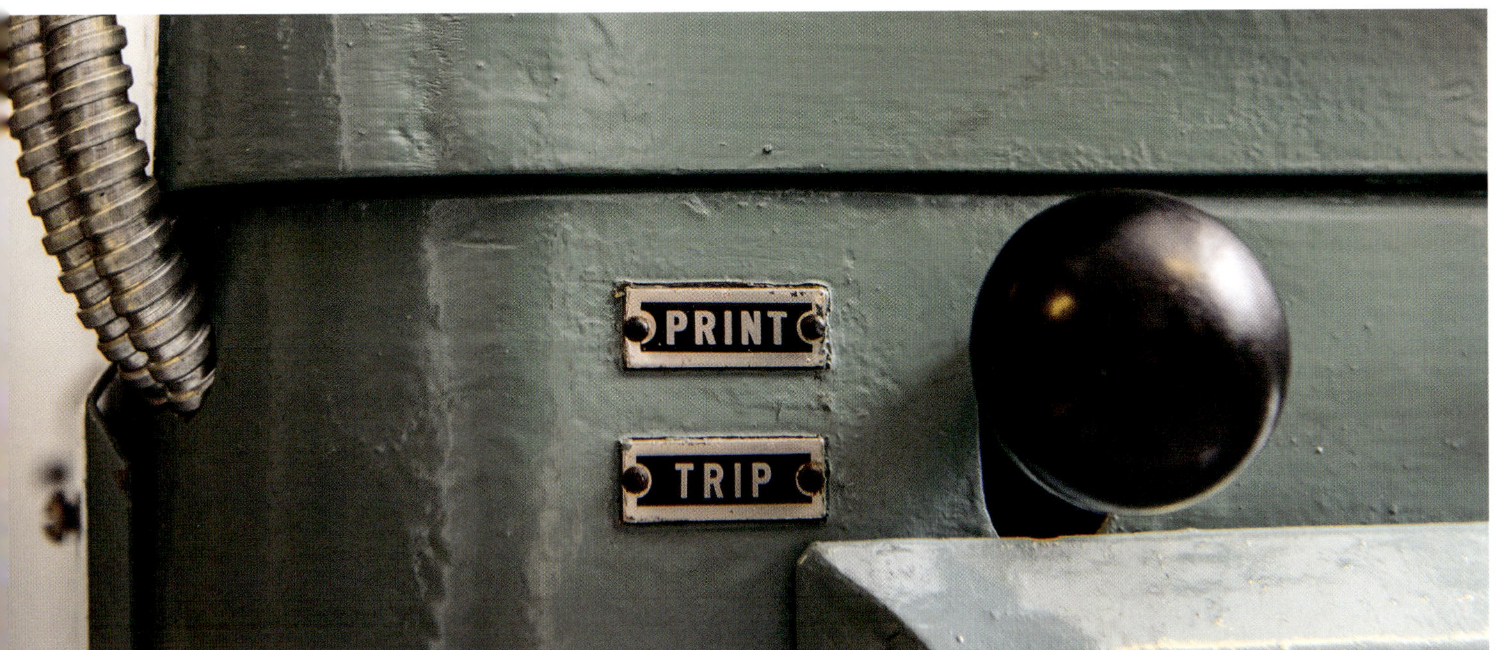

 Print/trip lever on Vandercook printing press.

For me, letterpress evolved out of a love of design and of the classical type aesthetic that was really founded in early printing. This, fused with the concepts of hand-made, traditional craft and mass production was a winning combination for me. I came to letterpress as a graphic designer, and I still approach printing as one. That is to say that I have a passion for design and I do not mind how long the printing takes to achieve it. Letterpress has practical limits but at the same time, anything is possible. Creating in a workshop brings me joy, and working with type feels interactive and responsive rather than the more passive feeling of designing sitting in front of a screen.

I have written this book to try to share some of my 20-ish years of experience working with letterpress.Turning to letterpress early in my design career offered me the chance to design and make.

Wood type.

This soon spiralled out of control and led me to buying, collecting and owning a large collection of both type and presses, teaching myself how to use, restore and work with everything letterpress along the way.

As a designer and printer, I have had to make letterpress work in the modern world – this is not a history lesson, instead it's about respecting the history of letterpress and seeing how it can work in the here and now, how we can preserve what we have and expand to the future. The layout of this book is such that you can either read it as a whole or dip in and out, and look at some pretty pictures along the way. The aim is to get you started printing (if you are new to it) or for the more experienced printer, show you how I do things, with the same open and honest approach I give when teaching practical workshops.

So, let's get printing.

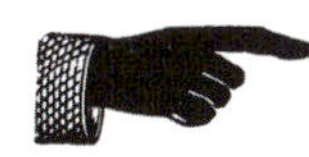

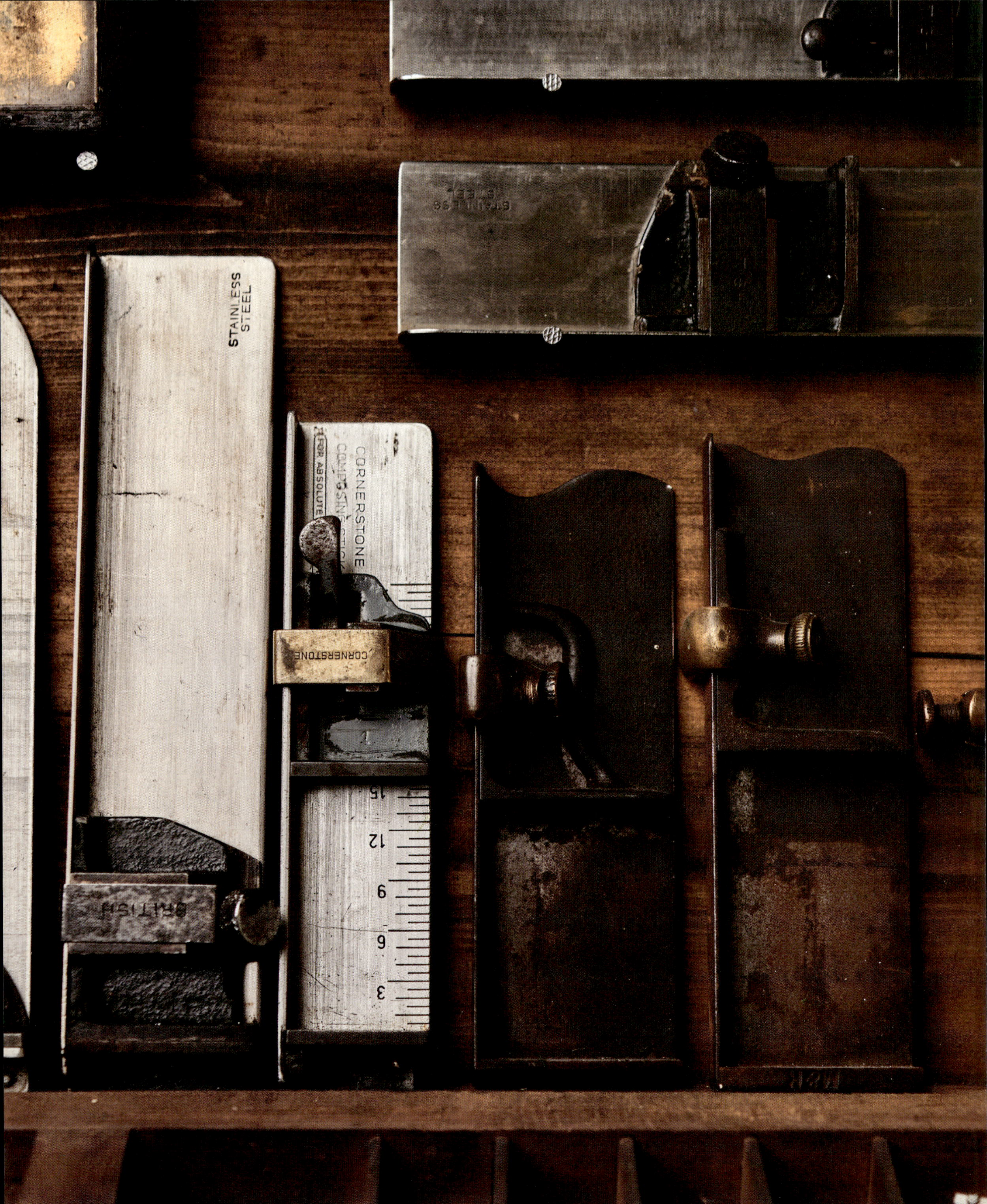
STAINLESS
STEEL
CORNERSTONE

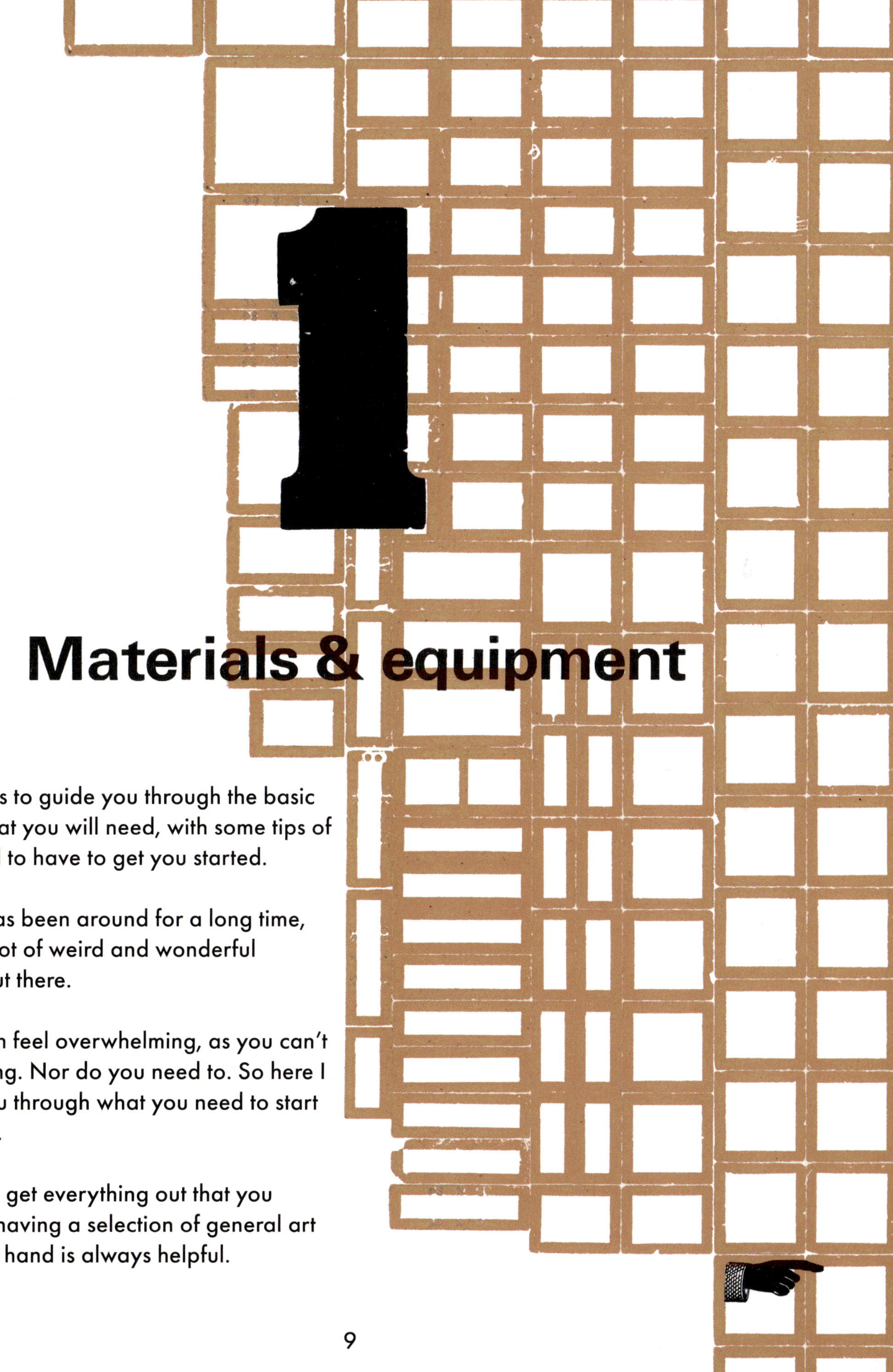

1

Materials & equipment

This chapter is to guide you through the basic equipment that you will need, with some tips of what is useful to have to get you started.

Letterpress has been around for a long time, so there is a lot of weird and wonderful equipment out there.

Often this can feel overwhelming, as you can't buy everything. Nor do you need to. So here I will guide you through what you need to start pulling prints.

A top tip is to get everything out that you may need – having a selection of general art equipment to hand is always helpful.

General handy stuff to have when printing

I would suggest always having a note pad, pencils, a rubber, pens, a craft knife, a ruler, scissors, tracing paper, a flat head screwdriver, a small flexible artist pallet knife and masking tape. Try to get organised and work tidily; aim for everything to have its place and stay there. It makes printing a lot more fun when you are not constantly looking for what you need. I am a fan of old tool boxes, and I have a general printing equipment one, which has all the useful day-to-day stuff in, so when I start printing I can just grab the tool box and everything is ready to go.

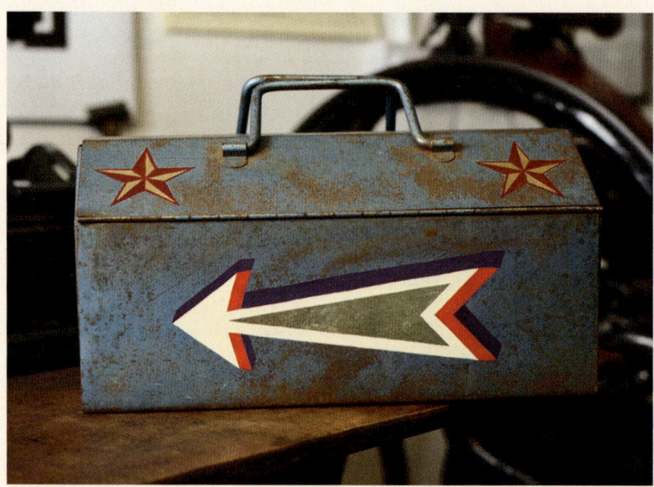

Repurposed & hand sign painted vintage toolbox.

Cleaning

You are going to need some rags. It's surprising how much material you can get through when cleaning up, so collect plenty. Old T-shirts and similar items that would not be fit for the charity shop can be cut up into perfect cleaning down rags. You will also need some cleaning chemicals. There are a variety of different options depending on your setup and where you plan to print. Low-odour white spirit works great on cleaning down type and rollers, but you do need ventilation so this may not be ideal for some.

Another option is orange oil, which I use when working outside of my own workshop. There are brands like Zest-It who sell large and more portable sizes. As you can guess it's made from oranges and does indeed have a strong orange smell which a lot of people seem to like – I am personally not a fan of the smell. It's a good idea to have rubbish bags on hand so as soon as you have cleaned your rollers, type, etc., you can bag and bin your used rags.

Invest in a storage box for your rags. You would ideally have one for clean rags and one for previously used but not really dirty yet! I have a very large vintage Swarfega tin that I use for storing clean rags and cleaning chemicals in and an old army ammo tin for dirty rags. Old army ammo tins can be easily purchased at army surplus stores and are not expensive, they also are often airtight and hold in any smells. Gloves are a very good idea to protect your skin when cleaning ink, I personally use black disposable gloves sold for tattoo artists as they seem slightly stronger than the standard blue nitrile gloves and are usually sold in boxes of 100 pairs. I usually get quite a lot of wear out of one pair so I do not throw them away after each use – they can be taken off carefully and kept in the rag storage tin. These can be purchased easily online with a quick search of 'tattoo gloves black' – just check what size you need before purchasing. A packet of baby wipes is always a good thing to have to hand as they are great for cleaning stubborn ink off hands, worktop or roller handle.

Type

Letterpress type has become highly collectable in more recent years. I was lucky that I started my letterpress journey some 20 years ago when the general interest was not massive, so purchasing type was not particularly expensive. Buying type now is pricey and once you start collecting, it does feel like you can never have enough. The truth is, you never can have enough – just accept that you are starting to collect items that were part of a huge industry and there is no such thing as a complete collection. The reality is that the type does lead the design and during the process of creating, you will find that you have favourite fonts that just work for you. These fonts often are not the largest size or the most interesting in design. My most used fonts are the simpler fonts with a good number of letters, they are not heavily worn but have a nice charm of character when printed (showing a hint of the wood grain) and aren't too large in size. Large fonts look great, but in reality you have only so much room on your sheet of paper and only so much space inside your printing press. If it does not fit then it will not print.

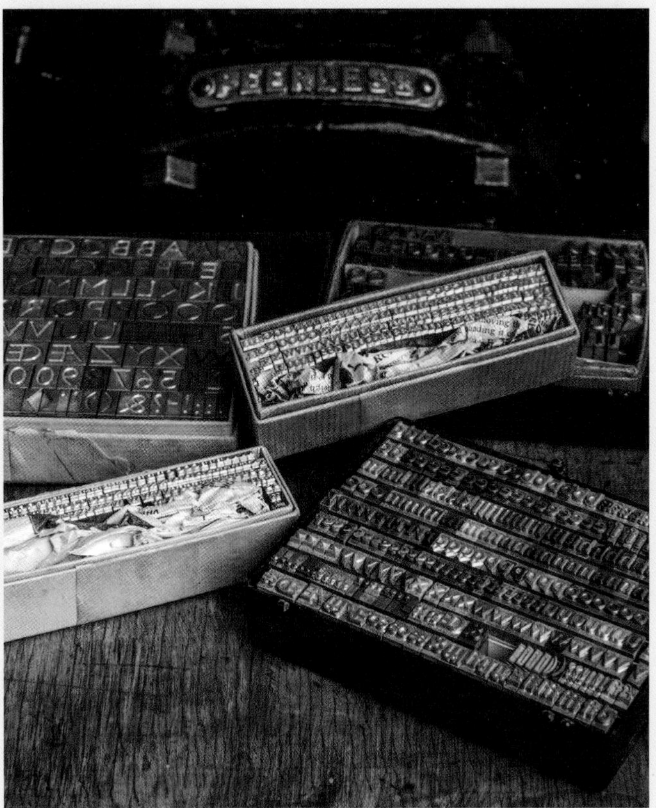

Small sets of lead type.

Lead type

Lead type is smaller, traditionally it was really only made up to 72pt size (about 25mm tall). This is due to the physical weight – when you have a full set of 72pt lead type you realise just how heavy it is and just why they didn't make it any larger. It's a good idea to have a collection of different-sized sets; you can buy them on eBay quite easily.

When you search for letterpress lead type you will find that popular fonts like Gill Sans will be more expensive. Look for badly advertised and poorly photographed items – they may not attract as much attention so you may get yourself a bargain. You can also search for letterpress cabinets and buy lots at once as this can work out cheaper, but they may not be fonts you'd necessarily choose. In the UK Adana made small type cabinets that sit nicely on a desk and look very smart, they come up regularly for sale on eBay and often will come with a small collection of different fonts – this is how I started with a small cabinet of type. It is quite good to start collecting small and slow as then you can learn what you like and where to spend your time and money.

Wood type

Wood type in the modern world is what people tend to visualise when they think about letterpress graphically and artistically. It was used for posters, advertising and all sorts of wonderful things. Wood is obviously a lot lighter than lead so the font sizes increased massively beyond the 72pt lead type size. Today wood type is expensive and it can be hard to find complete fonts. Part-fonts present an obvious problem of not having some letters, which limits what you can do.

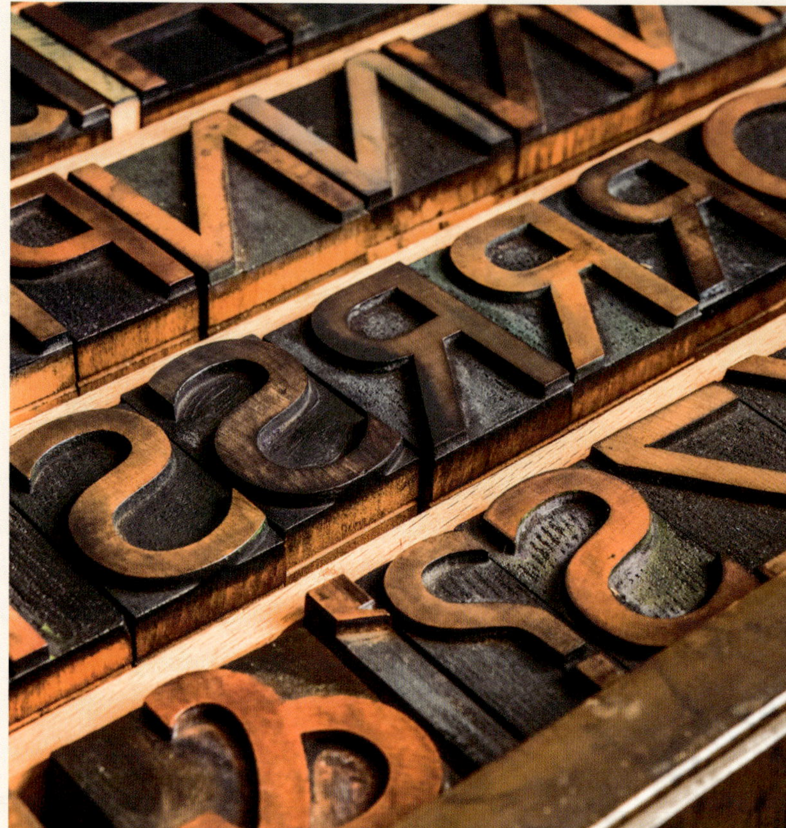

Complete set of wood type in case. ☛

Online there are many sellers who split up full sets of type to sell the letters individually. This is something I discourage people from buying, as ultimately, breaking apart full sets of type means they can never be used as they were intended. Aim to get one full set to start with. You can also find mixed cases of type online (a case is the name of the trays used to store the type), a mixed case will have a large number of different letters from different fonts jumbled together – usually the letters do not make up anywhere near the full font in one typeface. These can be quite good to own as individual letters can be inspiring and you can mix these to create weird and wonderful graphical works of art, or individual words made of jumbled letters. Unlike when a whole case of one font is broken down and sold individually, these cases tend to be the flotsam and jetsam of a print workshop. All letterpress printers have some random letters that are just nice to experiment and play with.

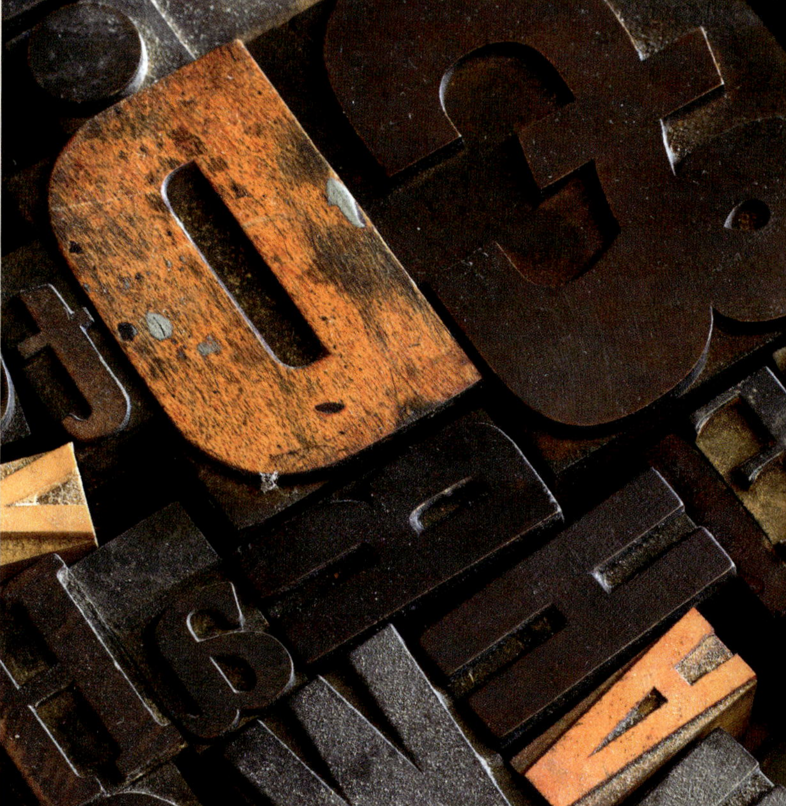

Mixed font wood type. ☛

Picture blocks

Letterpress was a massive industry with a lot of beautiful illustration and advertising materials printed, and as a consequence there are some wonderful illustrated printing blocks out there. I love my collection of picture blocks and am always adding to it. Car boot sales, antique markets and the like are great places to find random printing blocks. They often are quite cheap, and I usually only pay between £1-£3 per block. They're great to spark inspiration or to add something interesting to a design, and are just fun things to own.

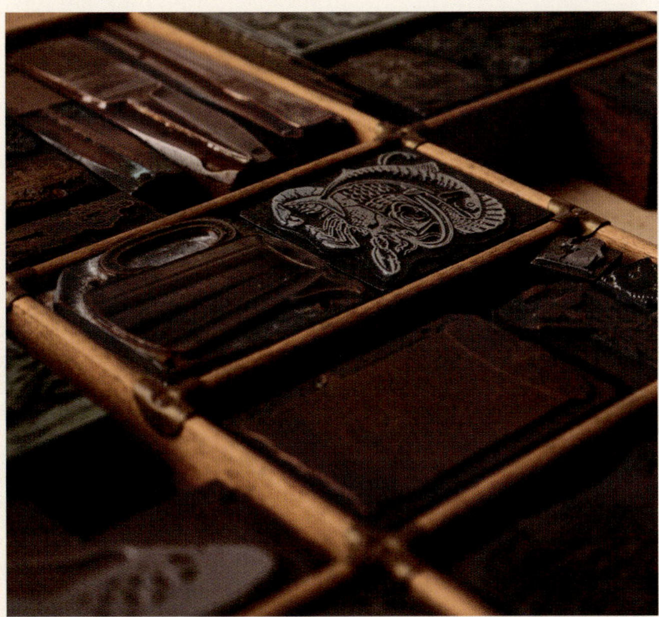

Vintage picture blocks.

Ink

Oil, water or rubber-based – they are all available; a lot is down to personal preference and what and where you are printing. Water-based inks are comparatively new in printing; great for people working at home as they're relatively odourless and easy to clean down with a rag. As these water-based inks are aimed at the newer market of creatives, they're often available in smaller quantities, which does work out more expensive when you consider the value. However, when you're starting out it is nice to have a selection of ink colours to experiment with whilst you learn and develop what works for you.

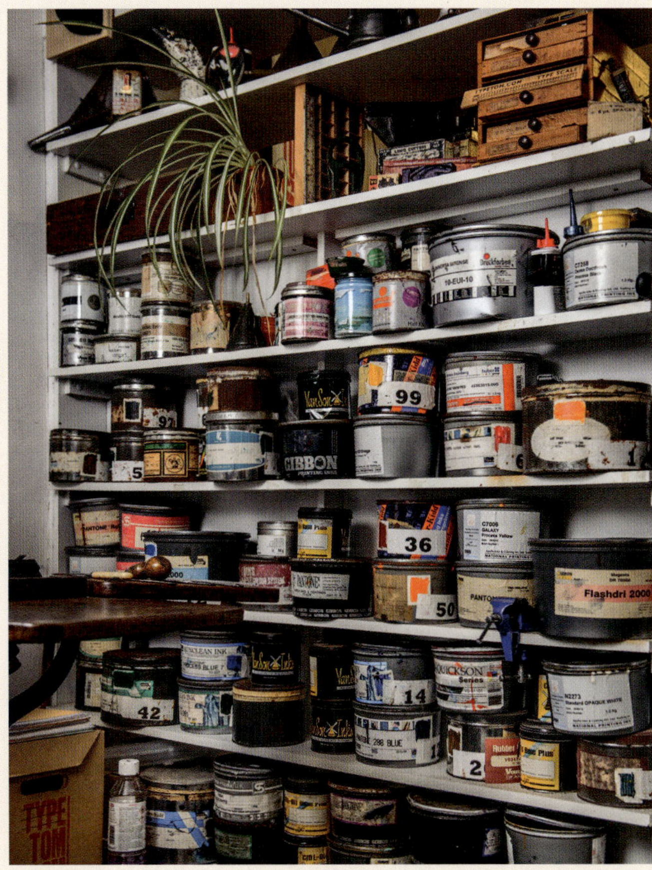

Collection of ink stored at TypeTom workshop.

Rubber-based inks, I am personally not a fan of, as they have an unpleasant smell – I wouldn't recommend them for people at home. Often these inks are more aimed at industrial or higher-scale printers. Rubber-based ink dries by absorption into the paper so can be slower drying than oil. It also does not really form a skin in the tin, which reduces waste and means the ink lasts longer, but it does go very thick with age and can be harder to work with (in my opinion). Rubber-based ink has a reputation for not drying on your press so it saves time on cleaning down, which is only really an issue for larger printers. I never risk leaving any ink on presses or rollers for more time than is absolutely needed, as it's not worth risking the time and money for new rollers.

Oil-based ink is what I primarily use and started printing with. You can now buy small quantities of oil-based ink in tubes designed specifically for letterpress, something that has become available as the interest and passion for letterpress has grown over the years. Modern ink is often a blend of linseed oil and soy, and it gives a slightly punchier, bolder, heavier or denser appearance than water-based.

Some of the letterpress ink colours that are produced now are bright and interesting, which is a really welcome addition to the age-old craft of letterpress. Oil-based and rubber-based inks do require some chemicals for cleaning down, which again means thinking about the environment that you will be printing in. You can now easily go online and search for letterpress ink, where you will find reputable companies such as Cranfield and Van Son inks. There is also an abundance of old ink still out there, sitting in tins wanting to be used. 'Old ink is good ink' is my motto. It is often also cheap ink! Most of the ink in my collection has come from when I've been collecting something else for my workshop and been offered a random box of stuff, usually for free. Often this ink is marked as litho or offset printing ink, but it works well for letterpress. Old oil-based ink in tins does form a skin, this is from the oil reacting with air around it and the process of ageing. You can simply use a fine pallet knife or wide flat head screwdriver to carefully break through this crust to get at the good ink beneath. You might find bits of the crust in the ink that can be picked out when putting the ink onto the inking glass before rolling out. It is surprising how long ink can really last – I have tins of ink in my workshop that are dated from the seventies and still can be used!

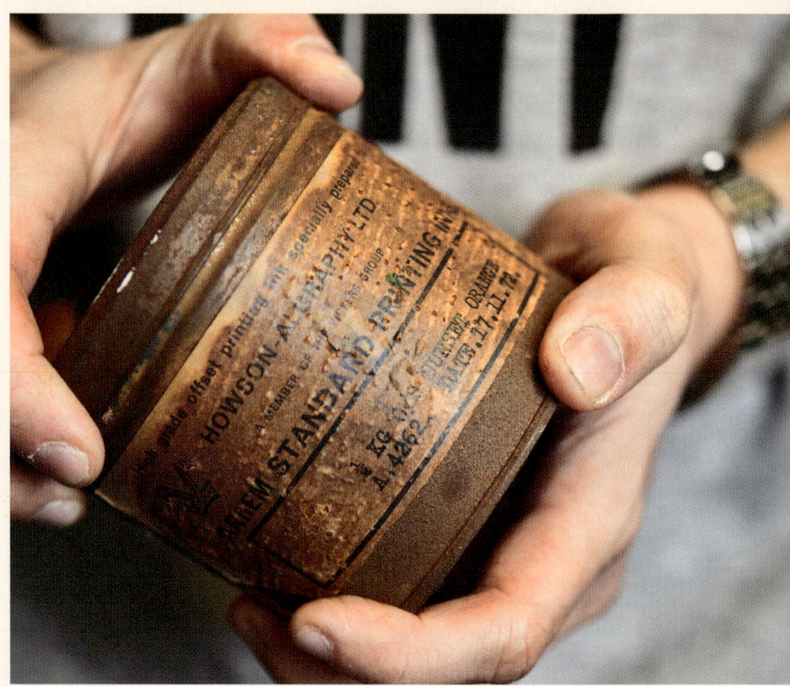

Tin of orange ink made in 1972 (still usable).

Paper

Paper is made in a variety of different ways; in the modern world most paper is heavily manufactured using wood pulp and different dyes/chemicals mixed in exact conditions and quantities to get consistent quality, texture and colours. You can still get handmade papers from specialist paper-makers; often made from natural fibres such as cotton, some are even made from more interesting raw materials like straw or elephant dung!

Different papers have different characteristics. Coated and uncoated papers vary in finish, affecting how much moisture the paper absorbs and its general appearance. Acid-free and archival paper are made to last the test of time, and if looked after well, will last a lot longer with reduced yellowing when compared to more standard paper stocks.

To start with, go to your local art store and spend some time browsing and touching paper – simply buy stuff you like. Get a selection of different colours and aim for paper that is not too textured – do not buy anything that feels like water colour painting paper.

Also buy some cheap paper that you will not be precious over. I usually print using a 160gsm smooth wove paper, which is an own-brand from my paper merchant. It is not the best paper you can buy, but it is very consistent and has a nice texture with a smooth, uncoated finish. It's also quite cheap, so when I am in the mood for experimenting, I'm not concerned by the cost of how many prints I am pulling.

Get a ream of A3 printer paper – you can find reams available at a stationery store that are around 120gsm. This gives you paper to play around with inking and colour to your heart's content pulling proof prints, then use your final paper choice for that perfect print. This gives you the freedom to experiment and see the printed results whilst keeping the process budget friendly, enabling you to save your better paper for final prints.

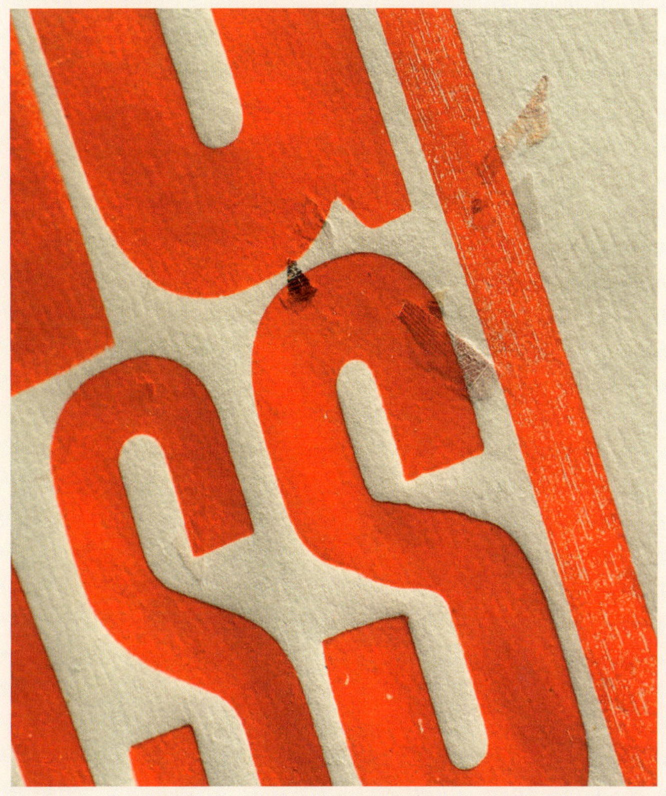

Close up of print onto recycled paper made with UK banknotes.

The interesting thing is that when I run workshops, students have a choice of different papers and they always seem to lean towards using the cheaper paper that is smoother and less textured. This is because with letterpress you are physically moulding the paper around the inked type surface to remove the ink and leave the impression and print of the type on the paper.

The more texture and the pulpier the quality of the paper, the more pressure you have to use to get a good impression, as you have to push the texture out of the paper to get the print. Depending on inking this often means you lose some of the very small and interesting detail the type has to offer. I have found through many years of printing that uncoated smooth wove paper is for me, as it offers the cleanest impression and the most control over the final print. However, it is fun to experiment, so it is always good to have a mixture of paper options. Just remember the most expensive materials do not automatically make the best prints, it is technique and the creative eye that does that.

Whilst textured paper does cause an issue with the printed finish, letterpress printing is not as limited as other processes such as screen-printing, as the inks used in letterpress do not really cause issues with wrinkling or shrinking of the paper. This means you can use very fine lightweight paper such as 33gsm onion skin paper (named for obvious reasons) or newsprint paper which is very cheap and often sold in larger quantities by kilogramme rather than by sheets. Whilst on the other end of the spectrum you can also print on super heavy weight cards and papers like GF Smith's 700gsm cards. I personally have always enjoyed printing on greyboard, which has a heavily recycled finish and is available in a variety of thicknesses.

Printing on super heavyweight card is great for items like business cards and wedding stationery, as it allows you to add more of a deboss (punching the type a little harder into the card to leave a physical impression of the type behind).

Inking plate

Inking plates are usually large (about A3 size) thick glass sheets that you roll your ink out onto. These can be purchased online and from art stores. You can also get plastic ones that have a lip around the edge. You do not have to worry about the ink running off the inking plate

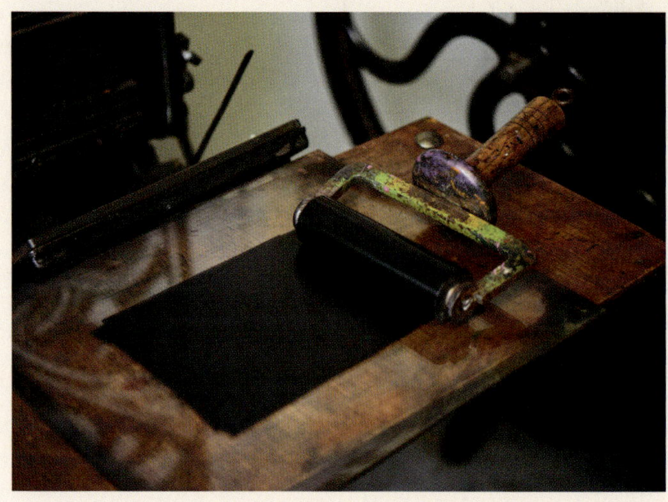

Inking roller/brayer on glass inking plate.

with letterpress, as the ink is thick and sticky. Buying inking plates from art material supplies can be expensive – I purchased toughened glass shelves from Ikea that came with nicely ground smooth edges. You can also think outside the box – if you can find a plastic/acrylic sheet around 3mm thick, that would work well. The advantage to using a plastic sheet is that they are easy and light to store away. If you're working at home and space is at a premium, this is worth considering.

Galley

A letterpress galley is a metal tray that usually has three edges on it. It's used to hold type, and in some cases to hold the type in when pulling proofing (test) prints. Some printing presses such as Farleys have an easy way to adjust the press height/pressure that the printing press rollers print at, countering the standard thickness of the galley tray, meaning you can print with the type in the galley. I personally only use the galleys for gathering type in, moving them around safely, and helping to transfer type onto the flat bed of my Vander-

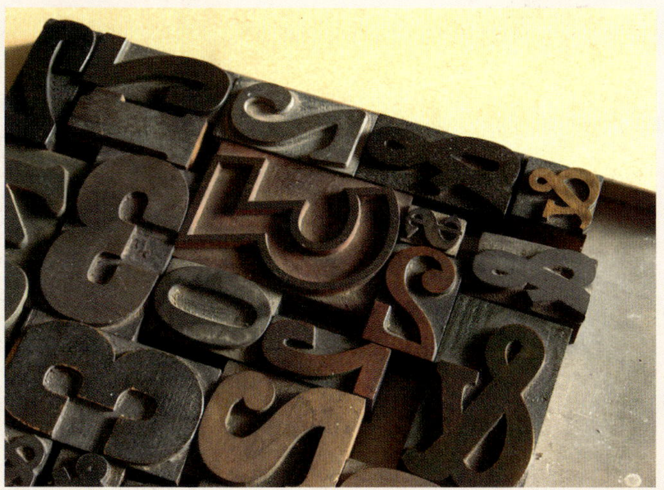

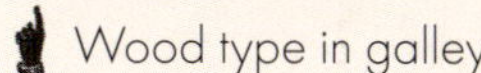 Wood type in galley.

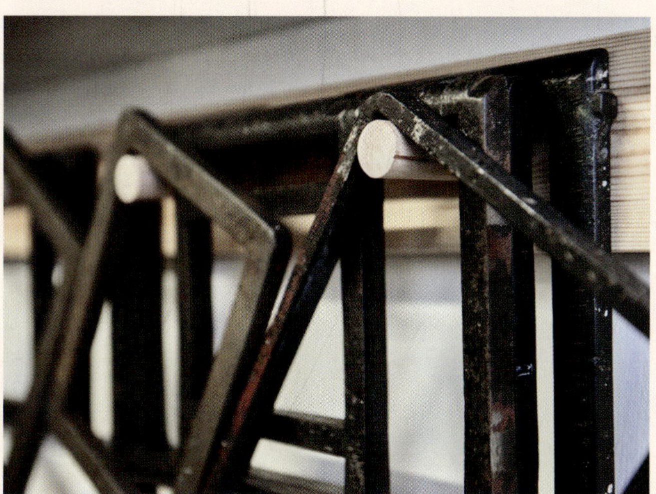

Chases hanging in workshop.

cook printing press. Some also use the galleys to store regularly printed compositions of type in, rather than disassembling. These galley trays are then stored in a galley rack – a tall slim cabinet that holds a large number of galleys.

Chase

A chase is a metal frame that you will place your type or blocks into then pack them in place using spacing material (furniture) before locking in place with quoins (expanding metal blocks) ready to print. Chases either insert into a printing press and rest on locators to make sure the frame is secure and unable to move during printing (this is the case for presses that have a clam shell-like mechanism like Adanas, Cropper Charlton & Co. Peerless, Golding Pearls, Arabs, etc.). Or if you are using a flatbed press like a proofing press, Vandercook, Farley or the like, the chase lays flat on the printing press bed. The chase size varies depending on the size of the press, so if you are purchasing a printing press make sure it has one – it can be very hard to find the correct size separately. It can, however, be a very good haggling point when purchasing a press without a chase.

Furniture

Furniture is the basic name of the spacing material that is used to pack out, space out, or surround your type, to then lock it in place. Furniture is usually made of wood (metal lead type has its own spacing material specifically for use with its relevant font). The furniture comes in a variety of lengths and widths and is cut to be lower than the type height. As the machining of furniture is done to a very high and exacting accuracy and standard, it is best to try to buy original wooden furniture rather than making your own. You really cannot have enough furniture as you will be using it to create your forme (forme – when type is arranged, locked out in a chase ready to print) that you will print from.

You often find furniture when buying other items of letterpress, as all printers required a lot of furniture so they kept hold of it. As you get started you can always browse your local DIY store's timber area for nicely planed timber. I remember in the early days buying some door-framing timber and cutting it down into lengths. Just make sure that any timber you buy is not higher than type height (UK height 0.918in).

Quoins and quoin keys

Quoins are expanding metal blocks that sit inside the chase between the metal frame and the furniture surrounding the type/blocks. The quoins have a mechanism that requires a key to be turned, expanding them to grip the furniture against the type and locking everything tight for printing. There are a few different types, makes and styles of quoins, the basic ones are Hempel quoins, which are triangles that when locked slide against each other

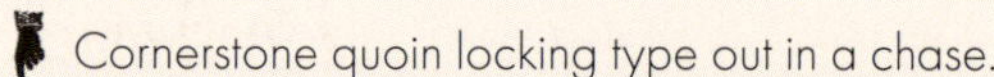

Cornerstone quoin locking type out in a chase.

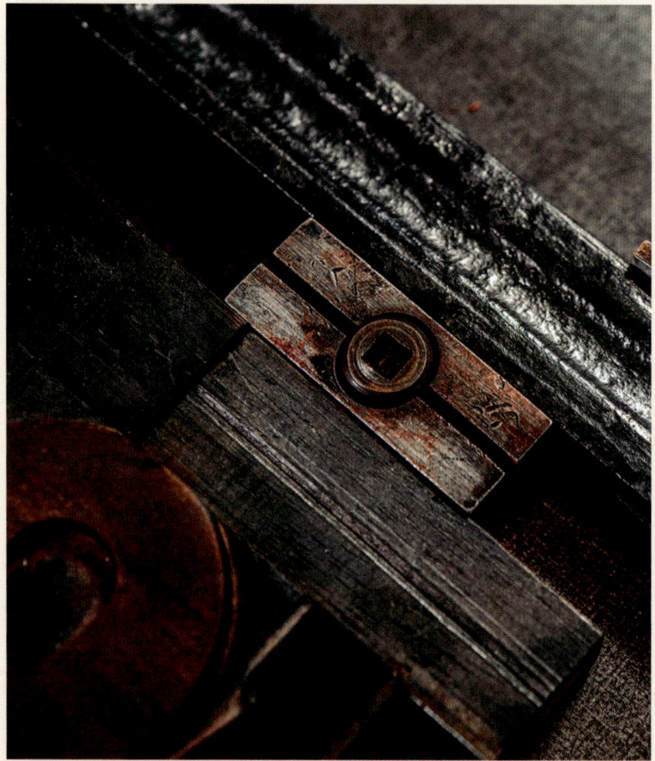

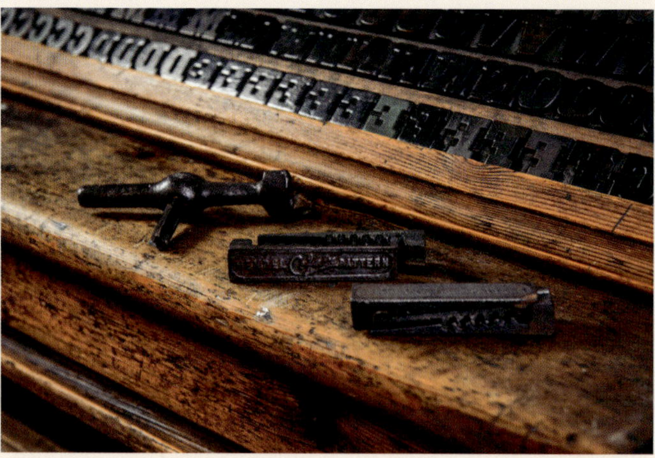

Hempel quoins and quoin key.

laterally to form pressure. These Hempel quoins are rarer and tend to be a bit problematic and fiddlier to use. In the UK the most common quoins are Cornerstone quoins that are straight forward and easy to use, and when locking type out they just expand and don't slide to lock tight. There are also Adana quoins that were designed for the smaller-size print area of the Adana hand presses. It is useful to have a selection of quoins but you can start off with just two quoins. All quoins are manufactured to be lower than standard UK letterpress type height (0.918in) so they remain in place without being printed. These can be found easily on eBay.

Galley magnets

Galley magnets are magnetic blocks that can be used on metal flatbed printing presses. They work by magnetically gripping to the print bed or a galley tray before being pushed into place up against furniture and type. Galley magnets can substitute quoins and can be used without a chase, although this depends on exactly what you are printing, and can be fiddly.

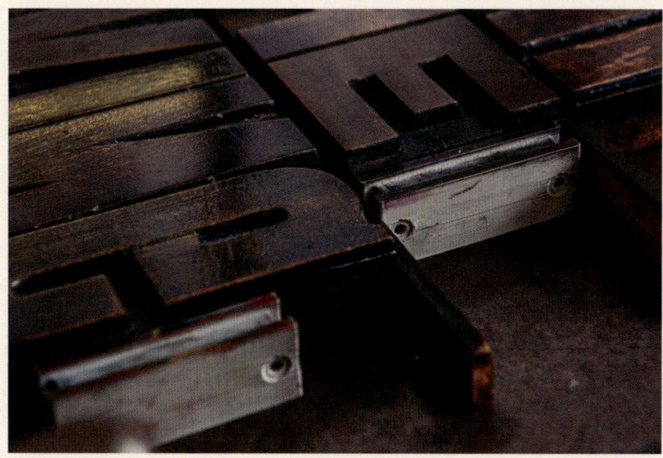

Galley magnets holding type in place.

Galley magnets are very useful when creating experimental prints as it makes securing type in weird and wonderful forms much easier and can be a lot quicker than quoins, as you do not need to worry so much about arranging furniture around all the type. Original galley magnets are a bit tricky to find and they are expensive – an alternative is bar magnets that work as galley magnets. Some online suppliers advertise bar magnets for letterpress – see what you can find. I decided to have a go at making my own galley magnets as the cost of buying the number of magnets needed for my workshop was too costly – making these are discussed in this book's last chapter Future-proofing letterpress.

Inking rollers

There are lots of different rollers out there, and often they are one of the most expensive items that you will buy for your printing. You really want to go for a medium soft roller that is not too big. Rollers that are advertised for lino printing tend to be of the right hardness. Ideally, go to an art store and have a look and a feel of rollers. You should be able to squeeze the roller slightly and there be some give. Have a chat with the staff in the store, most good stores have staff who have used the equipment and they can make recommendations.

It's tempting to buy really big rollers because logically it means less rolling, but in practice it means more ink, more space used up on your inking plate, which means more cleaning down. The most common sizes of rollers that I use are around the 6-inch and 3-inch-wide sizes. Using smaller rollers means that you can have two or three different ink colours rolled out on a single inking plate. It is important to look after your rollers and make sure that you clean them properly, as once ink dries on a roller it can be impossible to get off, and it can be ruined. Store your rollers away from direct sunlight and heat sources like radiators. Ideally hang your rollers – in my workshop, I put two screws in the wall and rest the rollers on their frame. Hanging a roller means that no part of the rubber roller area is in contact with a surface for long periods of time – this can cause flat spots on the roller. You can also screw a hook in the end of your roller if the handle is wooden, though it can catch on things.

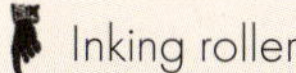

Inking roller.

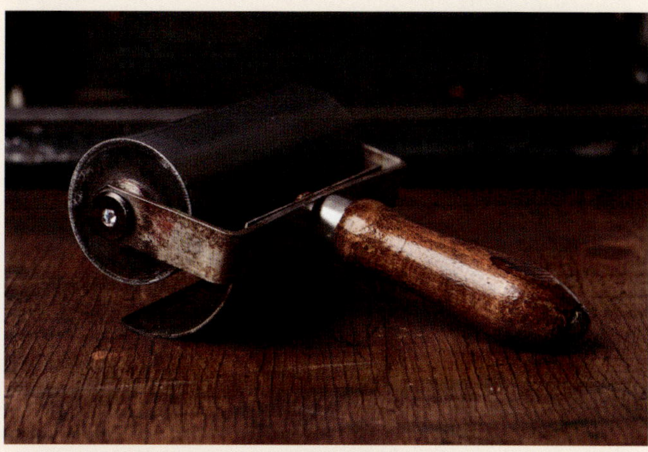

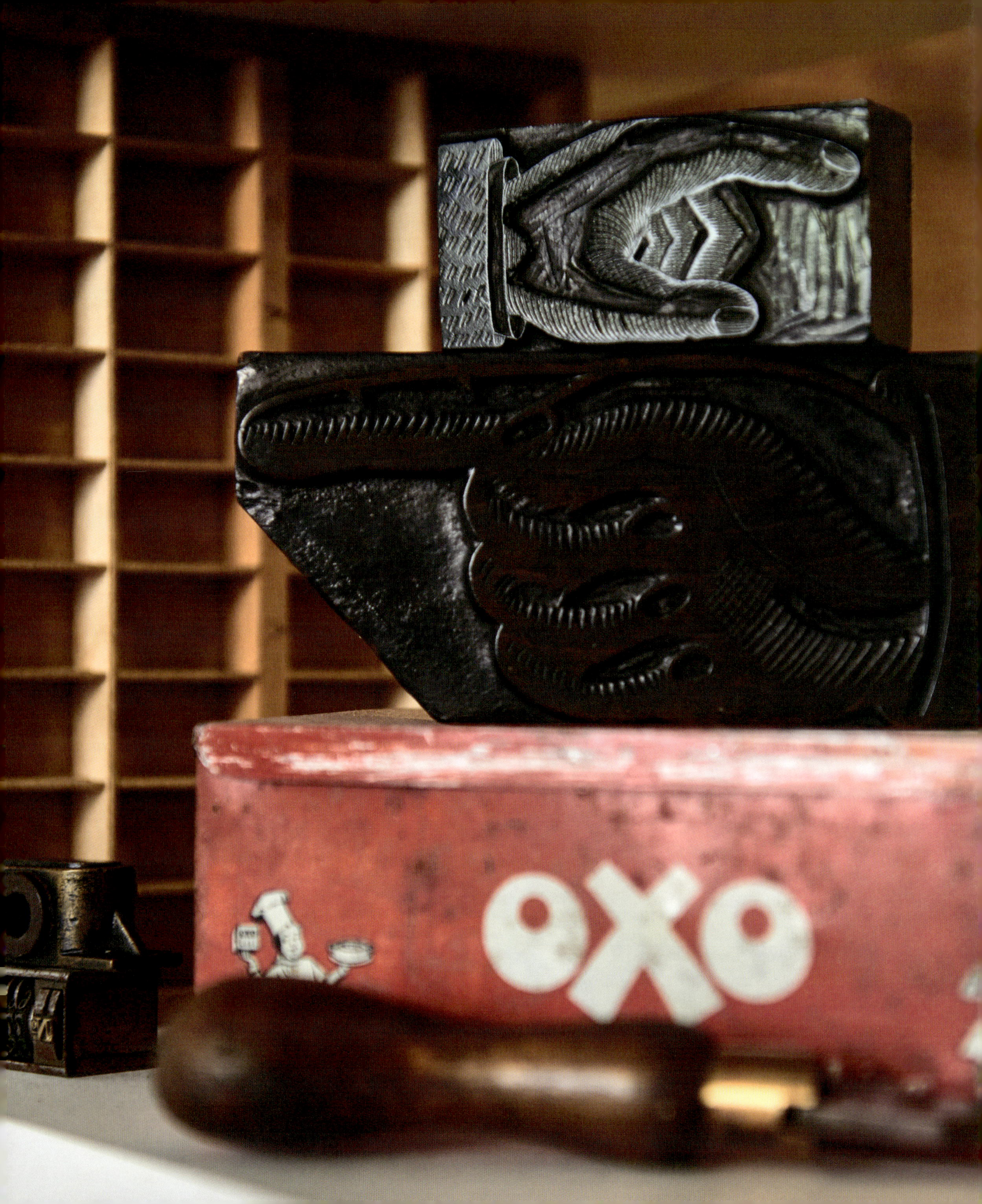
OXO

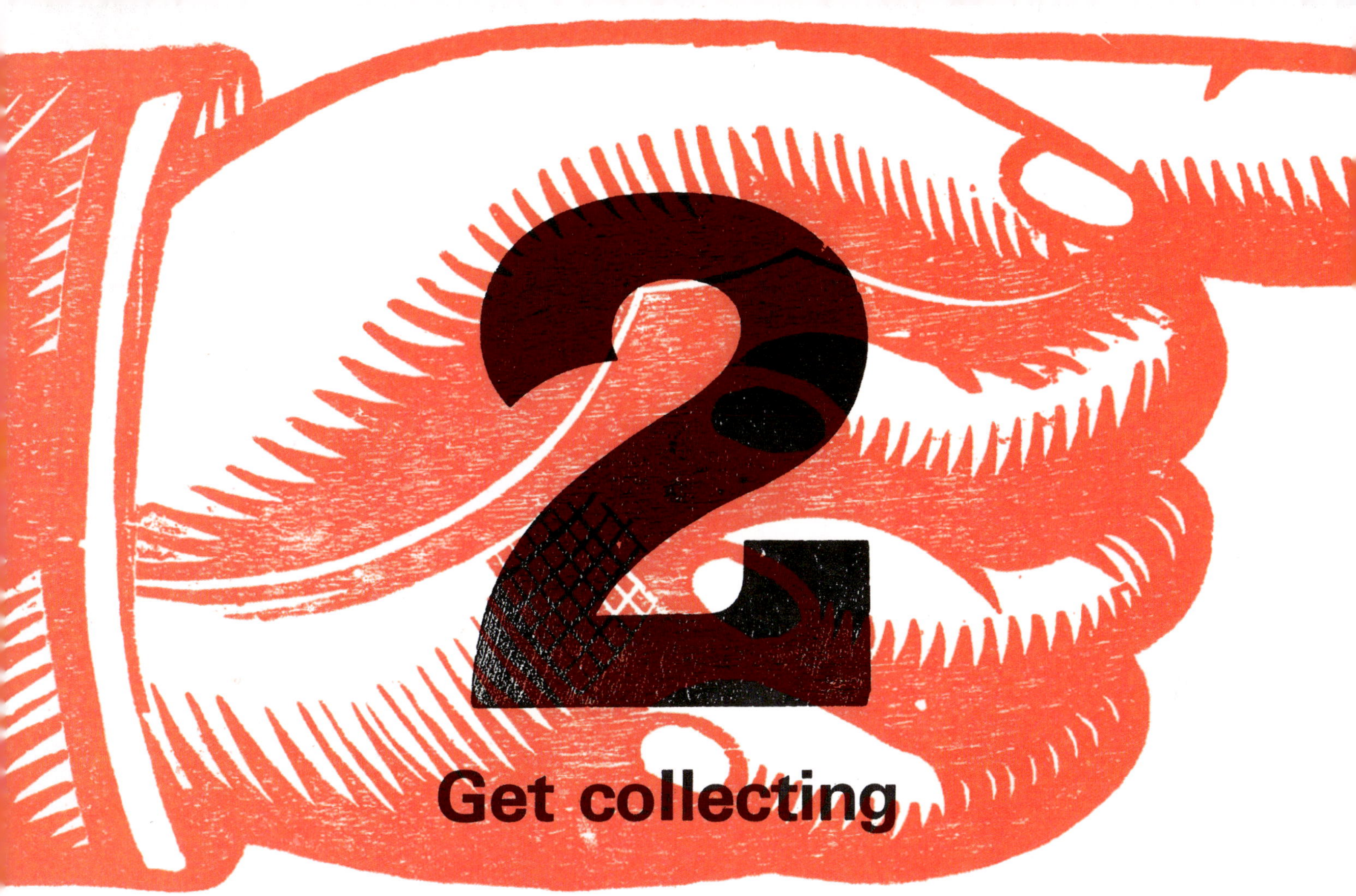

2

Get collecting

So, in Chapter 1 we saw some of the basic tools and equipment, and which items are useful to have in your letterpress workshop. Now, let's get serious and look at where to start! Starting out learning any new process and discipline can be slow and boring so let's try to avoid that and focus on what you can do to just start and get printing as quickly as possible. I personally believe the best way to learn is to do.

Expecting that you will not have every piece of equipment and all the type you really want, you need to think of it this way: you are starting a collection. As with many good collections, there is never really an end or completion, that is the fun part – hunting down the rare item, that perfect font, a quirky picture block or the new thing! This should be part of the process. For 20-odd years I have been collecting type, presses and the weird and wonderful, and it has made me really respect and love the craft and the people that developed it. Letterpress is about these items and the companies and individuals that forged the trade and changed the world with printed matter for the masses. The slow process of collecting, while it may test your patience, does mean you meet a lot of different people along the way whose experience you can learn from.

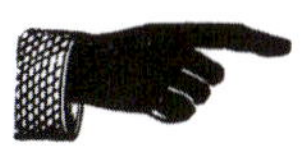

I often think about a piece of advice from someone I purchased a press from in the early days about press maintenance, which was as simple as 'keep it clean, keep it flat'. Twenty years on I repeat this to people on a semi-regular basis, as if you keep your press clean you can spot any problems and the machine is always ready to print. If you keep your press on a very flat surface then the press is balanced equally as intended, avoiding wear and tear that over a period of many years contributes to breaks and part failures. This chapter will introduce you to a number of printing presses and give you a general overview of them, with a chapter later on dedicated to their operation.

A very basic start...

Working on the principle that you are starting from scratch and with budget in mind, I have written up a very basic starting point. I will talk about printing presses as I love the interaction and connection between myself, machine and the creative process. However getting back to real basics is important and it is very surprising how much you can learn and in fact relearn by doing so.

Starting your printing journey can be as simple as buying a piece of lino, some cheap lino cutting tools and a small tube of ink from your local art store. Cut a pattern or a letter, or better still, both – this will give you the very basic principle of printing. Cutting a letter will teach you to cut a mirrored image of the intended design – the letter will be flipped. To make your first print you do not need a press, you can go really basic and use a baren (a flat tool used to rub on the back of paper to transfer ink from printing block to paper), or even the back of a wooden spoon from your kitchen (remember to wash it up well after use!). The basic principle is to ink the surface of your cut block then slowly lower your paper onto it, add a couple of sheets of scrap paper as packing sheets and rub in a circular and rhythmic fashion over the top of the paper, making sure you cover all areas of your printing block. You are then ready to see your print. This is the real foundation of printing and you can move from doing this to then trying printing with a piece of wood type or picture block that you have found – the principle remains the same. After these very basic steps, you can try mixing together traditional type, picture blocks and lino and seeing what is working for you. After these small tentative steps, you are probably starting to think about what's next...

Let's now look at a few different types of printing presses out there. I will focus mainly on presses that I have actually printed on. Where you are in the world will affect availability, but a lot of presses work in very similar ways. The information here can be applied across different presses, and is intended to make getting your first, second or third press that little bit less daunting!

Adanas and small hand presses

Adanas are small hand presses that were made in the UK from around the early 1920s till the late 90s. The most well-known model was the 8 × 5, so called because it took an 8 × 5 inch chase, though it is worth remembering that the chase size is not the print size. My first commission, to design and print a gift certificate was printed on an Adana. I designed the certificate to be 8 × 5 inches and realised that whilst the

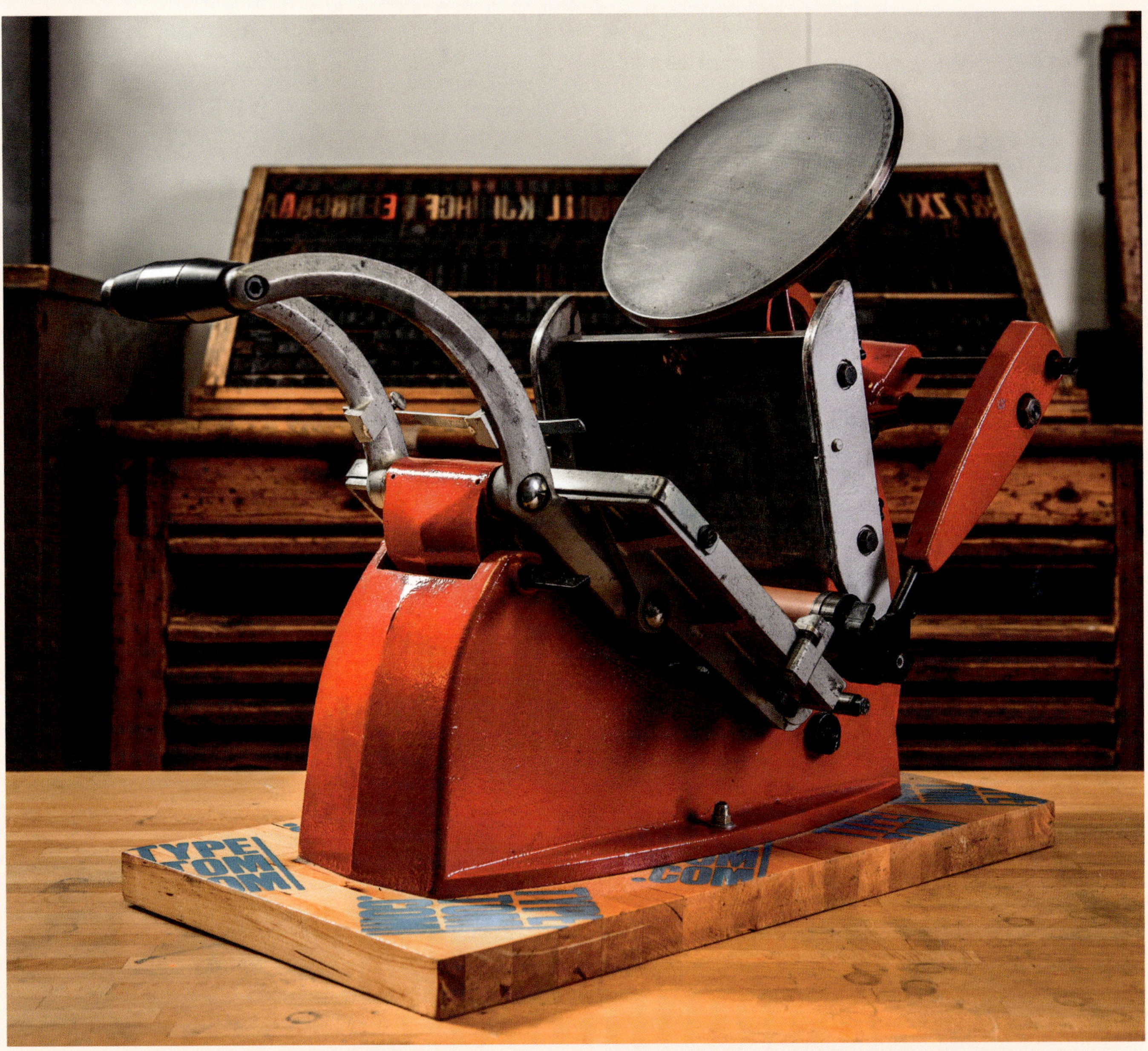

A restored Adana 8x5 model.

printing plate I had made fitted into the chase perfectly, it had to be packed out with card to secure it in place and because of the density of the design the rollers could not deliver as much ink as I needed. This meant I had to remove the rollers and hand-ink each print, which took ages!

The Adana offered an affordable small and easy option for the hobbyist printer at the time of its creation. The 8 × 5 is a very practical and easy-to-use machine that works on the same principle of the clam shell mechanics used by other platen presses (the platen is the flat plate where your paper rests for printing on, in these cases the clam shell-style mechanism pushes the paper which is placed on the platen up to your type to print). The difference being that it's small and intended to be used on a worktop, pushing the handle down to engage the mechanism as there is no counterweight or flywheel to carry the momentum and apply the pressure to print, just you and the small gearing of sorts that the Adana has. An Adana is a great starting point for anyone who wants to get started printing. I still use my first 8 × 5 for odd jobs, short runs and demos. They only print one colour at a time, and you ideally have to leave the prints to dry for 24 hours in between colours. They are ideal for printing greeting cards, wedding invites or some smaller business stationery on.

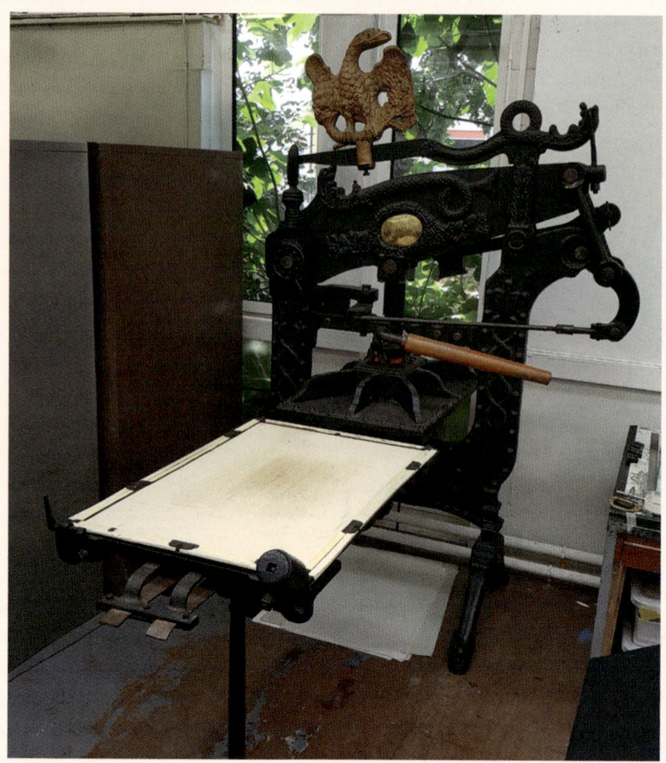

Columbian printing press at Ochre Print Studios.

Adanas are easy to purchase online through eBay where they regularly appear with small collections of type and small cabinets that Adana also produced. If you are looking to buy one, keep an eye out for one that comes with additional bits, be particularly mindful that rollers are expensive to replace so if the Adana has rollers or a spare set of rollers included in the sale, that means you may be saving yourself money in the long run.

Albions, Columbians and Stanhopes

For me these are the big three; they personify printmaking and they feel fantastic to use. Rarely do you become so at one with a machine and literally put your all into pulling the perfect print. The basic ways to spot the difference between the presses is this: Columbians tend to be the largest presses and every part of them is built to last with very thick and industrial casting, they also usually have a massive eagle counterweight on the top of the printing press. Columbian printing presses were the American-designed press, although most were made in England. Albions are more delicate-looking machines

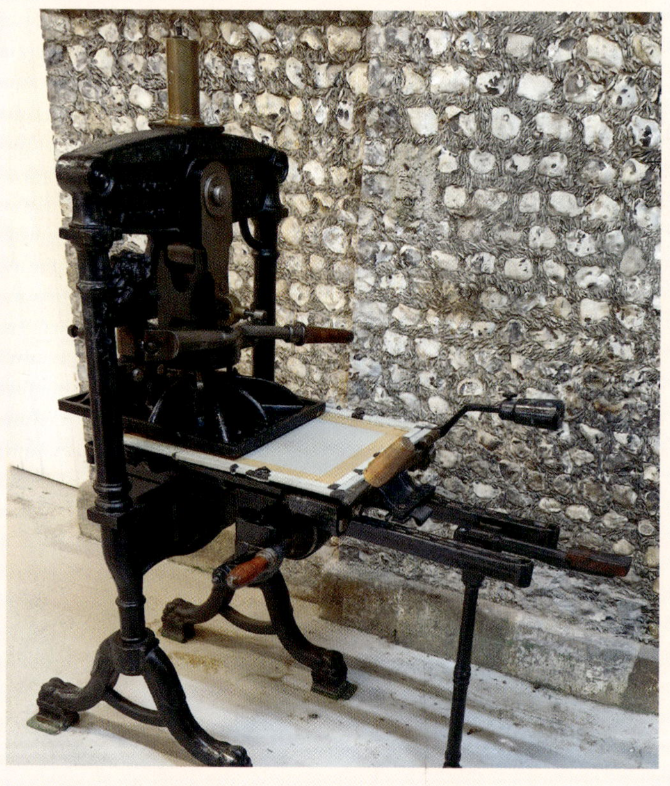

Albion printing press at West Dean College.

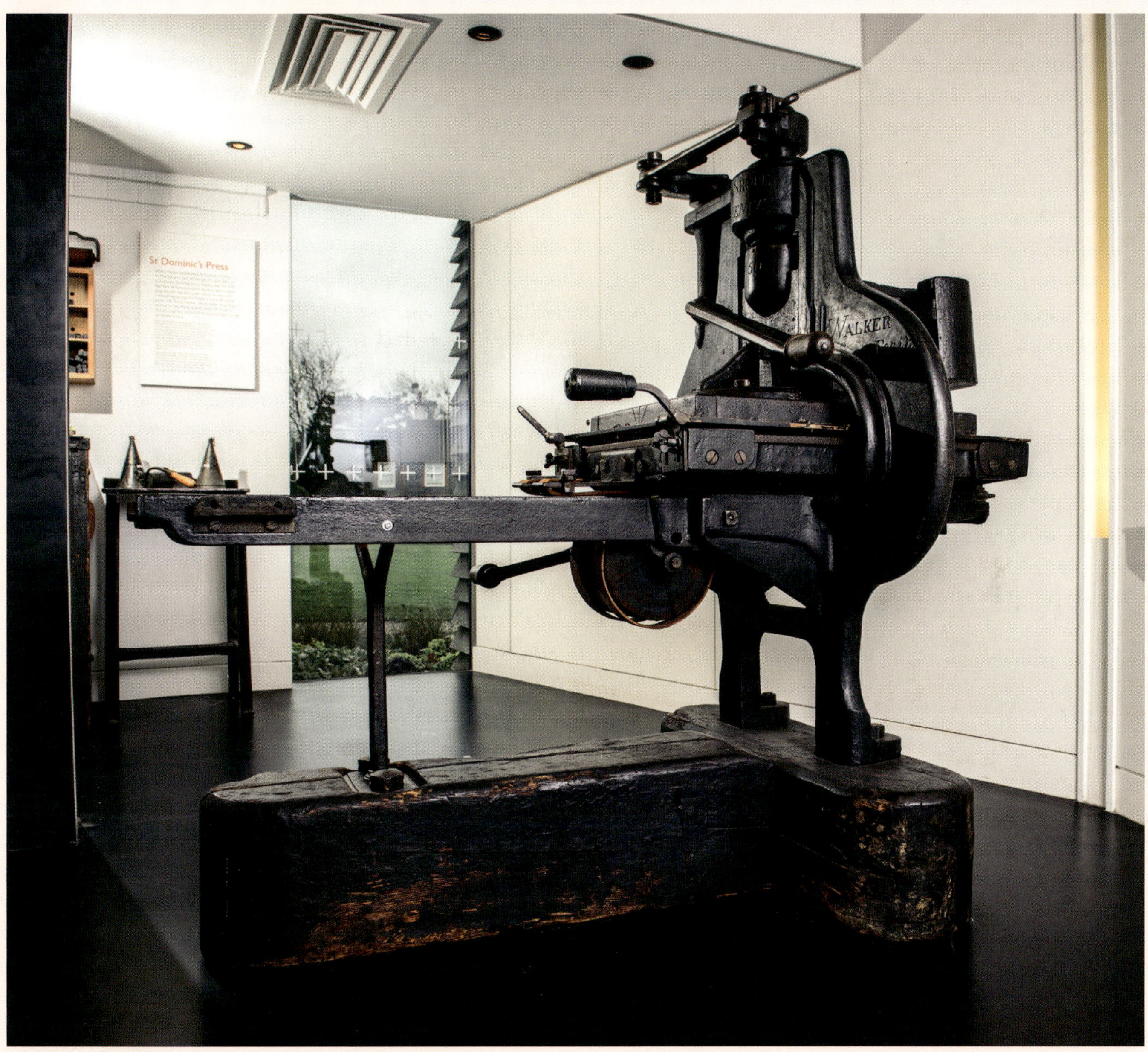

Stanhope printing press at Ditchling Museum of Art + Craft.

and usually have the name Albion cast along the top of the machine, they also have lion claw feet. Albions were made in the UK and are often now used for printing lino prints, as they came in a selection of sizes from very large to tabletop.

The Stanhope press was the first cast iron press of its kind (picture shown is of Ditchling Museum of Art + Craft's press, which was previously used by Erik Gill and was made around 1803). They are very heavy with incredibly thick castings, and easy to recognise as they are mounted to a very large wooden cross!

All these presses work in the same basic way though use slightly different mechanics to pull a print. You start by creating your design, comp-ing (composing) your letters, picture blocks or whatever exciting thing you are inspired to print. Then you lock out your type into a chase on the bed of the press. Once the type and chase are safely in place, next comes the inking (this will be covered in greater detail later in the book).

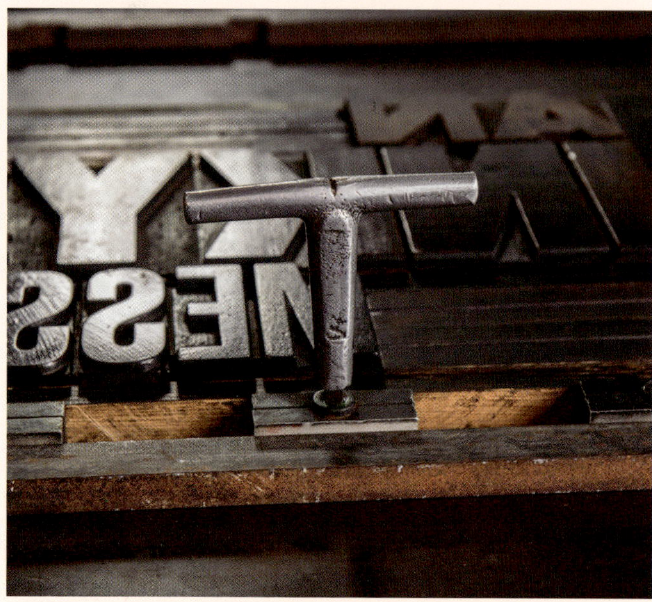

Quoin & quoin key locking wood type in a chase.

Once you have smoothly applied your ink you are ready to delicately and lightly place your paper onto your forme (type locked into a chase ready to print is called a forme). After this you add a couple of packing sheets to help aid pressure. This level and fine tweaking of pressure is ideally adjusted for every different design, as a single extra piece of newsprint can really help to make the impression on the paper and make the print come to life. Whether you are printing a page for a book set in a simple lead type layout or a delightfully inky wood type creation, both are aided immensely by these fine adjustments and finishing touches. So, the type is inked, the paper and packing is on, now you lower the tympan (a metal frame usually covered with parchment that is used to locate sheets for printing pages of books and gives correct packing pressure for printing). Next, you turn the handle on the side of the press, allowing the bed holding the chase and the type to slide on a cast iron track into the machine. The bed should come to rest with the surrounding edges of the bed area in the centre of the platen (the metal plate that is now hovering above your type, which delivers the pressure when printing). It is very important that you make sure the bed is in the middle of the platen area. The edges of the bed plate have a corner lip around them and if you misalign and pull with these under the platen plate then you could cause damage to the press. With all these presses, when you turn the handle to move the bed, do so slowly, and be mindful that the bed needs to stop and park with precision.

Albion printing press at West Dean College.

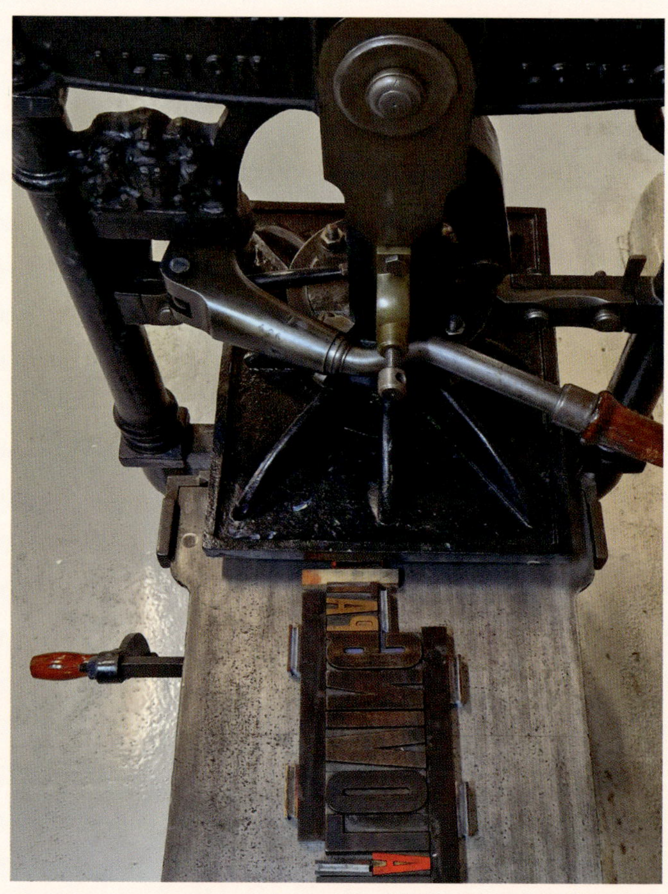

There are stops on most presses, but we want to stop and park the press not crash it – go slow and enjoy the moment and the process. Some of this equipment is amazingly old, and should be treated with care.

Now is the moment of printing. Double check everything is in place, grip the lever arm handle and pull towards yourself in a smooth, non-jerky, movement. As you are pulling try to visualise the paper being moulded around the type and the ink being transferred leaving behind the impression. If you visualise this moment you can try to keep the pull on the press as smooth as possible and you can really feel the pressure being applied to the type through the handle helping you not to pull too hard.
Most of the presses have a basic bolt-style mechanism that stops the lever arm at a certain point to help you not over-pull, but it is best to learn and develop good practice: feel your way and use the stop as a maximum pressure point. Pulling too hard on the press will not really help your print and will in the long run cause more wear and tear than is needed. Some people put their feet on printing presses to give themselves a better leverage! Please don't do this, looking at Ditchling Museum of Art + Craft's Stanhope, you can see the wooden base has a rounded area from the many years of heavy use. Often the feet on Albions and Columbians will have a shiny patch where people have put a boot on it when printing. If the press has been set correctly and you are using good printing practices with setup and inking, then this is really not necessary. I often talk about and show these worn areas to students when printing, I personally feel that putting your boot on an area of the press is as bad as putting your boot on someone's sofa when you are a guest.

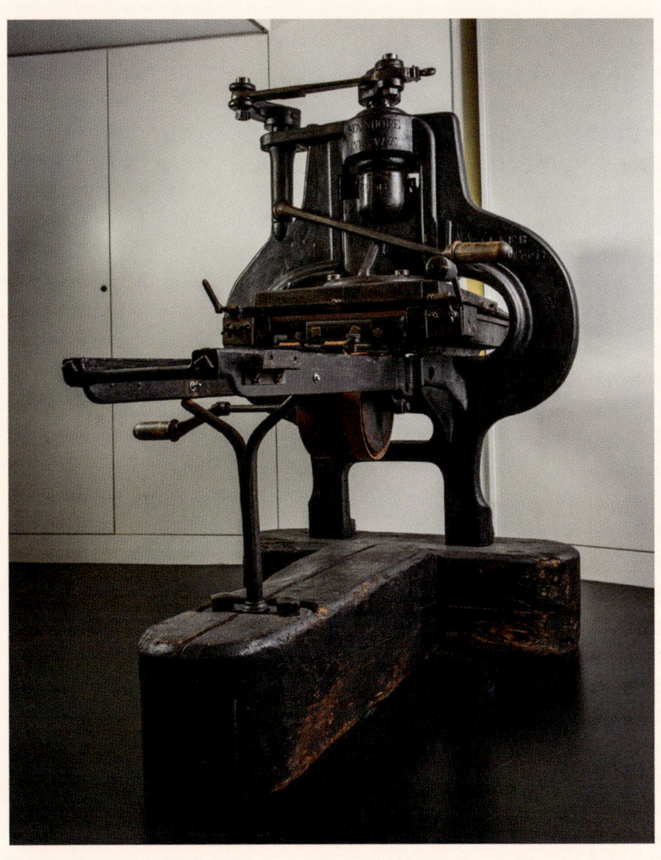

Stanhope printing press at Ditchling Museum of Art + Craft.

I love all of these presses, and I have spent many truly happy hours printing with them, although I do not actually own one! It is worth talking about how big some of these presses are and that you really need to be able to walk around them to use them to their fullest. In the case of a Columbian, this requires a massive amount of space in a workshop. They also are very valuable and command a high price, and could be viewed with the same logic of owning a classic car that needs a lot of maintenance and upkeep to keep them on the road. If you are going to own one, then you are a custodian, and you are investing not only financially but in the future of letterpress, too. I have come close on several occasions to owning an Albion but for various reasons, like money, space and conditions of the press, I've not yet acquired one.

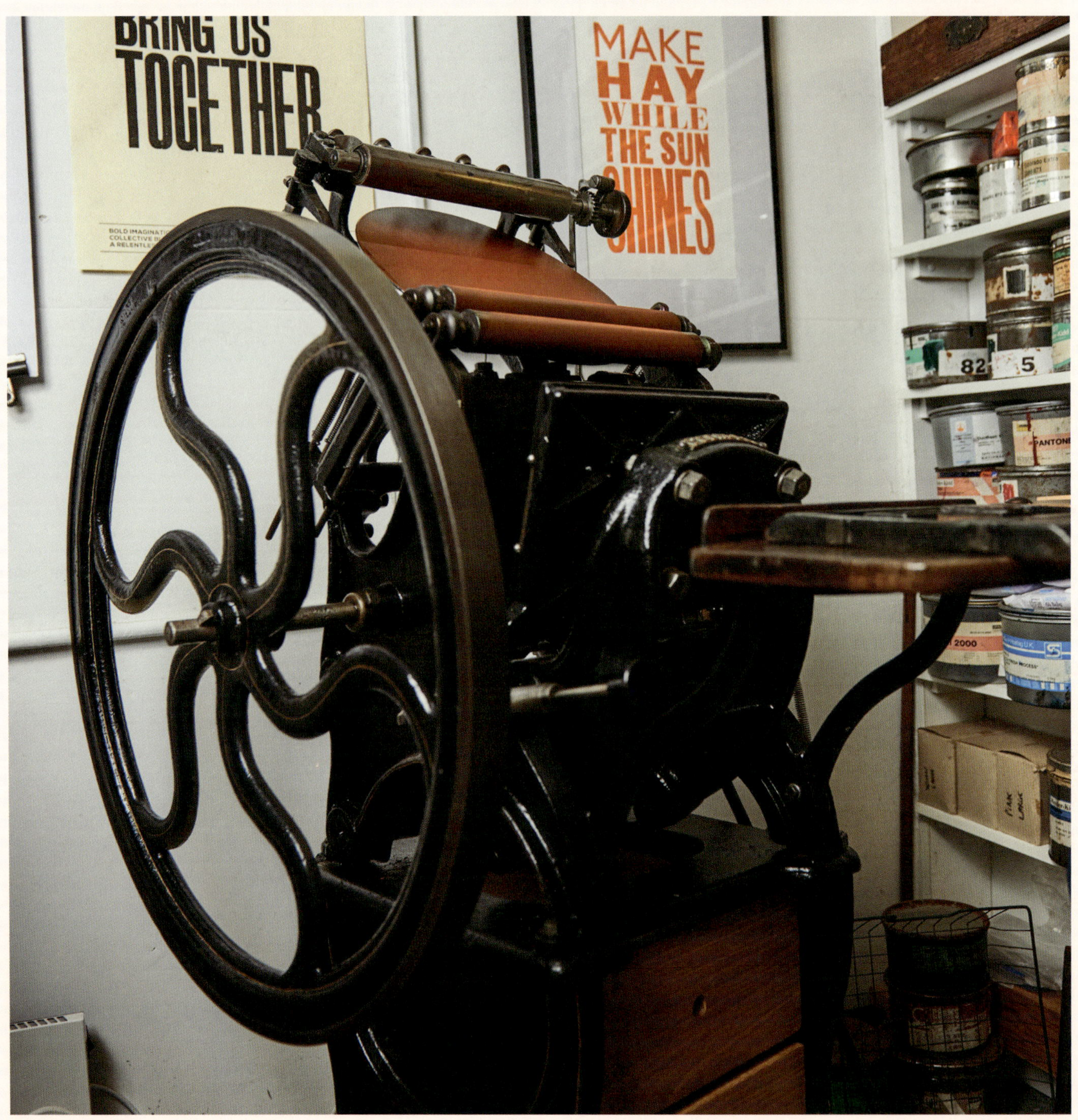

Cropper Charlton Peerless (platen printing press).

Platen presses

Platen presses print with a clam shell-style movement. The press is either powered by foot or by motor. I have a collection of platen presses that I use for printing products and stationery on. My presses are all foot-powered, and this demands that you learn the ability of standing on one leg and pushing down the pedal with your foot in a rhythmic fashion to keep the fly wheel spinning and the clam shell print area opening and closing. When the pedal is pushed down a series of different things happen: the rod that is attached to the side of the pedal pulls down on a rod that is attached to a gear on the upper side of the press, which is attached to a very large shaft that runs horizontally through the press just under the clam shell mechanism. On the end of this shaft there is a fly wheel attached. The fly wheel is very heavy, and when this series of motions happens the wheel starts to spin, and the weight and momentum from the flywheel will cause the pedal to rise once again, so you can then push it down again causing the perpetual motion.

Also attached to this mechanism are several other parts that mean the rollers will rise and fall over the type and climb up and onto the inking plate. The inking plate also rotates each time the rollers go down onto the type, meaning that each time the roller rolls over the rotating inking plate the ink has been agitated and is clear from any ghost inking that can occur.

In the case of my Cropper Charlton & Co Peerless there are two inking rollers that deliver ink to the type, and one roller that climbs high onto the inking disk plate and kisses with the metal inking fountain roller. This is to add more ink constantly to the inking plate as required. Whilst this mechanism is fantastic and always slightly amazing, I rarely use the inking fountain as I don't often do runs over 1,000 impressions, and cleaning down the inking fountain is a bit of a pain and quite a slow process. Ink can be added slowly with a spatula to the right-hand side of the inking plate and it will slowly incorporate in as the inking plate rotates round. When printing with one of these style of

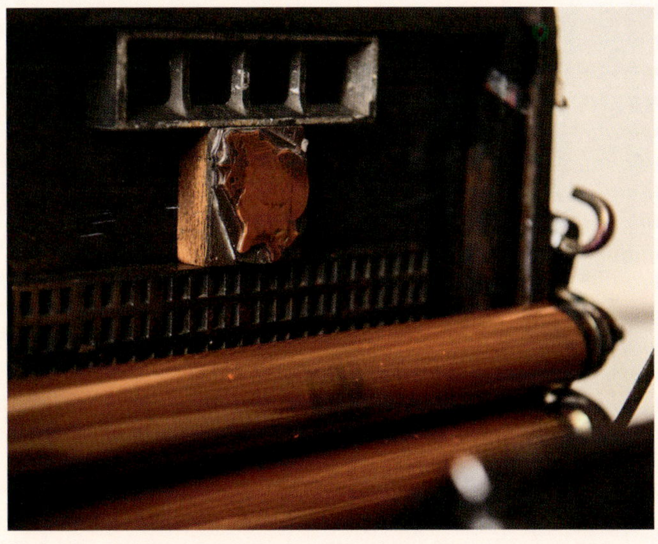

Picture block in chase, clamped in Cropper Charlton Peerless.

presses, the type needs to be securely locked into the press' chase, and this will then be lifted vertically and held in place using your press' chase mechanism. Some presses have a metal clip that's secured on the top of the chase with some location rests at the bottom of the chase.

Other presses like the Adanas just sit in place on some runners, or grooves. These presses are often referred to as jobbing presses, as that is exactly what they were used for – all sorts of different jobs. For instance, the press can be used as a creasing machine by removing the rollers and locking a brass type-high rule into the chase then adding some card backing sheet to the impression side of the clam shell. This is how I crease all my notebooks and greetings cards. It is worth noting that these machines are at the high end of being risky, even dangerous, as they move fast and the clam shell mechanism opens and closes quickly. It is imperative not to underestimate the level of risk of putting your hand inside a moving object – I have met a number of people over the years who have lost parts of fingers in printing presses.

Proofing press (cylinder press)

Proofing press is a generic term for a flatbed press that would have traditionally been used to pull test or proof prints on. They are usually heavy, and some come with their own stand, while others you can just lug onto a good strong table. As you can see in the image of mine, it is a very basic cast iron bed or plate where the type is locked in place, then the main roller has two runners that it runs on.

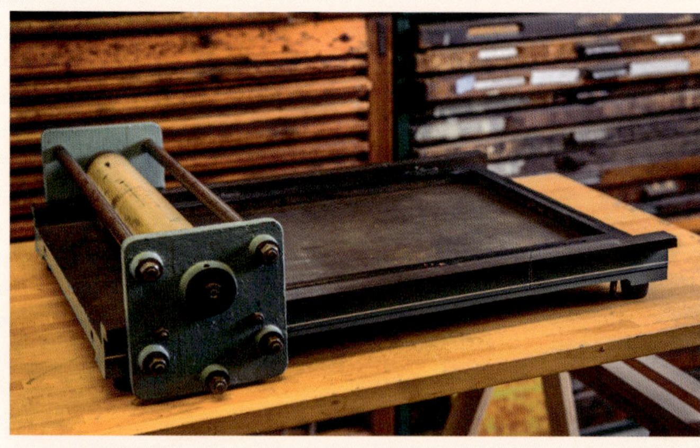

Basic model proofing press (made by George Pallister & Sons).

The end parts of the roller head on mine have eccentric turning bearings. Which means you can tweak the pressure of the roller by turning the bearing nuts. Ultimately, you put your type onto the plate/bed, lock your type out into the chase, ink, gently lay down a piece of paper adding a backing sheet or two then pull the roller head over the type to get your print.

The best examples of proofing press that I have used are Farleys. Depending on which model you have or are looking at, they range from very basic 'just-pull' models to ones that have their own metal stand with height-adjusting rollers and self-inking units. Farleys also often have a gripper bar that holds the paper in place whilst printing as paper slides, which can sometimes be a slight problem with proofing presses. I personally have always loved very basic proofing presses, they just feel fun and you feel very connected being the pulling power behind your printing machine.

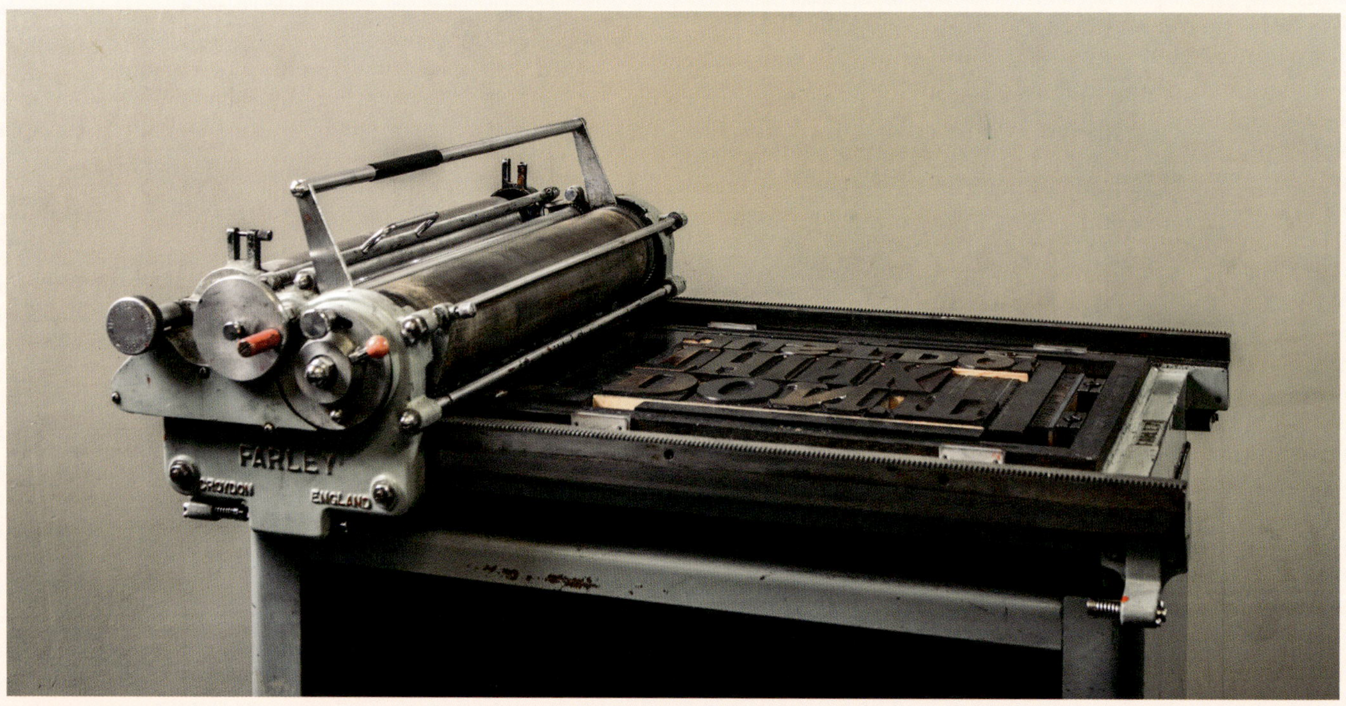

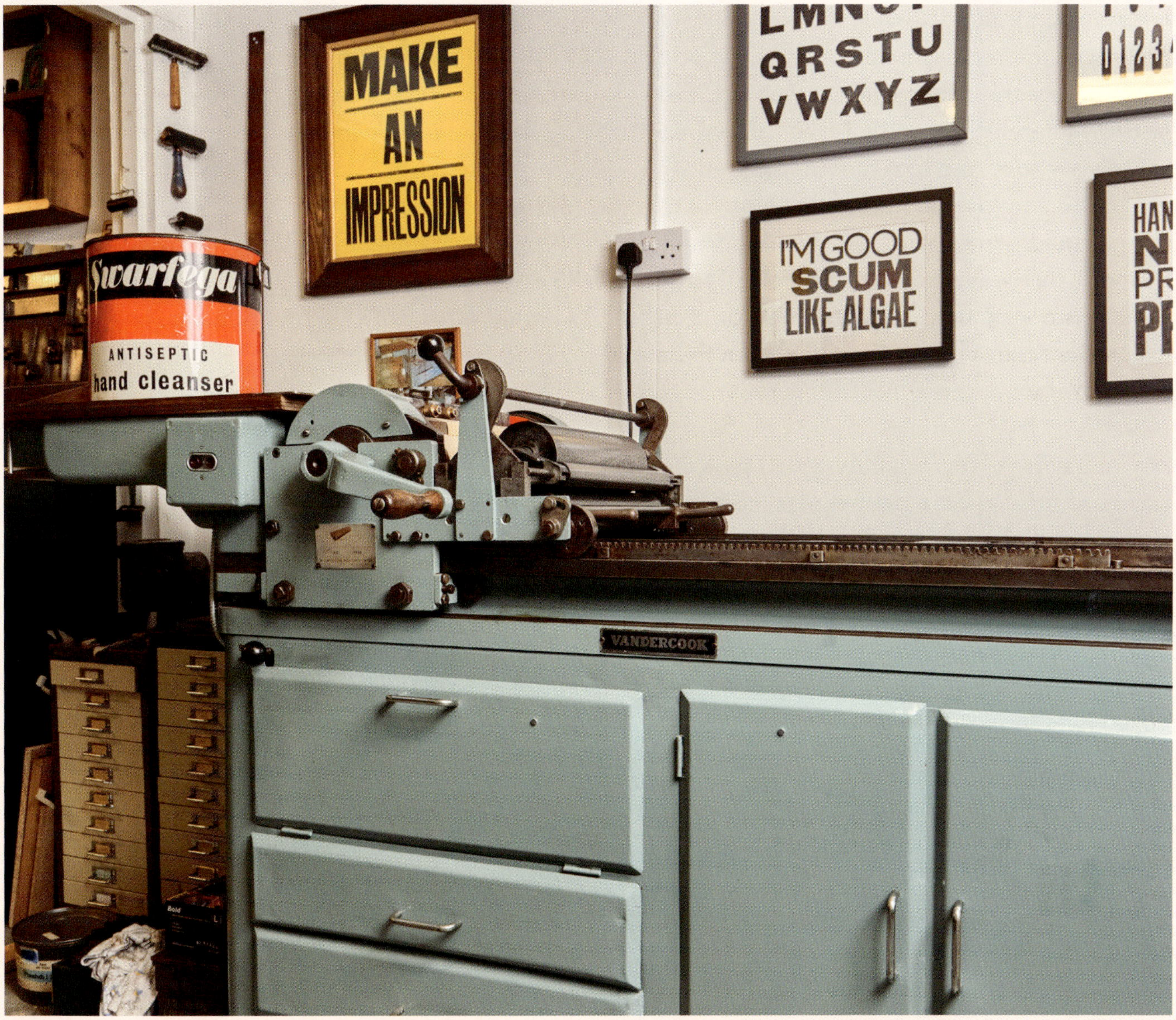

Farley proofing press at Ditchling Museum of Art + Craft.

Restored Vandercook 4C printing press in Typetom workshop.

Vandercook

The Vandercook is a very large proofing press, it is at the big end of the scale weighing in at around one tonne and comes in a variety of different models. The press shown is my Vandercook 4C, which prints on a paper sheet size of 39.5 × 55cm. I restored this press a number of years ago after it was gifted to me by its previous owner, having lived in a cow barn with some cars for a number of years. Needless to say, it was in a very sorry state.

The Vandercook has a motor that powers a very simple inking unit. This consists of a rotating drum that is connected to the motor beneath it via a chain. This metal drum then comes in contact with two larger rubber printing rollers, which in turn have two small and one large oscillating roller above it.

When using the inking unit, it allows for quick pulling of prints as you just need to put paper into the gripper bars by pressing down the pedal with your foot, slide in the paper, release your foot and turn the handle and walk along the length of the press while printing. As the handle turns, the rollers will roll the ink over the surface of the type, closely followed by the paper on the printing drum creating the impression, before the press head slowly hits its end and stops where the paper gripper releases the print as if by magic. Just to be clear, it's not magic. It's a very well-designed mechanism on the rear side of the press that is a bit like a 'train track', which means that after removing your print you can return the head to the start position to pull another print. This 'train track' mechanism means that on the press' return journey the impression roller rides slightly higher, so as not to take an impression onto your tympan sheet (a tough sheet of paper that is fitted to the impression drum).

Used & new Tympan sheets.

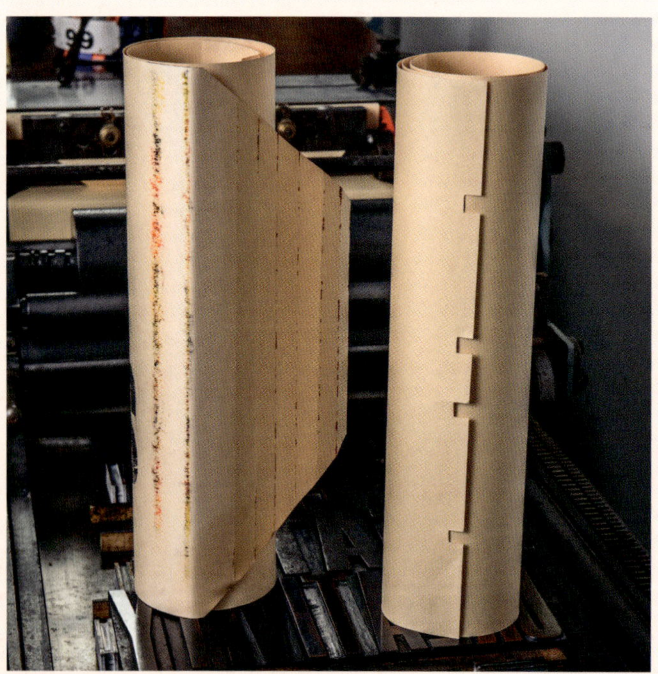

Traditional tympan sheets can be hard to get hold of. I purchased a pack of large, thin manila card for the Vandercook and I cut a template that I use each time it needs replacing. The Vandercook is a special press for me but it is very large, heavy and is a very expensive thing to purchase if you can't find a nice chap like Andy who gave me this one knowing that I would get it back up and running, and that it would be used and loved.

Type

Speaking as a collector and somewhat hoarder of type, this is a bit of a touchy subject. I love type and I have never felt like I have enough. This is part of the restrictive nature of letterpress, and to a certain extent I believe that not having too much type makes you a more creative designer, as you are forced to problem solve with what you have rather than everything you want. Type is a very expensive commodity today, and sadly prices people out of the market. But as mentioned in the previous chapter, look for part font sets, the random odd letter here or there to start with, then later look to buy your first case of type.

Don't buy big, start small both in terms of quantity and physical size. Large wooden type is a beautiful thing, but it's expensive, sometimes impractical, and you may not even use it much. Smaller wood type is much more usable as you are more likely to be able to form your word and fit it into a printing press. Lead type is currently a bit less popular to buy, and you get smaller sets which contain more letters. Lead type was a massive part of the printing industry, and so there's a lot left in circulation now.

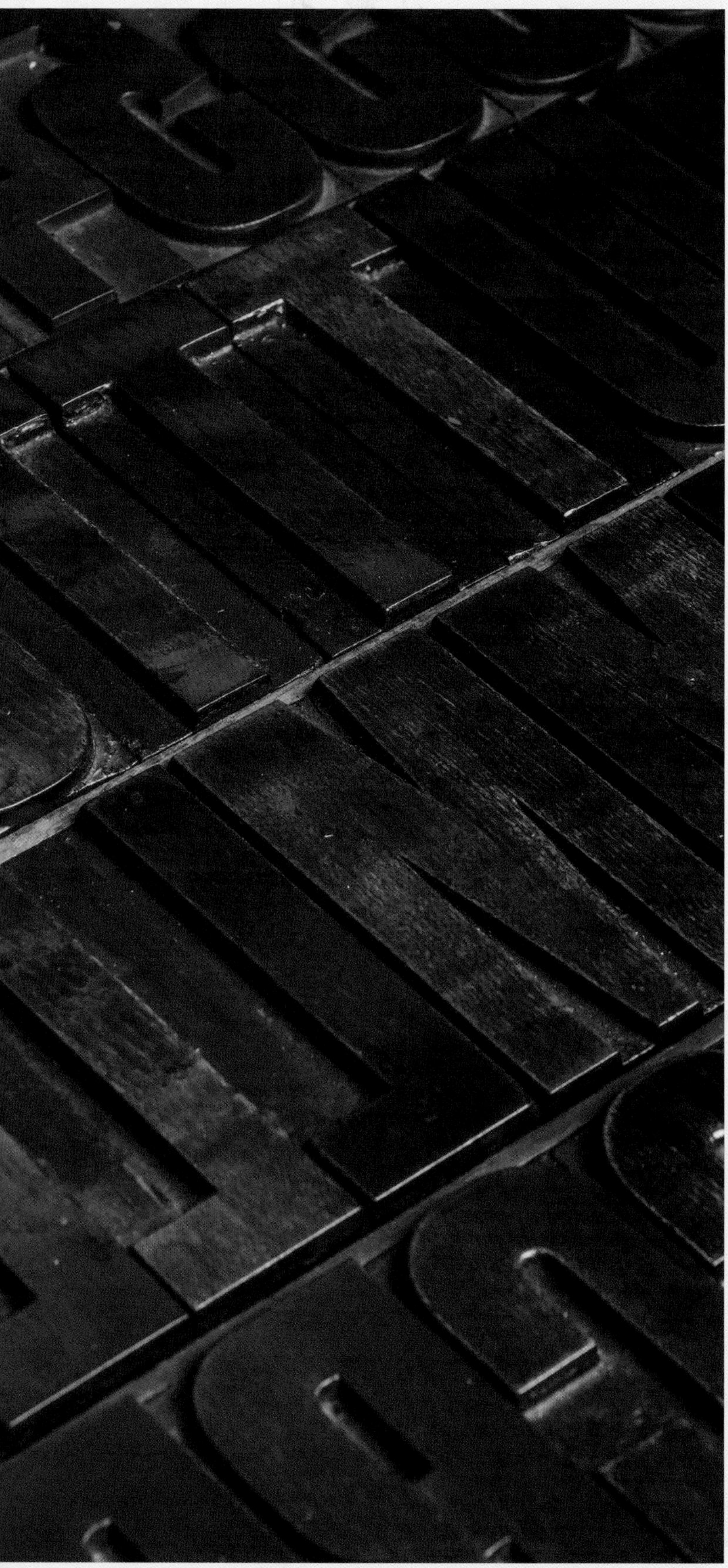

How I got started

Studying for my degree at the then-named London College of Printing gave me access to printing equipment, which I loved, and it was one of the reasons why I wanted to study there. Leaving college meant having no equipment and entering the real world. I joined a couple of print groups, one which had an open access studio. They mainly catered for screen printing and more traditional artistic forms of print like etching. This worked well for some things, but I always liked the idea of being industrial. As a struggling artist and designer, I started working with a friend; we got some early commissions and one was to design a gift certificate for a book shop, the client assumed that we would be printing the gift certificate whereas we assumed that we were just designing the certificate. With the client being very keen on the gift certificates being hand printed, we looked for companies that could offer us a short run, to no avail.

I ended up purchasing my first printing press, an Adana 8 × 5 found through an ad in a free newspaper, the Friday-Ad. For all of you who are not from the UK or old enough to understand, the Friday-Ad could be found in hard print at many shops. Think eBay, before the internet! So, with this first Adana the first commission was completed. Hand presses are hard work and physically strenuous when doing a 1,000-print run. They also are heavily limited by their chase size and the diameter of their rollers (as explained in the Adana section earlier). They're great for smaller print jobs, for example, small areas of type like printing business cards or more interesting short-run prints.

☛ Wood type.

After this first commission we quickly learnt that we really liked letterpress and printing, and that this could be a good USP (unique selling point) for the style of type and graphic design that we were into. We also saw that printing on an Adana worked, but at the same time was not enough for our next goal – releasing a range of products to show off what we could do, to try to get more commissions. This time I turned to eBay and found a large job lot for sale! Job lots and large amounts of stuff can mean a really good price, as many people don't want to purchase more than a single item. The job lot I purchased was also badly photographed and the listing mentioned that there was some fire damage. Believe it or not the auction price was not high, and I ended up with a lot of trays of lead type, quoins and quoin keys, some picture blocks and a large Arab printing press.

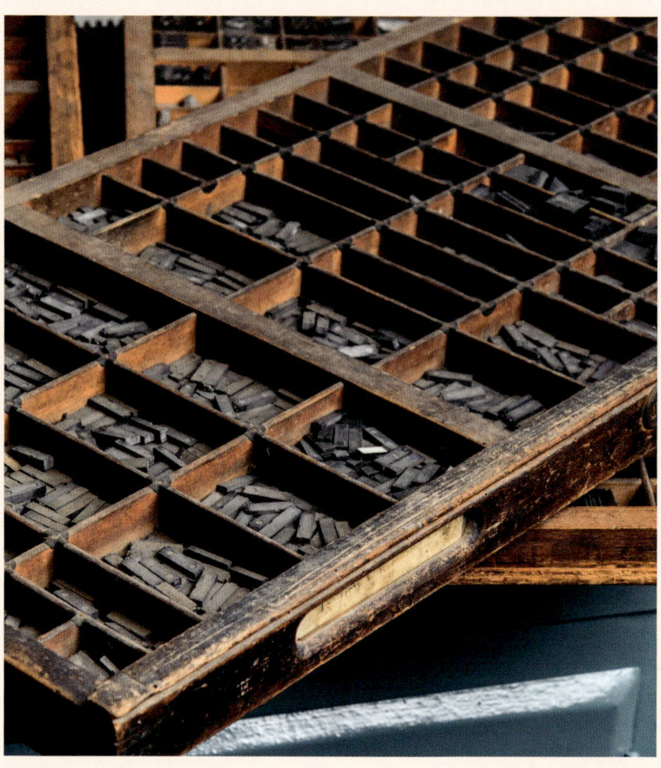

Collected cases of lead type.

The Arab platen press became the cornerstone of printing for us. It took a long time to get used to treadling a pedal and to operate the clam shell mechanism. This time was well spent; though at the time it felt very tedious and slow, learning on the job is sometimes the best way. The Arab press was very big and heavy and great for printing large things with its oversize A4-ish print area. I then went on to purchase smaller platen presses and ended up with a collection of Cropper, Charlton & Co. Peerless printing presses and a couple of others that operate similarly. I sold the Arab press when I was given my Vandercook to restore and print with, as it became somewhat a third wheel – I really needed to think about space and the future of the workshop. The smaller Peerless presses are great for longer runs and are nowhere near as heavy to operate, as all the parts are smaller and lighter, so easier to get going and keep going on longer print runs.

If I was starting afresh today with limited funds, I would look at buying a small collection of type, both wood (in smaller size) and lead in a variety of sizes. I would purchase an Adana 8 × 5, looking on eBay for one that did not look too pretty and which has rollers, then focus in on any adverts with other paraphernalia included and all in good condition. I would then look for the cheapest proofing press that I could find in working order. With the Adana you can print short runs of stationery like business cards (please print your own cool business cards, people always love a unique hand-printed business card) and maybe some products that you could look to sell. With the proofing press you can take your first steps with wood type poster printing, opening the door to creative experimentation.

Typetom collection of jobbing platen printing presses.

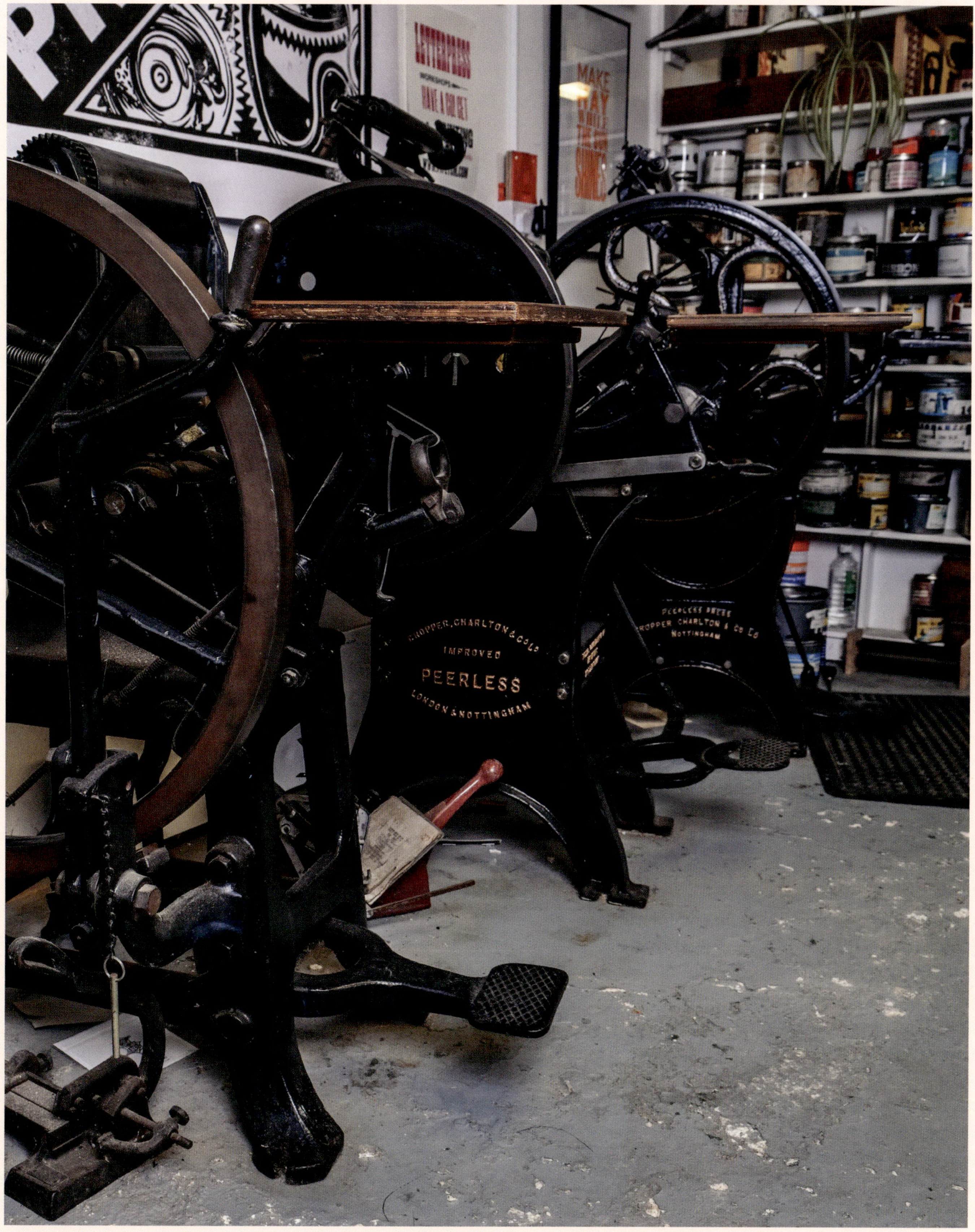
LETTERPRESS
WORKSHOPS
MAKE
CROPPER, CHARLTON & CO LD
IMPROVED
PEERLESS
LONDON & NOTTINGHAM
NOTTINGHAM

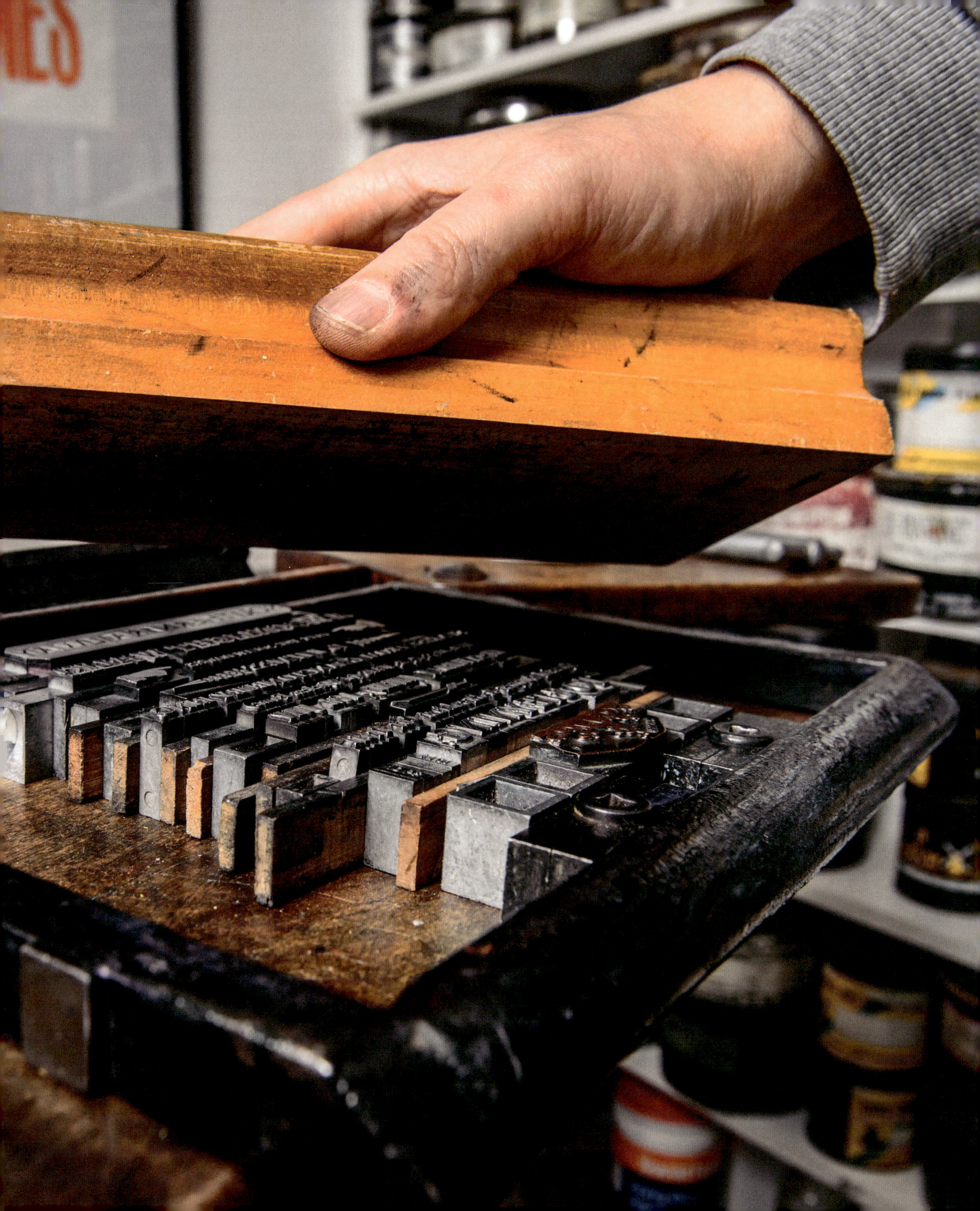

3

Working with type

Owning type and looking after your type is what we shall be looking at in this chapter. It is really important to me that when I acquire anything that is to be added into my collection, I spend time ensuring that it's all ok and ready to print with. We will start with looking at wood type, as this in my experience can throw up the most problems.

Wood type is a wonderful thing made from a natural material. While it is widely stated that wood type was most commonly made from hard maple (also called rock maple), the reality is that a variety of sources would have been used, with some manufacturers having better quality product and processes than others (exactly the same as today).

Other woods referenced as being used for type include boxwood, holly, cherry, poplar, birch and beech. Once a piece of type was made it was printed with again and again and again, leading to the user becoming its custodian. Now, way over 100 years since their creation, the type is dark, coloured from years of inking and printing, and it's very hard to identify exactly what type of wood was used. To me, exactly which wood is used for each font is slightly irrelevant. The important thing is to keep the type in good working order and do not damage its condition. Again, think of yourself as a custodian of your collection.

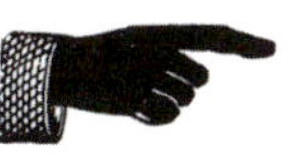

Handling type

Letterpress type should be considered precious; be careful when you are handling and carrying type around your workspace. It is very easy to drop a piece of wood type on the floor and sod's law says it will always land face down on a corner, denting it. Lead type is also very heavy, so when carrying a chase loaded with lead do so carefully and be sensible, only carry any type locked out in a chase on a galley. When carrying full cases of type, consider where you're going to put it before you remove it from its cabinet. Don't place it precariously, as I, like many others have done before, dropping an entire case of small lead type on the floor and spending a considerable amount of time returning it to its case. Don't stack type on top of type – it can seem like an easy option to carry a bundle across the room, but it's much easier to drop like this. Invest in a galley tray or just even use a normal tray. Don't place your galley tray on top of type – this is a good way to scratch it. Get into good working habits and stick to them; a clean and tidy workshop is a productive one.

Checking your type

When I first get any new sets of wood type, I carefully inspect it for signs of woodworm! Woodworm can ruin collections of type; it is really quite easy to spot the presence of these little creatures as they leave little holes and dust as they munch through your valuable type. I usually inspect any new wood type for my collection outside just to be sure about its condition. This is also a good place for a quick wipe over with a clean rag to get any loose dust or dirt off as a first pass. People buy rags for cleaning but I am a fan of recycling, so I keep any clothing or fabric that's not fit for a charity shop for my workshop.

If you think you see signs of woodworm in type, do not add it to any other type, as you will contaminate your collection. You could use a plastic storage box with a lid (not that I'm suggesting the woodworm would leap out seeking your wood type and attacking like tiny ninjas! But let's not risk it). I have been very lucky over the years and have not really had any problems

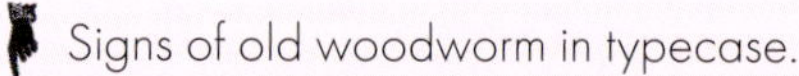
Signs of old woodworm in typecase.

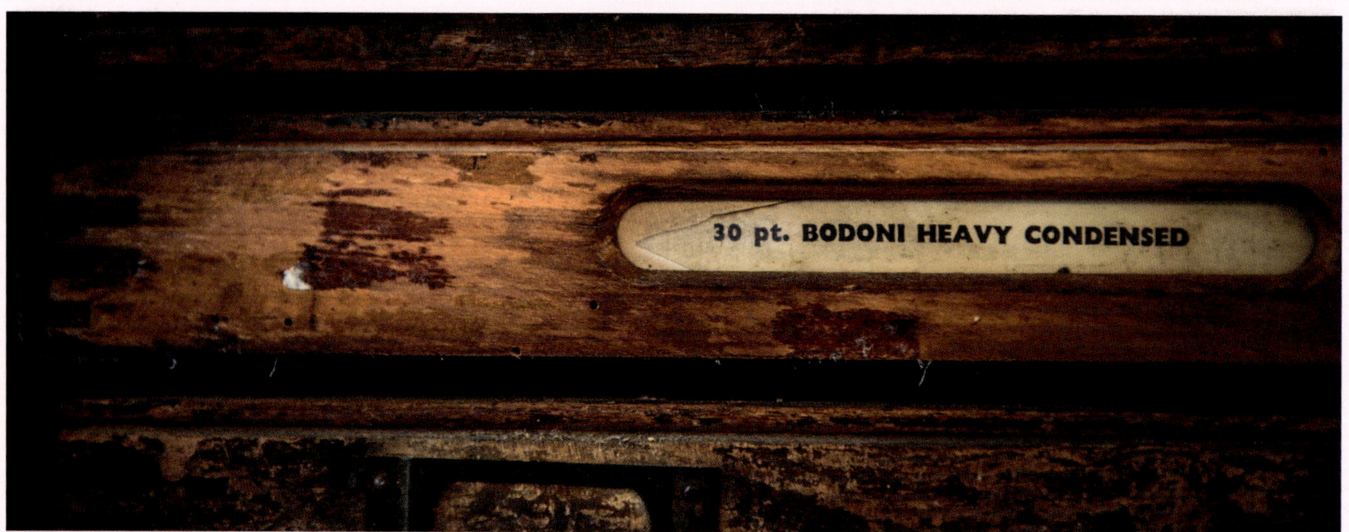

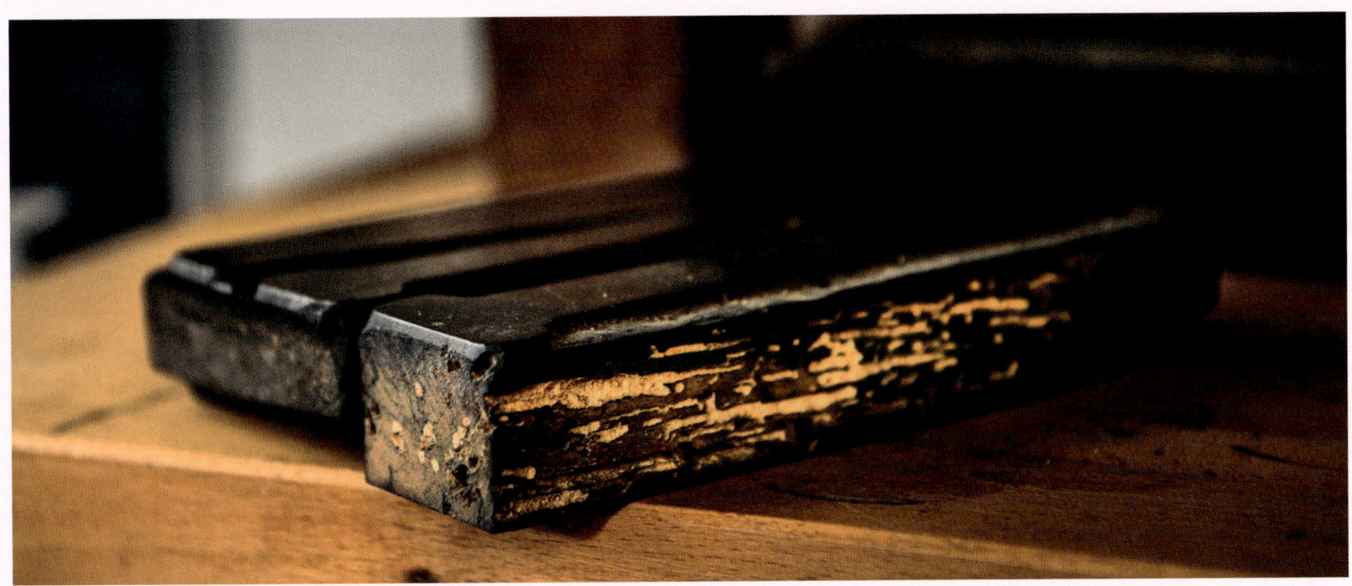

 Severe woodworm damage to wood type.

with woodworm in my type. I have had some issues with woodworm in old wooden typecases and type cabinets, however. For this I removed all the lead type that was in the cases, put the cases and cabinet outside and used a woodworm insecticide chemical, in this case, a liquid applied liberally with a brush or rag. I would not use this method of treating actual wood type, as wood is a natural and beautiful material that has a fine grain producing a delightful effect. If you apply any liquids that will soak in, then you risk swelling and blowing the wood, this really damages the grain, subtlety and fine textures for printing.

Now, how to treat your affected wood type. As said previously I would never submerge or put copious amounts of liquid on wood type. With a quick search you'll see that the internet is awash with ideas, including putting your type in Ziplock bags and into the freezer – apparently what museums do, where possible, to kill unwanted creatures in artwork and artefacts. Personally, I would use a high-quality woodworm insecticide and a blunt injecting syringe (not sharp medical-style) and inject a small amount into each hole. I wouldn't fill up each hole, as this would make it more likely to blow the wood's surface. I would then allow the type to rest and dry out slowly, isolate it for a sensible amount of time (depending on the space you have) and check for any changes. I am a big fan of taking photos to track progress – this is one of those times when working with old things in the modern world is wonderful. Then I would repeat treatment as necessary. Test any methods of treatment on a battered unloved piece of type first and see how it goes, take your time and do it properly. If I was given or purchased type that appeared to have a real infestation, I would not keep it, I'd either offer it to someone or sell it, clearly stating the condition that it's in.

Cleaning your type

Now that we have talked over the terrifying concept of an infestation, let's take a breath and assume that your wood type is simply dirty and old. The simplest way to clean type is to start by giving it a good wipe over with a dry rag to remove any dust or debris, and use a clean, dry brush to get into all those corners in either a sweeping or a rotating motion. I have used smaller wall paint brushes or art brushes to softly reach into corners and fine points. I collect old boot cleaning brushes that are often available at car boot fairs – great for giving type a quick once over.

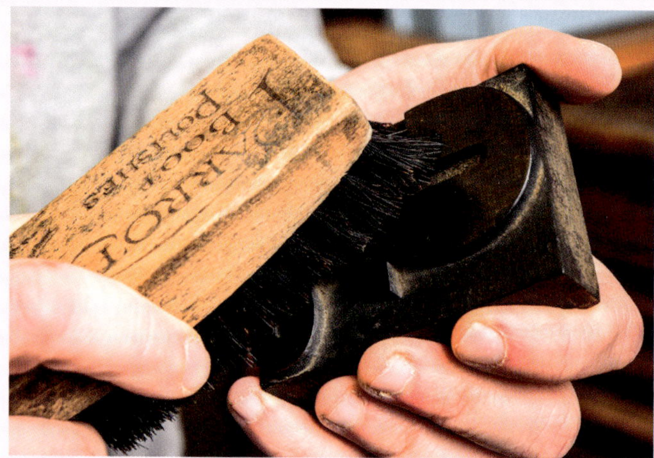

Cleaning type with a clean boot brush.

I always give type a wipe over with a clean rag with white spirit on, using a clean and light-coloured rag shows you how dirty the type really is. If the cloth seems very dirty, leave the type for a bit to air off, then wipe over again. You don't need excessive amounts of spirits; whilst it is tempting, it's better to use more elbow grease and less chemical. When using any chemical, follow the instructions on the bottle. I wear black plastic disposable gloves and make sure that my space is well ventilated. If you are at home and spirits would not really work for you, I also use orange oil at this stage, which is more appropriate for the home environment – it does smell unsurprisingly very orangey, so open a window.

Once the rags seem relatively clean (there will always be some signs of dirt), I leave the type to air. Afterwards, I personally think that the best way to clean the type to its former glory is to print with it. This sounds strange as you want to clean the type for printing, but when the paper is removed from the inked type it pulls any remaining grime from the type. If you use a bright colour you can really see this process working. If you are printing with an Adana-style hand press you can simply pull five prints, line them up as you go to see the difference, and continue until you get a consistent colour. Rather annoyingly, sometimes the specks of dirt create a lovely effect, like a patina.

Cleaning ingrained dirt out of type by repeated printing & wiping.

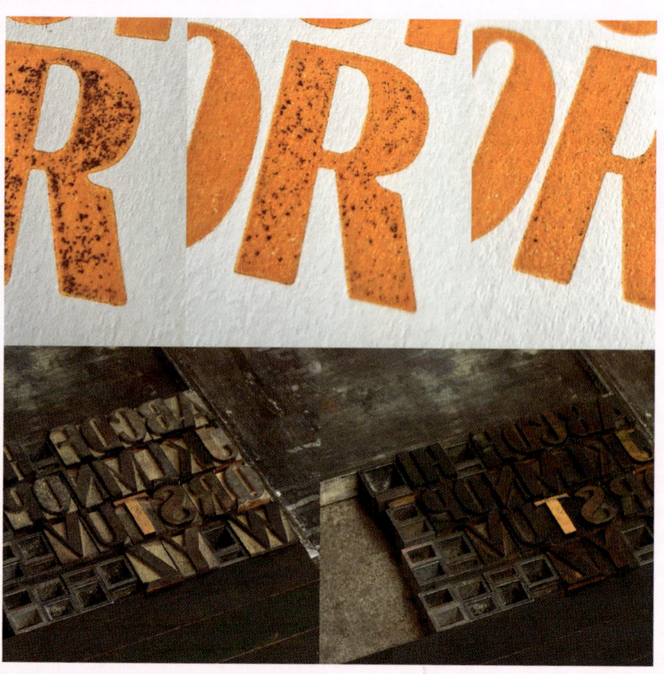

If you are printing with a proofing press or trying a DIY method of rubbing the print with a baren, and the type is showing quite a lot of dirt, you can aways give the type a quick wipe over with a clean rag to remove the majority of ink after the initial print, as it may taint the ink. Or, my preferred method is to pull a second or third print onto newspaper without reinking in between. If you have quite a lot of type then this step will save you time reinking. After pulling a couple of ghost prints (un-inked prints using just residual ink left after printing), reink and reprint, comparing to the original print to see if there is any improvement, and redo as needed. It is worth taking your time with this, as it gets you very familiar with your new type and its individual qualities. When I am doing this process, I like to set up a type specimen sheet – a simple print of the entire alphabet.

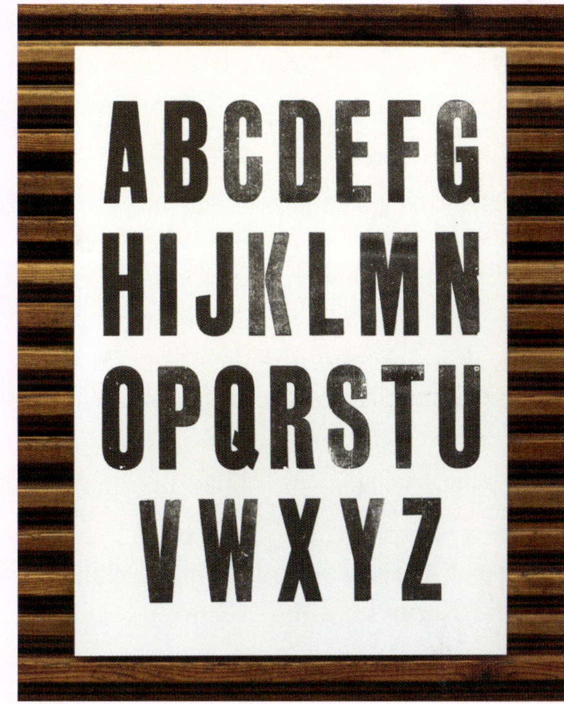

Specimen sheet print.

You're able to print freely without thinking of styling, instead studying the typeface for its inherent design.

After finishing printing, always clean your type well. Do not leave it to make a cup of tea; whilst the ink does take a long time to fully dry,

Cleaning oil based ink off wood type with rag wearing gloves.

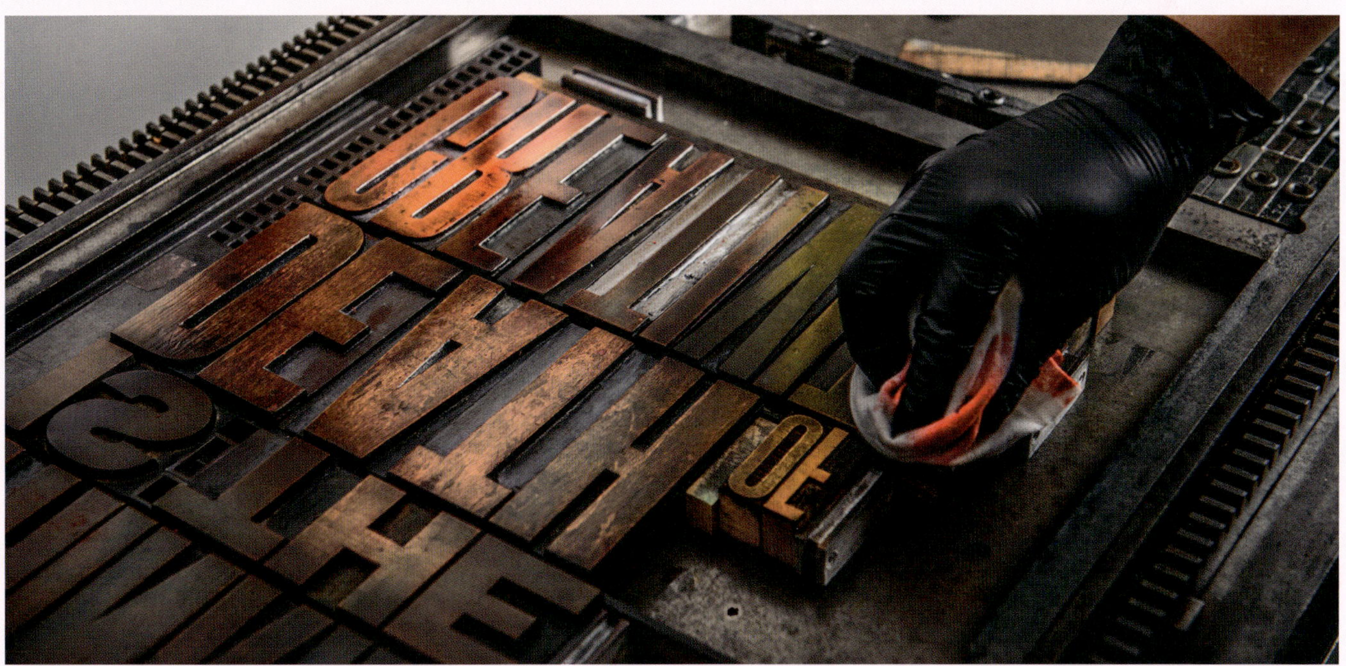

it will if you forget and leave it overnight. I'll admit, I've done it. Also put your type away after cleaning with a rag and whatever your chosen chemical is. Clean your type when it is all locked out in the chase, don't release the quoins and clean letters individually as this takes a lot longer. Then put the type away. If you leave it locked out in the chase and go a bit heavy with the cleaning liquid, it can seep between the letters, which then takes longer to dry and risks soaking into the type. Basically, work tidy and clean up after yourself.

I have also heard of people purposefully leaving a very fine coating of ink to set on the wood, creating a smooth top surface. I have never done this, and I've found that on the rare occasions that I have left ink to dry, it becomes a real pain. As I described earlier about cleaning the fine details of the type by printing, this also happens to hard ink when you print. If, for example, the dried ink is black and you then want to print in yellow, some of the dried black ink starts to pull out into your yellow. If you are only pulling a few prints this is not really a big problem, but if you are pulling a run, it can be very surprising how dramatic the colour change is from the first print to the 50th. It's hard to spot it happening until you have finished and compare prints. To really understand why someone would choose to apply a top coat of ink to their wood type, you really need to understand the very basic step that went into making wood type.

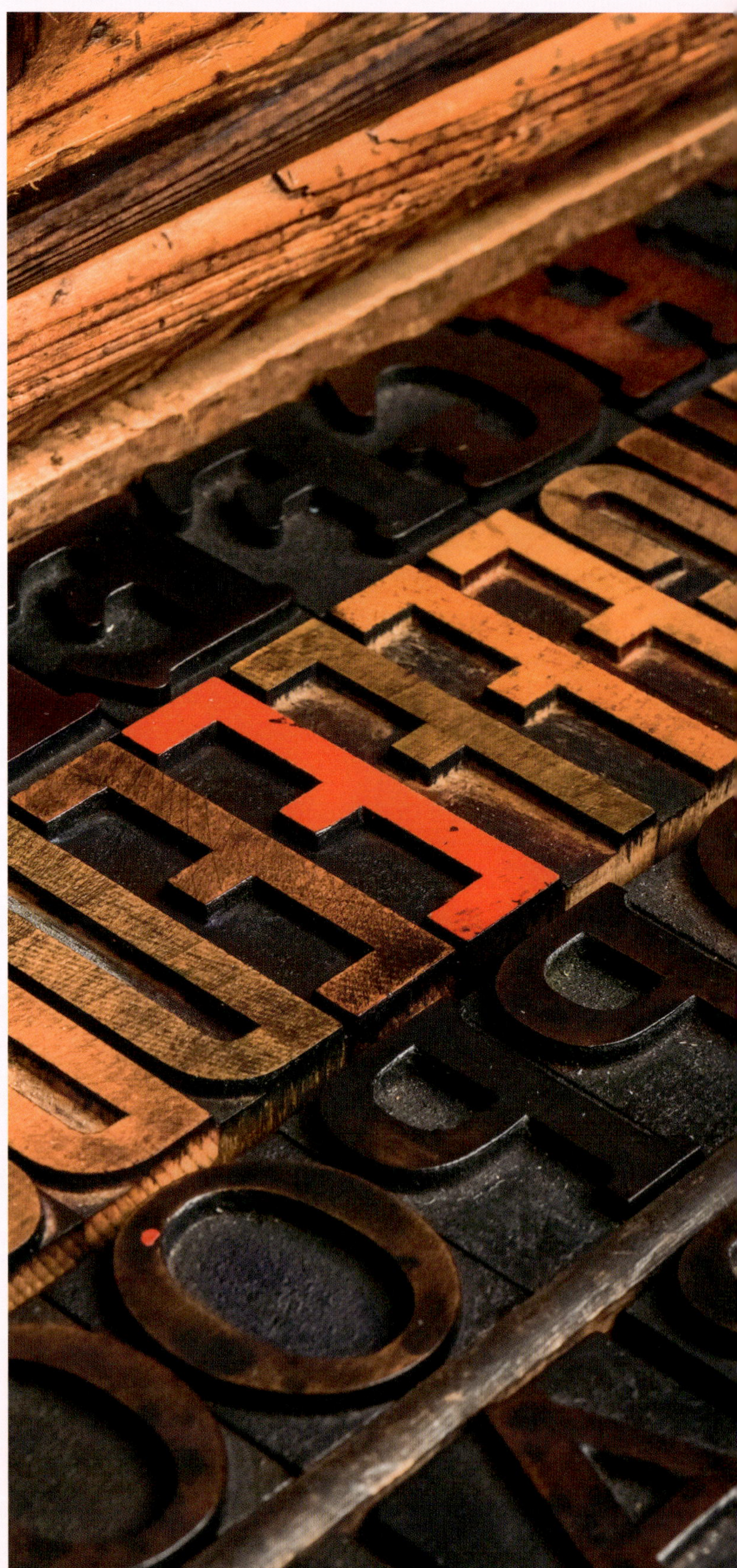

Dried red ink on letter E wood type. ☛

How type was made

The wood used for letterpress wood type was traditionally made from end grain, this means that your printing surface is not the long side of the timber that you would see when buying a plank of wood, it is the end, which features rings. It is worth saying that larger sizes of wood type were often made from side grain – you can tell the difference by giving your wood type a close inspection. This timber would be aged (left to slowly dry to become stable and minimise warp), and then be processed to be the correct height for type before layers of shellac were applied to the perfectly sanded and finished surface. This was all before the actual cutting of any letters happened.

Fonts were cut using a pantograph router (a spinning cutting bit), a device that allowed the scaling and controlling necessary to create different size fonts. Using a physical template of the individual font's letter on one end of the pantograph and the spinning cutting bit on the other end. The existing template letter would be traced around with the pantograph's non-cutting end and when set correctly, the cutting end would cut out the bulk negative areas of the type, leaving a perfectly sized and cut piece of new wood type. This was slow work, as each letter had to be cut individually. Next, all the small points and corners of the type had to be cut by hand with a blade, as the rotating cutter would leave rounded internal corners.

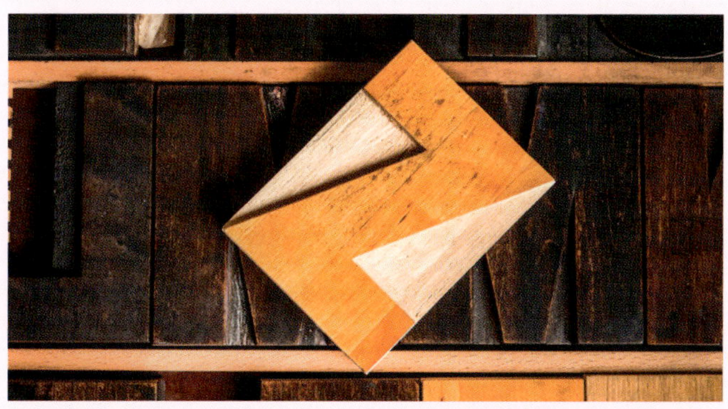

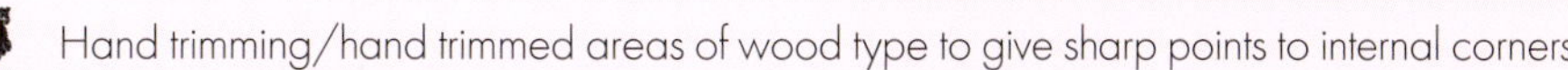

Hand trimming/hand trimmed areas of wood type to give sharp points to internal corners.

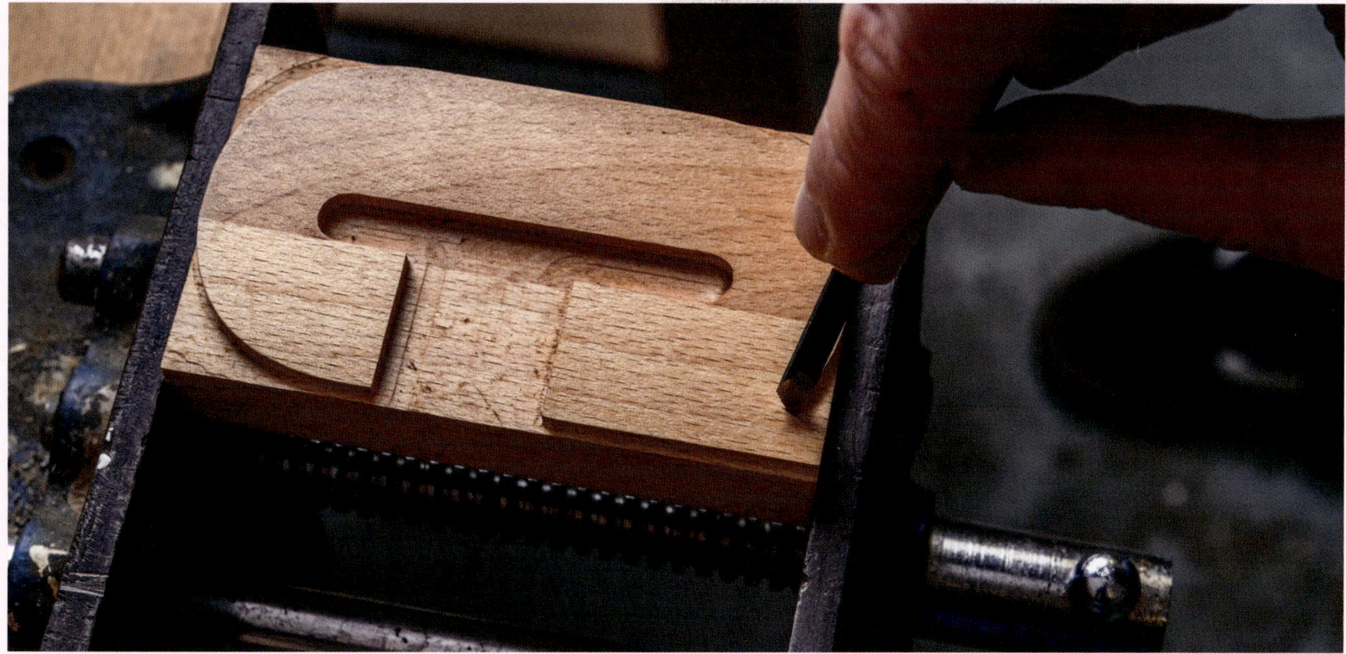

If you look at a piece of wood type closely, you can often see the pass marks for the cutting router bit as the operator would move it across the wood to clear out the areas of the type that you do not want to print. You can also often see the very precise cuts that the skilled craftsperson made to perfect the corners and points that couldn't have been cut out by a machine.

So, to get back to why someone would leave a top coat of ink on their type. They feel that the shellac finish has worn away, and that a coat of ink will act like the original finish. This is something I have never done, and something that I have discussed and disagreed about with another printer. Another issue that I have seen when purchasing wood type is that the top surface has been lightly sanded to (I assume) look more aesthetically pleasing! Be careful when purchasing any wood type where the top surface looks like clean new wood – it should have a similar colouration and visual on all sides. If the wood type has not been badly sanded and the overall height of the individual letters has not been really damaged, it should still be useable – but beware. I treat this type exactly the same as any other case when printing, though I always remember that if it is printing with very slightly less press than surrounding type, then it is probably due to this issue.

Lead type

Lead type is what I started with, as it was cheaper to collect and I began with small presses, so it made financial sense. The lead type that I have in my collection ranges from the truly tiny 6pt type, which is incredibly hard to see, ranging up to 72pt. 72pt was really the largest size that lead type was made in; beyond this size is generally wood, which is far lighter. When I have people in my workshop, the easiest way to demonstrate this is to ask someone to pull out a case of 72pt lead type

Wood type that has been sanded.

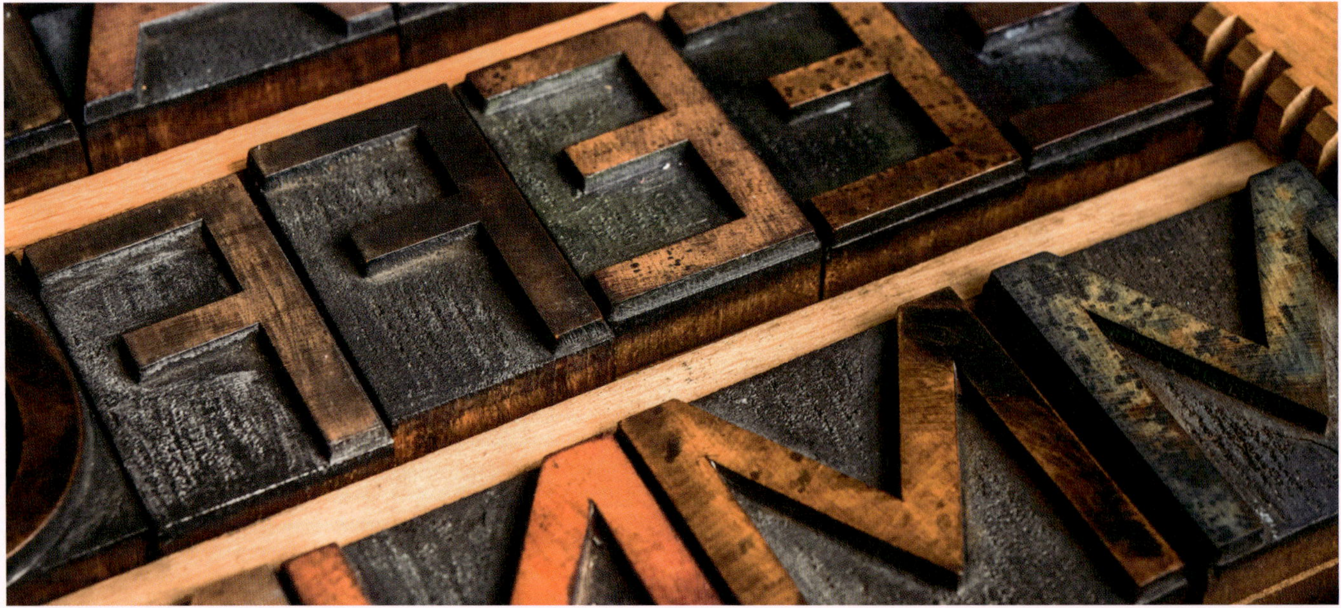

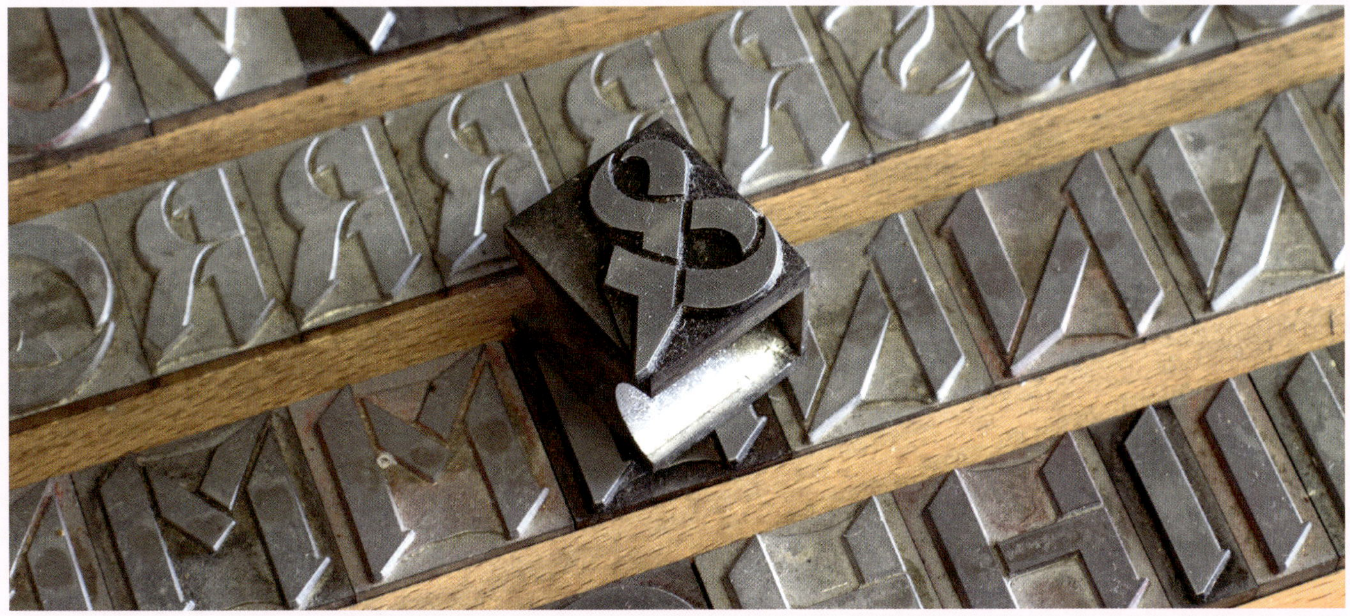

72pt (point) lead type.

– it is surprisingly heavy and each time I work with it I always feel slightly amazed at just how much lead must have been used for each set of type. As mentioned earlier, you can buy small sets of lead type for not huge amounts of money, and have a bit of variety to play with.

With smaller sets of type, it's easier to see the condition than with wood type. Being made from lead (a soft cast metal), the type can get crushed, dented and damaged from setting up and printing. An easy mistake would be dropping a locked-out case of lead type on its face side. Another common mistake is to incorrectly set up your printing press pressure, applying too much and crushing the type during the test print. For instance, when setting up an Adana to print, there's a bar that you set to hold your paper in place for each print. If you get this in the wrong position during setup and misalign so it lines up with your type, when you push down with full force you will crash the metal bar into the lead type crushing part of the type flat. Once you have damaged type like this, it is sadly unusable. If you do this by mistake just learn from the experience. Remember not to push too hard on test prints, to double check everything as you go, and remember that mistakes happen.

Cleaning lead type is not very complicated. Again, use low odour white spirit or orange oil depending on the environment, always ventilating accordingly. In my own workshop on the south coast of England, that would be low-odour white spirit. When working at external workshops or at events, I use orange oil. Only clean down any type when it is locked out, with lead type which is small it is very annoying to clean each tiny letter individually.

Try not to overload the rag with chemicals and soak the type – it's very easy to flood the smaller parts of font with chemical, which can bleed into your ink when pressing.

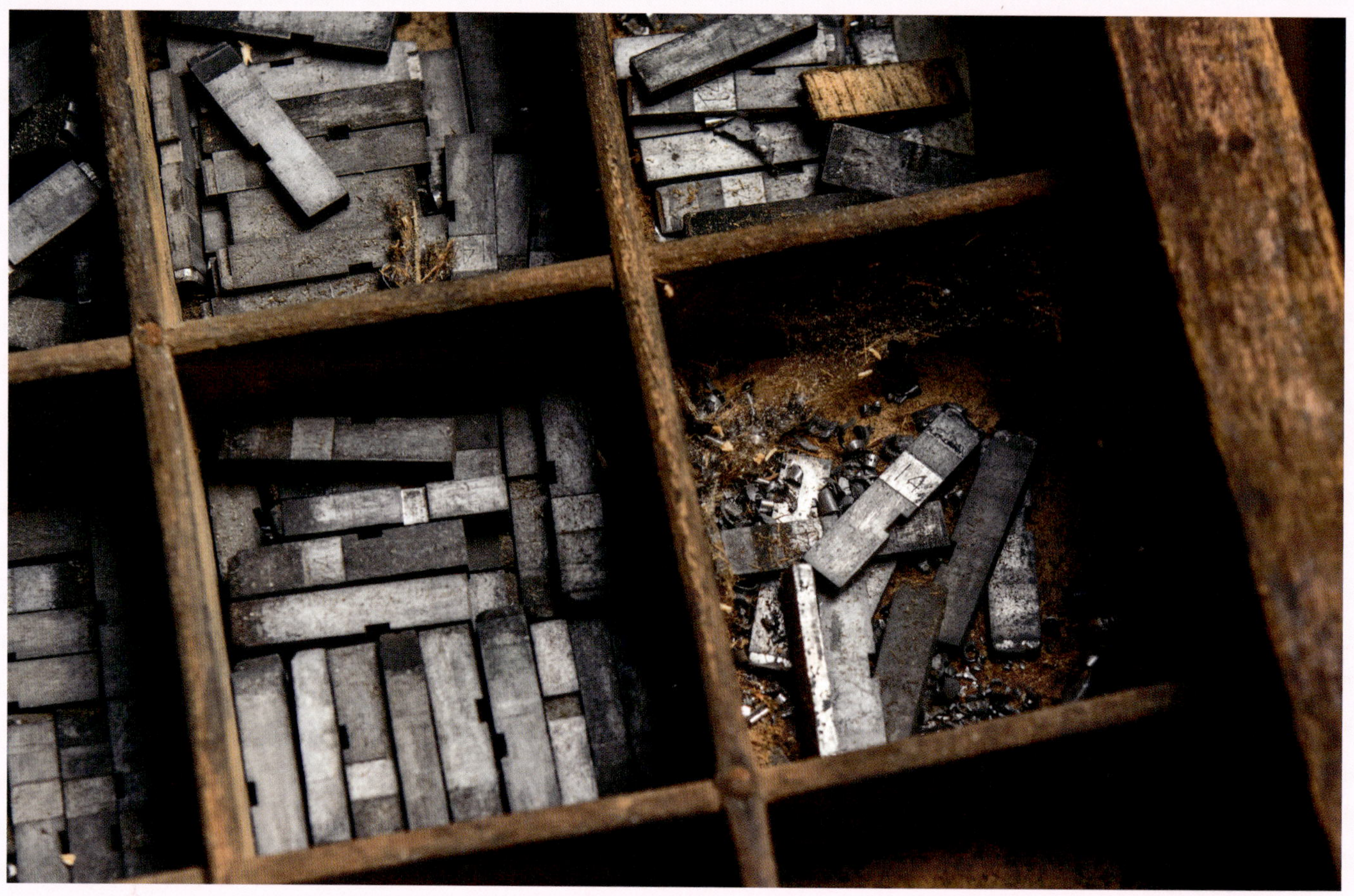

Dust, dirt, shards of metal & spider webs in a type case.

Now, your type may be dirty when you get it... Dust, spider webs, dead insects, sawdust and the odd mouse dropping are all things that I have found in cases of lead type. These can be cleaned out in a very obvious fashion, remove all the type and do a general dust of the case – ideally outside as you really don't want to breathe it in. Then give all the type itself either a quick dust, or if needed, a wipe over with a rag and low-odour white spirit. As I have mentioned before, printing and using the type as intended is a great way to keep and maintain it. If your type is a bit worse for wear with ink dried into the crevices, then you have to get a bit more involved with cleaning. I keep my family's old toothbrushes for just these sorts of issues. Lead type has the advantage over wood type that you can soak in in small batches – don't soak whole sets at once. Work with a small amount at a time, soaking in white spirt. I like to use my old electric toothbrush to scrub the type clean. If it doesn't shift it on the first go, re-soak and scrub again. It can be a slow process, but it is worth taking care so as not to cause damage. For this activity I work outside, to minimise fumes exposure, and also because I like working outside when I can. Wear gloves, a mask and some eye protection – common sense and good practices are a good thing to develop for all working activities.

On occasion, you find that lead type has developed a white, almost rust-looking growth to the surface. It feels like sandpaper and is quite disturbing. This is lead oxide, and some refer to this as lead type blight. Lead oxide is not good for you, so cleaning this should be done carefully. If the type is very badly oxidised, there may be pitting to the top printing surface. To clean, soak in vinegar for a day then rinse, dry and use an electric toothbrush to scrub. Please do this outside, be careful and use a mask and gloves. Depending on how badly oxidised the type is, you may need to repeat soaking again. As with cleaning lead type generally, taking your time and being gentle is the way forward. As this is a slow process, you will learn the best way that works for you. After getting the type back to a good clean condition I soak the type in white spirit and wipe clean, leaving for a while to air off, then spray liberally with WD40 as this gives the type a good protective coating. Leave this over-night then wipe off the oil using two passes with two different rags. This should leave the type clean and not oily.

A good thing to add to your useful-things-to-collect-and-not-throw-away list are the plastic takeaway food containers that come with lids, I often use these for any cleaning activities, and they handily stack on top of each other when you have quite a lot to do. I've also heard of people using small ultrasonic jewellery cleaners and getting good results. I did purchase a cheap one online, but found it was not as effective as my normal method. It is always worth experimenting to see what works for you, though. If your type is in really bad condition, think carefully about your time and whether you feel confident dealing with it. If you don't, there is no shame in moving type on to a new home – just be honest about its condition if you are selling, giving away or swapping.

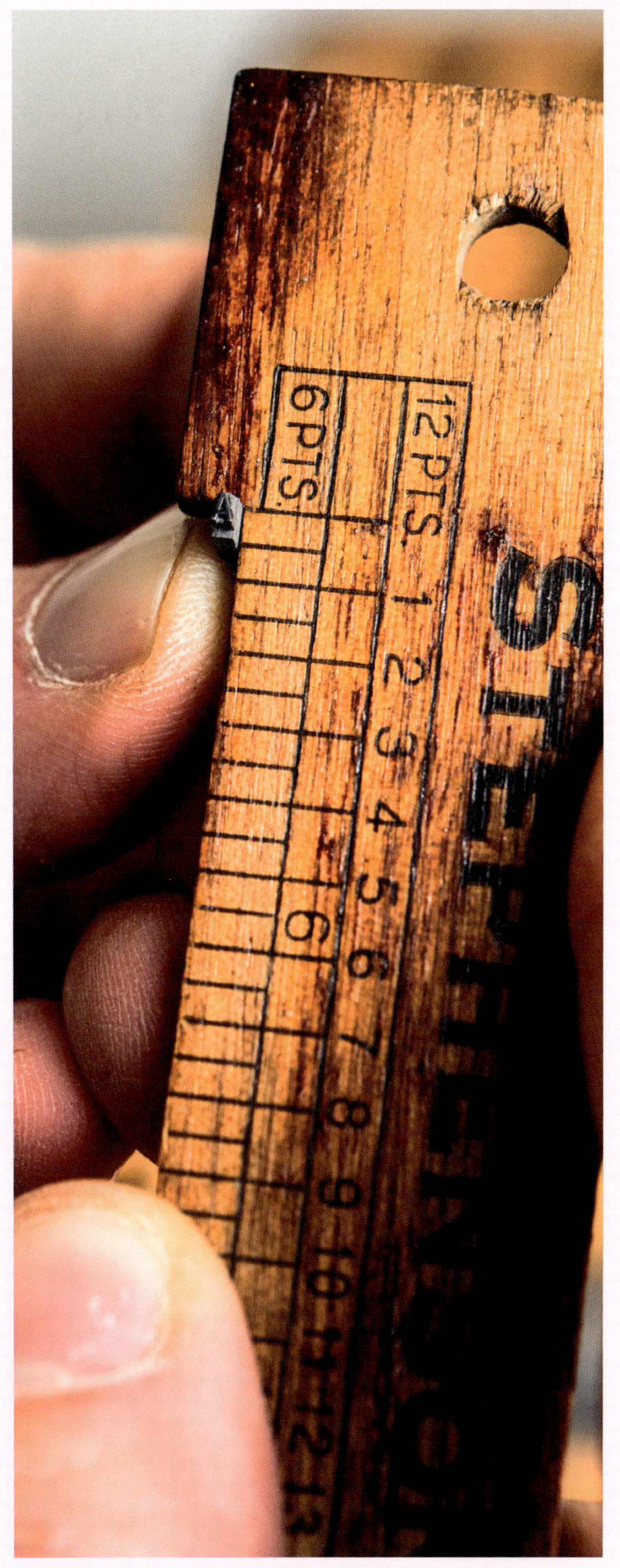

Tiny 6 point lead type in a type rule. ☛

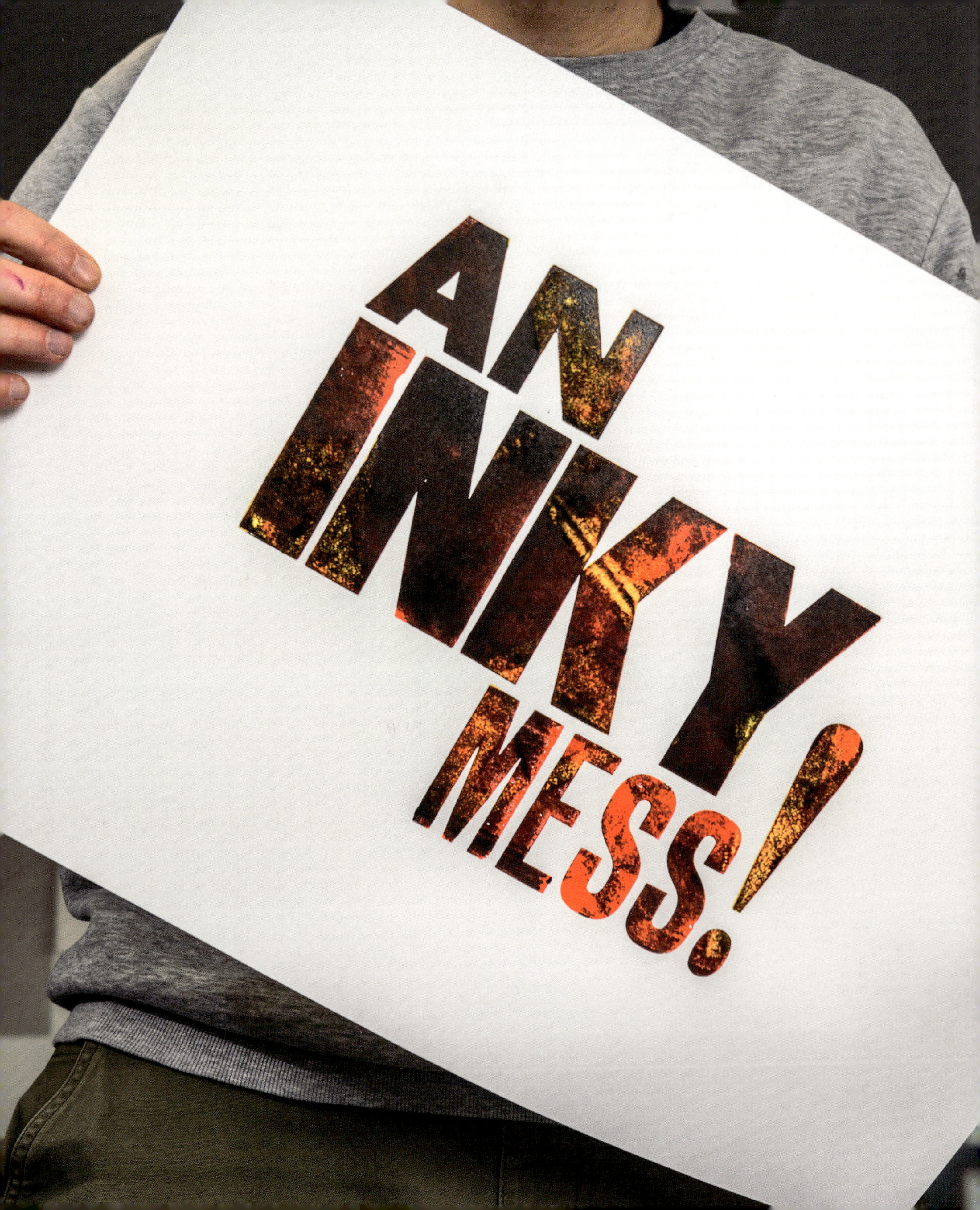
AN
INKY
MESS!

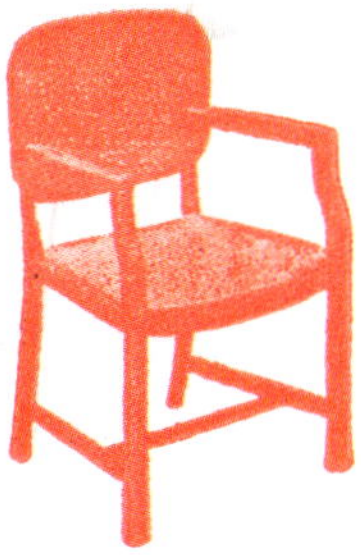

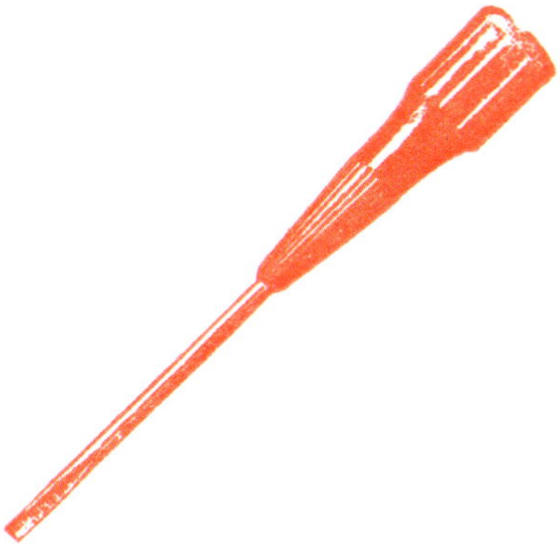

4

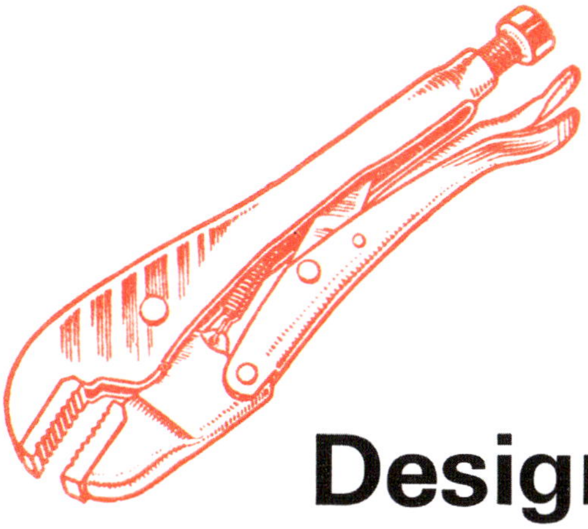

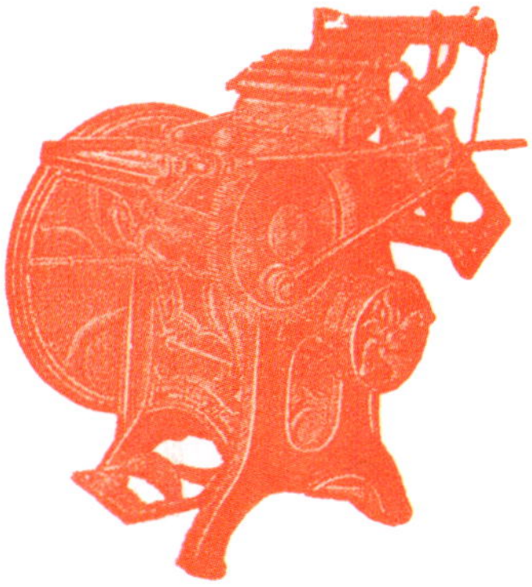

Designing with letterpress

I trained as a graphic designer, and I work as a designer first and printer second. This may sound strange and obvious, but you will find that as you work, play and enjoy your time printing, you develop different instincts as a designer, printer, maker, artist or whatever you consider yourself.

As a designer, I always get excited about shape and form and how the tactile and real nature of the printing process can interact with the overall design, and then as a printer how this is going to work on a practical level. This means questioning the number of colours and how they are layered, in what order the colours should be printed, whether it is a product or a personal project, and questions like 'is it financially viable?'. I decided a long time ago that some things will require more print processes than may be financially sensible.

But it is about process and doing something that you love, so if it takes a bit longer, then it takes a bit longer.

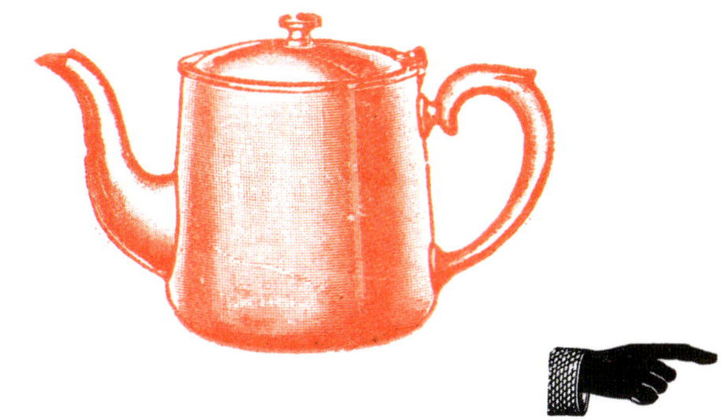

Designing and instinctive designing (wood type)

Letterpress is a very different process from design on a computer; a lot of people will have done design work using software like Photoshop, InDesign and Illustrator. They all have the same basic concept: almost limitless choice! Choice of fonts, colours, filters and effects, images, and sizes. Well, good news if you find these digital choices dizzying – letterpress is really about working with what you have and allowing the design to be created in an almost symbolic process of the designer and their objects. The reality of letterpress is that you can't have everything! With letterpress, sometimes you are really just grateful if you have enough letters – not joking. Sometimes you will need to think outside the box and be creative in your problem solving. The good news is that when you get into the zone, you can feel like a creative mastermind.

I always say to people during workshops that letterpress designs itself, and that the letterpress type and block dictate and direct the flow of the design, in turn dictating and inspiring colours and layouts. In this section I will primarily focus on using wood type and poster printing, though the rules and concepts of what we are talking about translate to lead type as well. It is great to just start off with the very basics, a sheet of blank paper, a phrase or just the words you want to print. This back-to-basics and free approach is how I love to start printing. You have set one absolute parameter that whatever you are doing has to fit on this sheet of paper. I insist during workshops that students have a notebook, and they must write out the phrase or words that they are going to print – try not to think when you do this and just write. This is always an interesting point of a workshop, as you find that people start designing without thinking about it. As a rule, people don't write their words out in a straight

Wood type including part/incomplete fonts.

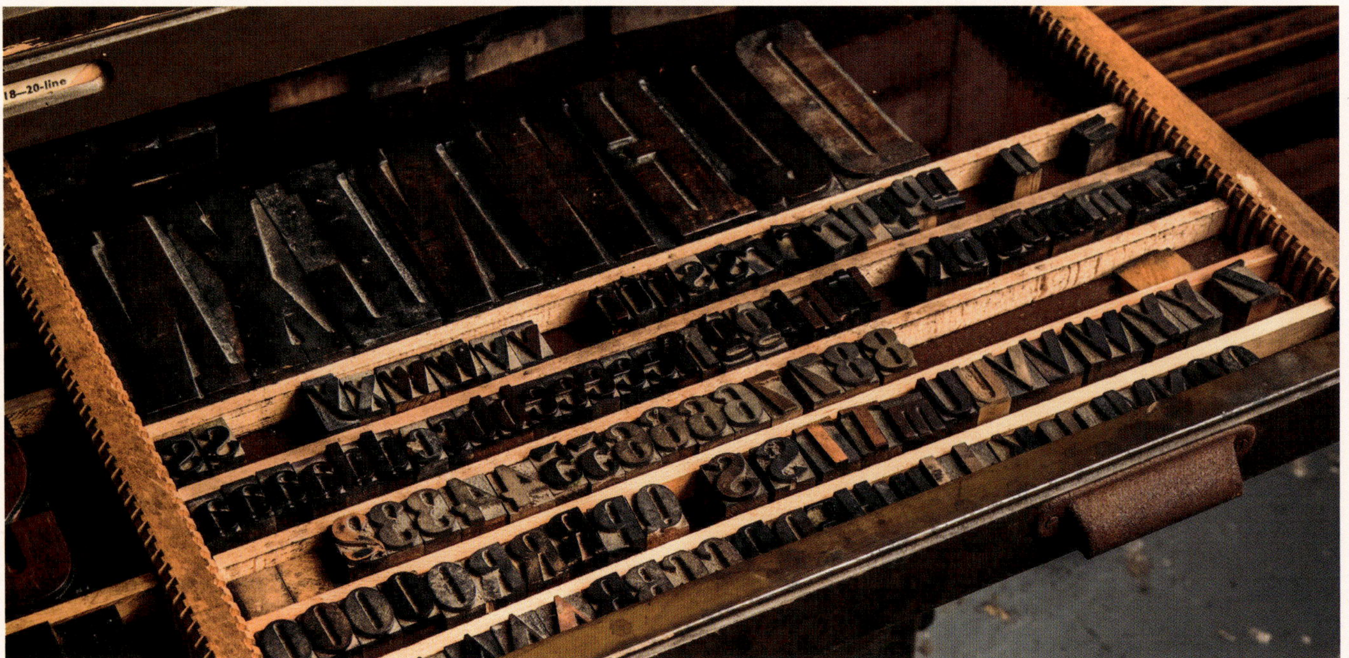

line. Instead, they usually write already with an element of design, for example, centre-ranging a short phrase over three lines. This often answers some basic questions about the design, but they may not have thought of basic things like do you want to print the design landscape or portrait? Are there priority words that need to stand out? This is what I consider natural and intuitive designing to be: working from gut feeling. This is my happy place for designing, printing and making.

Often it can be hard to design in a purely instinctive fashion and sometimes it's not possible at all due to client restraints. Practice makes perfect, and when I hit a block, I will fall back to what I do with others during workshops. The first prints I pull with participants in workshops are random word prints. Working as a group, each one in turn will pick a random word (there are lots of word-generating apps out there). I tell them that the word doesn't matter and it's just about getting hands-on with the type and pulling their first print – which is sort of true! I tell them to go and pick a set of wood type they like.

When picking the letters out of the case to form your words, don't try to spell backwards. This happens a lot when printing with people new to letterpress, as the letters are mirrored. Somehow when people see that the letters are flipped, they assume that they should work backwards, spelling the word in reverse. Simply spell the word as you always have, but as you select the letter put them down in reverse, right to left, for example, T R A I N = N I A R T. Whilst this seems very simple, it can get surprisingly complicated looking at letters in reverse.

Once the wood type has been selected, I get each person to put their word on the bed of the printing press. This is when things get interesting, as each person puts down their word how

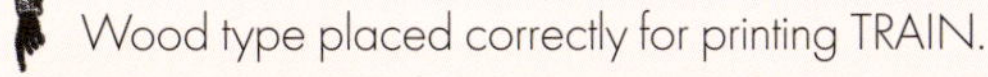
Wood type placed correctly for printing TRAIN.

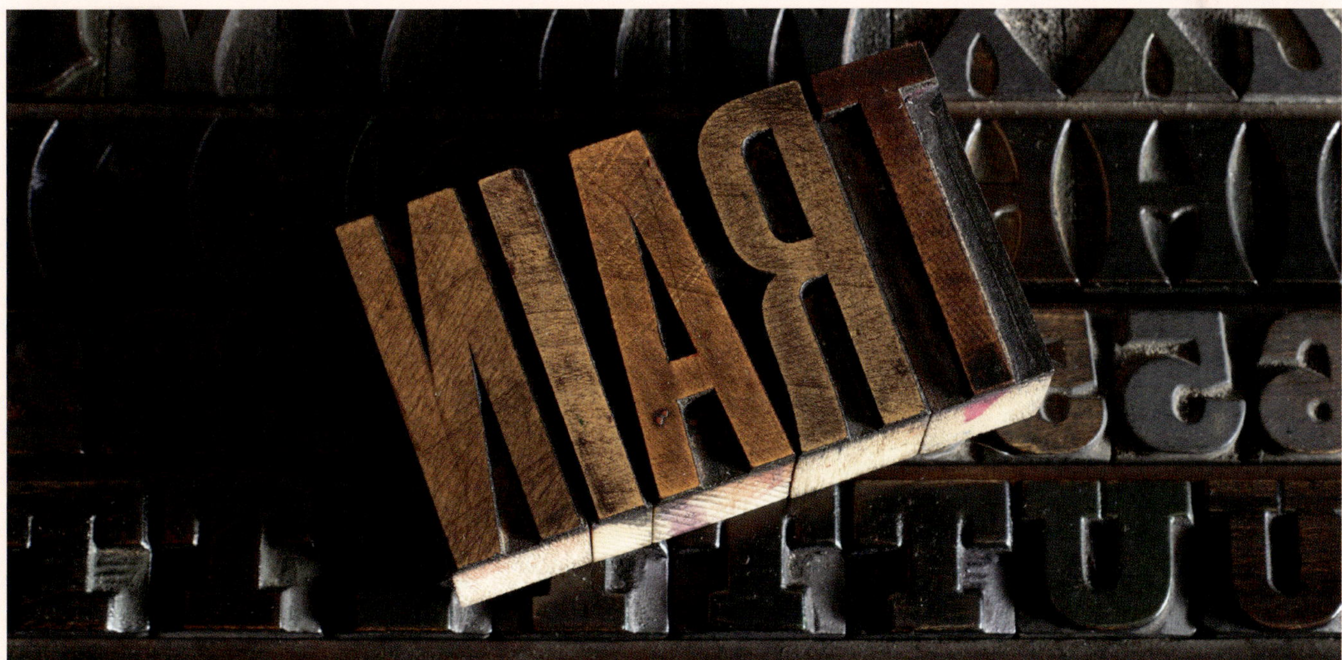

they see fit. This can make for some design clashes. One person may like everything very ordered, so would naturally like straight lines in a static arrangement. On the other hand you get people who like effects whereby letters are not in lines and appearing to fall apart or jump around higgledy-piggledy. Whatever happens, all the type is on the bed of the printing press ready to print.

Quoins, galley magnets and furniture are used to secure everything in place, ensuring that there will, ideally, be no movement of the letters once locked out. When you create any sort of scattered, deconstructed or unusual composition with type it is very hard to lock letters fully in place at strange angles, so galley magnets are ideal for this. Remember that you can use the galley magnet on either the long side or the short end to hold the type in place, depending on how tight space is. I always create these prints in black, as I only want to look

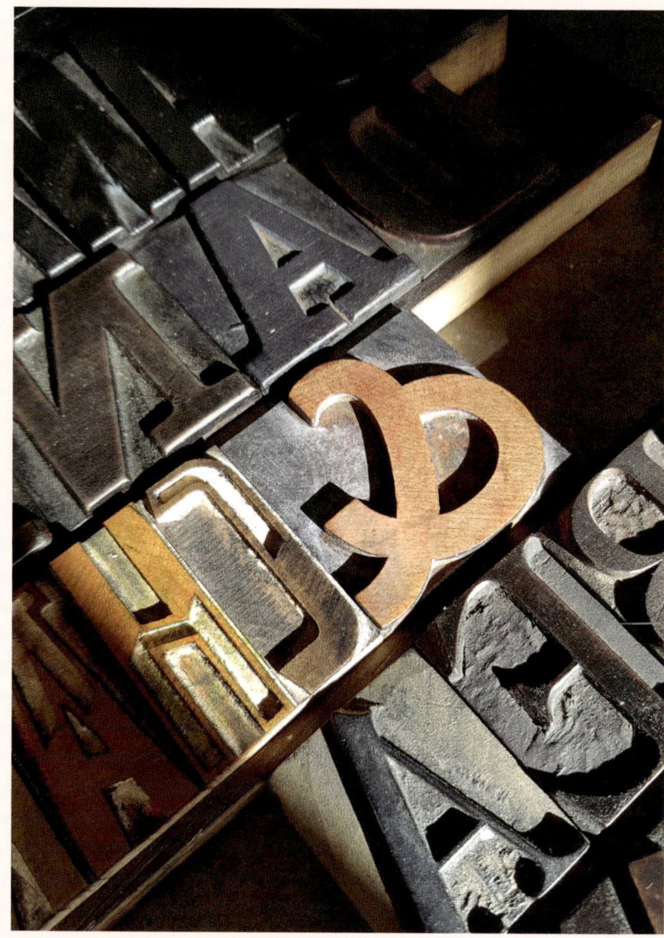

Arranging wood type.

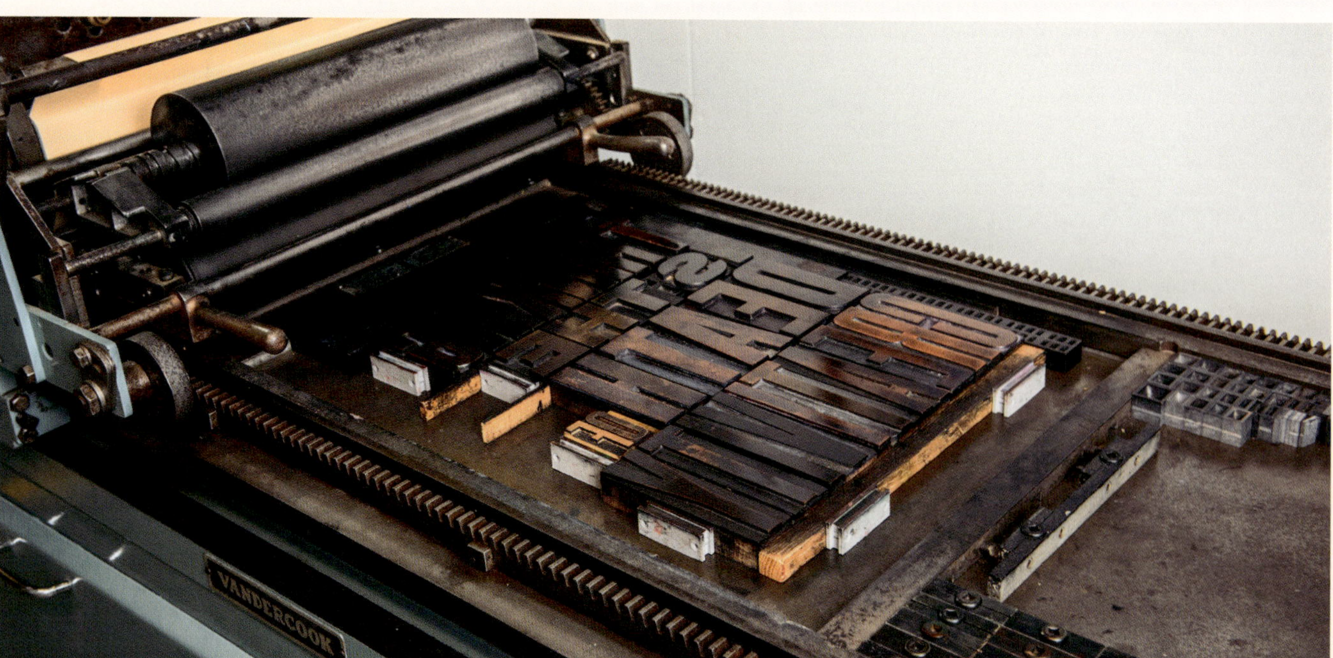

Wood type arranged on Vandercook using galley magnets.

at the form and layout of the print and design. Thinking too much at this stage is not a good idea, so I don't usually introduce colour choice. Ink the type rapidly and thoroughly, and pull the first print. The first print is usually always a poor one – this is when you can see how to improve with some simple alterations.

These issues can be simple ones of mis-inking some areas, or a different density produced by over-inking some parts – badly worn type often has areas that will not print cleanly because they are slightly warped or dented. If the composition of the layout is not as liked, linespacing is regularly debated at this point; kerning (spacing) between letters is always interesting with letterpress. As each piece of type was made by craftsmen each having their own uniqueness, this in some cases is the design of the font and how the individual letters interact with each other, and also the physical sense of how much space was left around the letter when cut out.

Mis-printed area of type due to imbalance/small dent in the type.

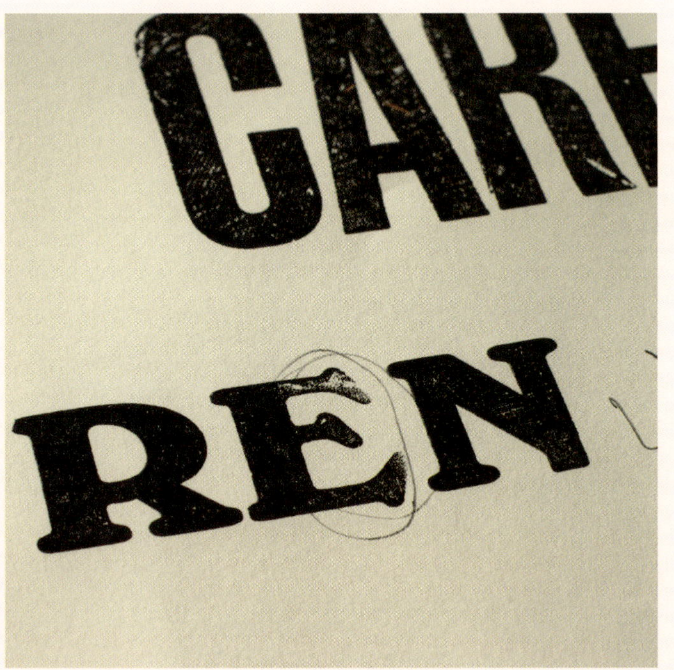

Always remember to look for misspelled words – check your spellings, particularly common words, as it is easy to miss the obvious mistake when looking at tiny details and slight imperfections of print quality. As soon as the print is pulled, I number each page corner as we go, until the print is right. This means that you follow any adjustment you have made and judge whether you're making improvements or creating new problems! Having prints strewn across the workshop and not being sure in which order they were printed does not help you problem solve, and it makes me feel like a dog chasing its own tail. This is when you realise how many options there really are with very limited text and fonts.

From here, letterpress takes over the design process. Some people like the small imperfection of type that's warped a fraction of a millimetre and isn't printing the corner of a letter. Some like heavy inking so everything looks very bold, while some go for lighter inking, so you still get all the boldness of the individual font, but you manage to pull the characteristic of the wood, making the print appear more three dimensional.

It's good to make changes at this point, and try different layouts. Change line spacing, play around with the kerning between letters, try without any added spacing at all. After creating a number of different iterations, you can look at them as a group and reflect on what you do and don't like. This also shows the real reason for using random words to practice printing: so that you don't care about the meaning of the words. They do not have a meaning. They hold no emotional attachment, and are there to help you learn more about what you like and what you think looks good. Once you've discovered the joy of just playing for playing's sake, it can really free the natural designer in you.

Letterpress designing and printing is really about grids and forming letters and words in a style that suits the individual designer. This depends heavily on how legible you want the type to be; in some cases it may not need to be read easily and will just function as a shape or abstract element. With different type layouts and structures of design you can also influence the way the viewer reads and interacts with the print. This, as a designer, offers you a real chance to make your piece beyond that of normal design and print. The small and simple changes employed in a process like this can really help you learn quickly and pick up on different effects and possibilities.

Kerning – make hay while the sun shines

I know that this concept of type doing the designing can seem like a rather strange notion, so I thought it would be good to run through a couple of designs where the type really takes over and directly leads the design. The first print here was for a pop-up event where I would be printing in a very large marquee in a field for an event celebrating crafts. The phrase was selected: 'make hay while the sun shines'. The first word I picked was 'hay' in a very bold font, which became the core of the design and dictated other fonts and the overall paper size. Just to be clear, I don't feel that this is one of my best designs, I just remember that the process that went into it felt very right.

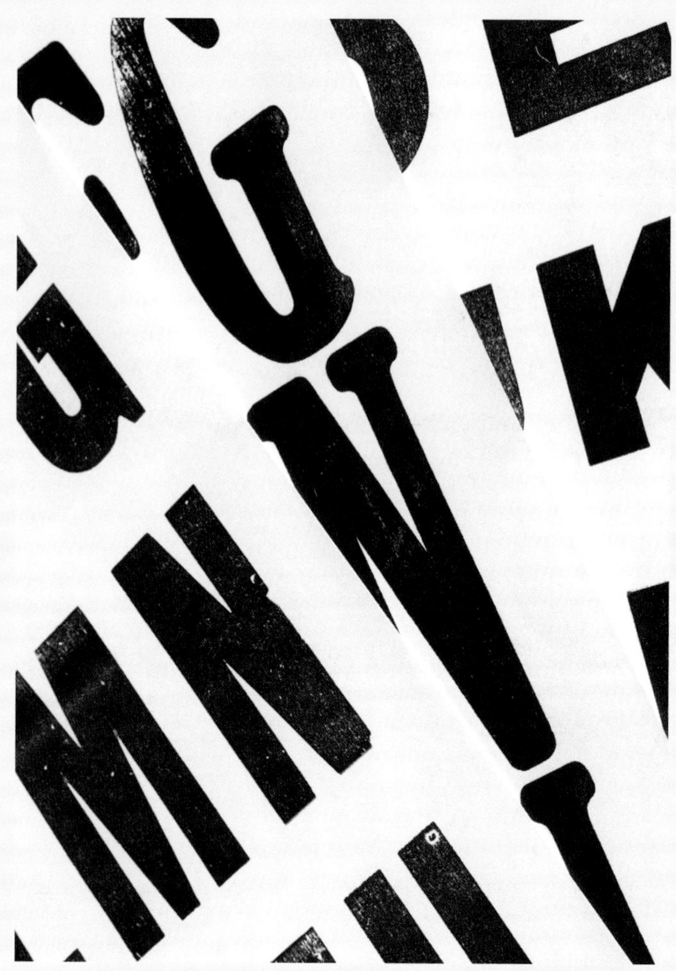

Natural differences in prints.

The word HAY is a difficult combination of letters for letterpress, when you consider their shape and where the letter is positioned on the block. H fills all the space of the block, A fills the base and middle third of the block, and Y is basically like A but upside down in terms of space usage. So, the visual problem when all the letters are pushed together without kerning is that the H and A are very close to touching at the bottom. A next to Y leaves a very defined angular space when in fact there is none, with the two wooden blocks touching. The resolution to this is to space (kern) out the H from the A. The spacing in this case looks very odd, but when printed it looks correct.

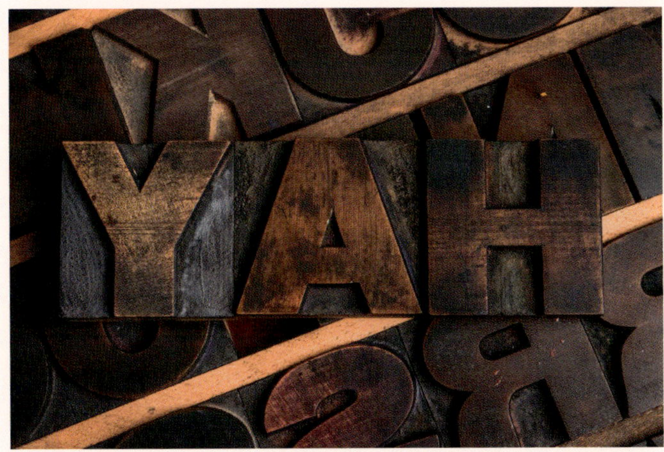

Wood type placed with natural spacing of the type.

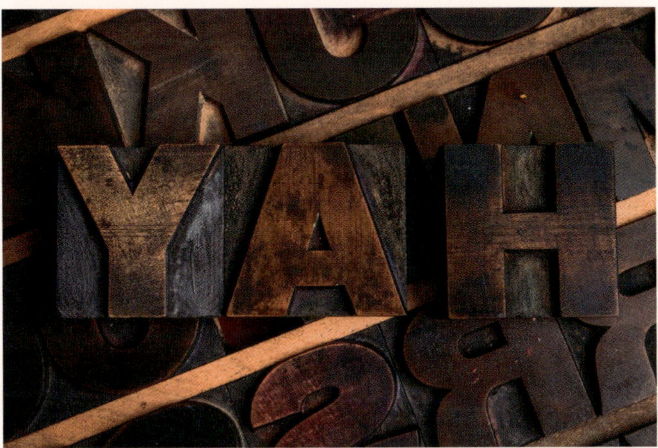

Moved to create more natural looking spacing when printing.

After the HAY was spaced, I realised that another font, similar to Gill Sans or Johnson in design, would fit really nicely, so MAKE was set. These two words dictated the width of the design from here in. Next came SHINES, which is a very close fit for the width of the design. I wanted a large and bold font to make the word shout. For the final two words, I was really looking for what fitted in the space and looked good – which in reality is a big part of designing and making. After all words were chosen, the type was then kerned with small pieces of card rather than the slimmest furniture, to make all the words the same width. With letters like M and H, the blocks are usually cut very close to the edge of the letter. This exact width from the edge of the letter to the edge of the block was not always the same though, as each letter was cut by a person on a circular saw. Whilst these were very accurate, at the end of the day each block is handmade. For a design that features straight lines of text in relation to each other, it is worth paying great attention to the small details, packing using a small slither of card if they do not magically align. For me, it is the little tweaks that really give that extra lift to a finished print.

Make Hay print.

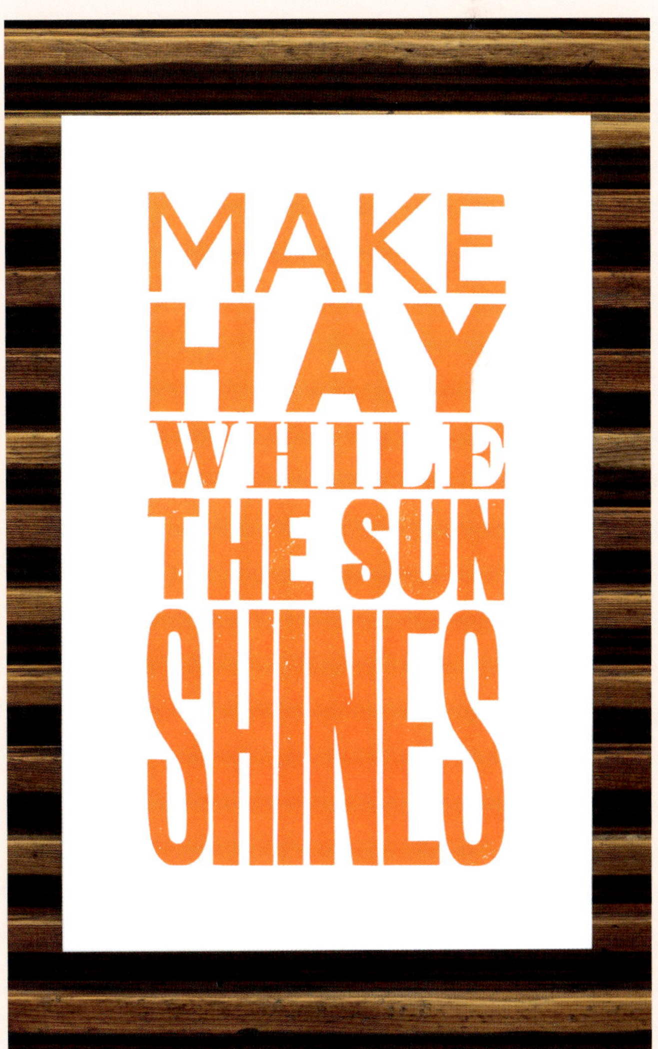

Visually affecting a design

Sometimes the issues of kerning can be a real pain. People often talk about the natural spacing between the letters just being part of letterpress and its aesthetic. I personally disagree, and think that you should always look at the spacing and make even small adjustments to make the type flow as is intended for the design. It is important to remember that the kerning of the type affects the way that words are read; it can slow it down or speed it up. This can allow you, the designer, to add a deeper and richer experience. Sometimes designs can be really difficult to get right; letterpress can have an odd effect whereby type looks really good laid ready to print, you can even feel very confident at this point, but then when you print it, it doesn't feel quite right, or is sometimes totally wrong. This is part of the process of dealing with non-digital design, as you cannot truly see results until it is printed. This can be tricky, as you can spend a lot of time in the setup phases just pushing the type around and not getting very far. When you design digitally, you get instant feedback and live results. However, whether you design digitally or with letterpress, you are building designs. With letterpress you are just building physically with blocks, so it will often feel slower and, on occasion, lacking in finished results. There are things you can do when you have moments of feeling that a design should work but doesn't, when you feel that you are ready to give up. In these moments it is good to stop, have a cup of tea, and try to look at the design in different ways.

To use another print as an example, 'the will to do will see us through' was a phrase I loved as it rolls nicely off the tongue. This was an occasion where I selected all the type that I wanted to print with, and as I set up the type on the press bed, I felt positive that it was really working together. When I pulled the first print in a single colour of bright red, I didn't like it. When I was selecting and setting the type, I wanted it to be crushed together and slightly uncomfortable to view, with some of the type jumping and jarring a little bit. This was done by selecting different size and boldness of fonts, and keeping the line spacing to a minimum. The first thing I really disliked was the closeness of TO and DO compared with the gap from DO to WILL. This issue is the same as previously seen with HAY, but with a different outcome.

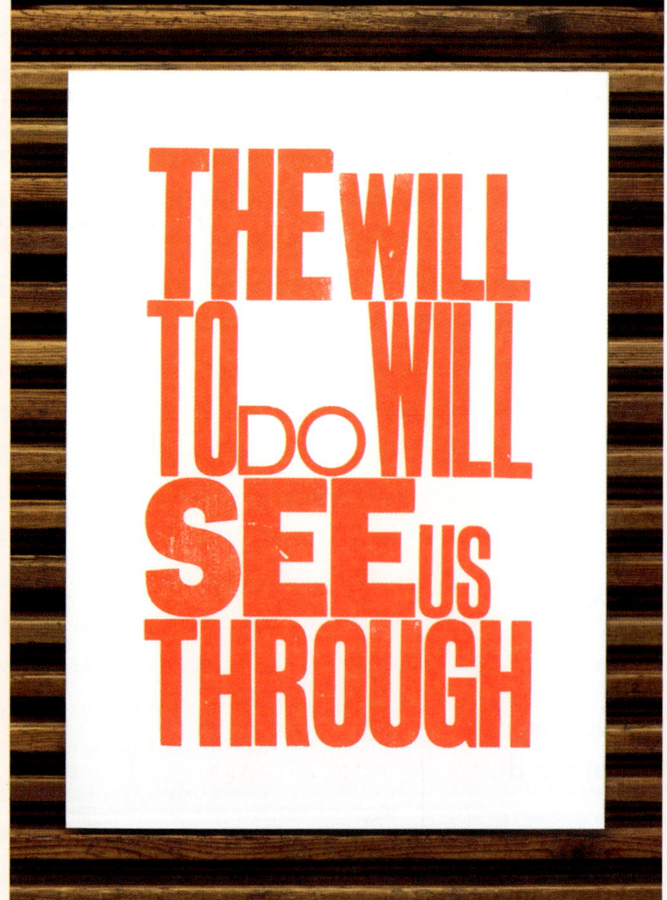

One colour option on the will to do print.

All the words in this case were pretty much touching with no spacing. It was what I was going for, but the space between DO and WILL really ruined the overall effect. After pulling this first one-colour print, I tried making various alterations to the kerning and line spacing to improve the look of the design. I got to the moment where you keep making lots of changes, but nothing really improves and all you seem to be doing is create new problems.

I ended up going back pretty much to the original setup and then thinking about filling in the negative space above DO. I tried finding a picture block from my collection that could work in the space but it just looked naff and wrong. I tried something I love to do, which is printing the actual letterpress furniture to give a shape and texture. Furniture can be great fun to print with as they often have lots of bangs and bumps, which can give some lovely effects when printed. Printing a block in this space did not work and it looked clumsy and heavy. At this point I was kind of annoyed with the design and thinking about just moving on and giving up. I had a cuppa and a little think about colours – maybe a multi-coloured print would be the way to go. A simple technique is to pull quick prints in different colours then cut and mix them around on a table to see what works. Note: doing this with not-yet-dry prints can be messy!

I couldn't really get the multi-colour print idea to work, and looking at all the different iterations lying around, I felt that what I did like about the design was that it felt like it was set almost in two triangles, with the individual words holding each other up in a very precarious way. Almost like the words are stepping on each other. So, in a moment of just being unsure what to do but wanting to do something, I inked the entire design in red then took a roller with black ink on it and quickly and purposefully inked some of the letters to highlight the stepping effect of the design.

Suddenly, I liked it. What I had also done is create a design that is hard to repeat, as the two inks are on the type at the same time. So when you go to re-ink the red, if you touch any of the black ink, you will taint your red when you take the roller back to the inking plate.

Red with black areas inked version of the will to do print.

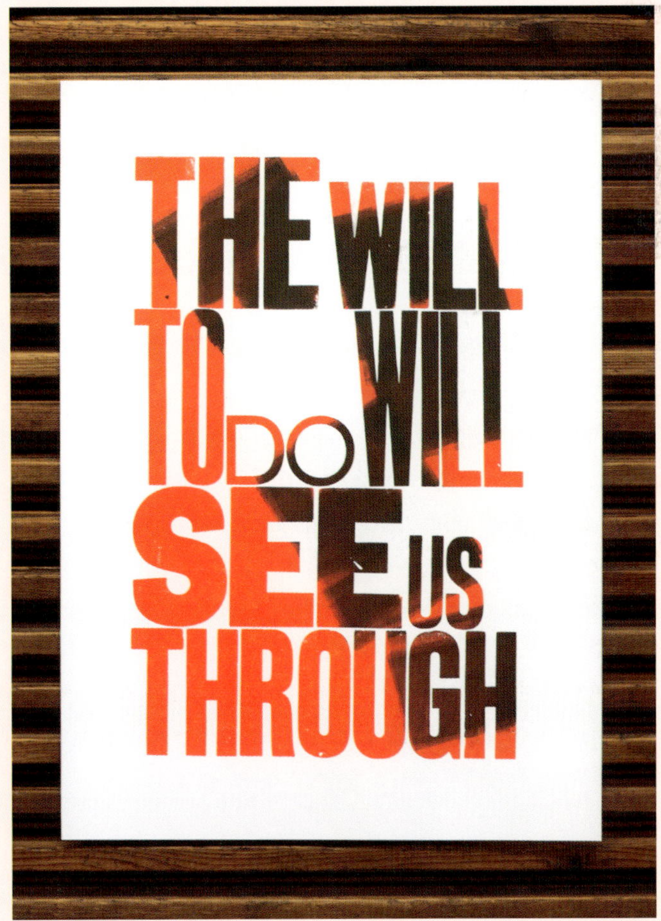

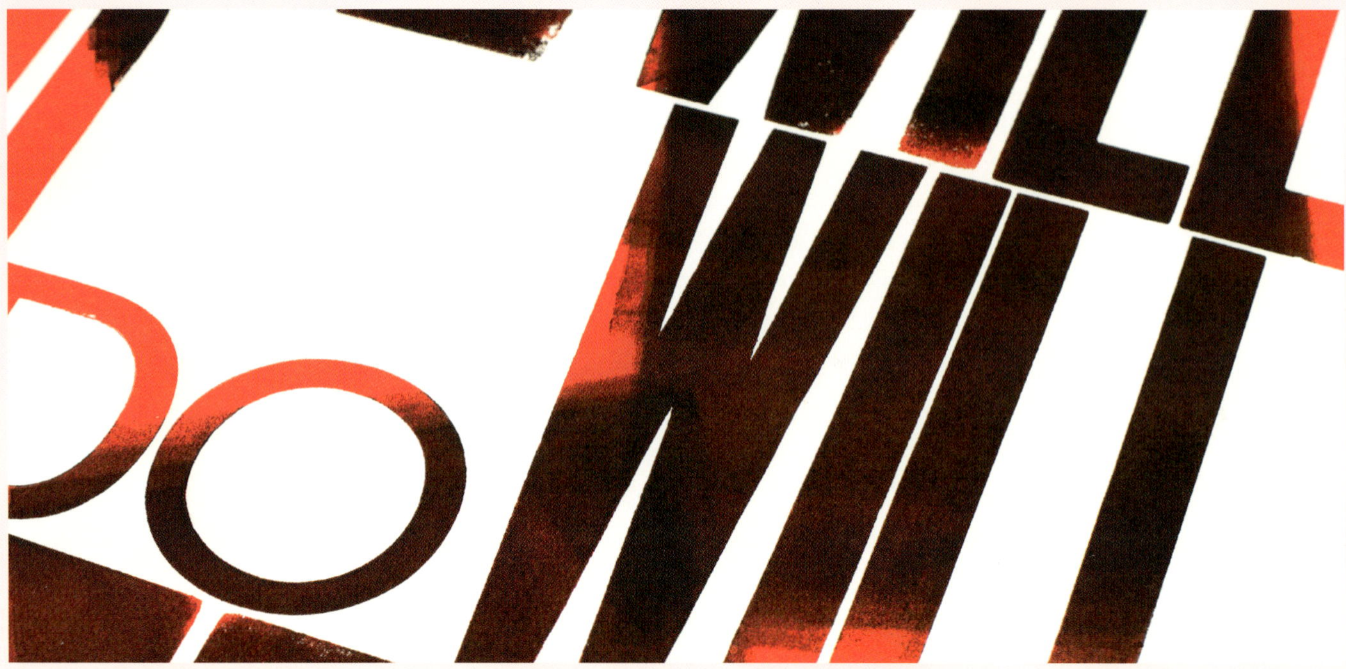

Close up of will to do print red and black.

This means prints like this are quite unique and really, one-offs, though there are techniques that you can use to make it workable for short runs or limited editions. This style of inking is something that I have become very fond of over the years. I consider it disrupting to a design, creating a level of visual noise to make the viewer read or see what you want them to. This can be used subtly by having very small areas affected. Different colour combinations can impact the effect, with some being very complementary and some being intentionally jarring and difficult to consume visually. This, to me, can add a very exciting element to a design and feels exhilarating and risky when printing.

Not enough letters, and other problems that can mess with your design

This really is a letterpress problem; you will always find that no matter how good your collection becomes, there will always be times when you quite literally run out of letters. When this problem occurs there's very little you can do, and the obvious answer is to change for a font that has the desired letters. If you do have the correct number of letters available for some words but not all, then you can consider multiple prints so you can then free up the required letters. The downside is that this is more time consuming, and it can be difficult to get everything lined up correctly in the finished print – it is surprising how the naked eye can spot something being very slightly out of alignment, even by fractions of millimetres. You can always try to make a feature out of the problem and use another letter from another font, which can look interesting and work well for certain designs. Depending on the font you are using, you may find that you have a similar-looking font that fits in and is hard to spot.

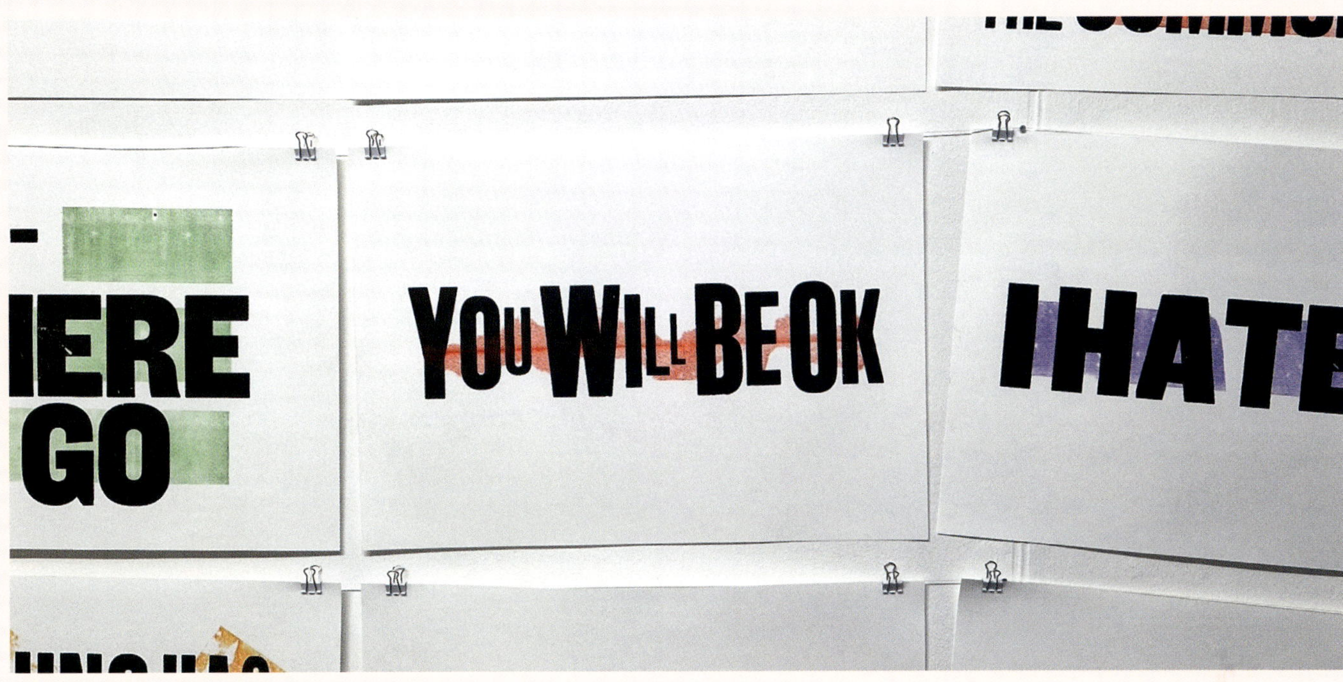

Using multiple fonts for words.

Another common problem when using wood type is the chosen font won't fit in the space you have. This issue is more common when working with very large wood typefaces; annoyingly they are the cases that you are often drawn to as they can be really beautiful, feel lovely to hold, are impactful, and make designing exciting. But bigger is not always better, and the real-world problem with large wood type is that even when printing with a large press, long words are often out of the question. I have a particularly large font in my collection that workshop attendees are often drawn to, but I have to tell them that if the design is going to be printed portrait, then all you can really print are four-letter words!

Problems like not having enough letters in the font that you want to use are part of the process that you will go through as a designer working with letterpress. You will sometimes find this frustrating, but when you do manage to get the design to work, it feels so much more rewarding than any digital design. I like to think that designing with letterpress is like doing a puzzle: there are lots of pieces, sometimes everything looks the same, sometimes it doesn't fit, and sometimes you feel like you cannot see the overall picture of what you are trying to achieve. In the end though, with perseverance, you will achieve and finish the design.

Close up on print.

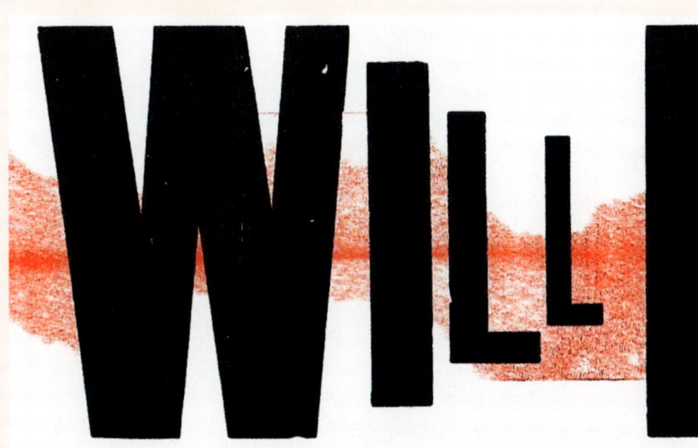

Lead type

Lead type works on the same principle as working with wood type. The clear difference being that the letters are much smaller, ranging from the truly tiny 6pt to the large and heavy 72pt (72pt equals 1 inch). With lead type you have to be prepared, as setting is fiddlier and you can drop a lot of words at once. For instance, if you are printing a greetings card and you want to put a little drop line of product information on the back of the card, for example, your artistic credit and professional information, then you really need to know the width of the card you will be printing on before you start. If you are working with larger bodies of type, you need to be mindful about how much type you have, or plan what to do if you run out of letters. Say you want to set long lines of type, but you are aware before you start that you may not have enough.

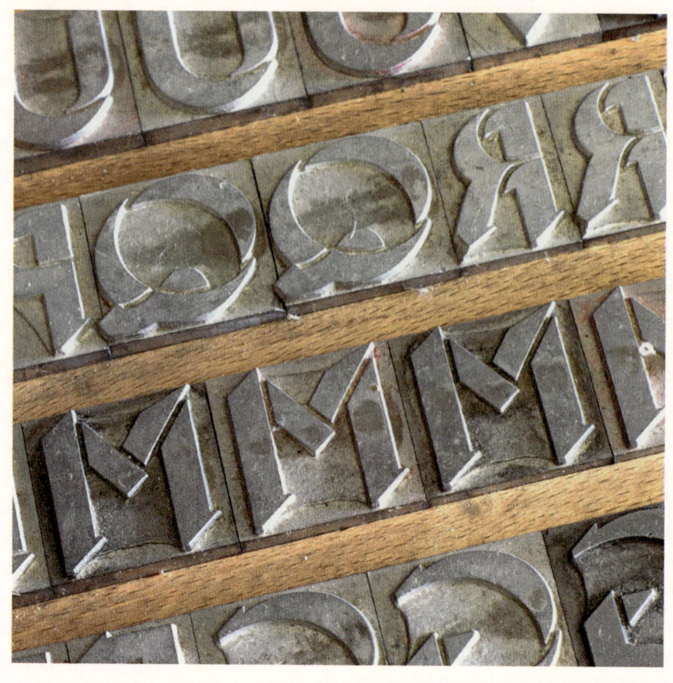

72pt (point) lead type.

Maybe changing font for each line or paragraph is an option. You should also consider mixing fonts and how the viewer will and can read the text, depending on purpose and audience.

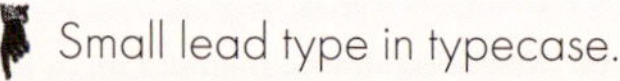

Small lead type in typecase.

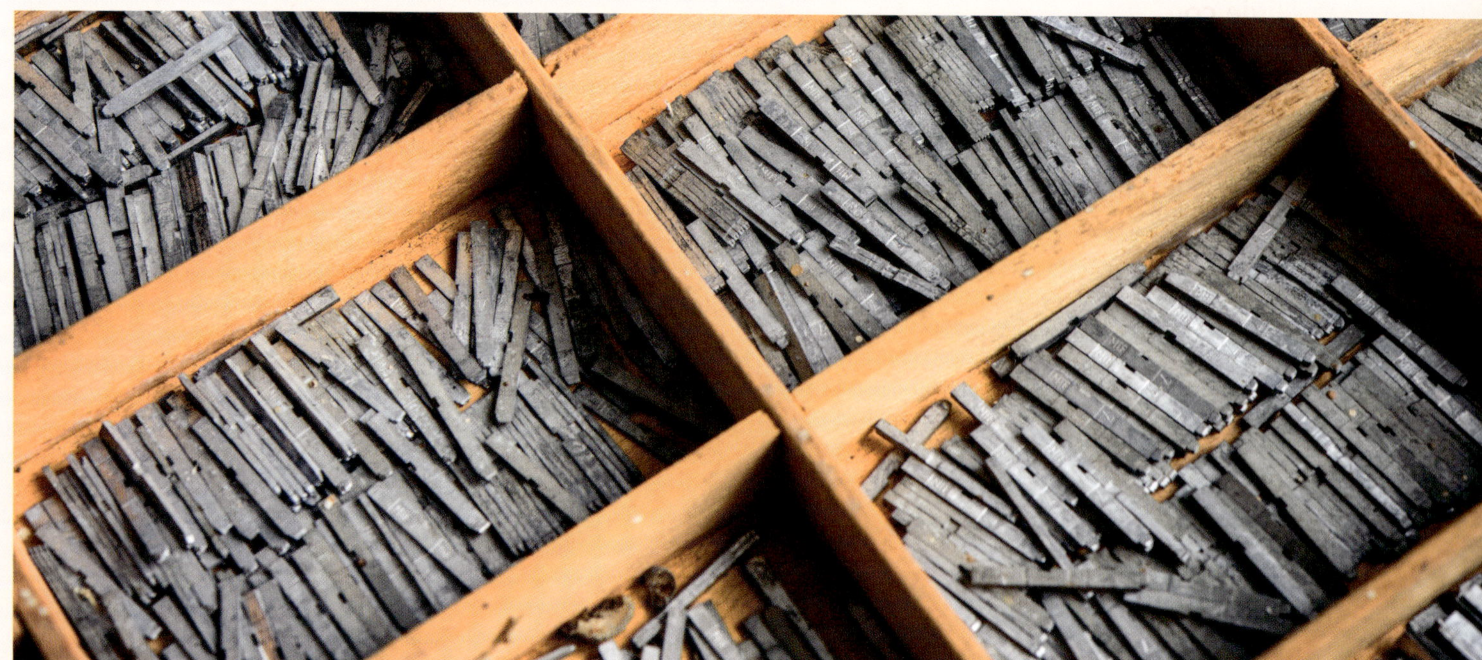

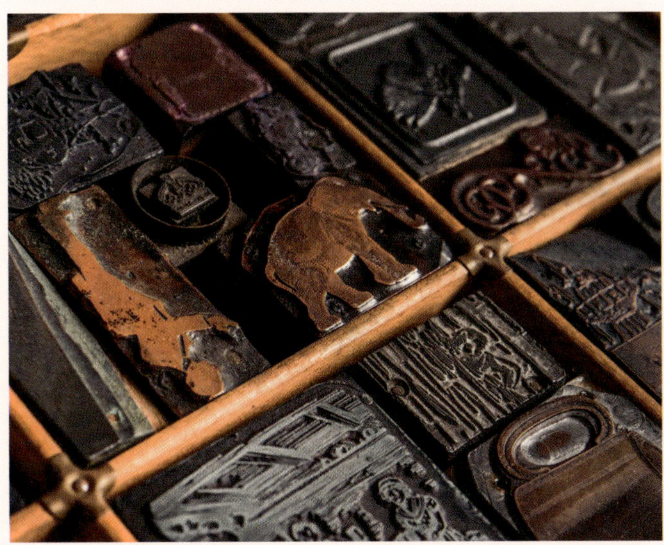

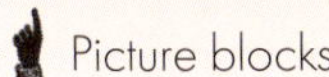 Picture blocks.

Picture blocks

Picture blocks are one of my great passions in letterpress; they can be weird and wonderful. I cannot collect enough, and when I find any, I pretty much always try to buy them. The picture blocks would have originally been made for a very specific purpose, usually for advertising or illustrating text. I love that now, we have very little context of how they were used. They are long disconnected from their original purpose, so they can be very inspiring and spark crazy ideas. I also find that they can make designs feel quite playful, and add a sense of nostalgia or history. Some will sit in your collection for years before finding that place in a design, or a client may just ask for an image that you have the perfect block for. One of my favourite blocks is a very small illustration of a tiny boxer standing on top of a haberdashery thimble. I assume this was to illustrate how strong the thimbles were… I haven't really put it to good use, but it makes me happy that it's in my collection and it makes designing feel exciting.

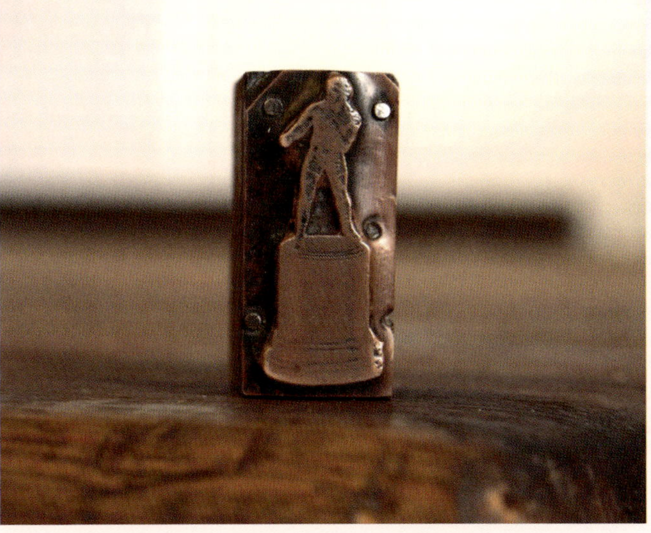

Tiny boxer standing on a thimble picture block.

Printing plates

Now we enter a slightly overlapping subject, where modern computer-aided design can be used with the age-old process of letterpress. Printing plates are not a new thing for letterpress, and have been used for a substantial amount of time. Printing plates can be made in metal usually magnesium or zinc though they are now more commonly made in photopolymer (plastic). Photopolymer is a light-sensitive plastic that is mounted to either a plastic or metal sheet. With either of these materials you can end up with a digital design that you are about to print with letterpress. Printing plates are used in a wide range of applications; for clients who want their company logo or branding on an item, printing plates are the only way to make this happen. There are people that work pretty much solely with printing plates, pulling all their prints from digital designs. I am not a fan of just printing with plates, I think everything has a place and can work together, but relying solely on digital design feels a bit wrong and somewhat misses the point of the hands-on craft.

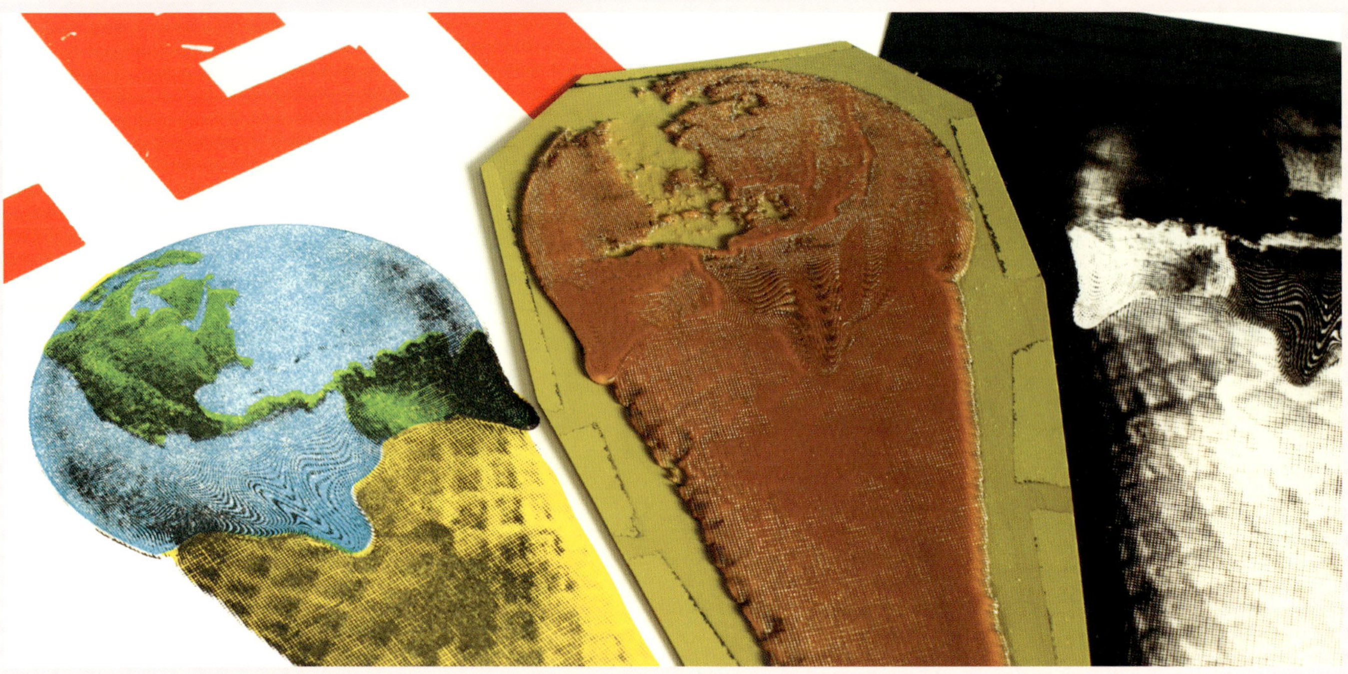

Photopolymer printing plate with example of print & negative film made and used to expose photopolymer when making plate.

That being said, if when you start up you are lacking in type, picture blocks and general stuff, getting plates made so that you can progress is a good idea. It is also possible to make photopolymer printing plates if you have access to a UV exposure unit, either at home or at a local print club. If you are buying professionally made printing plates, they can be ordered either mounted or unmounted. If you are ordering metal plates, I would always purchase them mounted and inform the manufacturer that you are using them for letterpress printing, as well as what sort of press you are using, so they will definitely be delivered at type height with minimal spacing around the printing area of the block. The reason I would always order metal plates pre-mounted is that the gauge/thickness of the material makes them a bit tricky to mount to a board, and also the cost of metal plates is a lot higher than photopolymer, so you don't really want to damage a metal plate mounting it. Photopolymer plates come with a backing sheet that is either a thin piece of plastic or steel, so they can be taped down to a mounting block (you can find metal blocks that were made to mount printing plates onto, which makes them perfect type height).

Lino

Lino is worth mentioning, as in principle it's the same as a printing plate, it's just hand-carved. There is something to be said for carving out your own illustrations, or for the adventurous, letters. In the modern world printing presses like Albions and Columbians are commonly seen printing lino cuts, and they work perfectly for it. Again, you can mount the lino to a block. It can take a bit of time to find the correct size block, and you can improvise with some MDF and some card packing underneath. Lino can offer a nice alternative to plates, as the end prints do show that they were hand cut and the images have some soul, while plates can look

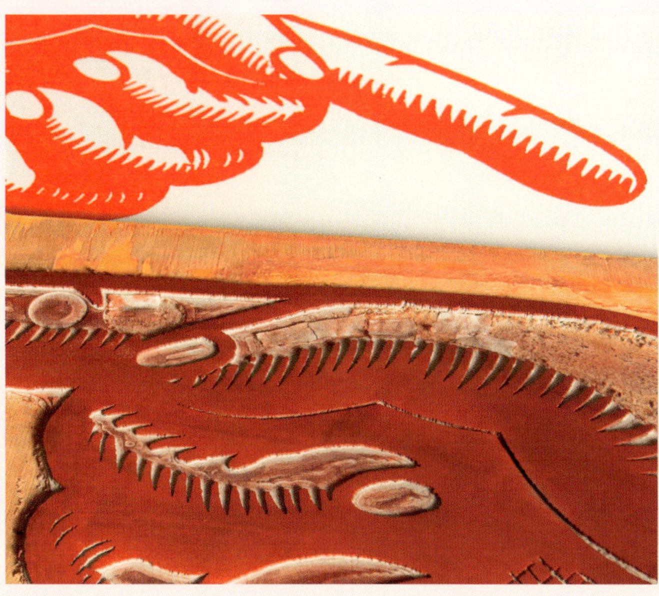

Hand cut large lino version of original printers fist.

a bit flat, sterile or worse, digital. A lino block can also be great if you want to add areas/ blocks of colour to a print. Lino takes ink really well, and the slight give of the material (that you do not get with wood or lead) does have a slight texture of its own. You can of course cut a letter out of lino, which can be a great help to supplement missing letters or just need to boost numbers in wood type.

Additional letter R cut in alternative lino material.

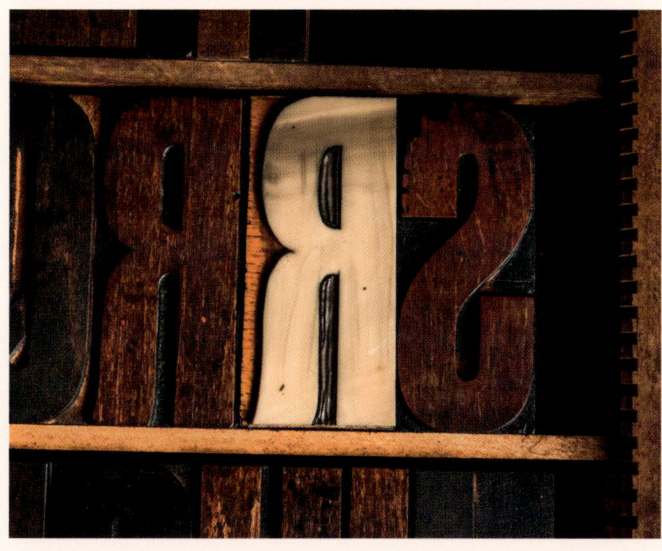

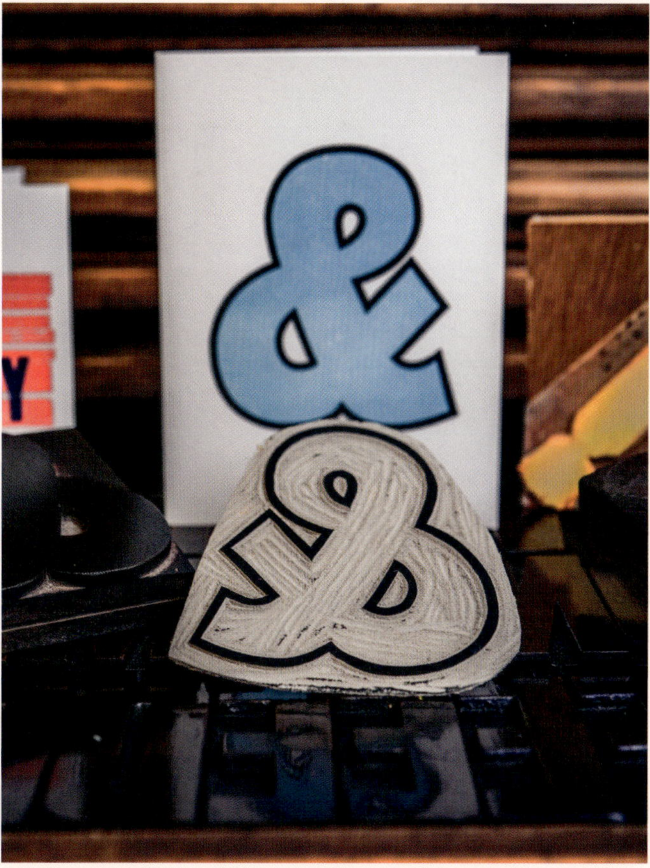

Lino cut outline to overprint on prints from original wood type &.

In summary

Letterpress can be very limited in the sense of objects, letters, print size, and so on, but you are only really limited by your own imagination and drive to design and print. You are not fixed to only using one of the mentioned mediums, so you can and should mix wood type, lead type, picture blocks and lino all at the same time, as they can work in harmony and create that perfect unique print. Be creative, try to just be in the moment and enjoy the process. All these areas and how to print with them will be discussed later in the book.

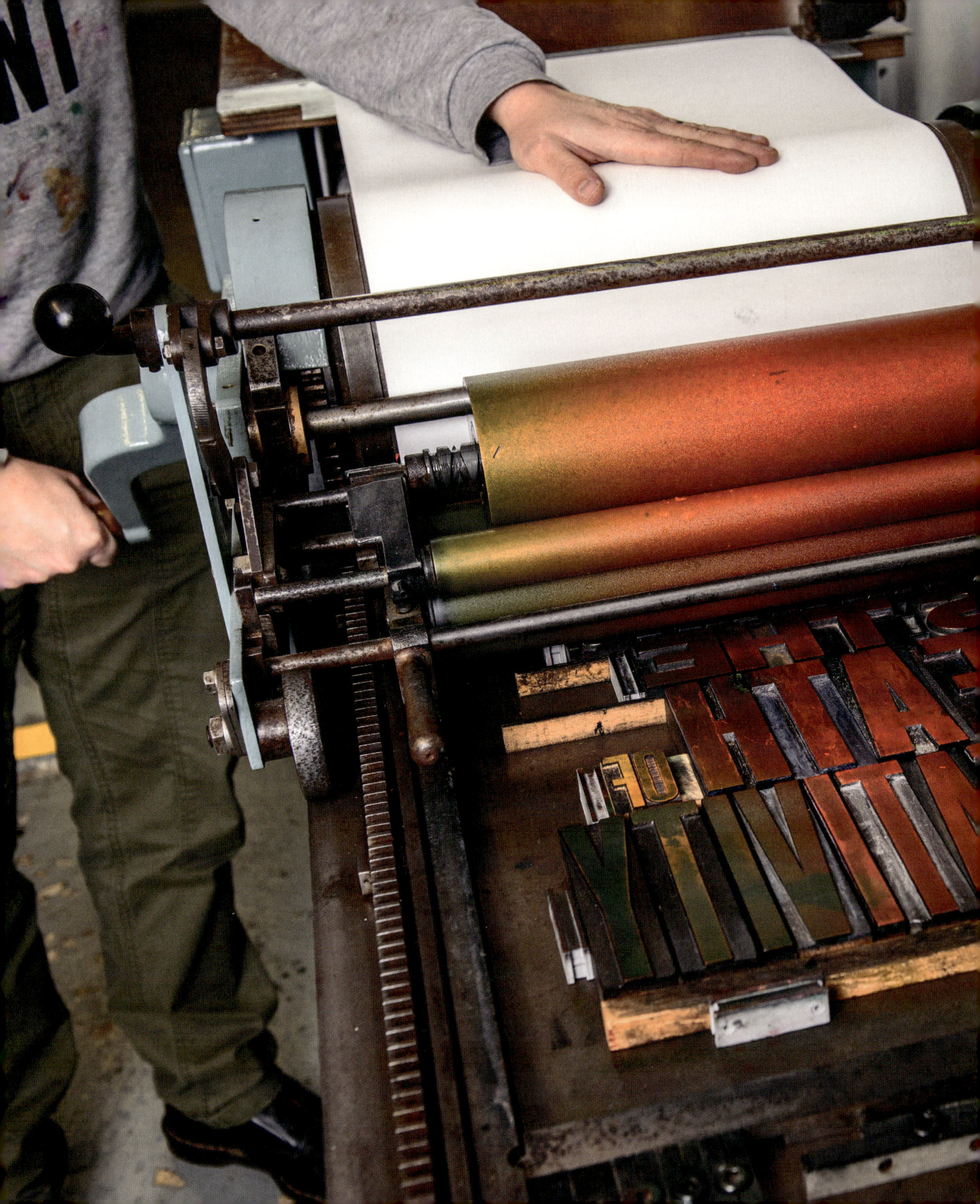

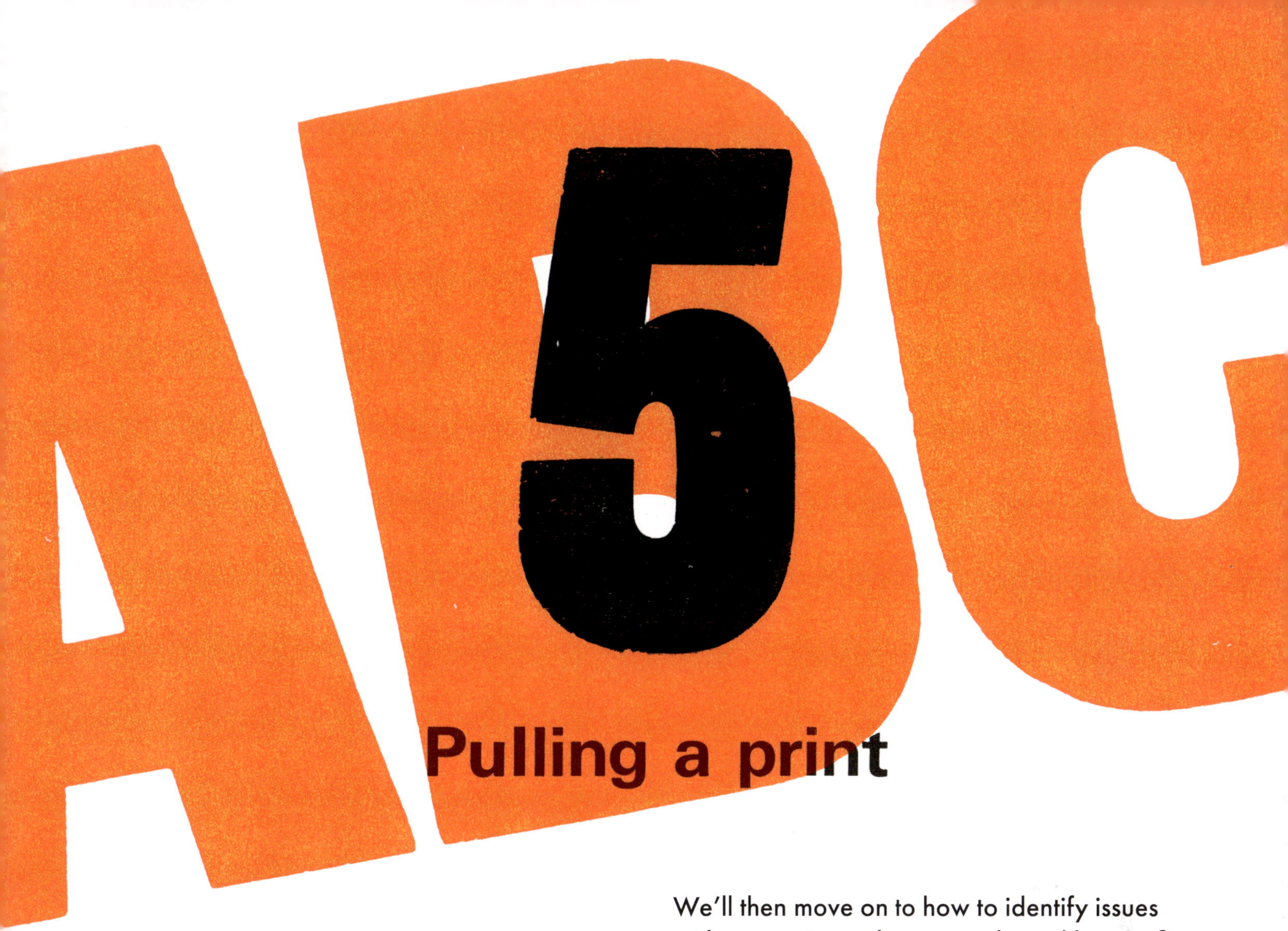

5

Pulling a print

So, you feel ready to get your type out and get printing – good, let's go. In this chapter I endeavour to give you gentle pointers, tips and cheats that I have learnt over the years of how to get the desired effect for your print.

I will talk you through setting up type for printing, locking it out so you are ready to ink, then print. We will look at printing using a variety of different machines, and how each one has its own unique place in a workshop.

We'll then move on to how to identify issues with your prints, what not to do and how to fix an issue. This will include things like areas not printing, dents in type, bold inking, deboss and correctly setting the pressure for printing, getting your print where you want it on your page, how your chosen paper affects the finished print, good inking practices and the all-important life skill of not losing your mind trying to get the elusive perfect print.

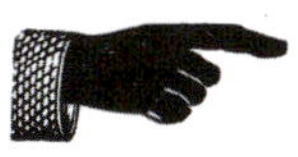

Planning your print

Always start by writing down what you want to print, even if you just scribble it on a random sheet of paper, this gives you a basic reference point and a quick visual of how long the words are in relation to each other. It may sound very simple, but it helps you to avoid mistakes like picking a large wood type font that will not work, either by emphasising a word that you do not want emphasised or by being too big to fit on the paper, or even worse, it won't fit in the press or the chase. A quick and easy way to see if the type is working on your desired paper size (without having to go back and forth to the press to check) is to simply put a sheet of the paper you are working with on your work surface, and put your type on the sheet to see how it fits.

After writing down your quote, phrase or random words, take a minute to think about a couple of things: do you want the print to be landscape or portrait, and importantly do the words look like they are going to work best landscape or portrait? How many lines of text does it roughly look like you are going to be printing? You can always write out the text a few times with different layout options – even if your handwriting is terrible like mine, it is still a useful visual aid. Taking a minute to think about what you are about to do can save you a lot of time longer-term.

Decide on any important words that you might want to draw attention to. If you are struggling to work out how the words flow and how to translate them into a graphic print, then read them out loud. Doing so allows you to feel what the rhythm is, which words stand out, how they could look printed, and be interpreted.

Wood type M.

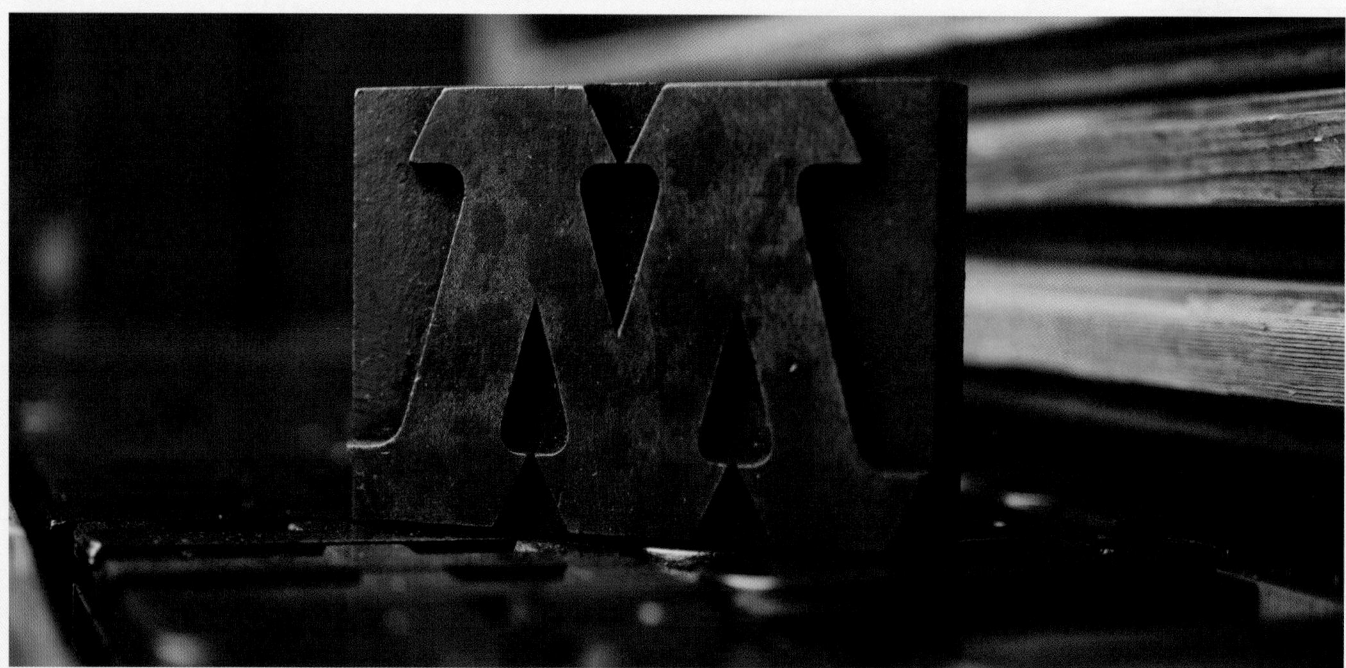

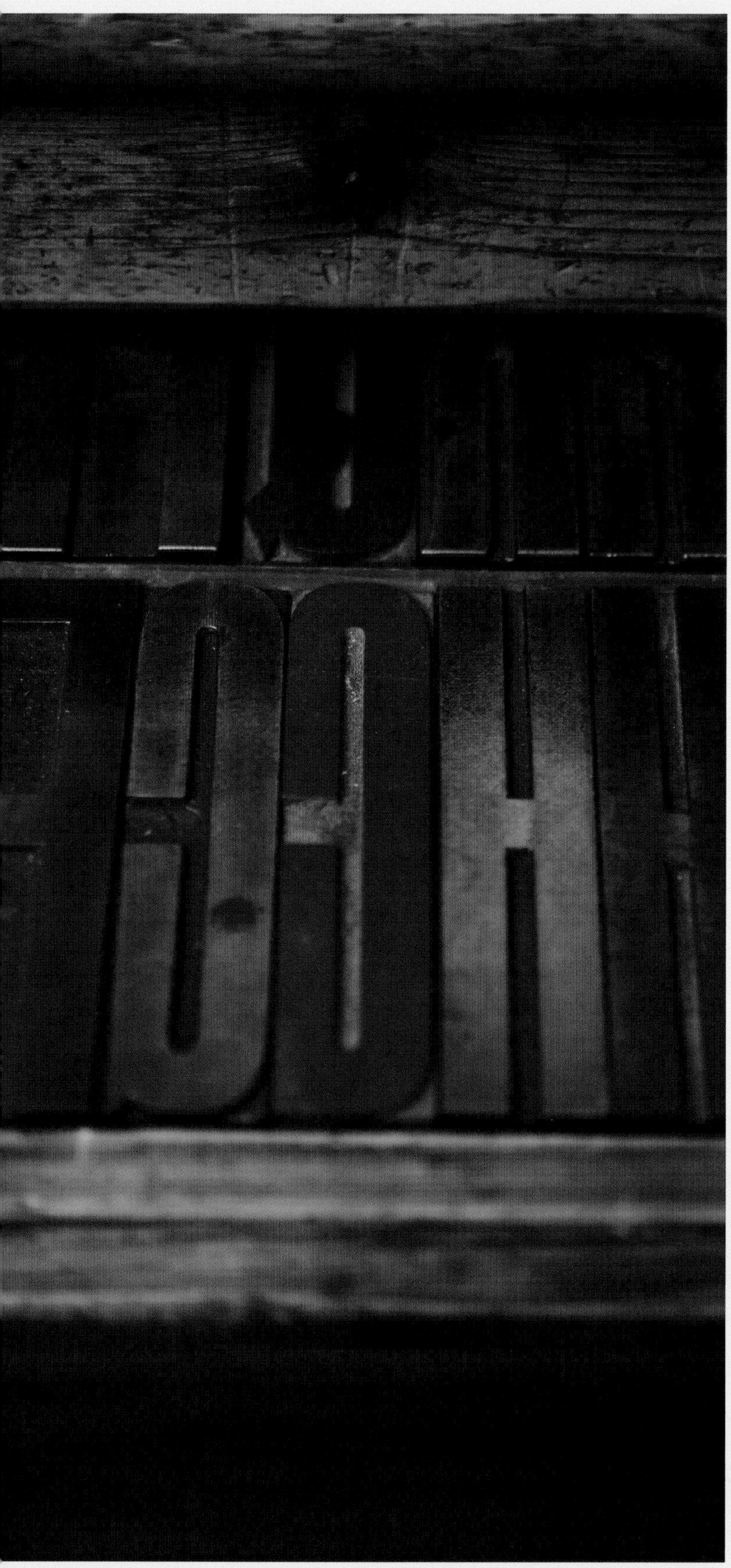

Selecting your type

Choosing your type can be difficult, you can face a variety of issues: you cannot decide what you like, you may have too much choice, not enough choice, one font doesn't seem to work with another, you can't imagine what it is going to look like, you can't find what you need for the space you have, or it's just not working. Try not to box yourself into a corner. I often find it's easiest to start with a word that you find interesting or exciting. Sometimes individual words have letters that have interesting shapes, and some fonts have some very different and exciting interpretations of letters. As you get used to handling type, you'll start to notice some of the interesting design elements that fonts have and you will be drawn towards them. Stay open minded, and if you find yourself getting lost or stalling and not being productive, simply compromise and select something even if you are not convinced it's right, put it down on the sheet of paper on your work bench and move onto the next word. Nothing is set in stone and it can all be changed.

While designing, sometimes it can feel like type flies out of the cases and falls perfectly into place, other times you feel like you have gone through all of your type 100 times. It's part of the process to work through it, pick stuff up, see how it works. Over time your natural impulse and inclination to design will take over and you'll feel your way through the design process. Try not to think too much – I genuinely believe that thinking is the death of creativity, and it does not help. Don't think, just do!

☛ Large wood type in case.

Only when it comes to selecting type, start to think practically. Always select the individual letters in the order they are spelled, then put them down in reverse. I notice that more spelling mistakes happen when letters are just gathered quickly, for instance if you know a word has two e's, picking them both up at the same time seems easier, but stick to the correct order. With wood type if you pick the letters out in spelled order into a galley, then carry the galley to your working area, transfer the letters to the position you want them. This way you spell the word twice, so it makes it easier to spot silly mistakes.

It is very easy to make mistakes, you can never really check yourself too much. When choosing type from a cabinet, there are a few practical things to keep in mind. Make sure when you slide out a case (tray) of type not to pull it out too far, as it will inevitably drop on the floor and probably onto your feet. Some cases can be very heavy. You can always pull out the case beneath the one you want part way, to provide support. I recommend (if you have the space) to remove cases from cabinets and put them on your worktop. If you are having to carry around loose type in your workspace then it is worth using a galley or suitable tray to carry the type on. Whilst I love the signs of age and use on type, new dents and banged corners are something that no one enjoys. If you are lucky enough to be working with larger collections of type and there are many cases to pick from, remember where the type came from, this is essential as you have to clean down and put the type back after you have finished printing. Repeatedly opening and closing cases of type in cabinets in the hunt for your type is not fun.

When you have your chosen type roughly laid out on your piece of paper, draw around your type blocks with a pencil, then write which

A full case of wood type pulled out, supported on case pulled half way out below.

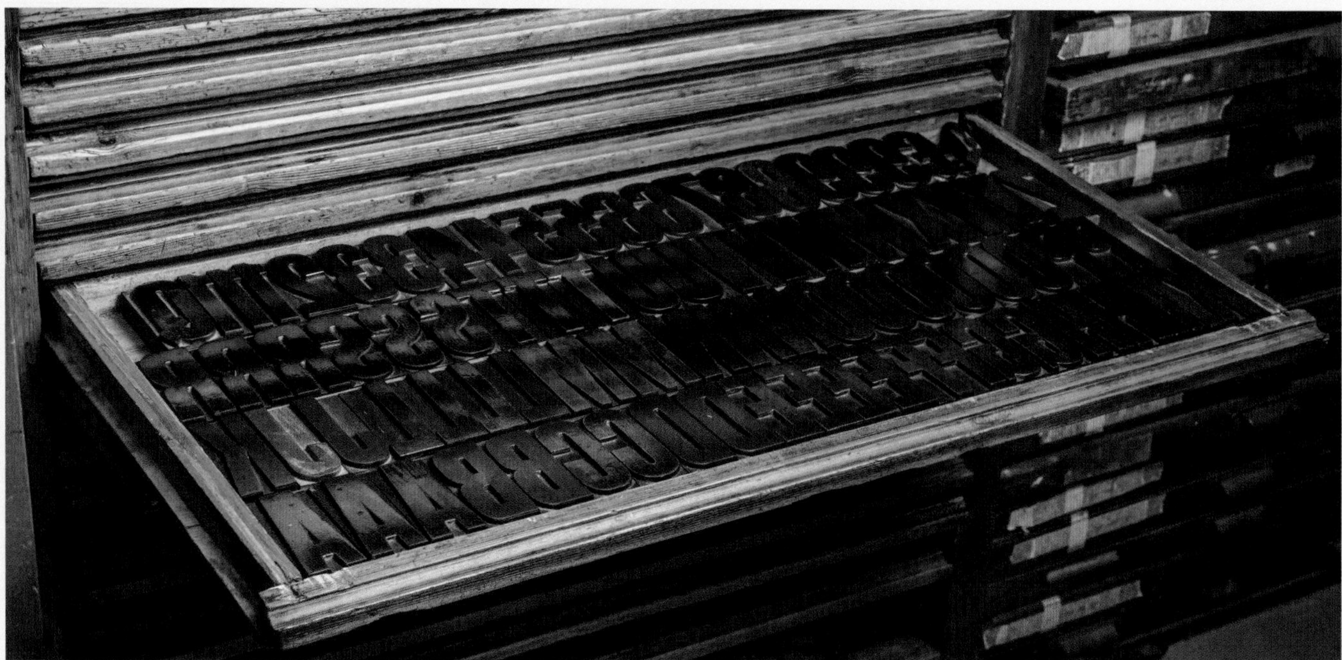

word is going in each space. You can also make any notes that come to mind including where the type came from. Small activities such as these make for smooth working processes in day-to-day printing. Now it's time to transfer your type to your printing press. In this case, we're working on the principle that you are printing on a proofing press, so the type is printing on the flat base (bed) of the printing press. Transfer your type slowly in individual words if need be to the printing press. If you move type in the order that you set out your design, then you can simply put the letters back down in the same position on the printing press. You can use your sheet of paper either as a reference, or place it onto the bed of the press and put your type on top of it once more. You can then find a suitable moment to slide out the sheet once you've started locking out your type, or leave it in place while you are still learning.

Selecting and comping lead type

As mentioned above, I recommend removing your case of type from cabinets and with lead type this is much more important. Full cases of lead type can be very heavy, so make sure if you are removing the case from the cabinet that your walking path is nice and clear. When carrying the case, you cannot see your feet and you really don't want to trip over carrying type. The more you work with lead type the easier you will find the letters you need; as you'll see, the cases have a layout a bit like a keyboard. If you are composing with lead type that is not of a large size, smaller than 36pt, 48pt or 72pt, I would always recommend working with a comp stick. It can be tempting to try to cut corners and not use one, but dropping lead type once you have set it is particularly demoralising and easy to do.

A case of lead type with comp sticks above and a type case layout (cheat sheet) resting on top.

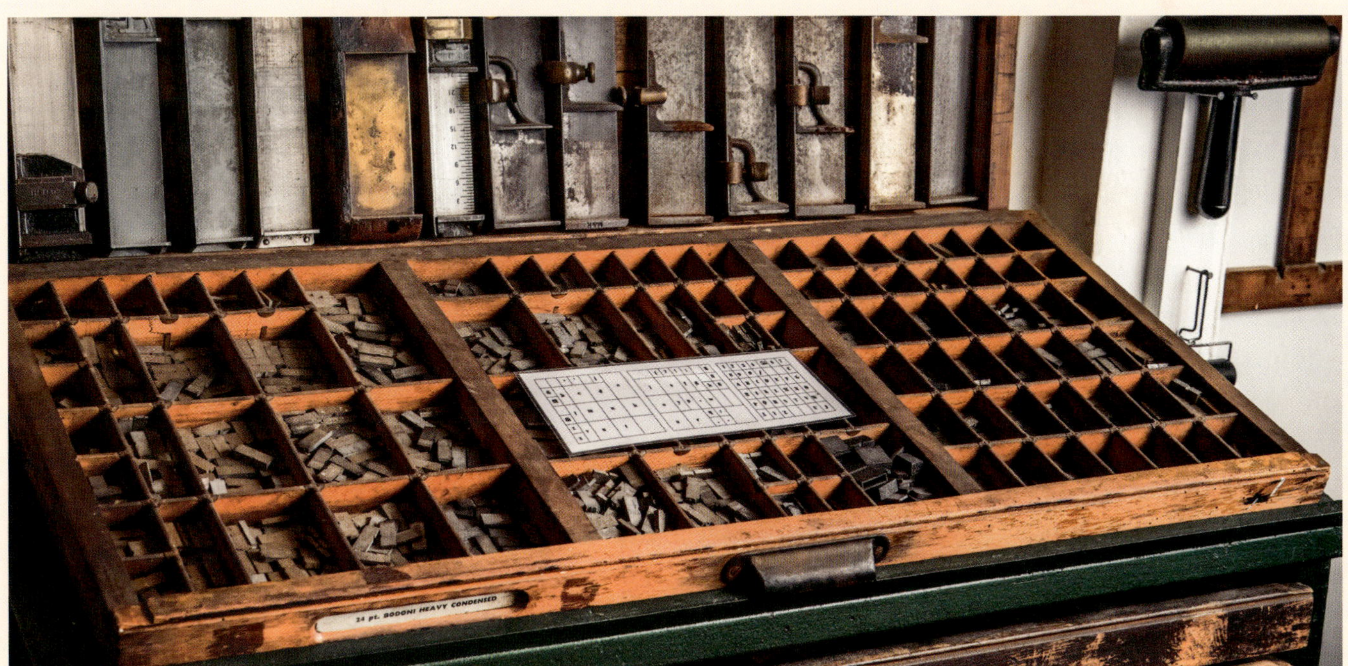

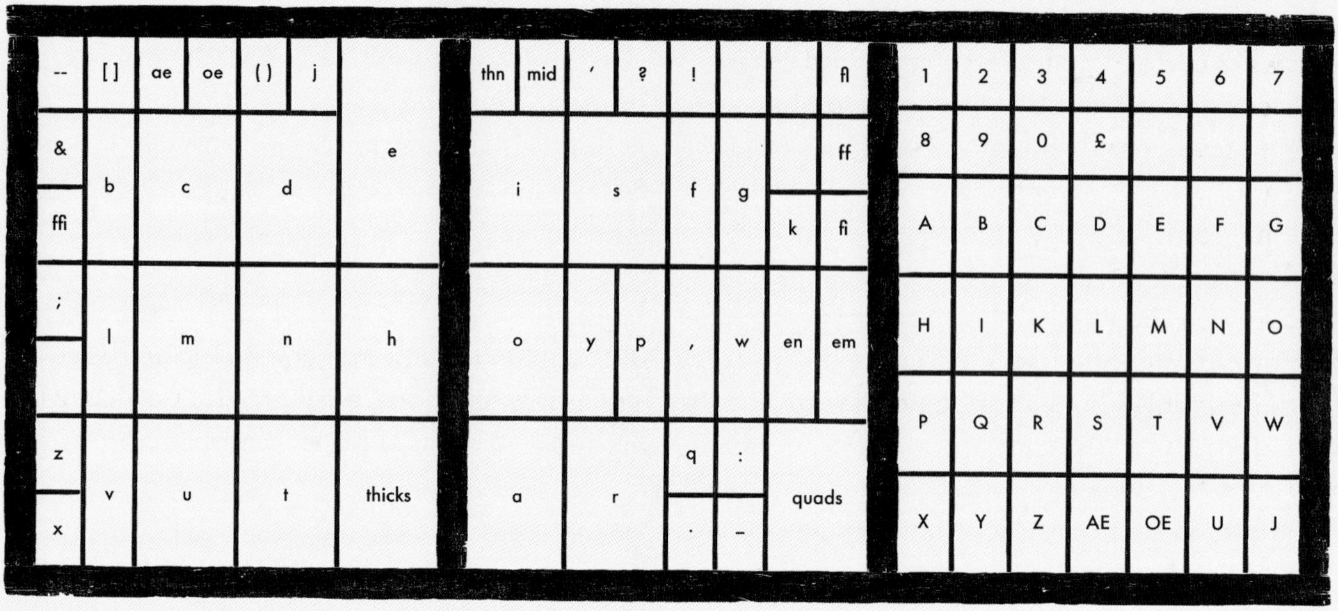

-- [] ae oe () j
& b c d e
ffi
; l m n h
z v u t thicks
x

thn mid ' ? ! fl
i s f g ff
k fi
o y p , w en em
q :
a r quads
. _

1 2 3 4 5 6 7
8 9 0 £
A B C D E F G
H I K L M N O
P Q R S T V W
X Y Z AE OE U J

Type case layout plan, there are many different layouts this is the most common in my workshop.

The first thing to do when using a comp stick is to work out how big the space is that you are going to be printing in. Once you have done this you can loosen and adjust the width that the comp stick is set to. This means that when you set your type, you won't get the length of the line of type that you are setting wrong. Holding the comp stick in you left hand (if you are right-handed) with the bottom ledge of the comp stick resting across your four fingers you want to be able to push your thumb into the bottom corner of the width adjuster that you have just set.

The basic process is that you pick each letter, adding them into this corner in the correctly spelled order, then put the individual piece of type upside down and back to front in the comp stick. You will see and feel that each piece of lead type has a 'nick' on the body of the type, which is there so that you can feel the bottom of the type and know how and which way to put in down. Once each letter is in the correct position in the comp stick, you push your thumb onto the nick of the last letter placed to make sure that the letter does not fall over as you go. This sounds complicated and fiddly – it isn't, it just takes a little bit of time to get used to the process. Soon it will feel no stranger than using a keyboard on a computer.

While you are setting your words, you need to also add spaces in between them – there should be spacers in each case of type. You will find that there are slightly different sizes of spacers to help you get each line of text set to the same length. If you are adding a gap to the bottom of your picked type and your next line of text, add this now rather than later, using leads (thin lengths of lead). While setting your type in the comp stick isn't really that fiddly, what is tricky is transferring your type to your chase and then printing press. This is another moment when it can all go wrong: you can drop your type. Before you do go to move the type, get organised, make sure you have space for what you are doing both in terms of where you will put down your comp stick, and have your chase and tools all ready and to hand. When moving the type from the comp stick you should always make sure you have put a reglet (the thinnest pieces of wood furniture) or a correctly sized piece of leading above the top and below the bottom lines of the type to create a firm grip. I would strongly recommend as you learn to do this to put your comp stick on the bed of the press, or a very flat worktop if possible, then it is more a case of sliding into place rather than lifting up and then putting down. Also, if you have space in your design, you can lock out your type in a chase (in the case of printing with an Adana, this is essential) then move the chase with the type locked in place around on the print bed. Whatever you do, do not walk around your workshop carrying type.

Setting your type (wood and metal)

Now your type should be sitting on the bed of your press. If you are doing a traditional and simple layout style – straight lines of text – then it is quite easy to add furniture as you put down the type. Keep a spare long thin piece of furniture on the bed so that you can push the whole word together as one into place – it just makes it quicker and easier to do, particularly if you are working with smaller wood type. If you are working on a more complex layout, sometimes it is easier to put the words down so that it looks right. From there, you can start to build up the spacing material you need to create the desired layout.

As a rule you want to be able to lock out the type as securely as possible, so take your time and fill the spaces well. Ideally you want to use as few pieces of furniture to fill each space as

Picking & comping lead type into a comp stick, holding the type in place by pushing thumb on the nick of the last letter.

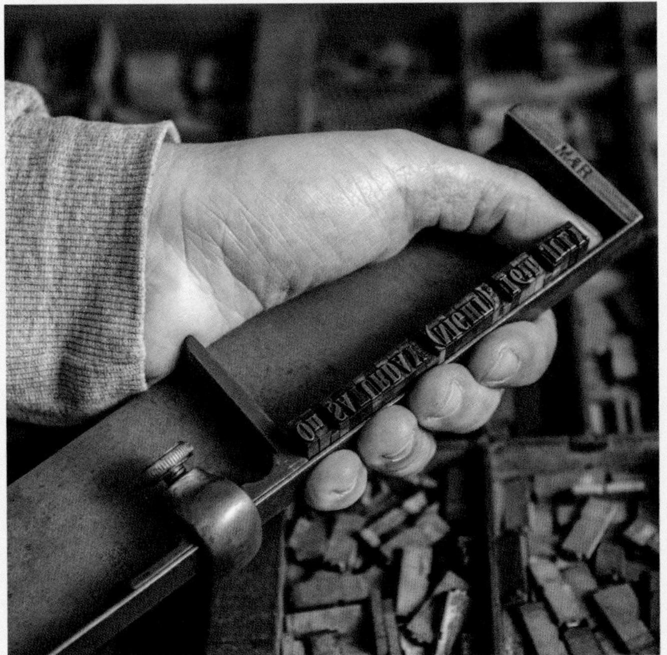

Moving wood type into place on the bed of a printing press, using furniture to help move a complete word.

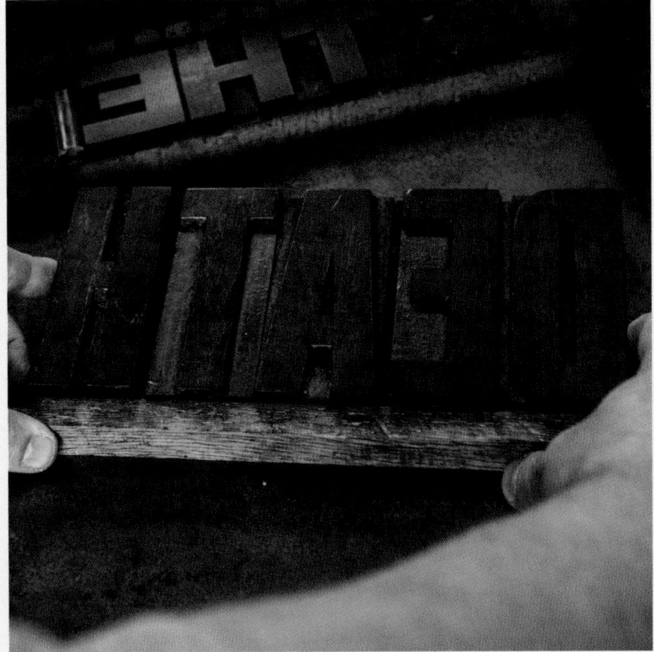

possible, so see if you can find a piece of furniture that's just the right size. What you really want to avoid is using lots of skinny individual pieces of furniture to fill a space, because when you lock out the type you will find that when compressed, they want to move more than one piece of wood ever would. This can make locking your type firmly more problematic. It's hard to comprehend how old some of these items may be, with wooden furniture and wooden type you have to accept that over the years the blocks have expanded, contracted and warped. We're talking about often tiny fractions of a millimetre, but it's enough to make some lockups testing. This part of letterpress becomes like a jigsaw.

It's worth noting that some layouts are so strange and awkward that they make the concept of packing out every space near impossible, or just so slow and laborious that it makes for diminishing returns. If type is at jaunty angles or an odd-sized picture block in the middle of type is causing you real headaches to lock in place, then aim to just get at least a piece of furniture at the top and bottom of each word. It is worth thinking about how you are going to compress and pressurise this in place as you may not need any furniture around it and can instead rely on the type locking it in place, imagine your picture block becomes like a large spacer. Remember to leave a bit of space around the edge of all your type and furniture, as we will need to put a quoin in to lock it in place, leaving room for galley magnets. Sometimes an ugly setup is something that you will have to do, but remember it will not be seen in the print.

Lead

If you are working with lead type then arranging your spacing material is much more important as you're working with much smaller print surfaces and you need to make sure that every single letter is perfectly upright in order to get a clean print. If you do not do a good job on spacing the type, then it's likely to move slightly during the pre-print setup phase and you will end up with a common problem of letters not printing cleanly or some letters not printing at all, as the type height is not 100 per cent flat. Fortunately, with lead type comes lead spacing. The advantage of using metal spacing material is that it doesn't compress like wood, so you don't have so much of a problem using multiple pieces to build up your setup. With lead type it may be fiddlier and more important to get all parts set well; all the parts that you are working with are designed with this need for near perfection in mind. In a way, the difficulty is just the learning curve of being hands-on with type. We have all dropped or knocked over type, or just done a sloppy job of setting – I find I learn better from my mistakes than my successes.

If you are working with lead type being printed in a press with a clam shell mechanism like an Adana or a Peerless rather than a flat bed of a proofing press or an Albion, then you will be locking your type out in a chase and then placing it into the press. The moment when your type is lifted into the press is the time when gravity is not your friend, and when it becomes worthwhile having done small setup improvements, like adding an extra piece of spacing to a line so there is a perfectly straight line of lead to the line above.

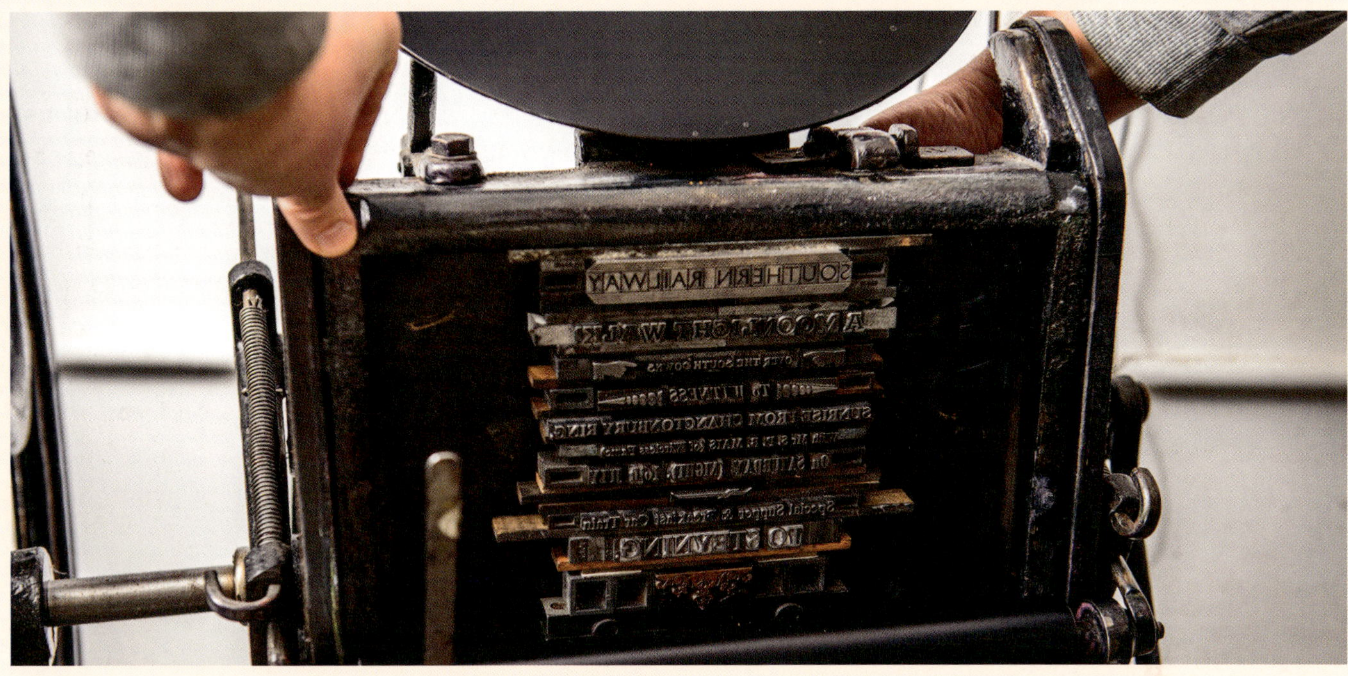

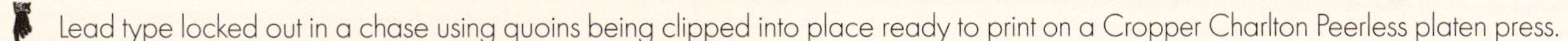
Lead type locked out in a chase using quoins being clipped into place ready to print on a Cropper Charlton Peerless platen press.

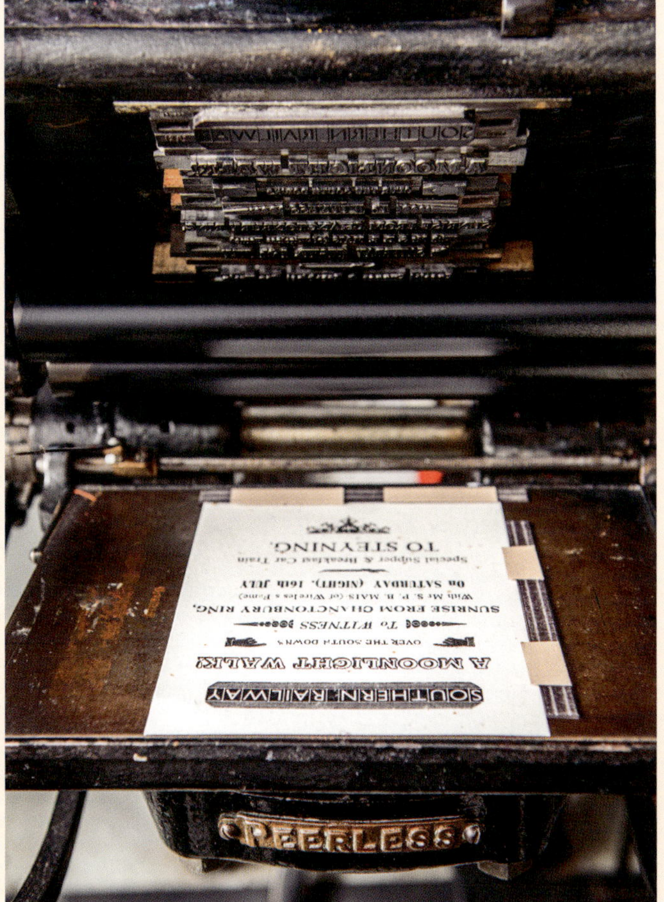

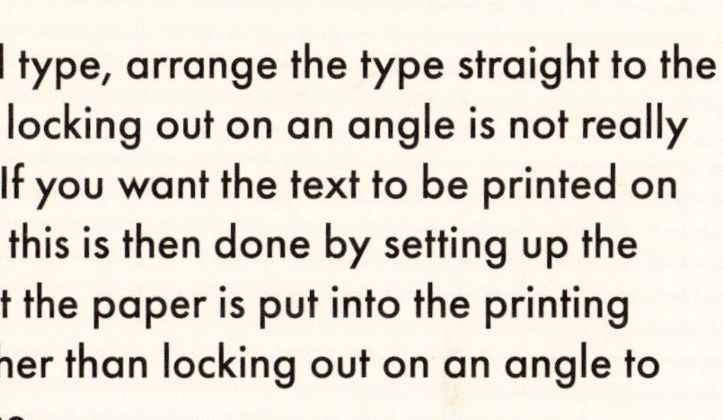

With lead type, arrange the type straight to the chase, as locking out on an angle is not really possible. If you want the text to be printed on the angle this is then done by setting up the angle that the paper is put into the printing press, rather than locking out on an angle to your chase.

Locking out (galley magnets and quoins)

Now you should be at the point where you are ready to secure your type in place, whether that is in a chase or straight into your proofing press bed (if you have a lockout bar). If you are securing into a proofing press, or a chase in a proofing press, you are working with your type on the flat bed of the press. This means you have some flexibility and choice of how to lock out your type: by using quoins placed at the bottom of the chase or lockout bar, or securing your type in place with galley magnets, or, both at once.

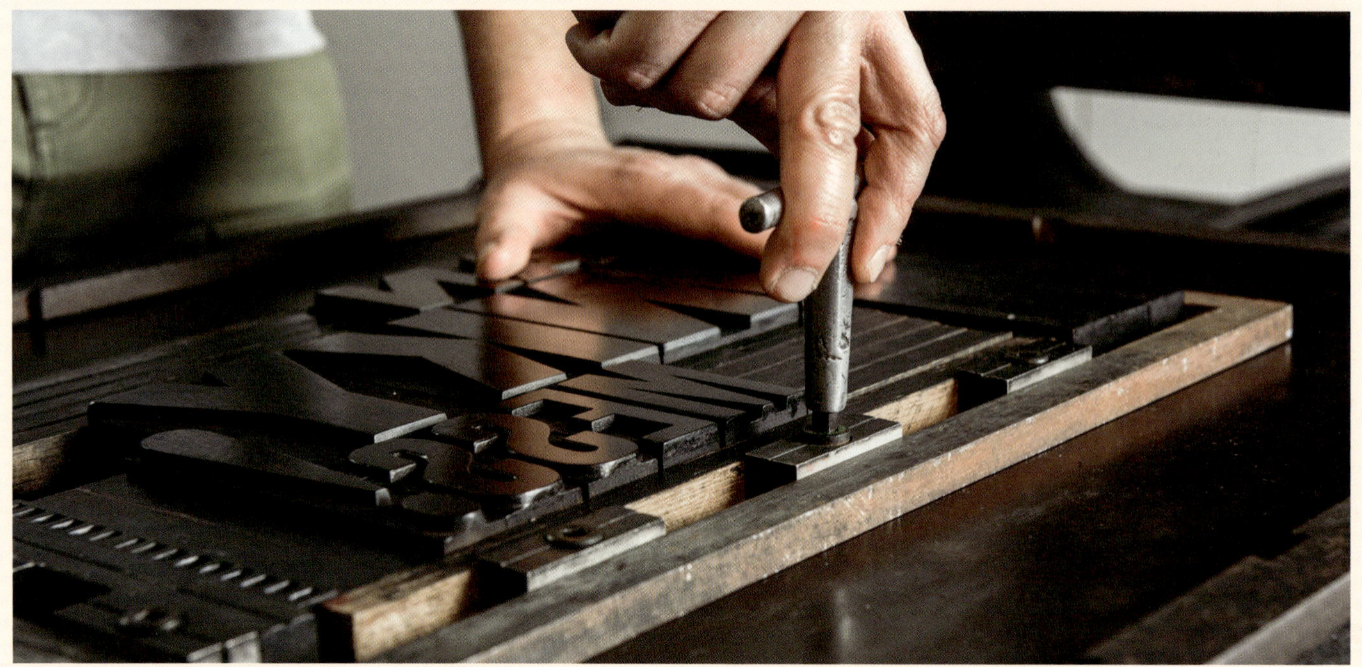

Wood type being locked out in a chase using quoins and a quoin key on a Stanhope printing press.

We will start by looking at just using quoins, bearing in mind that there are different sizes ranging from tiny Adana quoins, which have their very own tiny quoin key, to large quoins that are really two quoins joined with a long bar. For the purpose of keeping this simple, we will talk about using the most common and accessible cornerstone-style quoins, which measure 5 × 1.7cm. Hopefully you have left space around your type and furniture, if not, make some, because we need to put two quoins at the bottom of your type/chase, and some down the length of the press. The number of quoins you will need down the long edge really depends on your individual setup, if you are using large word type spaced over three lines, then the quickest and easiest method would be one quoin on each line of type.

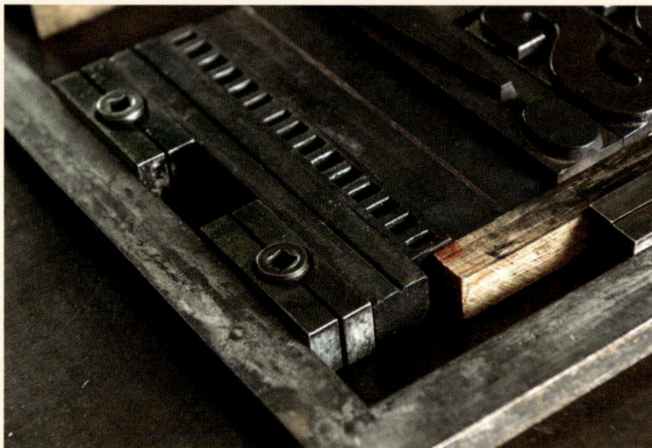

Starting with the quoins at the bottom, put them up against either the frame of the chase, or if your press has a built-in frame of some sort (e.g. lockout bar) place it against that, then tweak the furniture you have to fill the space up to the quoins as much as possible. When the gap between the furniture and the quoin is very small, ideally one or two millimetres, you can start to tighten the quoins. Insert the quoin key and turn it slowly clockwise to expand the quoin out, and anti-clockwise to release it.

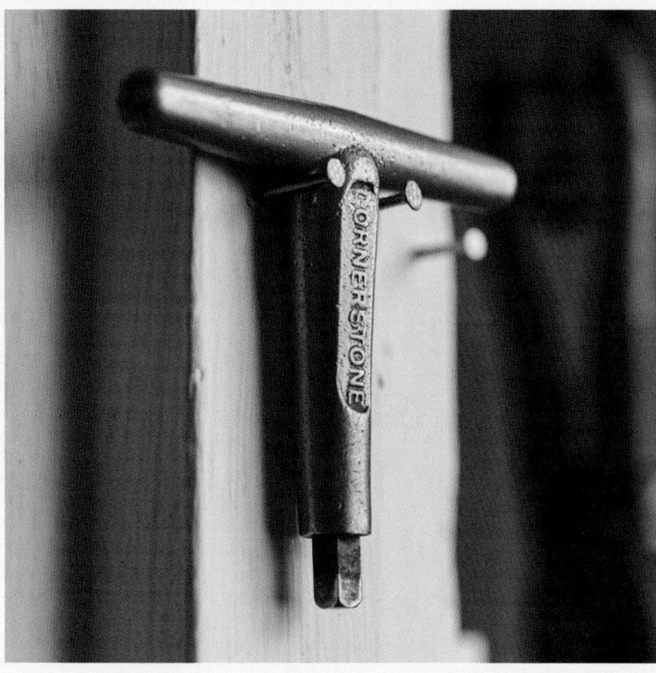

Quoin key made by Cornerstone.

Quoins have to be tight enough to hold the type in place but not over-tightened, as this causes the type to bulge or lift – tighten the quoins slowly, one by one. Usually the middle letters in words are the most affected by lifting. Lots of people when they first pick up a quoin key hold it like it's a knuckleduster! If you hold your quoin key open-handed, turning using your thumb and ring finger, then you don't have such an unnecessarily hard grip, and you can really feel the pressure from the quoins pushing out into the type. An easy way to check if your type is bulging is to tap the top of the wood type with your finger, and if you can hear and feel it move back down, it's bulging.

Now you can repeat the process along the vertical length of your press, placing quoins as they are needed. If you are struggling with not having enough quoins, look at how you can space furniture along the side of multiple lines of type at once. As you develop with printing you can put quoins in closer towards the type, as that can sometimes help secure and avoid issues like bulging but to start with, I think it is best to keep them on the outside edge of everything. One simple reason for this is it keeps the quoins as far away from your type as possible, which is exactly what you want if you are inexperienced at inking type, as it is very easy to slip and ink the top of the quoin. At best this is a pain to clean, at worst it will somehow get onto your print, even though it is below type height.

Sometimes you'll have more difficult setups in which type is all over the place, with words going up and down the page, text bouncing around or you've used multiple sets of type to form one word. You will struggle with quoins, and it's possible that the setup will look chaotic with some letters looser than others. But you will still get a print. Each print may be slightly different if you're pulling multiples. For these sorts of tricky setups, I recommend using galley magnets.

Some see using galley magnets as cheating a bit, but I feel that if it prints, it works. Galley magnets are very strong magnets with a frame around them, and they really snap down onto the cast iron bed of a printing press so make sure that your fingertips aren't in the way. If you are lucky enough to have plenty of galley magnets then the lockup process can be quick. You are aiming to do the same as you would with a quoin. If you have enough galley magnets then you can be very free with how you use them, and may not need to use so much furniture to pack out your type. Instead, you can put furniture top and bottom, and then place galley magnets on each side of the set

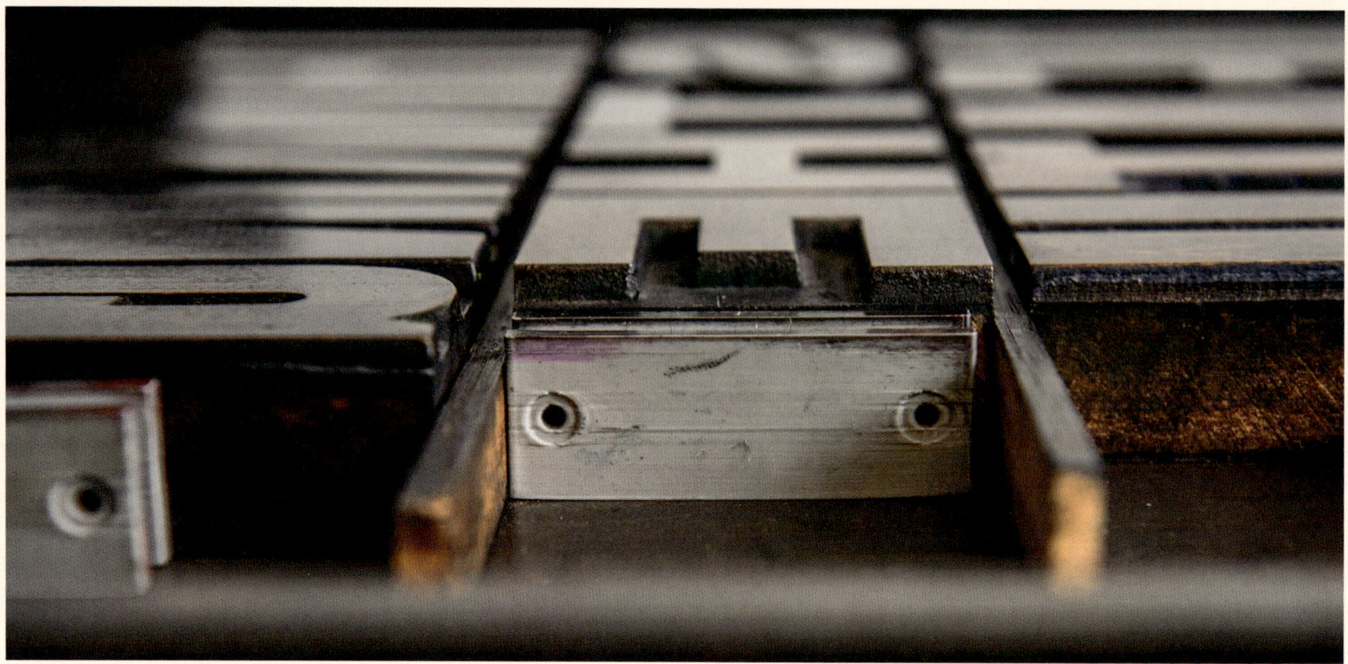

Galley magnet being used to hold wood type in place.

type. If you only have three or four galley magnets then you really don't have enough to do this for a full setup.

You can also use both quoins and galley magnets. For instance, I often set up a design with furniture between the lines of type, lock them out vertically with quoins, and then use galley magnets to secure the type at the end of each line. This way you get a good mix of securing the type nicely, but at the same time not spending too much time on something that may need adjusting very soon.

Locking lead type in a chase

If you are locking out lead type in a chase that needs to be moved and installed into the printing press, then you need to take care. If you are working with a small chase like the 8 × 5in chases that come with Adanas, then try to find some small Adana quoins, they work exactly the same as the more common sized quoins but they do not take up so much space.

Whichever size quoin you go for, follow the basic principle that you need to pack out your type with spacing material, then lock it in place by putting a quoin in the chase and turning to

Small quoins with matching quoin key.

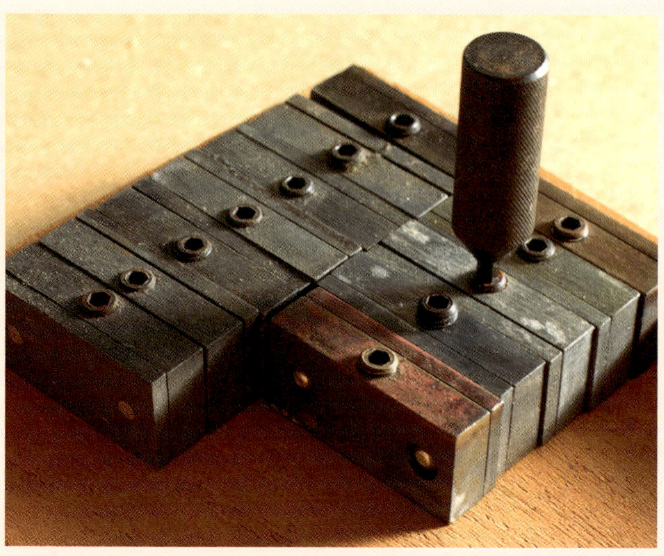

expand the block to lock tight. Again, do not overtighten, but you do need to be sure that the type is tightened enough to hold all the individual pieces of type securely in place. When you think you have tightened enough, lift the chase off the work surface only a tiny amount, and see if any of the letters move. Put it back down and adjust the tightness of the quoins if needed.

If you are having problems with tightening the lead type and keeping the top surface of all the type level, there is a tool called a printer's planer. This is a very flat block of wood that has a nicely shaped groove in the sides of the block for holding, the purpose of the printer's planer was to put on top of the type and then give it a little tap when it's not 100 per cent level, then retightening and checking. As a printer and a collector, I have planing blocks in the workshop but rarely use them. I've always felt somewhat nervous hitting down on my type; instead I favour a slower and gentler approach of just holding the wooden planer block on top of the type and lightly pushing down whilst tightening the quoin.

Printer's planer used to check type is level.

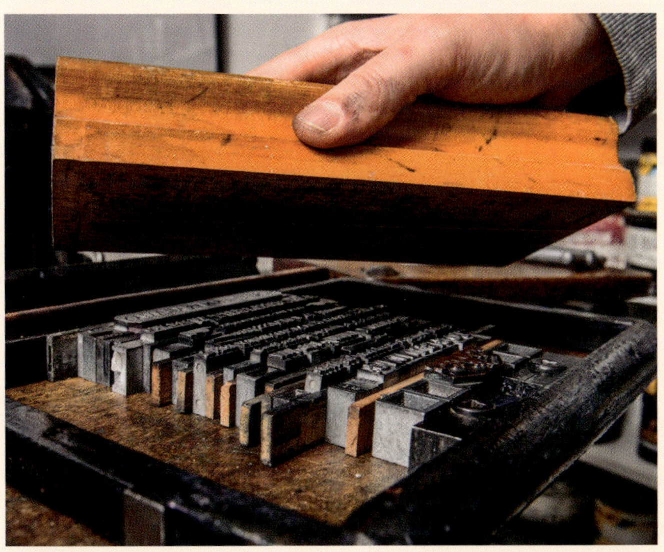

I have also found that making sure that you are working on a very flat worktop offers a great deal of help with final locking out. Wooden worktops look lovely but often are not 100 per cent flat, so using a wooden planer to bang down your type onto an undulating surface makes no sense. If you are working on a natural surface, you can always get a cheap piece of melamine or laminated kitchen worktop offcut using that as your area to lock out type on – look at DIY shops' timber scraps bins, they often have offcuts for free. As long as your type is as flat as you can get it and you don't have any rogue high letters, you should be fine to move on to printing. Just be slow and mindful in the next steps of inking and refining the pressure on the press to get the perfect impression and print. You will find that type can and will pull itself into place during test prints, though it is best not to rely too heavily on this.

Inking and pre-print

Pre-print

Let's look at printing with wood type on a flatbed press. You have your type either locked in your press or locked in your chase, and it's time to get inking and printing. Before you roll out your ink it is worth doing a blind print run (printing without inking to get your pressure using packing sheets correct), especially if it's the first time you are printing on your press. Lay a piece of paper gently onto your type and pull the press over it (proofing press printing). Was there any pressure between the press roller and the type? If the answer was no, then you need to use some sheets of paper as packing sheets, or if you have a printing press like a Farley then you can tweak the pressure by adjusting the roller height and adding a packing sheet. These sheets can be old misprints or newsprint. Place the extra sheets of paper on top of your original paper and pull again; hopefully this time you will start to feel pressure and the paper squeezing between the roller and the type. If not, add a couple more sheets until you do.

Once you start to feel the additional resistance on the pull of the roller, then look closely at the bottom sheet of paper that is in direct contact with the un-inked type (after you have pulled a blind print). You are looking to see if there is any deboss of the type into the paper. A deboss is when the paper is pushed hard enough to mould around the type and leave a physical impression – ideally, we don't want this. In the modern world letterpress prints are often associated with this deboss, but in reality, good quality printing is achieved without it. Traditionally, deboss could cause issues – think of a beautiful letterpress-printed book with its double-sided pages. If it was heavily debossed when printing, then the other side of the printed page would be very hard to read. The deboss is due to too much pressure and packing.

If you over-pack and over-pressurise when printing, you will fundamentally lose the tiny nuances of the individual pieces of type. Often the print will not have such crisp lines on each letter, as the paper is forced around the edge of the type, causing a very small amount of blurring. Also, the more pressure you put on your type, the more wear and tear you will inflict. I personally want to keep my type printing for my lifetime and beyond. Start light with the pressure, and you can always add another sheet of packing when you are actually printing. Doing this rough setup without inking just means that you are not getting into an inky mess and wasting materials.

Pulling a print on a proofing press, fingers wrapped firmly around printing bars whilst printing.

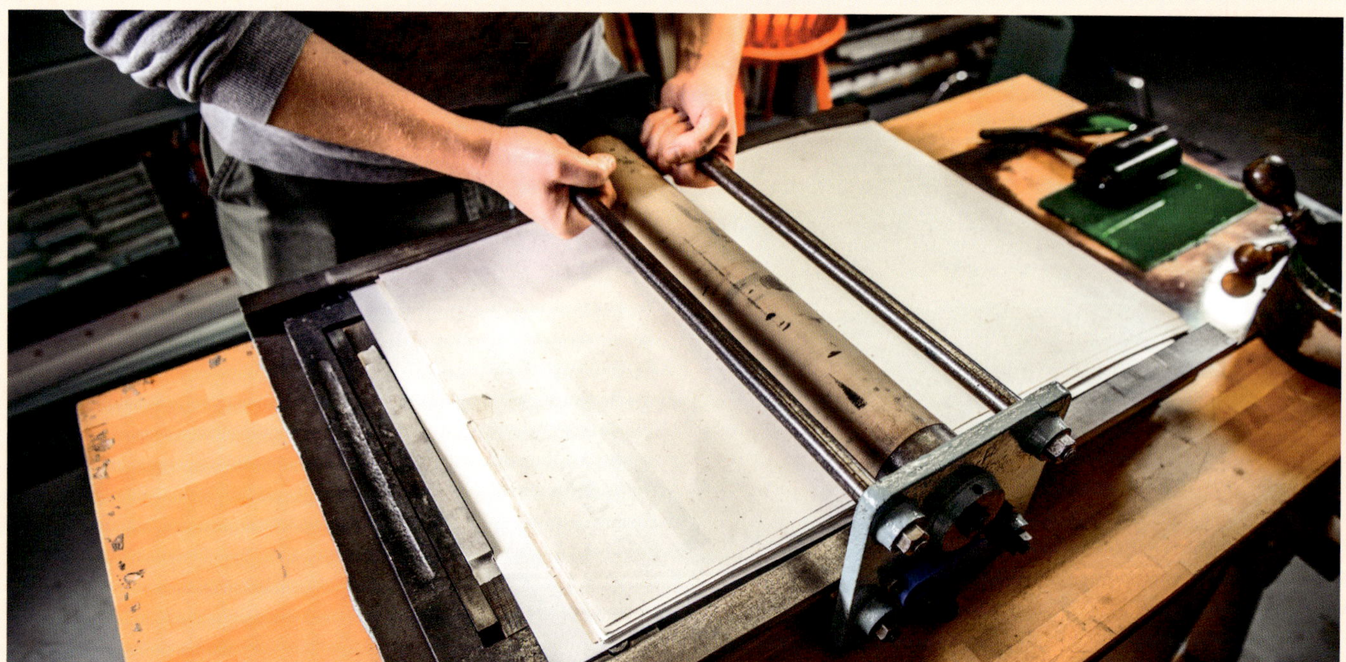

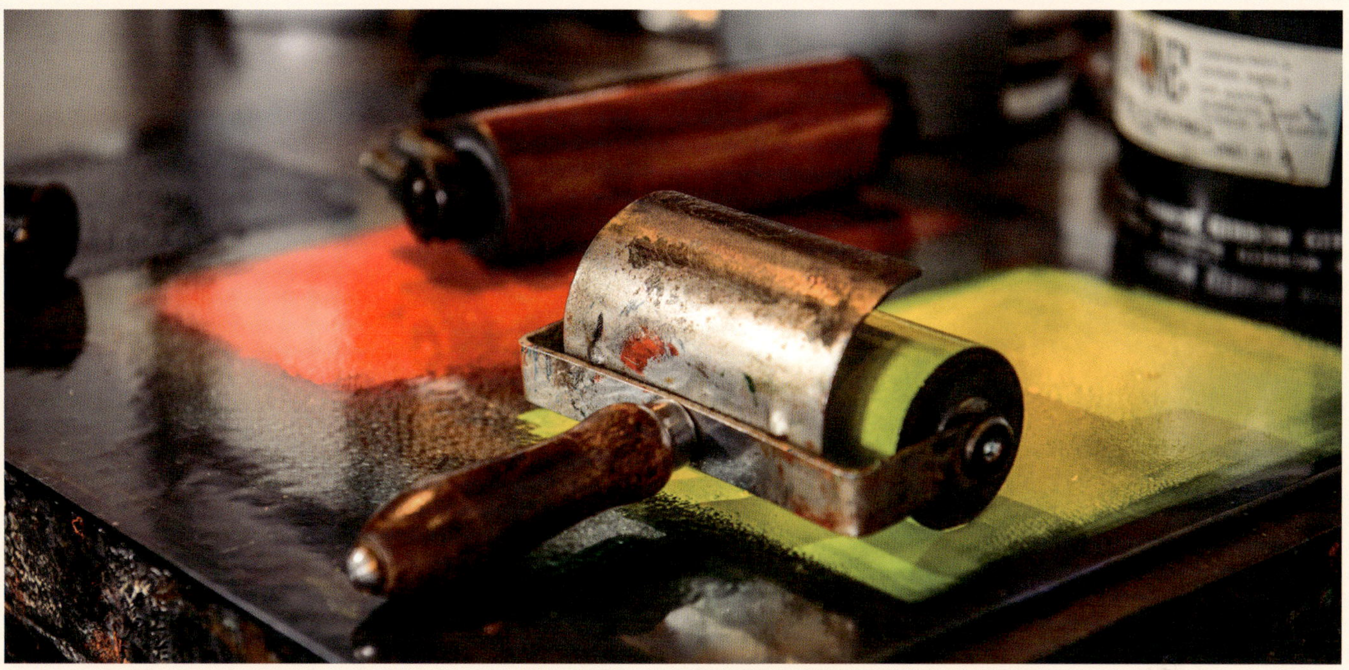

Ink rolled out evenly on inking plate and rollers.

Old screwdriver used to open & collect ink.

Inking

Take your inking plate, your ink and your chosen roller (brayer – roller for transferring ink). Bigger is not always better; choose a roller that will easily cover the area you need, but also think about whether there are any tight corners to get into. If there are some parts close to the corners of your press roller, then don't go for a large 6-inch roller, use a 3-inch or 4-inch instead. Using a pallet knife or screwdriver, smudge a small amount of ink into a line roughly the width of your roller. Start to roll out your ink: push your roller back and forth to start with, then from the bottom of your ink to the top, lift, then repeat from the bottom. You are aiming to have a rectangle about 25 per cent wider than the width of your roller, with the ink rolled out about 20cm long. People tend to ink the entire plate – this is a terrible waste of ink and just makes for more mess to clean up.

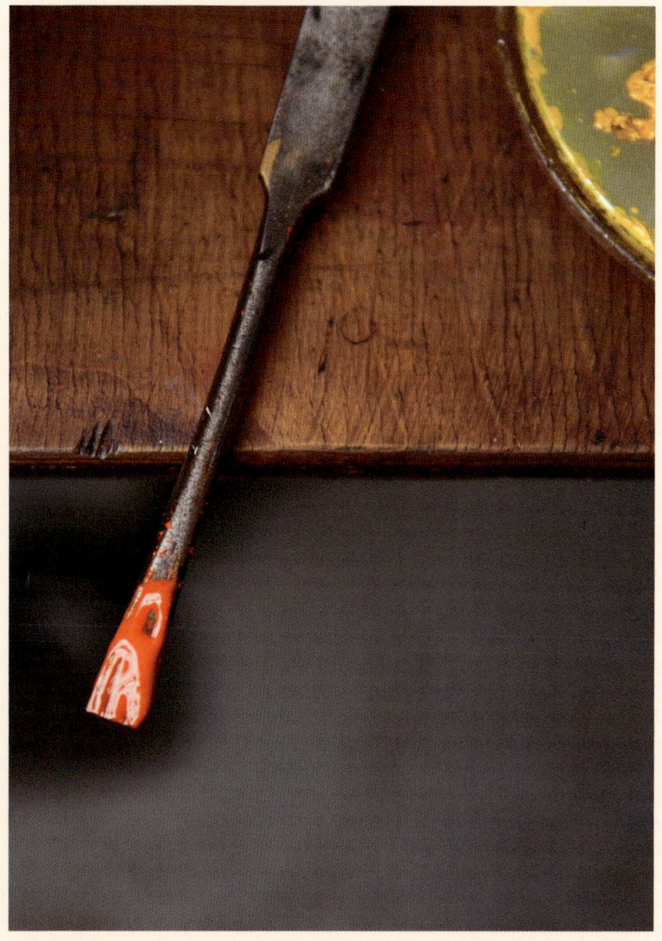

The amount of ink you will need for a design will vary depending on its size – you'll get used to gauging it quite quickly. As a basic rule you want the ink layer to be quite thin, unless you're going for a particularly inky finish. The roller should make a satisfying static noise when the ink level is right, but if the ink appears to be wet, drags on the roller and forms little peaks, then there is too much ink.

It's not serious if this happens – just extend out the rolling space. Remember to rest your roller handle on a dry area of the plate – I don't know how many times I have picked up an inky handle. A packet of baby wipes near your printing area is always handy.

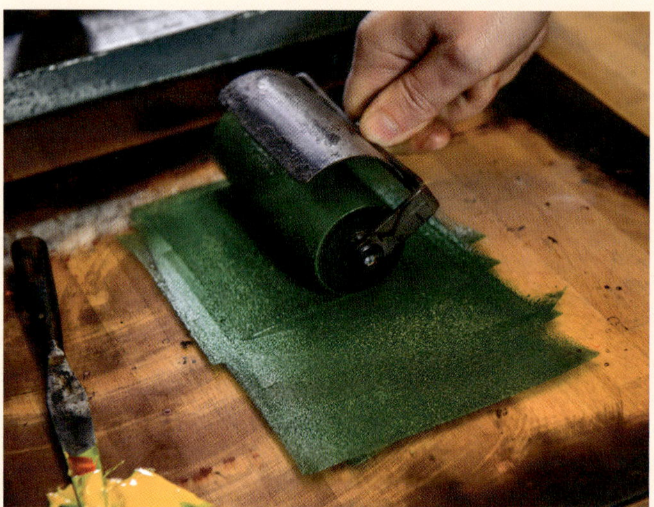

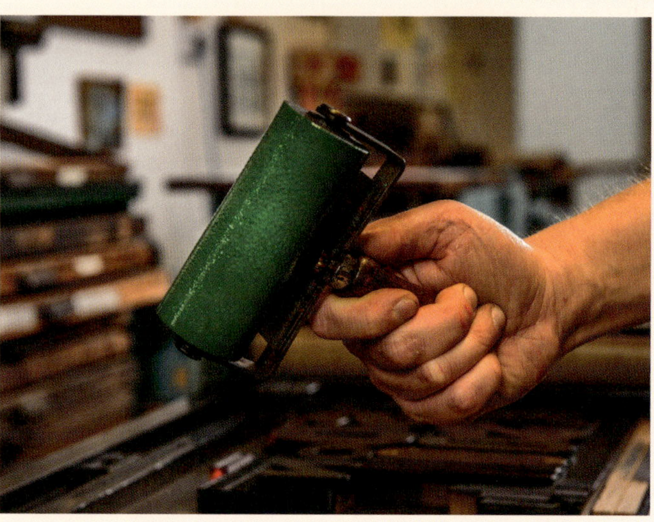

Mixed ink being evenly rolled out, making sure ink is the right density/thickness.

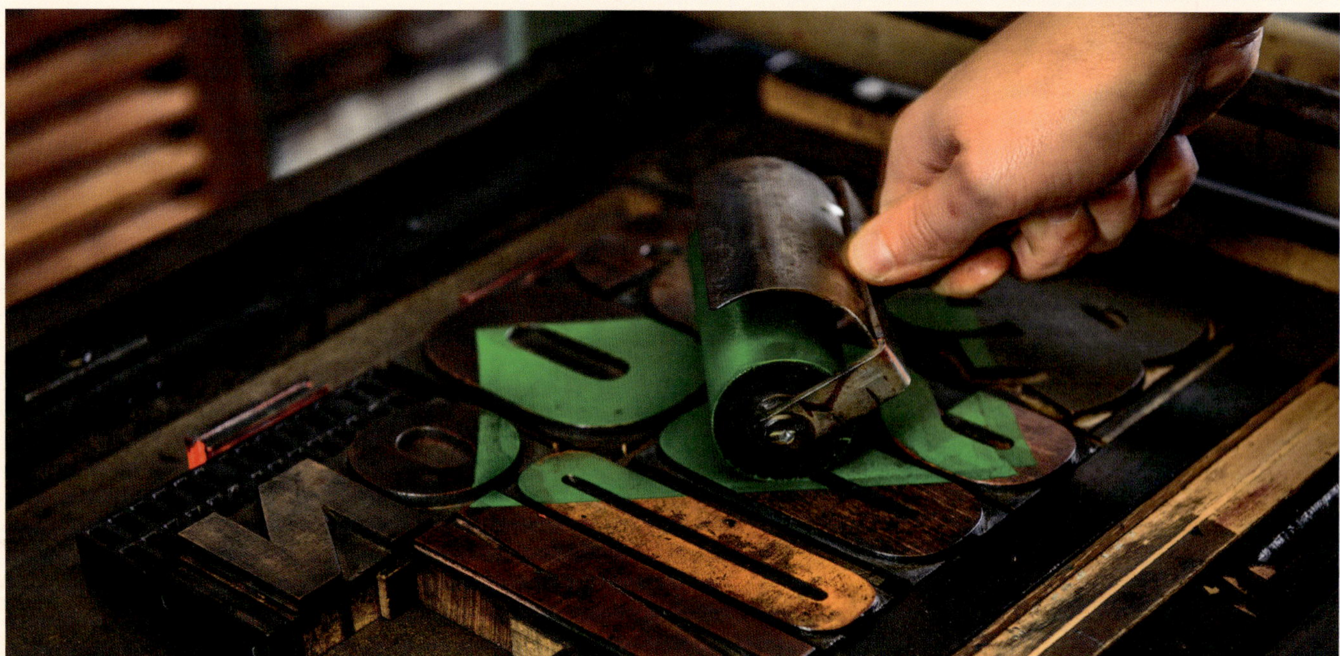

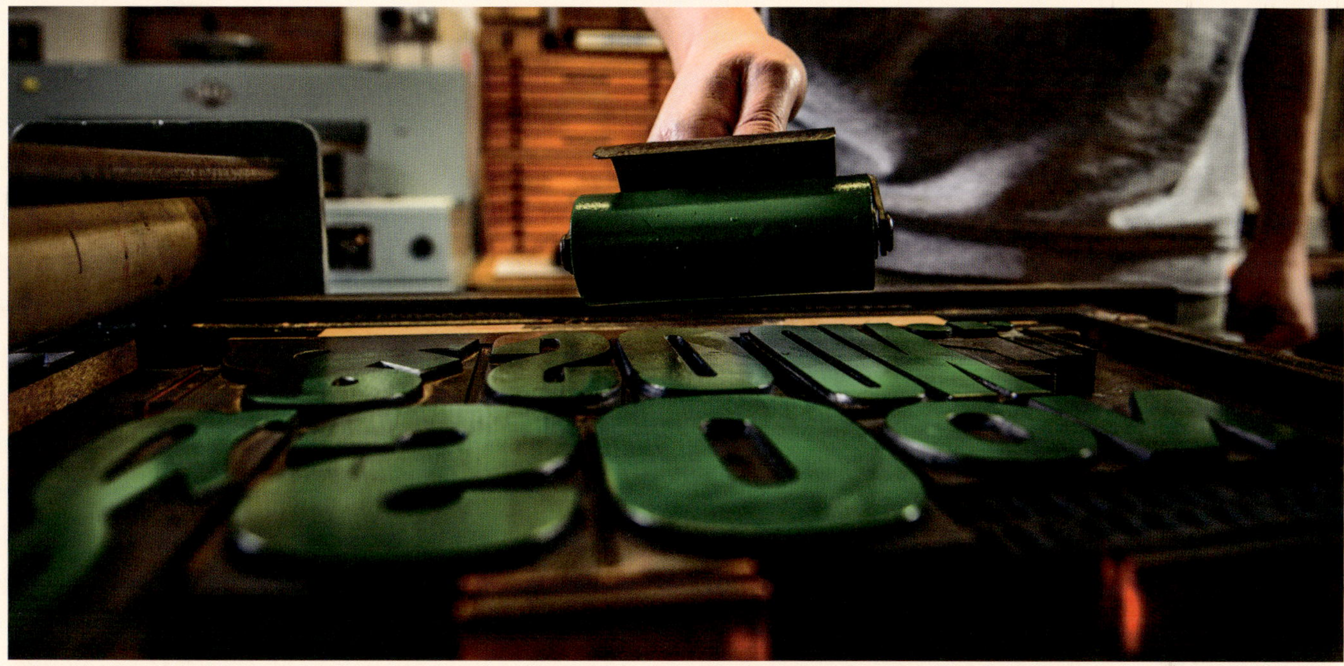

Inking wood type.

Depending on the design and layout of your type, hand-inking is a very basic process, but there are a few tips that help control the outcome and consistency from one print to another. Lightly lower your roller onto your type; as soon you make contact, start to roll. Don't push down too hard – the ink could collect unevenly around corners and edges. It can also make the roller skid. I always apply in sections at a 45-degree angle to the line of my type, meaning I am not going in straight. This way, the roller is less prone to bouncing up the side of letters and inking the edge.

As you notice the roller is lacking ink, gather more in the same manner. Try to lift the roller in a smooth motion off the plate, as if you stop then lift, a line of ink is created on the roller. Once again lower your roller gently onto the type and cover the parts that are not yet inked. This process may need to be repeated a few times.

With type in awkward arrangements, you may need to roll in a straight line to reach some angles. You will inevitably get to a point where you will ask yourself, 'Is there enough ink?' If I am feeling unsure, I always do one more very quick 'inking for luck' – a thin application, just as before.

Final quick one for luck inking to make sure no areas missed.

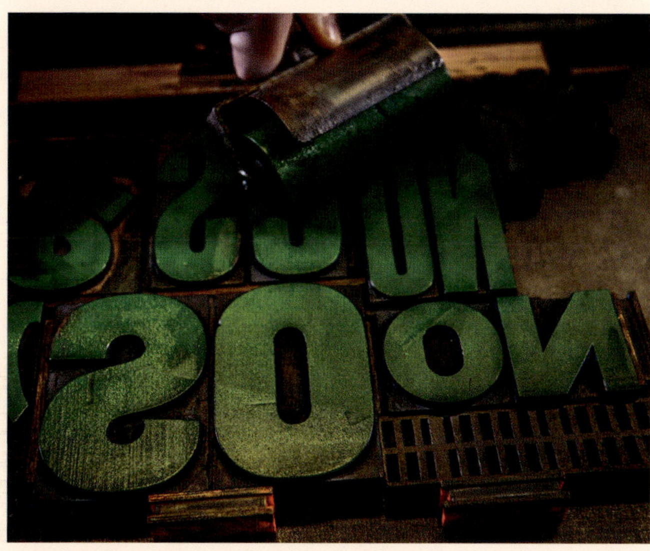

Pulling a print

It's far from ideal to get everything ready to print, only to then drop your paper onto the ink. Depending on what sort of press you have, some presses like Farleys have gripper bars that you can slide your paper into, holding the paper in place as you pull a print.

Gripper bar on Farley.

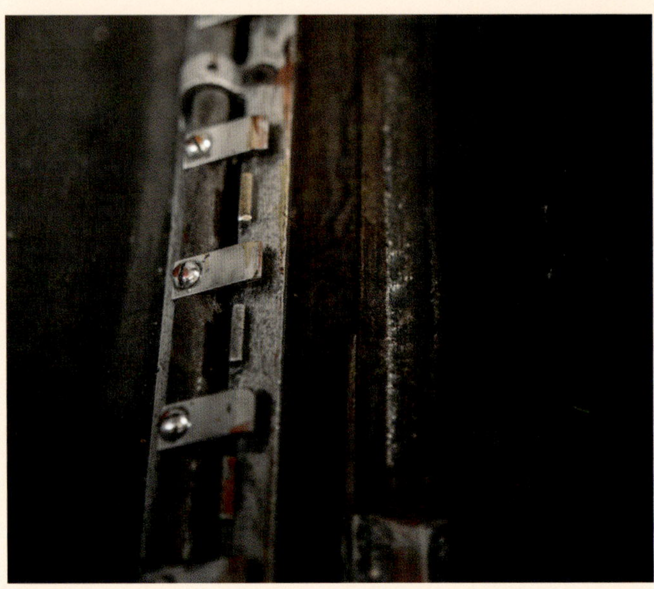

Gripper bar on Vandercook.

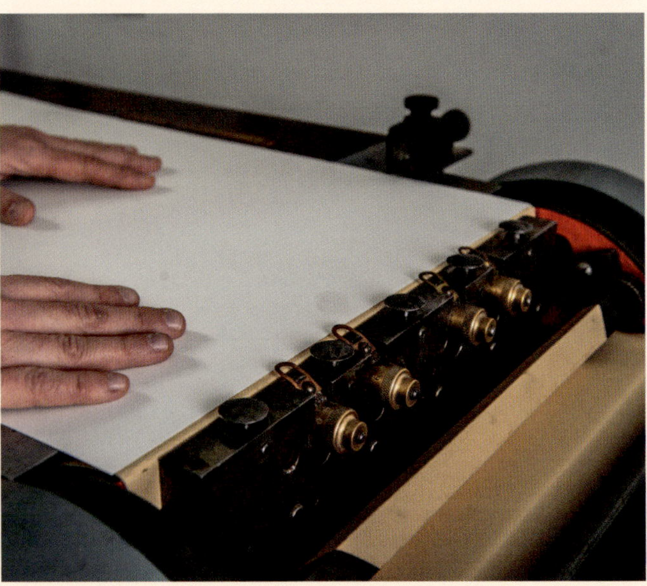

Other presses like Vandercooks have mechanisms where you slide the paper from an end table onto the start of its impression drum, and it holds the paper whilst it prints. In the case of a Vandercook it holds the printed sheet of paper on its printing drum after printing, so you do not have to peel the print off the type after printing.

If you are printing on a basic-style proofing press or a very grand Columbian, Albion or Stanhope, then you are going to have to place your piece of paper onto your type. With a basic proofing press you have to glide your paper down towards your roller, lowering onto the type as you would put a sleeping baby into a cot! A quick tip if you have no end stop or paper gripper mechanism: make yourself a rudimentary stop, or as I like to call it, a butt edge, to push your paper up to as a starting point. Simply take a 72pt piece of furniture, the longest piece that will fit in your chase/ press. With masking tape, attach a thin piece of furniture flat onto the surface. Place it at the top of your chase/ print, and slide your paper against the ledge to always have a safe starting point.

Placing paper for print on a basic proofing press.

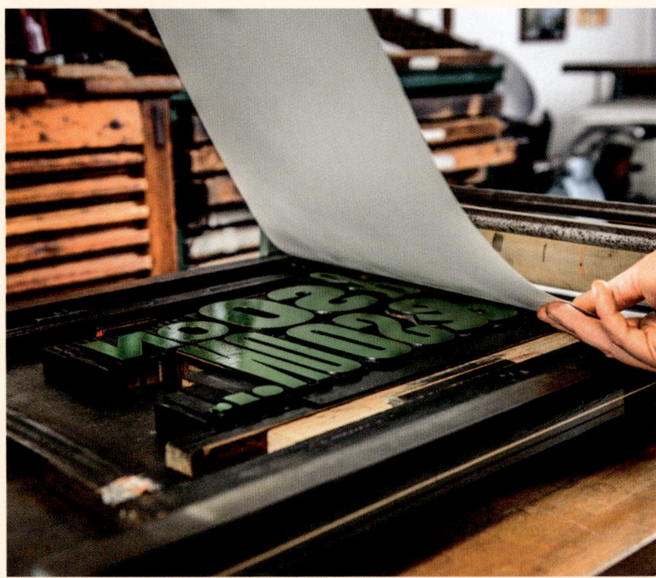

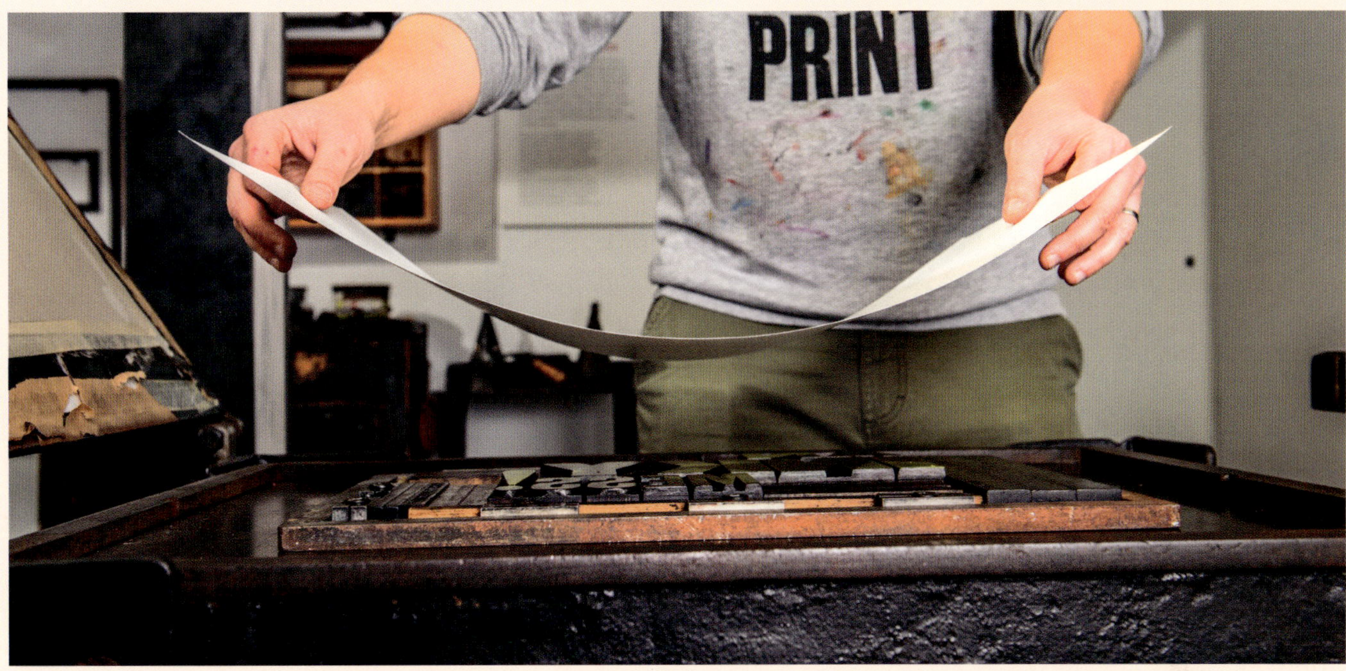

Placing paper for print on a Stanhope press.

Placing your paper onto type on Albions, Columbians or Stanhopes is tricky, as really you have to gauge by eye where the paper goes. Stand confidently by your press, hold out your piece of paper, gripping the short sides with your arms outstretched. Lower the paper about half the distance to the inked type. Now try to work out the alignment of where you want your paper. Once you feel you have the paper in the perfect place, slowly move your hands towards each other to let the paper sheet loosen and bow down in its centre, then lower your sheet onto your type. Do this smoothly and decisively, do not stop mid-way, if you touch the paper onto the type, you cannot adjust its position anymore. If you are finding this particularly difficult or you really like to get things perfect, then there are a couple of simple tricks you can try.

Placing packing sheets on top of printing sheet (gently).

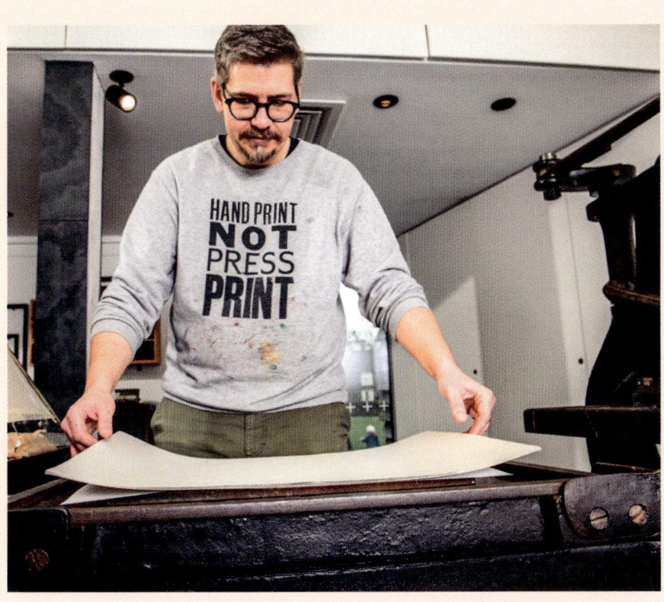

With your type set exactly where you want to print, measure out where you would like your print to be on your chosen sheet of paper. Then using a ruler, measure where the paper needs to be placed perfectly on the press. Mark the line of where you want your paper to be with masking tape and repeat on the other edge of the paper; you now have an X and Y axis to align to. Now your paper is laying on your inked type, at this point I often will give the prints what I call a 'loving pat' – a very light touch of the hand across the areas of the paper that I now have type under. Now put in place the packing sheets that you worked out earlier. Try not to slide these around too much on top of the printing sheet.

Now everything is in place, if you are on a basic proofing press, place your hands tightly around the area to be used for pulling. In the case of Farley's they often have a black plastic-like coating to indicate where to put your hand. Think logically before pulling the print and never ever, no matter how tempting it is, put your hand in any area of a moving part or where the roller goes. It is easy to have an accident – I speak with experience! Also make sure your printing press is securely placed and is not liable to move – this can be an issue for table-top presses. You can always try some anti-slip matting under its feet or screwing a small piece of wooden beading around the edge of your worktop if this is an issue.

As you pull the roller you will feel the resistance of the paper moulding around the type. What you are aiming for is a smooth and steady pull, trying not to slow down or stop mid-print. If you do come to a stop, you have too many packing sheets and too much pressure – you'll need to write off the print, back up the roller gently and start again once you have remedied the problem. You have just pulled your first test print. Making sure your hands are clean, lift the print from the bottom edge of the paper. Gently and slowly peel the paper from the print, using your thumb and forefinger. Take care – as you get to the end of the print the paper can release more quickly and slide on the type, leaving you with an inky mark. As soon as you have released your print, put it onto your worktop to inspect.

Pulling a print on a Farley, clearly indicated area where to hold when pulling a print.

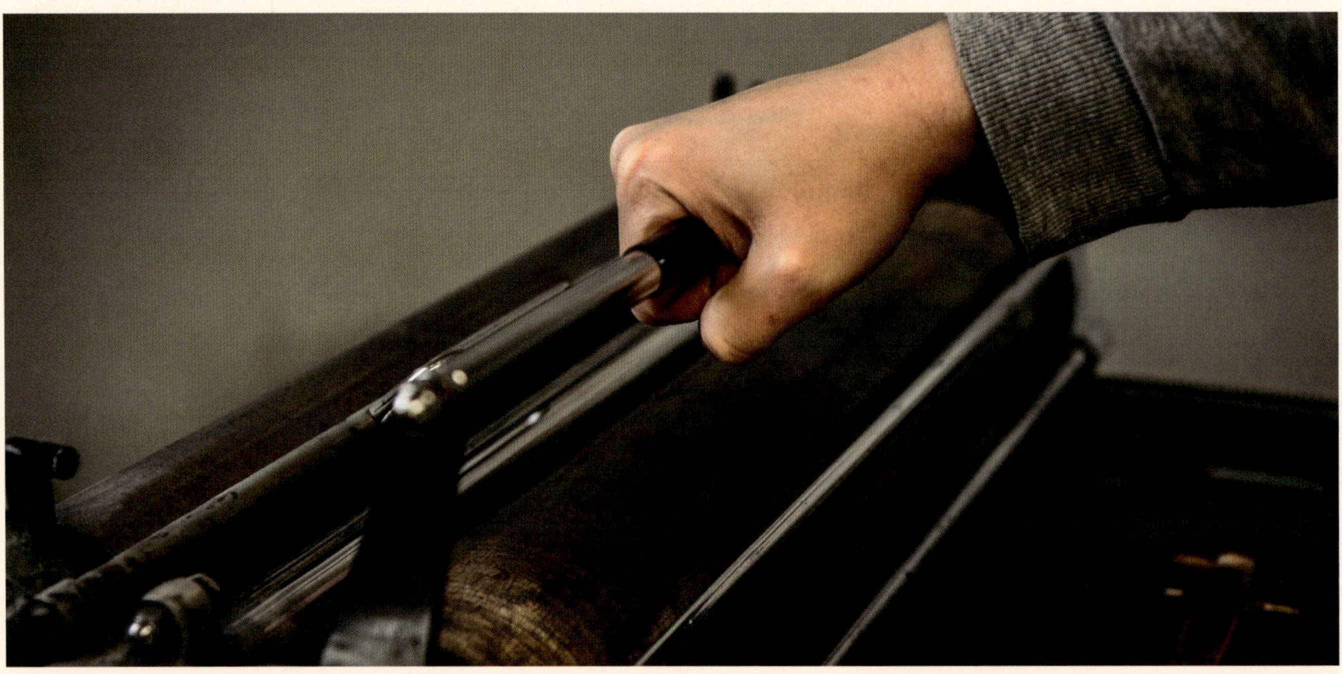

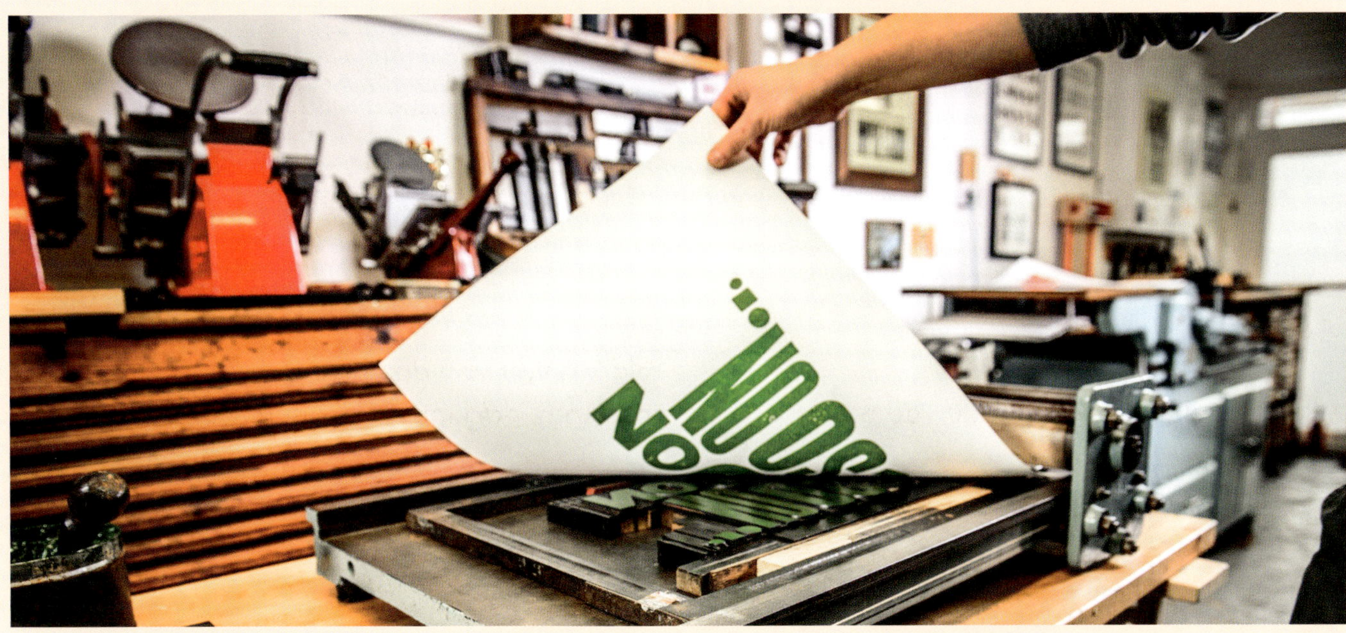

Gently & slowly revealing a print being careful not to pull quickly flicking the paper as the last part of the print is revealed.

Check your spellings, kerning and line spacing

The first thing to do with your test print is to check for any spelling mistakes, no matter how simple the words are. I always number prints with a pencil in the top right corner when doing test prints, so I can see developments and identify their order. Next you can look at the design with a critical eye. Ask yourself the basic question: do you like it? If there is something that you don't like, just change it. Now is the best time to make any major changes before moving on to final tweaks. If you are changing fonts or type, remember that it is best to clean the letters whilst they are locked out, as this is quicker and less messy. For any changes to the design just follow the previous steps and repeat as necessary. Whenever you make any changes, you will need to do another test print. This time, it will be slightly more difficult to see where there is or isn't ink.

Hopefully you are happier with the design, and now you can move on to look at the kerning and the spacing of individual letters in words, as they can look very different when printed. If you are not sure about kerning, question whether it's easy to read the individual words. Try to make the spacing between letters look as similar to each other as possible (as a basic rule); aim for what looks natural when the words are printed. The same then goes for line spacing between lines of text or words; do the words look crammed together, or are they too far apart and appear disconnected? Make small changes and pull test prints, enjoy the process of physical and manual design. You can keep test prints and reuse them for further testing in the future to save waste. If you want to add kerning or line spacing, release the pressure from the quoins and slide galley magnets out of the way as you go. You want to let the type be just loose enough to make the changes you want to. A quick tip: use thin pieces of furniture to help slide out individual letters or widen spaces, making it easier to get things in place.

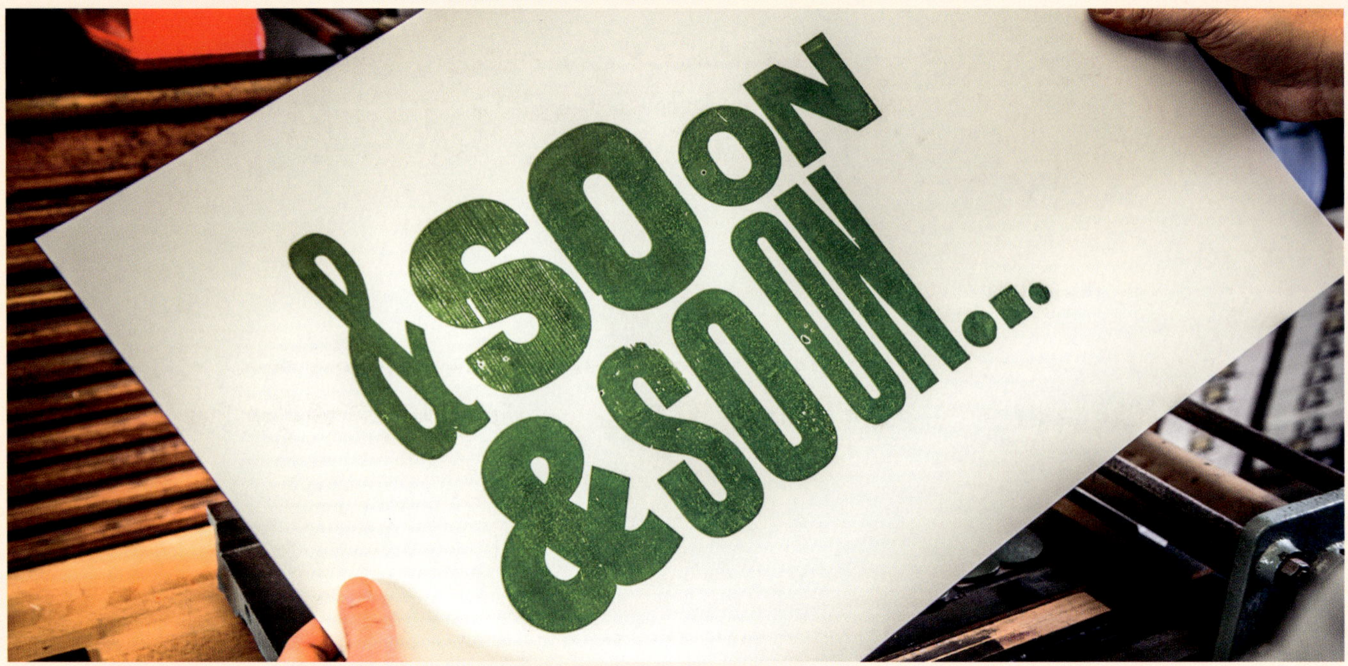

Checking the print for issues - inking, type, deboss, spellings! etc

Checking your print

Now you have your design set, turn your eye to the details of the print, are all the letters printing nicely? Is one letter printing less cleanly than the letters next to it? Is a side or corner of a letter not printing well? These are all part of letterpress, and they can be tweaked to get all you can out of each letter.

Firstly, look at the print overall, is it looking pretty good? If you feel like you did a good job of inking but your gut feeling is that the print should look a little punchier, then add another sheet of paper to the packing. Turn over your sheet and look to see the deboss – when prints are even, the deboss is also even. Compare the two prints against each other. If all you have changed is an extra sheet of packing, ask yourself, does the print look any different and did it feel very slightly physically harder to pull the print? If you cannot see any difference or improvements and you could not feel any greater level of resistance, you may need to add another piece of paper. What you should hopefully notice, by adding one sheet of additional packing and inking the same as the last print, is that the addition of only one sheet will increase the pressure and improve definition. It can be hard to work out if you have a pressure problem or an inking problem. If the pressure feels firm, and the print has not improved, try adding some more ink to your inking plate, roll out and print again. If you have patches in the print that are lighter than others, this may be where you have not done the best job of inking. For this, be more mindful to go over all areas of type and blocks, and always do one final inking for luck if you are not sure.

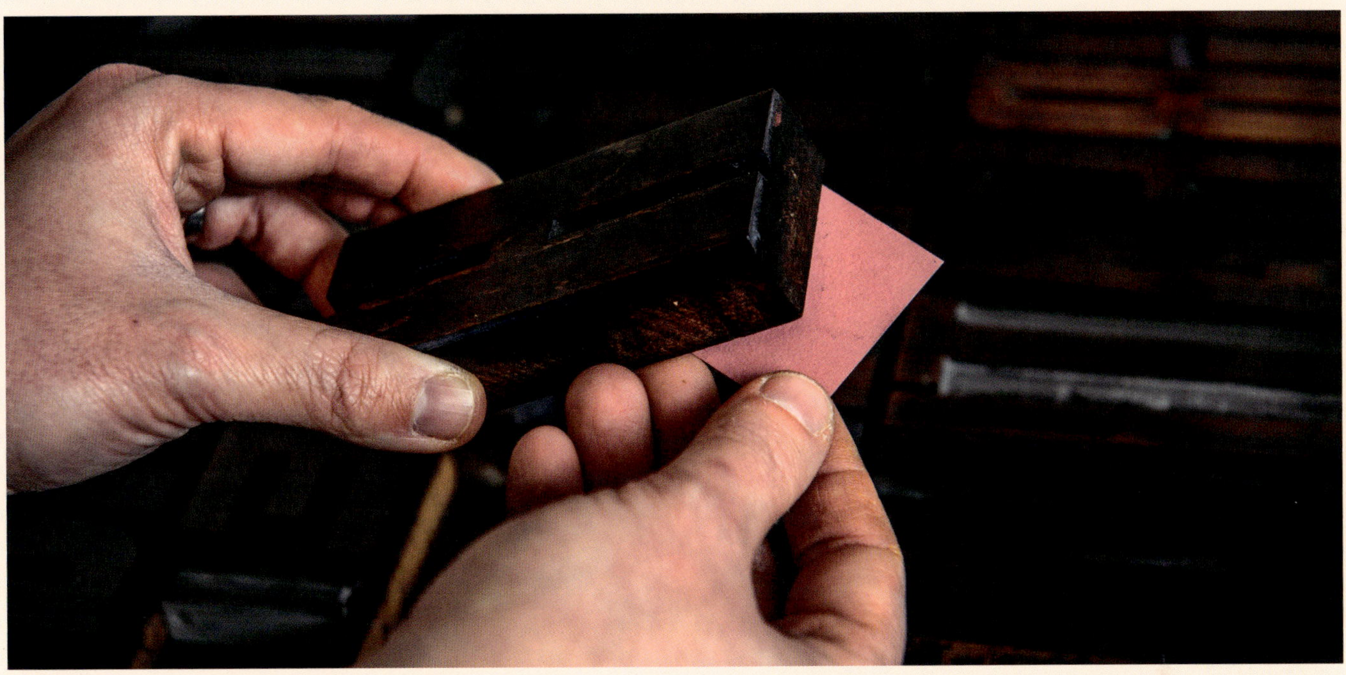

Packing a piece of old wood type to adjust the print height of the type.

Tweaking for a perfect print (adjusting type)

If your inking and pressure are good and still some areas are not printing nicely, maybe a section (probably a corner) of a letter is not printing well. This is a common problem when printing with wood type, the issue is likely to be that the type is very slightly low on one corner. This can be from years of hard printing, or perhaps the block has been dropped. For this there are both quick fixes for the current print, and longer-term fixes. The quick fix is to loosen your quoins/ galley magnets, remove the offending piece of type and put a small piece of paper under the problematic area. Or, place a piece of masking tape on the bottom of the block where the block has the issue, then return the block into the form, and try again.

Sometimes, annoyingly, you get letters within sets that have a slightly different height. This can be due to age and the quality of the timber that was used, with expansion and contraction of the wood over a long period of time. For this a piece of paper or card covering the whole area of the letter should raise your type. The best way to roughly know how much packing you will need can be seen by looking at your last print – if you only see a small difference to the other letters, a piece or two of paper should suffice. When the letter doesn't print at all, I would first look for a replacement from its type case. If one can't be found, then start packing with one piece of 300gsm card, and work your way from there. Do this slowly and take test prints as you go.

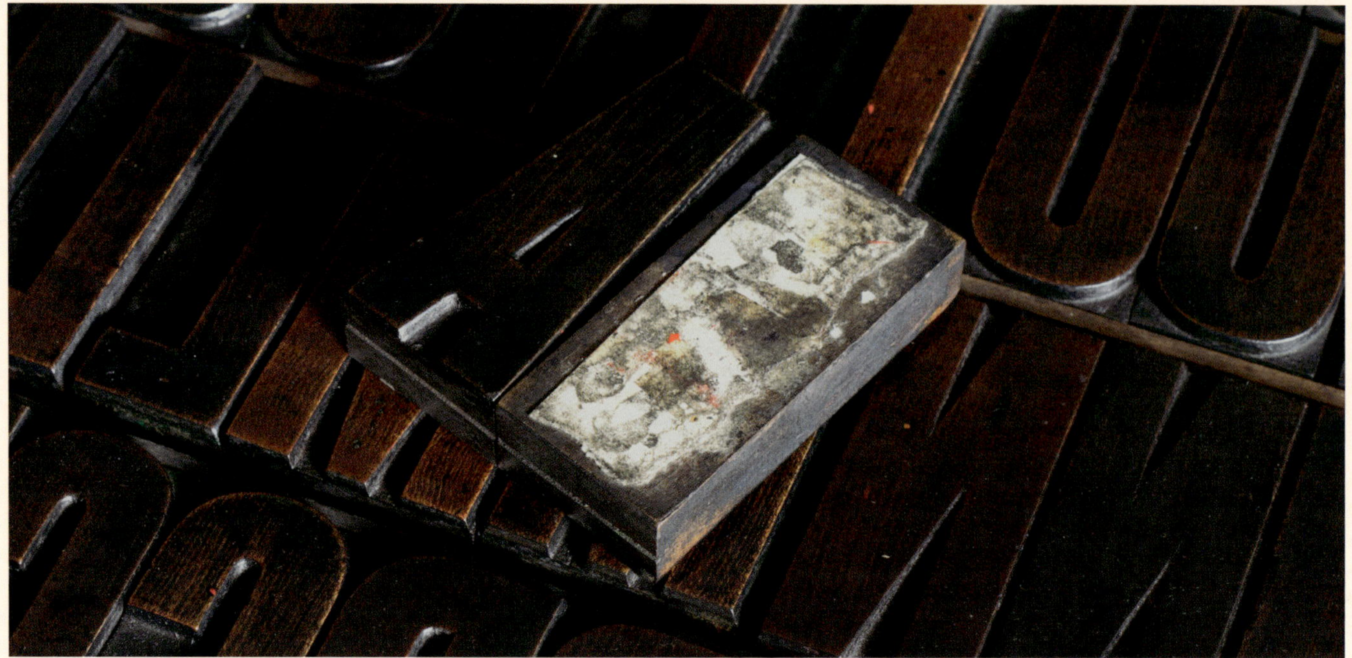

Old type packing.

For a longer-term fix to this common problem, you can use a type height gauge to measure your set, applying layers of brown tape to the bottom of type to reach a uniform height. You might find some ancient-looking tape on the bottom of letters in your collection where this has been done before.

Printing

Once you're up and running, you'll need to add more ink to your inking plate periodically; try to keep an eye on how the ink looks on the prints, as it is much better to add ink little and often than to run it down to producing a bad print. You will find in time that making small adjustments and refinements to the prints will become second nature. You'll start to be able to read your print, know what the problem is and how to solve it quickly.

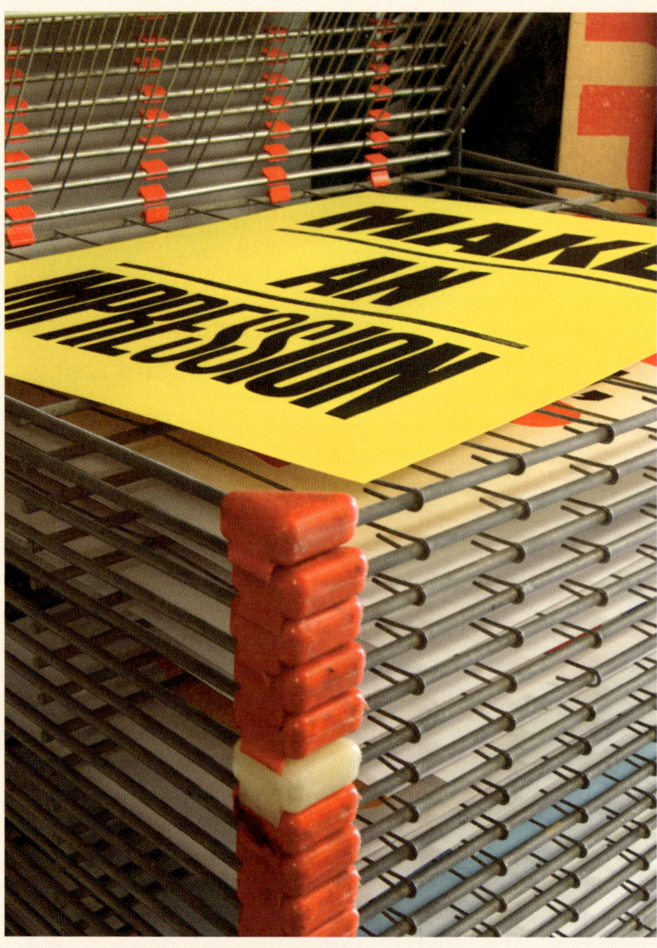

Prints on drying rack.

Have a think about where your prints will dry. Oil-based inks take around twenty-four hours to dry (depending on conditions). A drying rack is ideal, either floor-standing like you see in a lot of screen-printing workshops or for that traditional letterpress workshop feel, you can get hanging ball drying racks. Otherwise, worktop or floor space runs out surprisingly quickly. Think outside the box when it comes to what will work for your space – I remember seeing someone using vintage vinyl record racks as a small vertical drying rack.

If you find that something has suddenly changed in your print, stop and check your type, quoins and galley magnets. Remember to check that you have not over-tightened your quoins, which can cause old type that's worn around the edges to creep very slowly.

Now that you have finished printing your type, it is time to clean down. As mentioned in Chapter 3, use two rags; first, one that's been previously used, and then one that's clean – or clean-ish. Start on your type, then your roller, then your inking plate. Clean in order of what has the least to the most mess, for example, the inking plate is always last. Then put all your type, rollers, inking plate, etc., away so that when you next want to print everything is clean, tidy and ready to go.

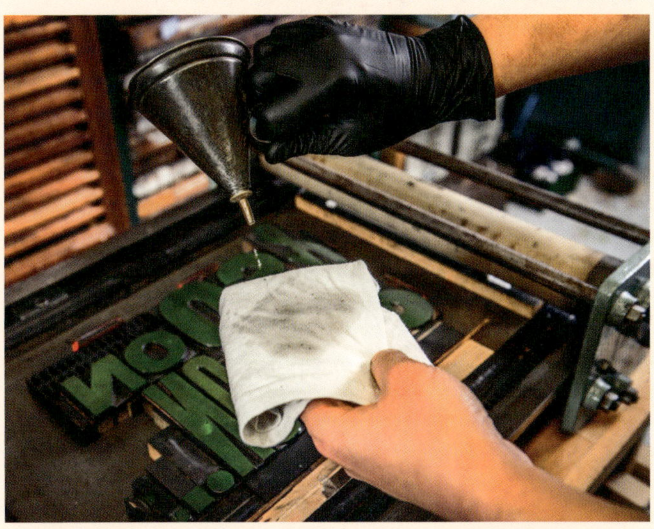

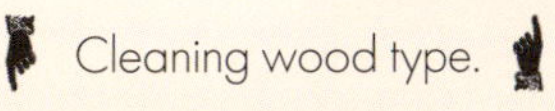

Cleaning wood type.

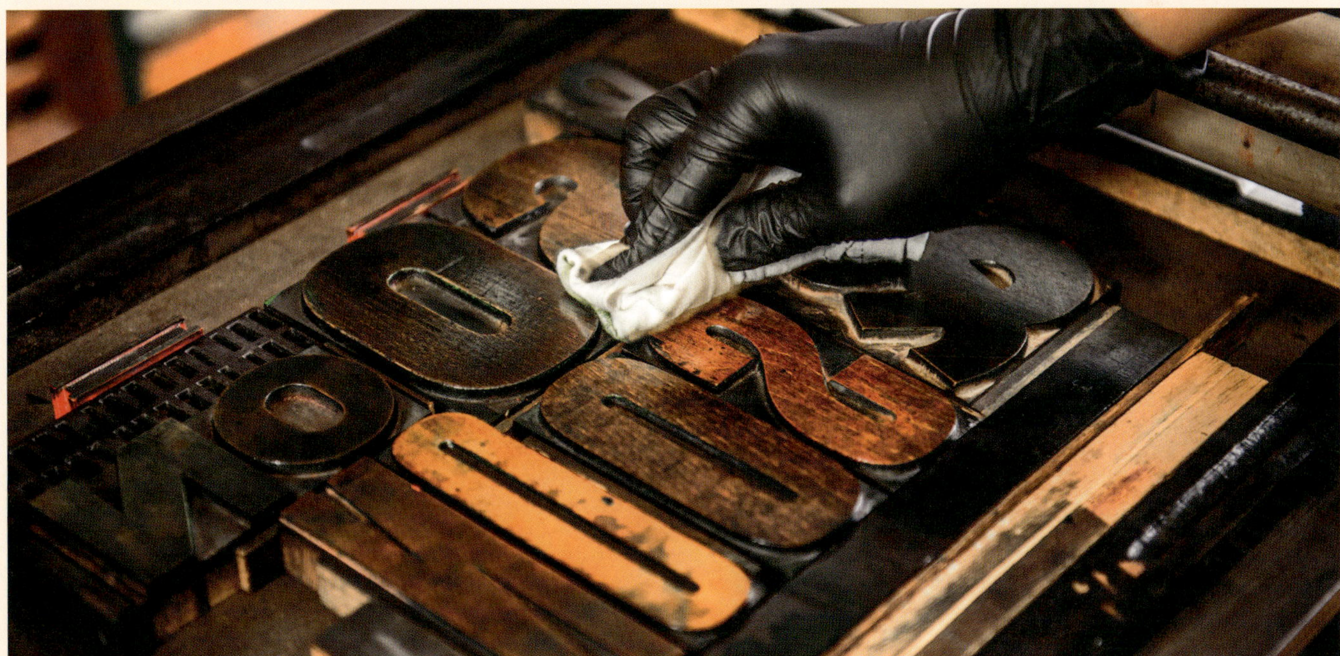

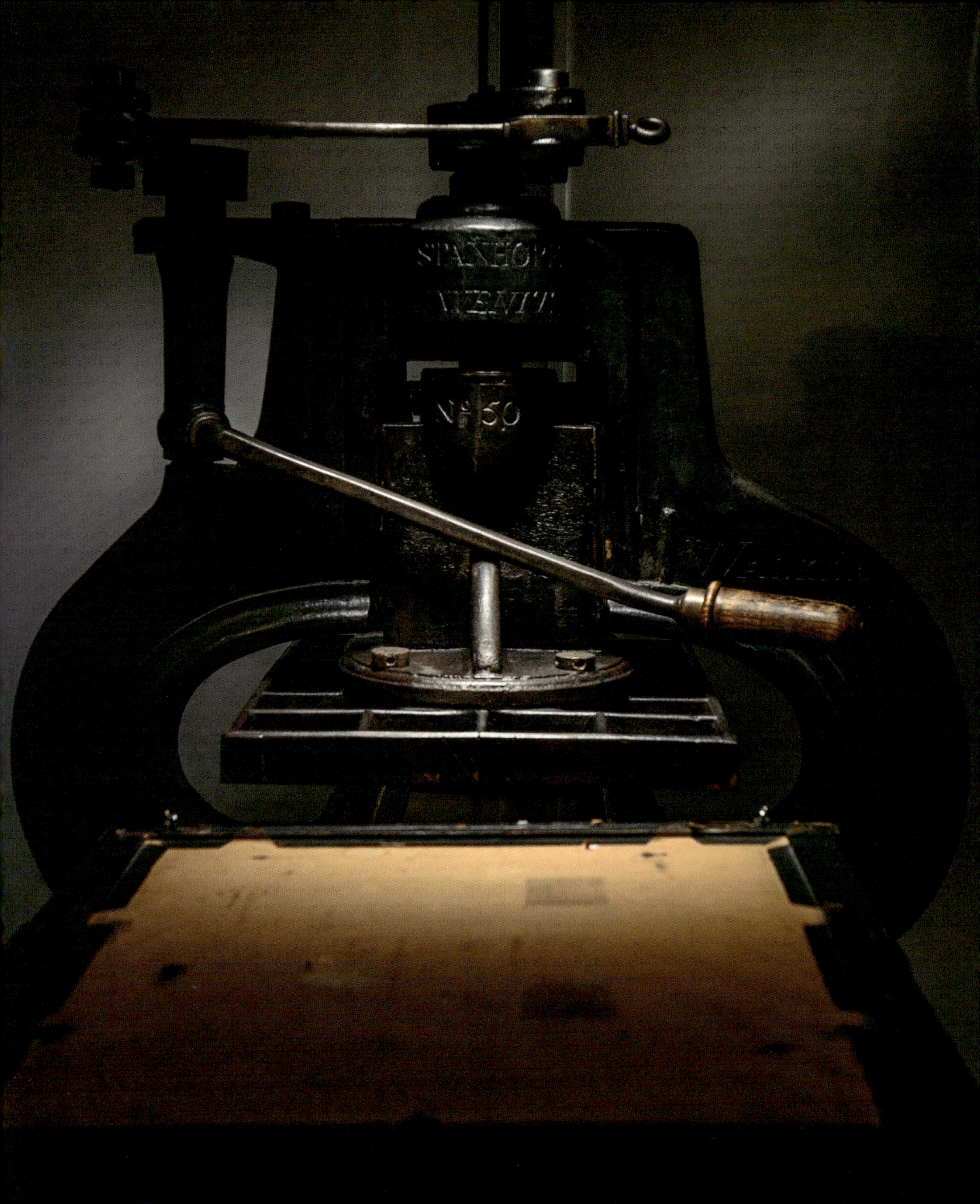
Nº 50

6

Printing presses

There are a large number of different presses out there, made by a variety of different companies. Some are better-made than others, and some designed with inventive solutions to the challenges of printing with a printing press. In this chapter I will look at handling different machines, in the order in which I purchased them or learnt to use them.

All these printing presses form the backbone of my creative life. Whilst all machines have their differences, they all have areas of common usage and operation. So don't worry if you don't have the exact press I am writing about – there are so many that we can't cover them all.

We can, however, group them into presses of a similar ilk. While parts may look different, their basic process is likely very similar, if not the same. I have found that working hands-on with different machines and learning by doing has broadened my processes of printing and creation.

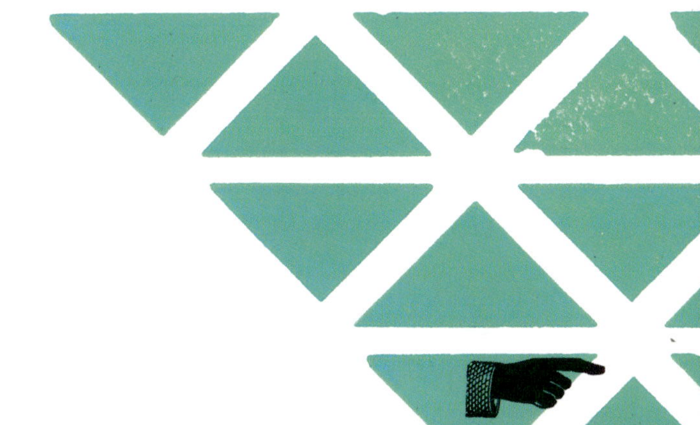

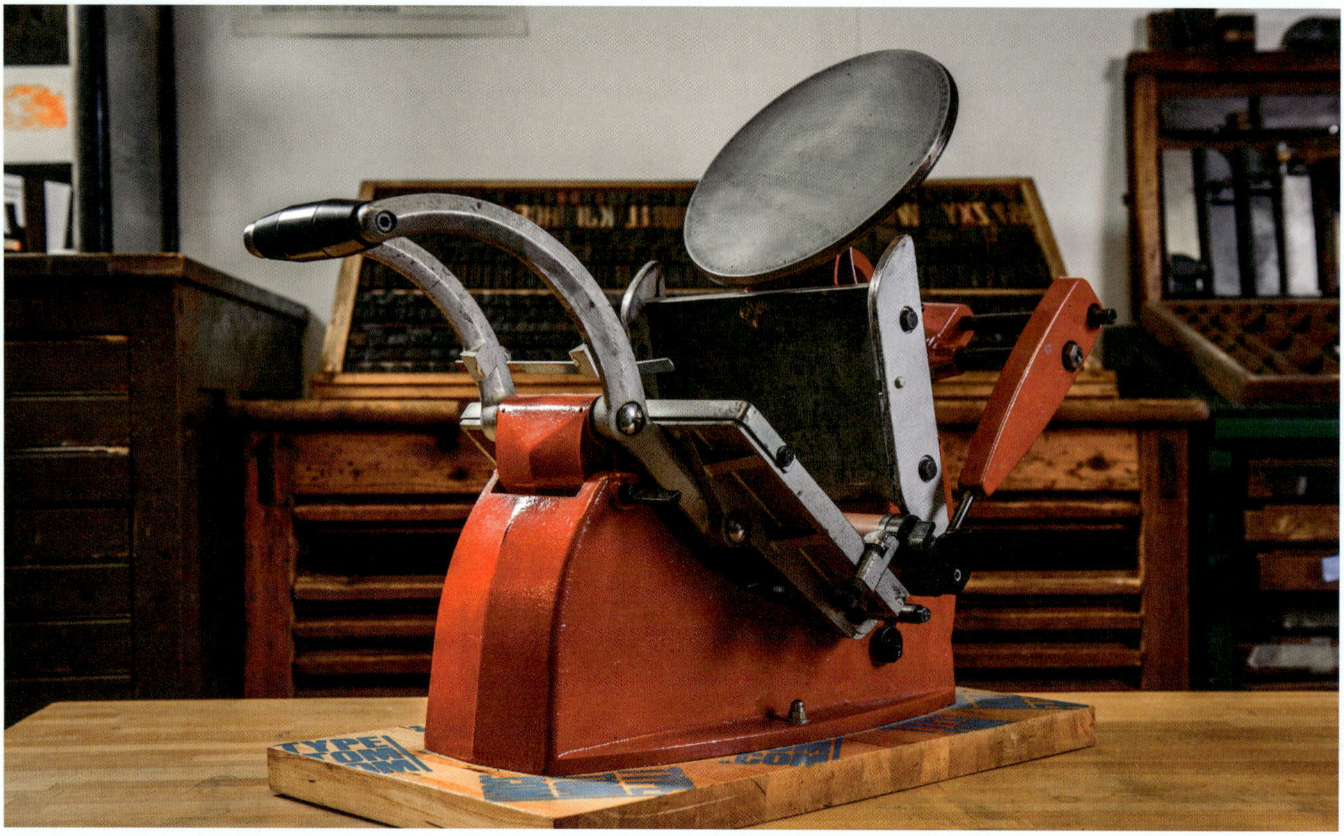

 Restored Adana's 8x5 model. 

Printing on an Adana

An Adana 8 × 5 was my first press purchased to print an early commission on. For me, the Adanas are special little presses that offer a gateway to learning. I recommend anyone who is thinking about starting letterpress printing to get one and have a go. They are great for small runs of prints, ideal for starting out on printing items like business cards and greetings cards.

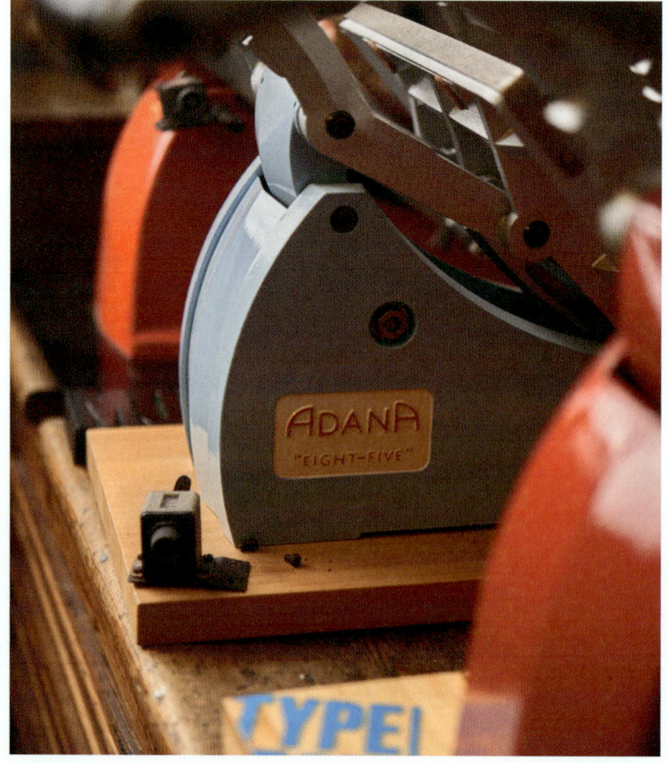

Adanas were first made in 1922, and were very popular in their time with hobbyists and businesses. You will often find Adanas in small print workshops, where they're still used for jobs like creasing and die cutting. Though Adana stopped production, you can still find them

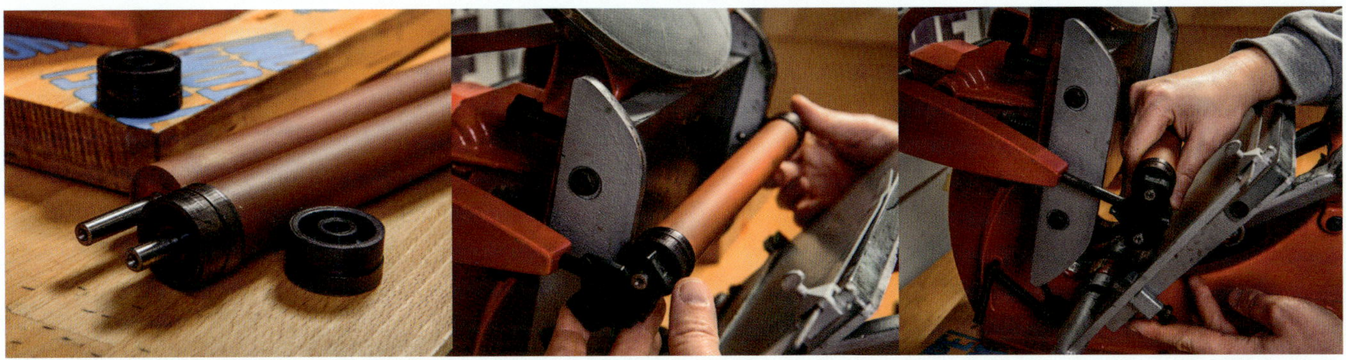

Adana roller trucks, and how to install/remove rollers.

regularly for sale on eBay, and being sold by traders on Instagram and other social media outlets.

For printing on an Adana, you can only use an Adana chase to lock your type out in – these were custom-made. Let's assume you have set up and locked out your type, put this to one side for the moment. For a quick overview, the Adana works using a clamshell-style opening and closing mechanism to print; when you push down the handle, it closes the clamshell and makes the impression, when you lift the handle, it will open so you can remove your print and then insert a new piece of paper.

Adana 8x5 chase.

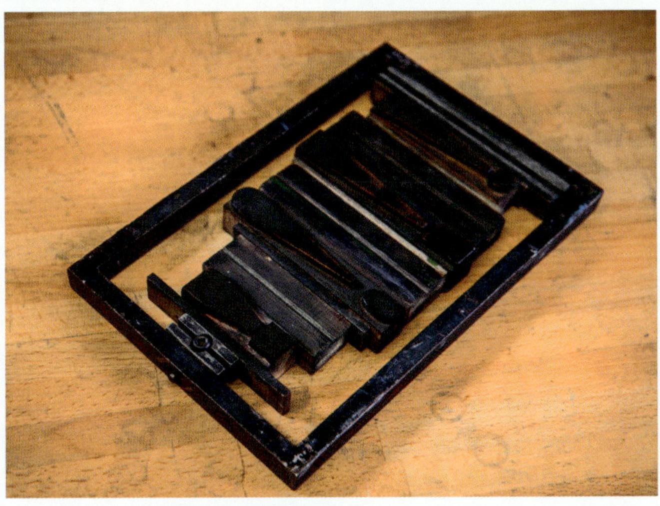

There are two rollers that rise and fall in perfect timing with the clamshell mechanism. As the clamshell closes, the rollers ride up the tracks, inking the type, and then up onto the circular inking plate where they collect more ink as the press prints. Just before the rollers reach the inking plate, the plate rotates, to reload the rollers with fresh ink. If the inking plate didn't turn, you'd run out of ink very quickly. If you're very lucky you may find an Adana that has the addition of a small inking fountain. You can fill this with ink, and the press will automatically collect more as it prints. Whilst this saves you time having to stop and re-apply, it does require cleaning down after use, which is always slow. I don't have a Adana with an inking fountain, and it's never been an issue.

To get printing, install your rollers by pulling forward the sprung roller holders, put the bottom roller in first then rock the roller holder up to fit the top rollers. Do this process in reverse when removing the rollers at the end of printing to clean, this is the least messy way. Once the rollers have been installed, lift the press handle, to ensure that the rollers are in their lowest position with the clamshell mechanism open.

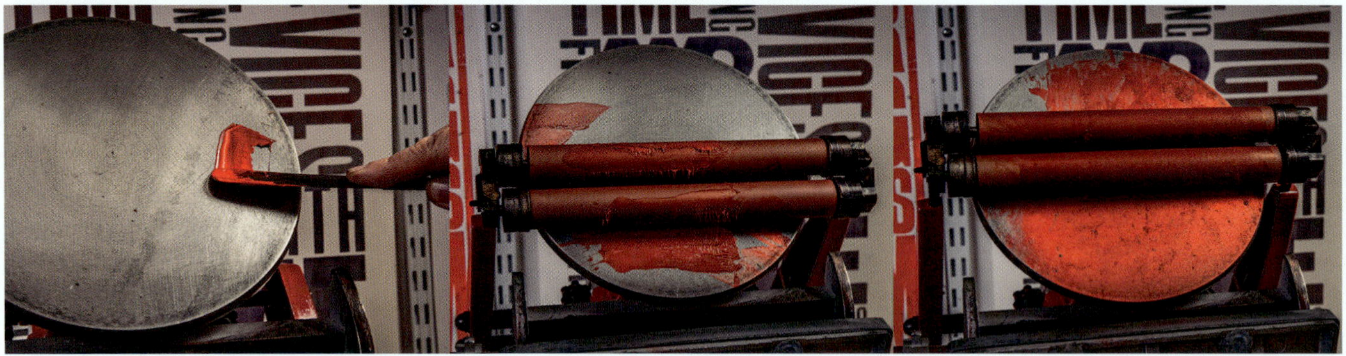

Applying ink to inking plate/disc and using Adana mechanism to evenly spread ink.

Now is the time to add some ink – place a small amount of ink onto the inking disc, ideally you will be doing this with a fine pallet knife or even an old flat-headed screwdriver. Try not to place a big blob of ink on the inking disc, instead draw the ink across the disc into a fat line, this will save time getting the ink rolled out evenly.

Now is a fun part, you need to push the handle up and down repeatedly, probably around 20 times to get the ink evenly smoothed out on the inking disk. This gives you a good chance to get used to the opening and closing mechanism for printing. Always leave your Adana with the handle up and the mechanism open. Never leave inky or clean rollers resting on the inking plate as this, even in a relatively short period of time, can cause damage like flat spots to occur on your rollers.

Pressure

On the Adanas there are a couple of important parts that you now need to focus on. The pressure of the print is controlled by four impression screws, which when tightened, cause the type bed to rise and create a higher level of pressure. They also work in reverse to release pressure. If these four screws aren't adjusted uniformly it will cause the pressure on the type bed to be uneven and skewed. When you first print on your Adana, try to get the type bed pressure as equal as possible – when adjusting the impression screws do so in equal fractions, for example, a quarter turn each time. It is safest to always start printing with the pressure set a little on the light side, then you can slowly turn up the pressure to get the desired impression.

Impression screws, turn right to raise plate, left to ease back.

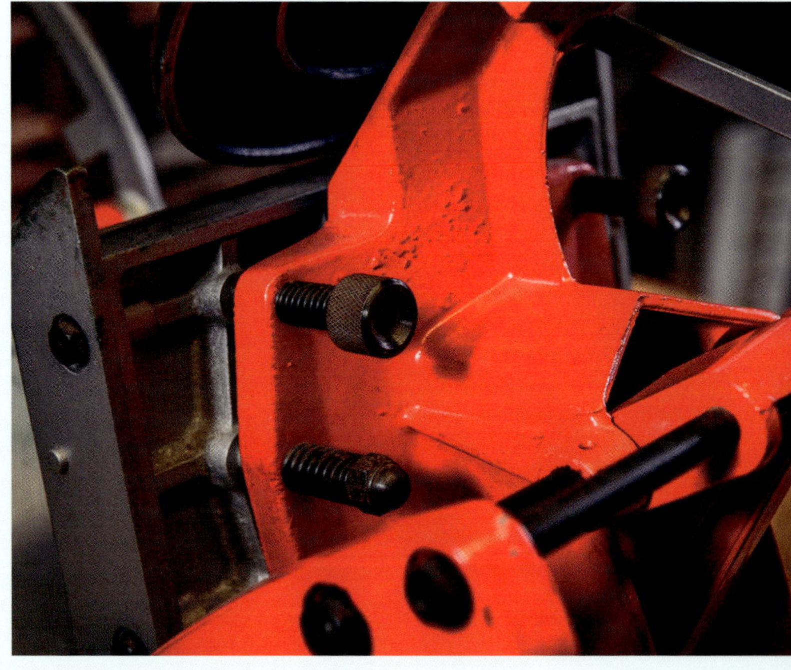

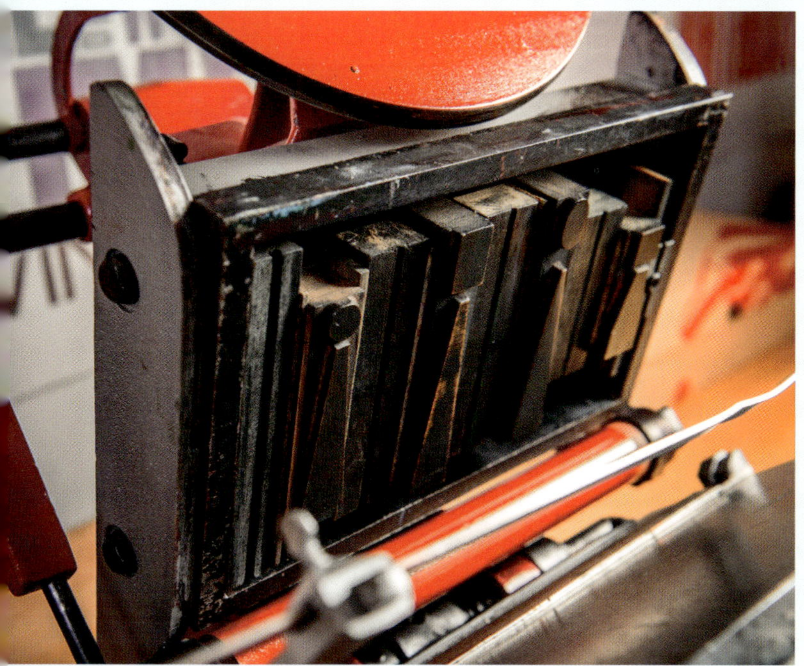

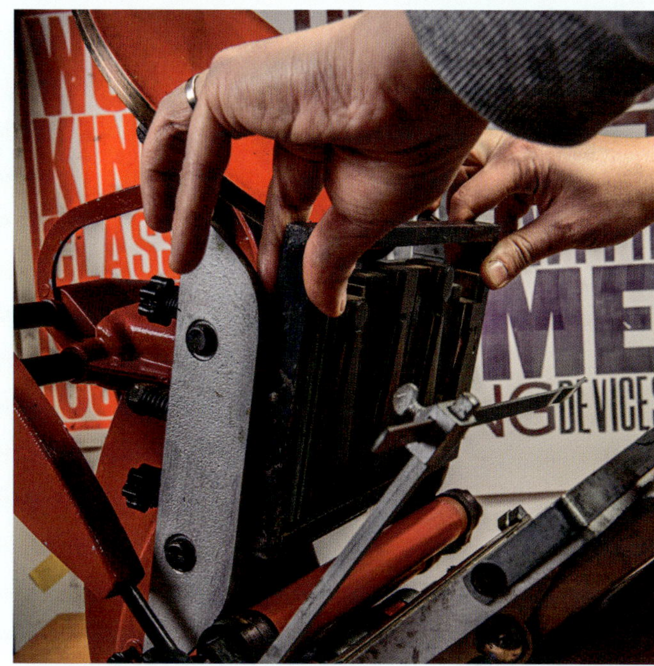

 Installing Adana chase.

Lay gauge

Next up is the lay gauge; a great little device that makes printing a joy. The lay gauge is a bar that your paper sits on when you are printing. It is adjustable to whatever position you want (depending on what you are printing), and once set up perfectly, your paper will always rest in the same position. When setting up your Adana, start by loosening your lay gauge and placing it at the bottom of the platen, so that it's well out of the way of any areas being printed while you are setting up. One of the common mistakes to make is to place your lay gauge in the wrong spot where it can clash with your type – if you push the handle down hard with the lay gauge bar aligned with your type then the type will probably be damaged.

Chase

Take your chase (with all the type locked perfectly in place) and lift it vertically, you will notice the small pin on each side of the chase, these are registration pins that you need to line up with the grooves that run down towards your press bed. This can be a little stiff and you need to get everything very straight and square in order to slide it down nicely. A tip is to get the chase sitting at the beginning of the grooves, then push gently on the front of the chase above where the pins are, to make it slide smoothly into place. Never wrap your finger around the top of the chase when putting it in place, as they can be heavy and can suddenly slide into place, catching your fingers.

Pre-print setup

Adding a backing sheet of paper or card to the platen area gives softness to the bite of the impression and helps with your overall print. An ideal material is a thin manila card. This card can also be a nice colour, so can work for printing on as well, for things like small note-book covers.

At the top of the Adana platen, you will see there is a rod that can be rotated forward to hold a backing sheet in place. Cut your piece of manila card to roughly the same width as the platen area, slide it in between the bar you have rotated forward and slide under your lay gauge. Crease the card over the top edge of the platen and rotate the rod back, clamping the card in place. You can now simply tear the piece of card that is flapping by the handle, hold the card flat and tighten the lay gauge, securing it at the bottom of the platen.

Test print and paper alignment

Slide a piece of plain paper down onto the lay gauge and add a little piece of masking tape onto the top edge of the paper, just to hold it in place for the moment. Now gently and slowly push the handle down, the inking rollers move over your type and ink it, the rollers move up onto the inking plate collecting more ink and the clamshell closes. You should now be able to feel the type impact onto the paper. The pressure and resistance should be quite light and you should not have to force the press to print.

You will notice that the arms attached to the handle have a resting point on the body of the Adana's frame at the front of the press, these two areas should touch without lots of pressure and once they have touched, no matter how hard you push down, the pressure on your print will not increase. This is a safety stop, stopping you from forcing too much pressure onto your type when printing.

Open the handle and leave your print taped in place. Have a look – is it a good print? Are all the areas printing nicely? If some areas are printed less cleanly that others, this is where you need to adjust the impression screws to raise the pressure in those areas. After each adjustment, pull another test print. If you have too much pressure across your type, turn the impression screws back to lower the pressure.

Adana lay gauge and DIY card gauge pin.

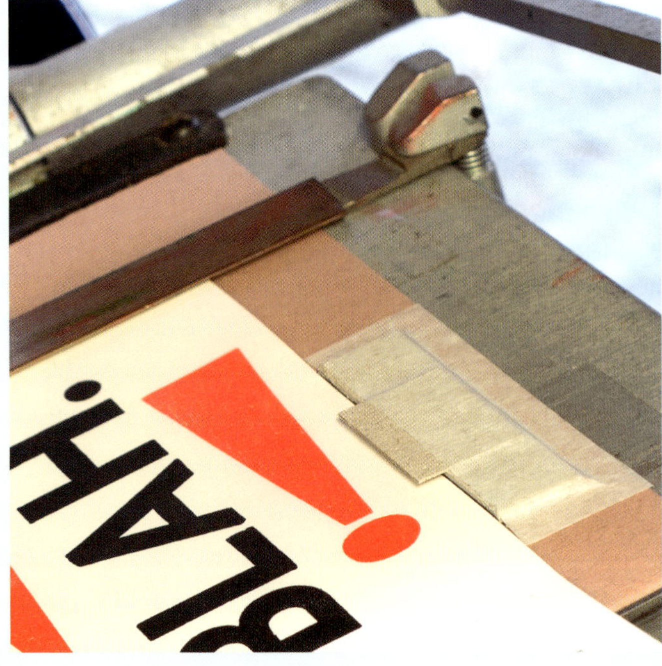

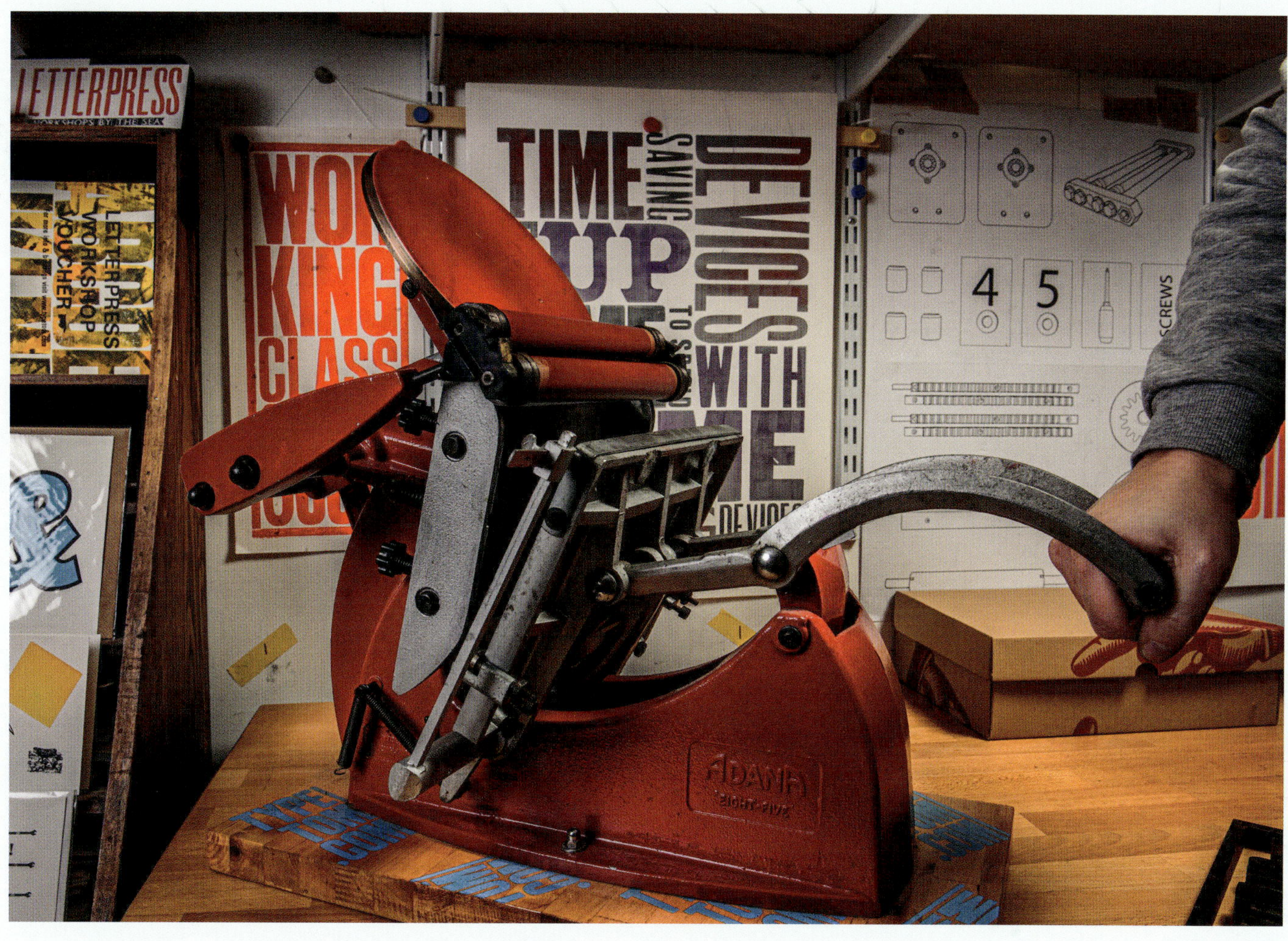

Pushing down on handle of Adana 8x5, rollers ink the type, print is pulled and rollers collect more ink.

Once you have a good test print, you are ready to do the final setup for the paper location. My preferred method for working out the exact location for printing is to draw where I want the print to go onto a piece of tracing paper (which is cut to the same size as the printing paper). This can then be lined up over the test print and the lay gauge pulled to meet the tracing paper, then secured in place by tightening the lay gauge thumb screws. You will also need to add a stop to the side of the paper to make sure that your paper is always in the exact same position. For this you use a gauge pin.

Gauge pins come in several styles. The old ones you stab through the packing sheet where they adjust into place. Or, there are simple self-adhesive ones, which are a piece of thin foam with an over-hanging lip of either plastic or card where your paper slides under and into place. I must admit to never having owned an official gauge pin, I have always used a piece of thick grey board and thinner piece of overlapping card to make my own, which are then fixed in place with a piece of masking tape. Having the tape on top of the sandwich of card and grey board means it's easier to adjust than a self-adhesive modern gauge pin that you can purchase.

Let's get printing

With everything in place, you are free to print to your heart's content. Depending on your print, print run length and machine, you will need to add ink to your inking plate as you print. You can do this by removing your chase, adding more ink and repeatedly pushing the handle up and down to get even ink distribution, then re-turning your chase and continuing to print. This is a bit tedious on longer runs so you can also add small amounts of ink to just the right-hand edge of the inking plate just outside the zone where the ink from the rollers hits the type. This slowly feeds the new ink onto the inking plate as you print. I recommend starting with removing the chase, then move onto the feeding the ink plate as you become more experienced.

If your print is quite large and takes a lot of ink, you may find that the paper gets stuck on the type, not falling back with the platen as the clamshell opens. For this you have a gripper arm. These are two metal rods that stay outside the platen print area if you are not using them. To use them, you should have an attachment that slides down on these rods (a gripper box), and you can then slide a bar (a gripper finger) that lines up with the top of your paper, outside of your print area, holding your paper onto the platen when printing, meaning the paper will return for easy unloading. The gripper arms are good to use but if you make a mistake and get the setup wrong, they will clash with your type and you will damage it. Again, take your time setting up and enjoy producing your print runs.

Once you have finished you will need to clean your type, rollers and inking plate. Remove your chase, clean your type, then remove your rollers. Clean your rollers first and finish by cleaning the inking disc and re installing the rollers – or keep your rollers in a special roller box or stand to avoid flat spots.

Printing wood type !!!! on Adana.

Cropper Charlton Peerless printing press.

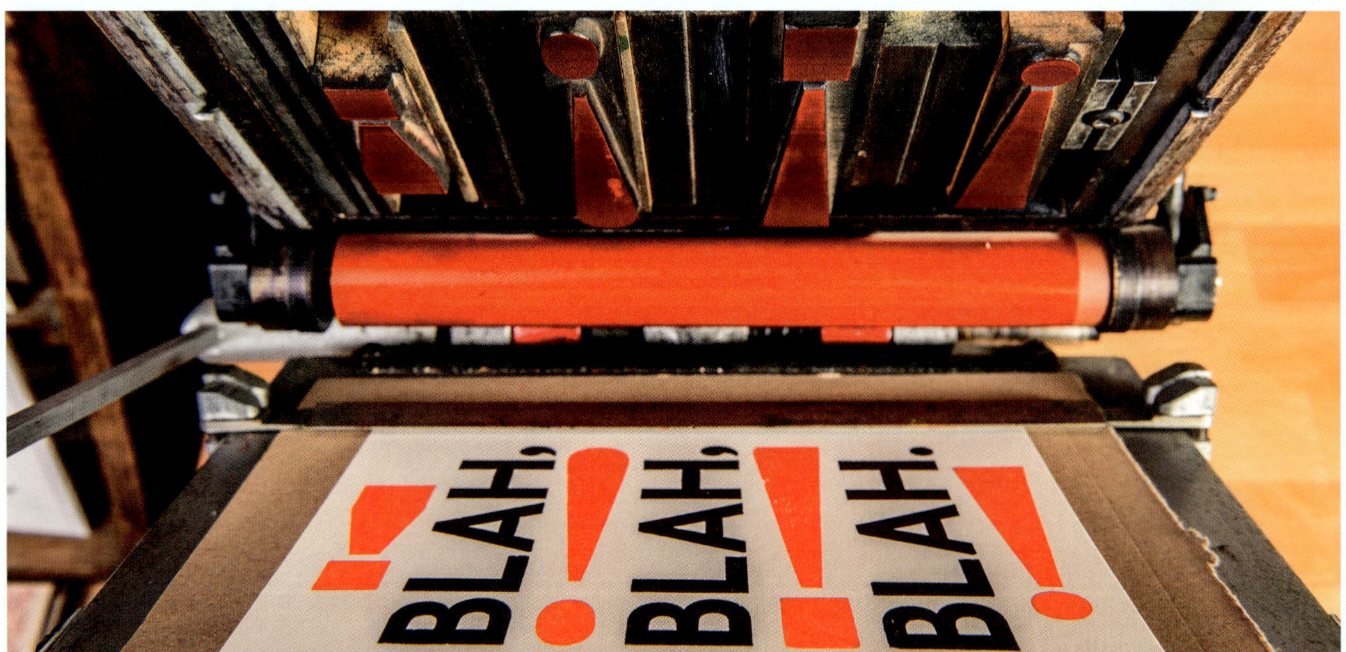

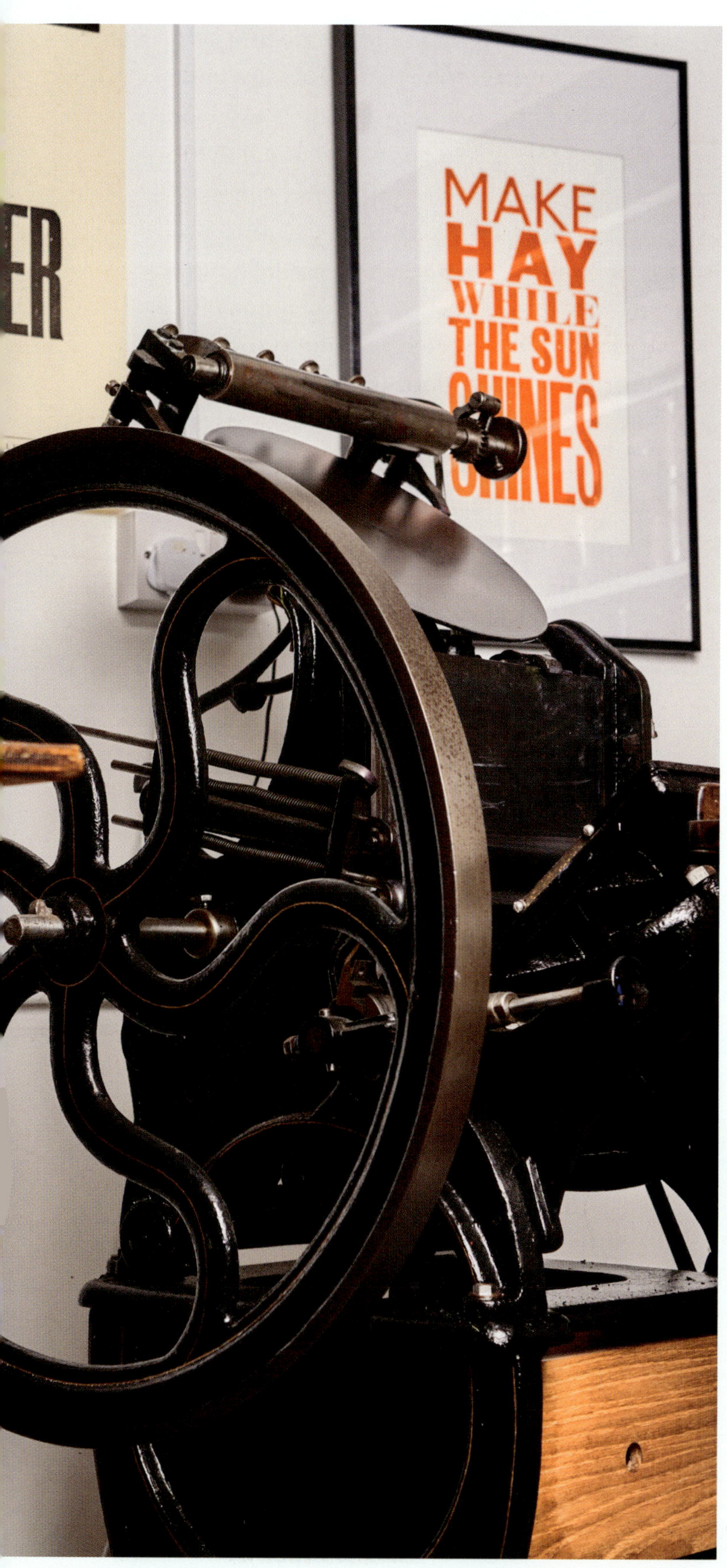

Printing on a jobbing press (Golding Pearl, Cropper Charlton & Co. Peerless and Arab)

From a hand-powered Adana 8 × 5, I moved onto foot-powered presses. Initially I purchased a very large Arab-style press and a smaller Cropper Charlton & Co. Peerless. It's worth saying that these are major upgrades from the easy-to-manage Adanas. Although the mechanisms on these presses work in a similar way, don't think that these industrial machines are at all like small-scale, hobbyist Adanas. They are beautiful old machines that deserve and command a lot of respect. If not operated correctly and safely, they can be very dangerous. If you do consider this upgrade, please take seriously my warning that all of these machines should only be operated with full regard to the risk involved.

The risk is based around the clamshell mechanism that creates your print – on an Adana this movement is slow and steady, while on jobbing presses like these, the operator is putting their hand into a much faster-moving mechanism. This section describes how I operate the press and navigate and minimise the risks involved. These presses are really for people who have experience with machinery and printing, they should never be the starting point of your letterpress journey.

Now to the basics of the machines. Similar to the Adanas, the platen area of the press is where your paper goes to print. You have the same bars that run along the top and bottom edge of the platen to clamp a backing sheet in place. Slide the card under the bottom of the platen first, then clamp and pull the card tight

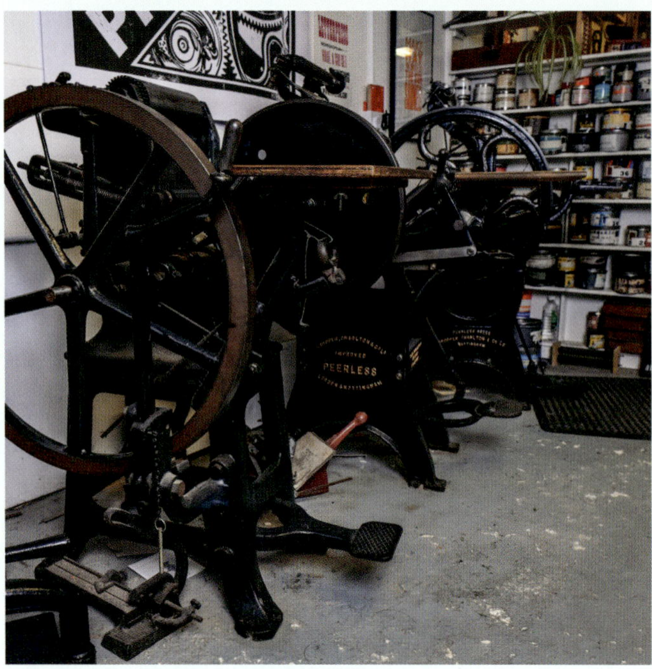

3x jobbing presses in TypeTom workshop.

at the top, hold, clamp and tear the card so there is no excess flapping around.

Gauge pins

With jobbing presses you do not have a lay gauge, instead you have to use gauge pins for the ledge where your paper sits. Follow the same process as described in the Adana section to locate the exact position for where your paper needs to be, which you can then tape in place, as the paper size you are using will probably be larger. As described earlier there are a couple of different styles of gauge pins, or you can also make your own with card and tape it in place.

Something that I do differently is buying thin, cheap strip magnets that are 12mm wide and about 2mm thick, being self-adhesive on one side. I then cut them into a selection of lengths, peel off the self-adhesive film and attach some overlapping tabs of thin card to make it easy to see that the paper has fully lined up when using them. A suitable length is then selected, and with the test print taped in place, the magnets are attached to the platen and slid lightly into the location. This is possible because these presses are made of magnetic cast iron, unlike Adanas, which are primarily aluminium.

Removing the test print, pull another to do a final check of location. If it's found to be slightly off, the magnets can be adjusted fractionally, before pulling further test prints. Once I have found that everything is in the perfect spot, I always put a line of masking tape over the top

Picture block printing on Cropper Charlton Peerless.

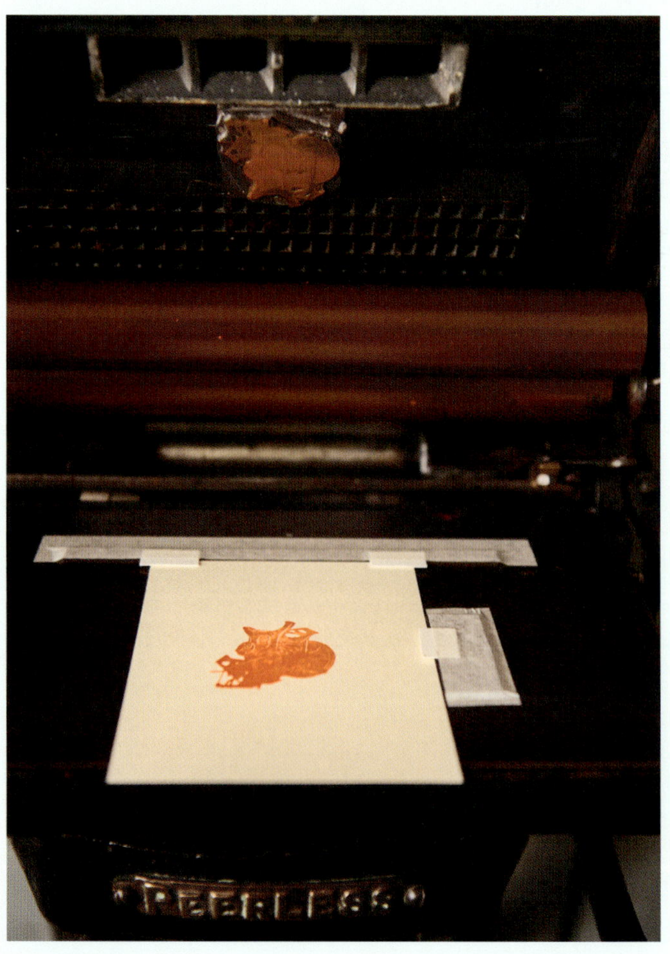

of the magnet just to make sure that there can be no movement whilst printing. It is surprising how hard it is to notice if there is some slight movement on a run, so it is best to be safe and make sure everything is as secure as possible.

Inking

Inking-wise, the disc and the roller mechanism is much like an Adana, with the rollers running up over the type and onto the inking disc. Usually there is a third roller on most jobbing presses, which climbs high onto the inking disc and lines up and lightly touches a metal roller that is mounted above the inking disc. This metal roller and housing assembly is the inking fountain. The inking fountain is where you can pour ink into, if you are printing very long print runs (thousands of prints). The flow of the ink out of the fountain and onto the metal roller is controlled by a number of screws. The screws are attached to a plate, that when loosened and tightened, allows ink to pass through the fountain onto the metal roller, which then allows a small amount of ink to be transferred onto the third inking roller through contact with the third rubber roller. Using an inking unit is not regularly required, and it is slow and messy to clean up at the end.

Pedal power

The drive and power for the printing press is delivered by your foot on a pedal, which is attached to a rod that's hooked onto a gear, which is attached to a large metal shaft that runs through the press. On the left-hand side the fly wheel is mounted to the shaft. The fly wheel is a large heavy wheel whose movement is initiated by use of the pedal. Once moving, the momentum from the weight of the wheel starts to take over the majority of the power that is required to drive the machine.

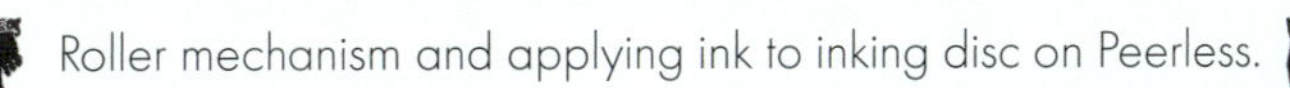

Roller mechanism and applying ink to inking disc on Peerless.

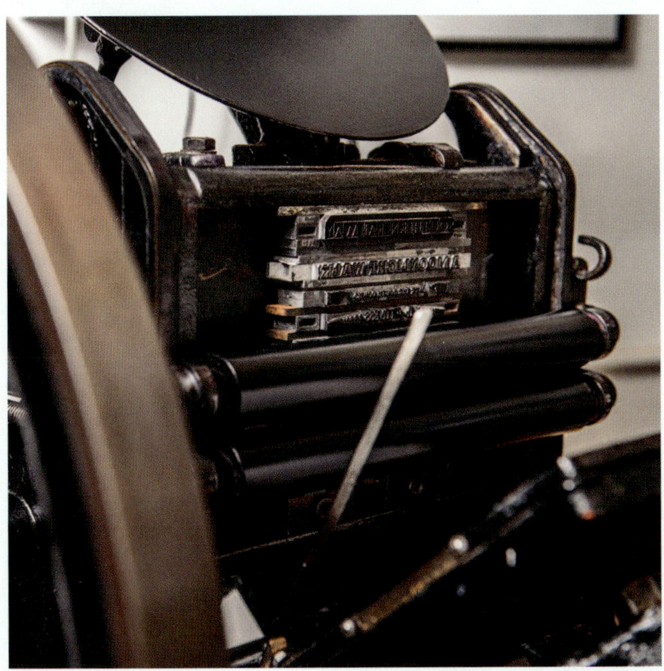

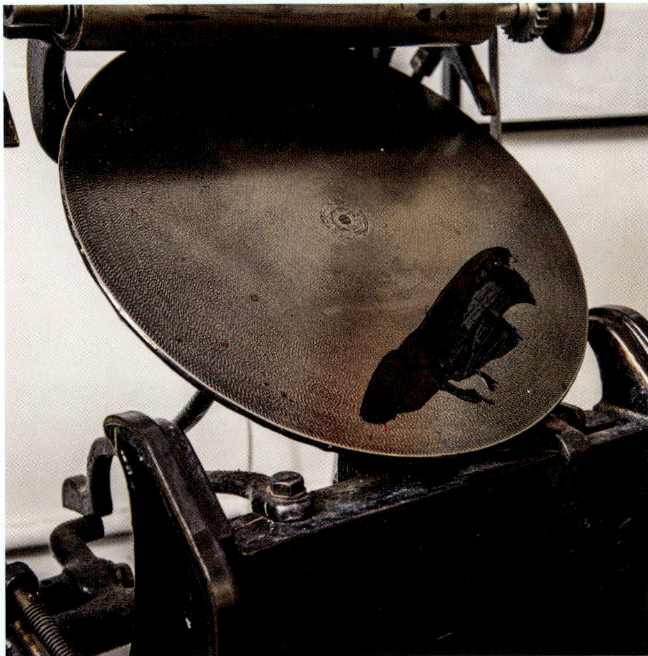

Brakes and impression lever

Some presses have brakes – often a simple arm with a pad that comes in contact with the bottom of the fly wheel to stop it. Other presses may have an impression lever instead. An impression lever is a rod that when you push or pull, causes the platen to move backwards and forwards. If a mistake is made you can push the lever and the platen will move to a position where it will not print. This can be done during the print run whilst you are pedalling, which means that you get another go at correcting your mistake. Usually, the mistake is not getting the paper or card correctly placed, so you can adjust then put the impression lever back into the printing position to get printing again. It saves a lot of time with a treadle platen press not to keep stopping and starting; it can also be tiring to keep getting the printing press and its heavy fly wheel moving.

Pressure

The impression screws that you need to adjust to pivot the platen into perfect alignment to print are usually located behind the platen; like the Adana, there are four screws that you tighten and loosen to get to the desired pressure height. They also have a locking nut, so that once you are in the right spot you can lock it there. This is useful for setting the platen solidly in place, but do not expect that you only need to set the pressure once for all printing. You'll need to tweak the pressure very slightly when you change what you are printing. The reason for this is that, unless you are printing exactly the same size print, the overall footprint of the printing area will change and you will need to tweak the pressure.

A good habit to learn is that whenever you set up for a new print, back off the platen a little, so that when you pull a test print the press is set

Impression lever and lever mechanism on Cropper Charlton Peerless.

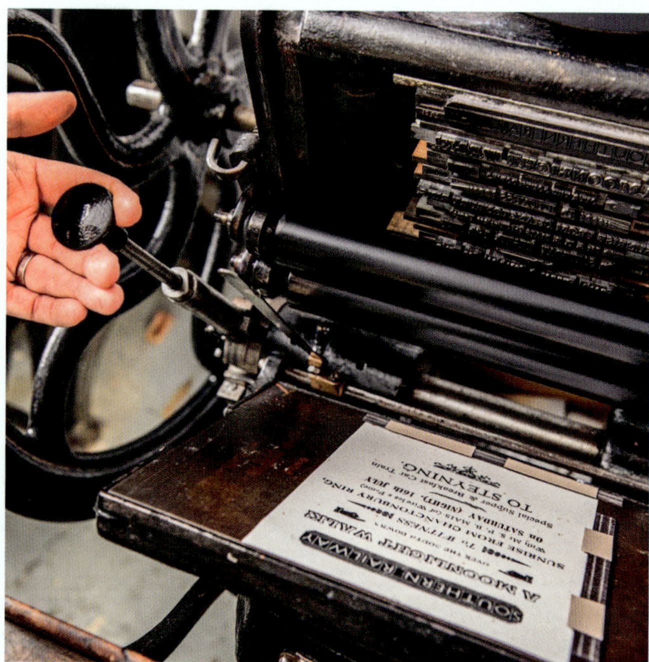

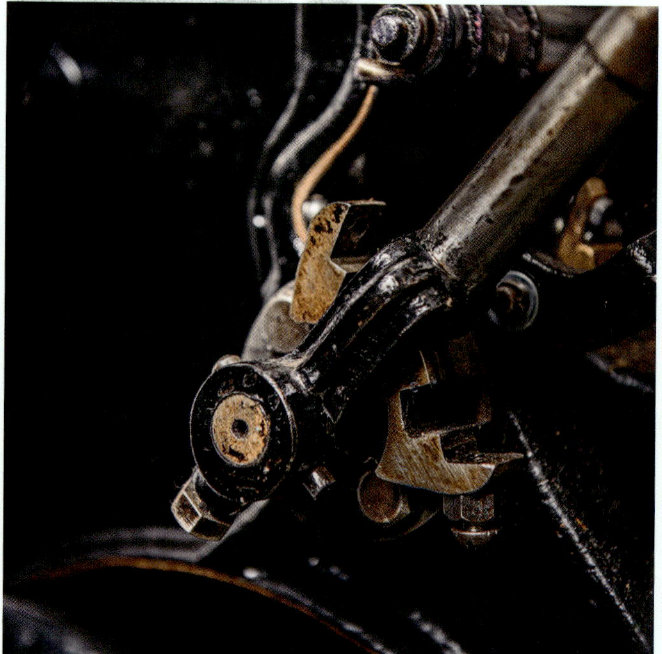

on the light side. You'll reduce the risk of damaging your type or making a mistake, and get used to the mechanism. The more you use it the easier it will be, and it'll soon become second nature to set the pressure.

Always aim the print in the middle of the platen for even pressure, and likewise setup your type in the middle of the chase. If you have to print in certain areas because you are restricted by issues such as paper size, then so be it. If you are printing in one corner of the platen then it is harder to get an even impression, as you are mostly printing over the top of one of the impression screws and have less ability to pitch the platen plate. Whenever I have to do this, I scribble down some rough notes on what I have adjusted, for example, top screw two turns left, and so on. With platen presses you will be using a spanner to turn the screws, as the presses are much bigger and heavier so all parts take more pressure weight.

Cropper Charlton Peerless impression screws.

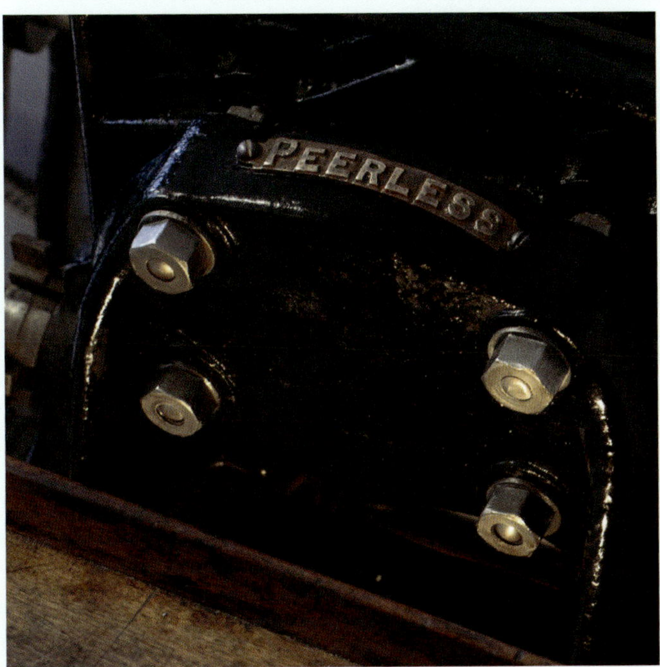

Gripper arm

A lot of these style presses have a gripper arm, or you may find you have part of the gripper arm assembly left. On these presses the arm is a simple length of metal that comes straight up the platen from the bottom of the clamshell. Again, when setting up, move these to an area where there is no chance of them clashing with your type. If you do not have the gripper arm part for your press (they are often missing as they get taken off, lost or broken) then it is not hard to make up an alternative arm, as often the attachment for the gripper arm is there (look for a rod with a groove running under the bottom of the clamshell mechanism).

I am a big fan of customising parts, and you can always bodge up a good rough part with odds and sods that are lying around a workshop. I remember once screwing a lollypop stick onto the gripper arm rod to act as a gripper arm! Yes, it did work pretty well, before making a final part in metal.

Lubrication

With old presses like these, it's important to make sure that all the moving parts are running easily with no grinding between any parts in contact. Regular oiling keeps them in good working order; look thoroughly over your press, you will find oiling points where you can take an oil can with a nozzle and add a few drops. Whilst there are the obvious places to oil, like the main shaft/bar that runs through the press with the fly wheel attached, you will also find oiling points around the gearing, inking roller mechanism and foot pedal mechanism.

I've found a common problem area on both of my Cropper Charlton & Co. Peerless presses, which is where the arm that is attached to the pedal hooks over the rod that drives the gears. Both of these presses had major wear on the hook area. For the worst one I found a piece of engineering nylon and cut a U-shape that fitted nicely inside the hook and then oiled the area well. This was intended as a quick fix but over the many years that I have owned the press the nylon has no real signs of wear, so it stays in place.

If you keep the floor around your press very clean then inspecting your press is not difficult, fine black dust by your press in a specific location can be a telltale sign of grinding metal. If your press is well placed and flat on a solid floor, regularly checked and oiled then really you should not have many, if any problems, but it is always worth being vigilant.

Let's get printing

You should have a small flat wooden worktop for holding your unprinted paper on, and a second worktop that rotates to give you a working area for holding your prints on whilst you print. Without your chase in place, apply a small amount of ink to the inking disc, smudging it in a line across the round inking plate. Put your tin of ink and pallet knife onto another worktop, the vibrations from the press when it is running can make things like inked pallet knifes fall and make a mess.

Your pedal is likely flat to the floor, as this is the common resting point that leaves the clamshell fully opened. You need to raise the pedal, to start the treadling, to move the fly wheel, to move the rollers, to ink the plate, to pull your print. To do this place your left hand on the fly wheel and turn slightly to raise the pedal. Be careful how quickly you turn this and where your feet and legs are, as once the momentum of the press takes over, the pedal moves fast and can hurt. Some of these presses can be scant on space, too.

With the pedal raised about halfway up, put your right foot on it and press lightly down – you don't need to push with all your might, you are just aiding the momentum. With the up and down motion of the pedal, the rollers will climb onto the inking plate slowly, one pass at a time, evening out the ink. It is easy to see this happen as the turning movement of the inking plate clearly shows where the ink is, and where it is going. It will only take a minute or so for the ink on your rollers and plate to be evenly distributed. Once the ink looks good, stop treadling the pedal and bring your press to a stop with the pedal on the floor and the clamshell open. Always aim to leave your foot pedal on the lowest position when bringing the press to rest, as this mean you are less likely to bang yourself on it.

Now clip your chase into the press. Unlike the Adana they do not have registration pins, the chases are usually a very simple rectangle of cast iron with a small lip cut out in the top. Look into your press' type bed and you will see there is a very basic stop of some sort, often looking like two small ledges at the bottom area. There's also usually a small arm just under the inking disc, that when pressed down lifts a clip that lines up with the cut-out lip on the chase. Slide the chase onto the bottom rest, push it up to be flat with the bed and press

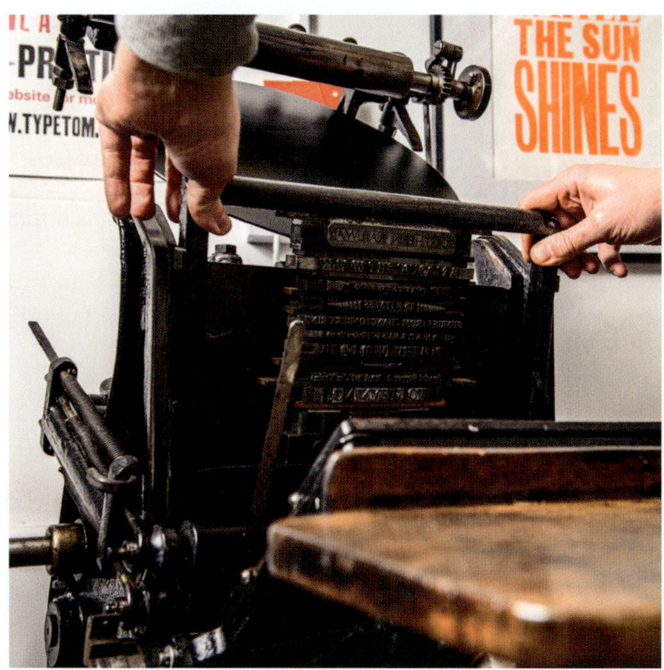

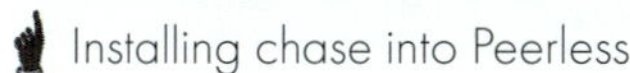
Installing chase into Peerless.

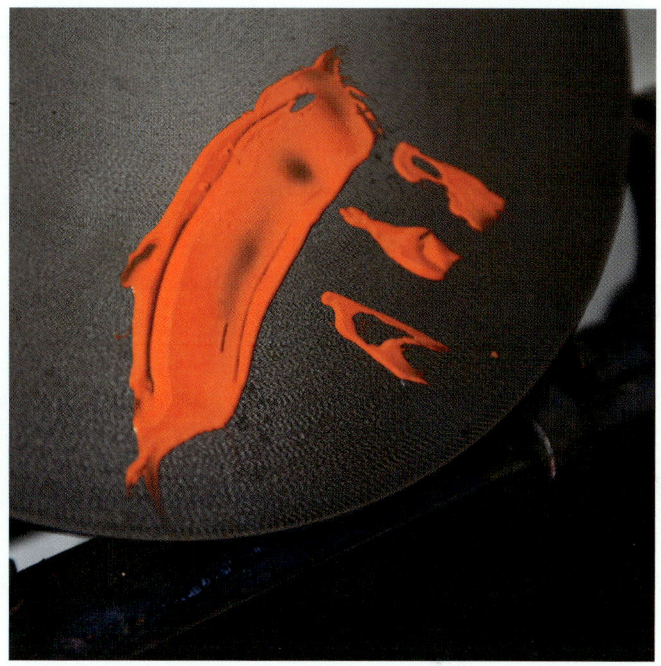
Ink on inking plate.

the arm to lift the clip and secure the chase in place. I always, out of habit, give the chase a little poke and pull just to check that it is secure and that there is no movement on the chase. At this point you need to check the pressure of the press and your type. Tape a piece of paper onto the platen that has a backing sheet of manila card on it, and gently pull your first test print. Leave your test print taped in place so you can see exactly where the print went. Always set up the test prints with light pressure, you can always adjust to increase as needed. For the first test print you could pull the print by turning the fly wheel by hand, which allows you to delicately check that the pressure is not too high, and removes the risk of damaging your type. Follow the steps in the Adana section for setting gauge pins, or my strip magnets technique. Take your time on setup, it can make the physical act of printing much smoother.

Press on

If your press has an impression lever, it's a good idea to put the platen into the position where it will not print. Turn your fly wheel to bring the pedal up and start treadling. The clamshell opens and closes, the rollers collect and distribute ink, and the press is ready to print. You are now standing on one leg, pushing the pedal with the other, the clamshell mechanism is opening and closing. Going at a slow pace, insert the paper down and onto the lay gauge you have created, or the gauge pins you have. Put the impression lever into the print mode, and your print will be made. Remove your print and then add a new unprinted piece or paper. This is a fiddly and awkward process to master, take your time and work slowly.

When starting out you can try to get used to the mechanism of the press by just pushing the pedal up and down, with the press un-inked and without type, just to get used to pedalling a press. With early setups, try to position your type so that when your sheet of paper or card rests on the gauge pins, it also extends outside the clamshell printing area when printing. This means that you can then load and unload your printing papers and card without having to put your hand in any moving parts.

Once presses like Cropper Charlton & Co.'s Peerless get going they print fast, so get everything ready to go, have your paper stacked on the left of the wooden work area and have something like a box lid ready on the right-hand side worktop ready for prints to be put into. When you are producing runs of prints it is worth interleaving scrap paper in between prints as you go, this means that you cannot get transfer of the previous print onto the back of your printed sheet. When you have finished printing, clean down your press thoroughly. On larger presses things like checking that the end of the rollers and the edge of the inking disk are clear from any tiny amounts of ink can be essential, as if there is the slightest amount of residual ink it will potentially taint future printing projects. Take your time and work smart with these presses.

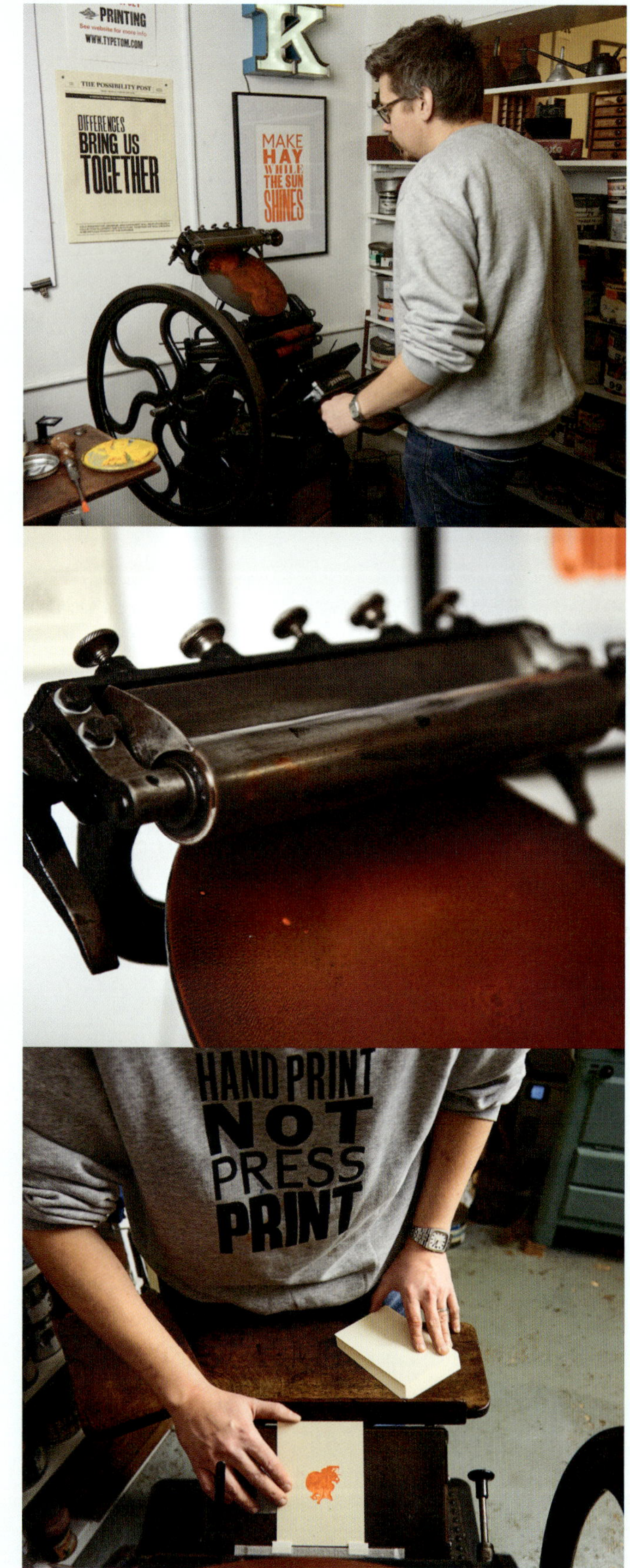

Treadling Peerless to evenly distribute ink, then printing picture block. ☛

Printing on proofing presses (George Pallister, Vandercook, Farley)

In this section I will talk about two presses I have that really cover the area of cylinder presses. At the very basic end, I have a George Pallister & Sons proofing press; at the more complicated and larger end, a Vandercook 4C. Both machines work differently from the previous machines, in that they do not print by using two flat surfaces that come together. Instead, they have a roller that goes over the type and compresses the paper into the inked type, moulding the paper around the letters as it rolls.

George Pallister & Sons proofing press

The George Pallister is a very basic model of proofing press that has a hard roller that's manually pulled along metal runners. Whilst this is a very basic machine it still is surprisingly clever; the roller has to stay as straight as possible when being pulled down the length of the press to print – if it's not straight, it can cause the press to jam, smudge prints and print with uneven pressure. Even on basic proofing presses like this there are still things that need to be set up and understood. The roller has two end plates, one either side of the roller, which are held together by a number of rods that are bolted in place to create a solid unit.

Keeping the roller running straight

On each plate-end of the roller there are a few things to discuss. There are two worm screws on each side, under which are ball bearings – it's these that are used to control the running of the roller unit. With an Allen key the pressure that is put on the ball bearing can be adjusted; if fully tightened the press roller unit will be locked in place. If too loose, the roller will skew as it is pulled down the press, this can then jam the roller at an angle.

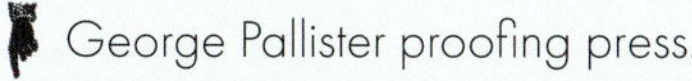

George Pallister proofing press.

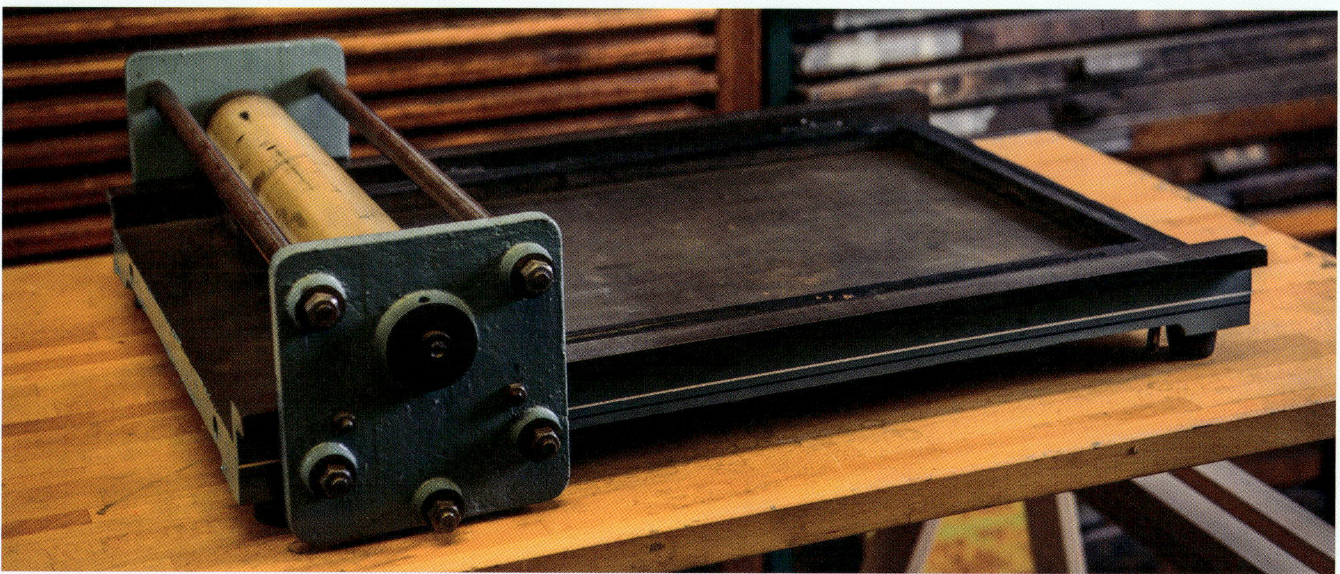

These small ball bearings need to have their pressure set precisely, so that they are just loosely making contact with both the sides of the press runners, for a gliding, not grinding motion. The easiest way to achieve this is to lightly tighten the bearing on all sides of the press then when you feel contact, back the screw off a little bit, pull the roller lightly and see how it feels – you get a surprisingly large amount of sensation through the bars as you pull the roller. If the pressure is set too hard the ball bearings can get flat spots and grind, you will feel it if you have tightened too hard as it will be very difficult to pull the roller. If you find you have a press which uses small parts like these, I would strongly recommend buying some basic spares for your press, things like ball bearings and worm screws are not expensive. Not all proofing presses use this mechanism to keep the roller running straight, so have a look at whatever press you have and study how yours works. Being able to understand how your press works really helps you understand how to print and how to solve issues.

Pressure roller setting

There are also larger bearings that roll under the runners on both sides of the press. These are mounted on an eccentric cam, which means that the mounting (the bolt) in the middle of the cam is off-centre to the roller bearings. When turned on their axis the bearing moves up and down so you can adjust and apply more pressure to the underside of the press runners. This is something that you want to take a little time with, your roller will naturally run very slightly off the runners when printing on this press, so the bearings are set so they are not pulling the roller down into the press too hard.

If you have a similar mechanism and you are struggling to set this, you can cut two strips of grey board card, place them on the runners,

Adjusting side ball bearings.

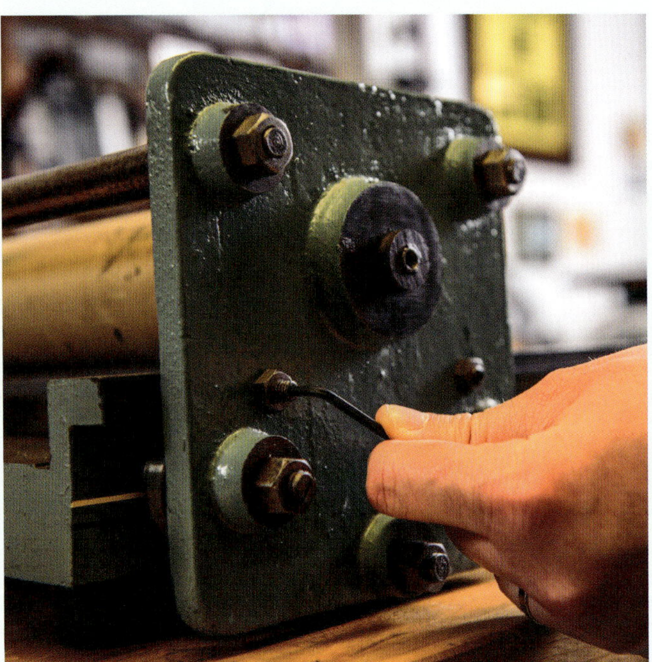

Adjusting roller pressure (roller bearings).

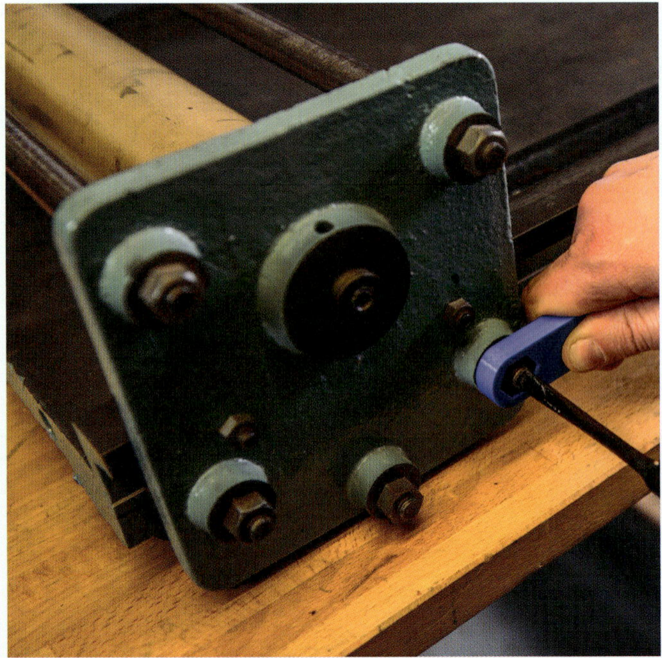

roll the roller assembly onto them then turn the eccentric bearing so they just touch the underside of the runners and roll off the cardboard. Then use a large piece of wood type on the printing bed with a couple of sheets of paper on top to test the roller height.

Using two strips of card helps to get the height of the roller equal on both sides of the press – tweak and adjust until the correct pressure setting is found. Use a thicker piece of card or a thinner piece of paper, or a mixture of both to really fine-tune the pressure and pull of the press. When you have this setup complete, you will be able to pull a print.

Let's get printing

This press is very basic, it does have a chase; I am not 100 per cent sure that it's an original chase, but it came with the press when I got it, so it is what I use. I lock the chase in place by putting it in the centre of the press bed, then I put two quoins down one edge of the chase and furniture on the opposite side, turning the quoins with the quoin key to pressurise the chase in place.

You can set your type as per normal in the chase area, I would always recommend using a 'butt' edge at the top of the press, so you have something to push your paper up to (as previously described in Chapter 5 Pulling a print). Add furniture and secure your type and printing blocks in place with quoins and galley magnets as required. With your type nicely locked out in the chase, you can run through checking how much packing paper you will need to get just the right amount of pressure to print. If you do this now rather than after you have inked the press it will save you time and you will reduce the number of test prints required.

Rolling out ink, inking type, placing paper, adding packing sheets and pulling print.

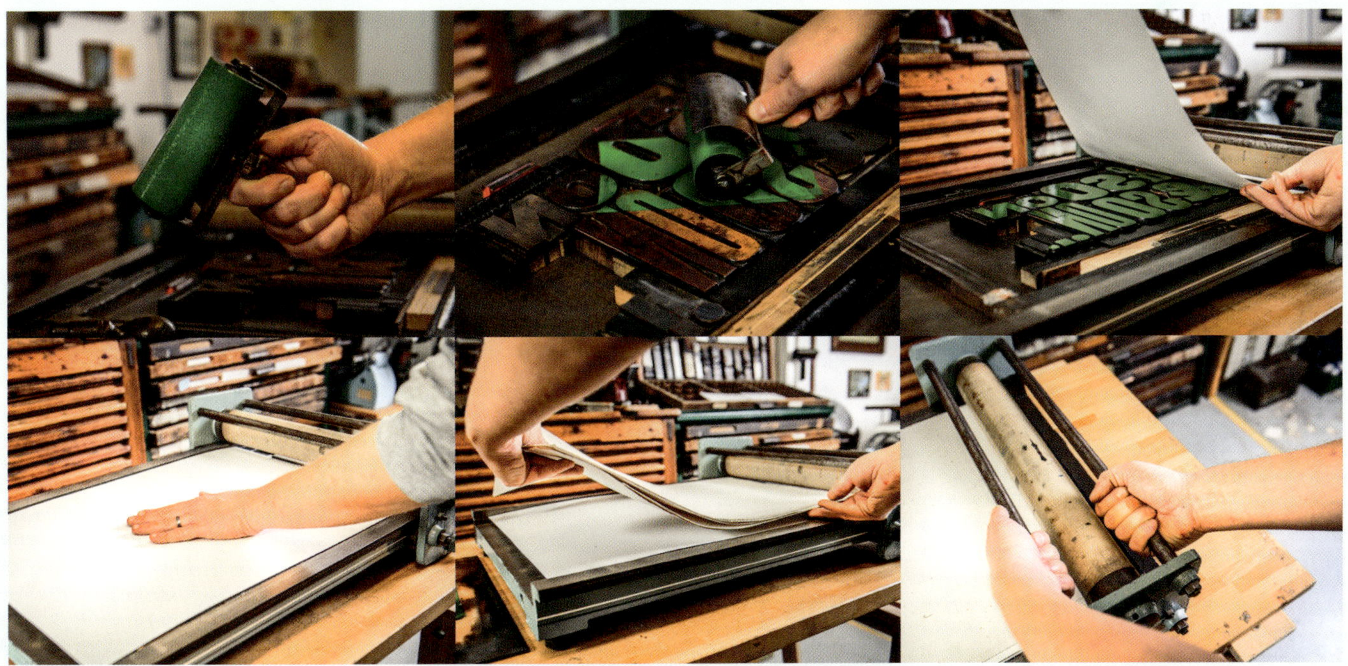

When you are fine-tuning your print, a number of fiddly and recurring issues can arise. Paper slip is a common problem with proofing presses, when the printing sheet of paper doesn't stick that well to the type and as the pressure rolls over the type, the printed sheet slides on the type, causing a smudged mess of a print. This problem seems to be more frequent with some modern water-based inks, which aren't as thick and sticky as good old-fashioned oil-based ink. This can also be worsened by the amount of packing you have and how much pressure you apply; too much pressure from over packing the print when combined with ink that is not wanting to stick to the paper is a bad combination.

Try adding a little more ink to your roller to help the paper stick to the type. After you have placed your paper onto your inked type, visualise where the type is under the paper and give the paper a 'loving pat' a light slide of the hand to aid contact and grip between type, ink and paper. Then add your packing sheets, removing a couple of sheets from the previous pull to lessen the pressure, then pull and check the print.

If you notice that the press seems to be printing lighter on one side of the press than the other, you have either set the pressure on the roller unevenly, or the eccentric bearing cam has moved, both of which you need to adjust. If you over-pack the press all sorts of odd things start to happen, it is sometimes hard to understand why something like the pressure has changed but usually there is a simple reason. When pulling a print, it is very important that you hold the bar or bars firmly above the roller, never put your hand in a place where it could be caught in any part. This sounds obvious, but it does get tempting when you have a slight issue to just hold things in place with your hand – do not even think about it! Wrap your fingers firmly around the bars and pull the press smoothly and evenly, if you can use both hands to pull the print do so. Remember to always clean down your type and press after using. Give your press a bit of a look-over once you have finished printing and cleaning down, as sometimes you can spot issues like a bolt coming loose before it has become an issue and fix as you go.

Gently revealing print.

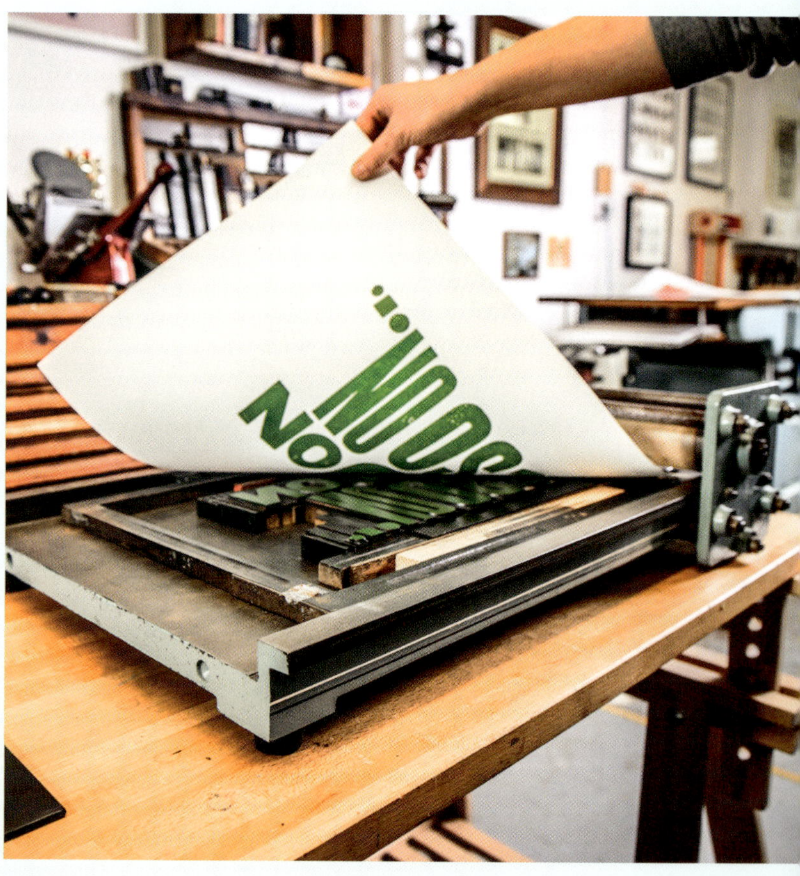

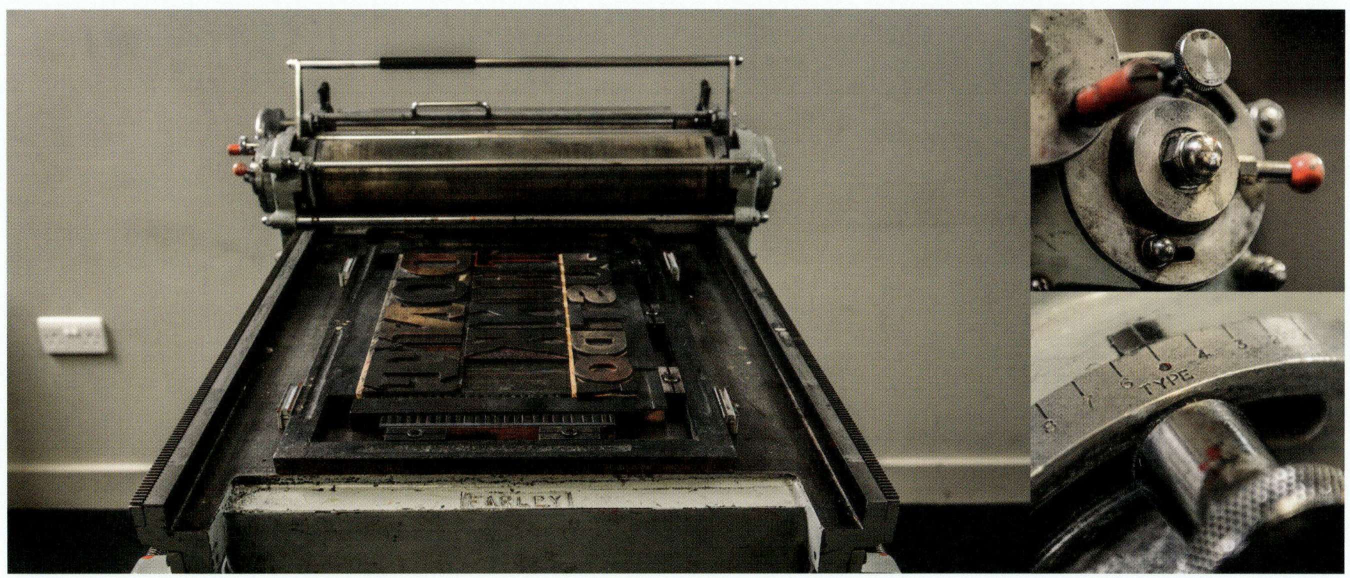

Farley proofing press at Ditchling Museum of Art + Craft, type height roller adjuster.

Farley proofing presses

My old George Pallister proofing press is a very basic model of a proofing press and is one that is quite rare, not having being made in great numbers. Farleys were at the higher end in terms of design and engineering, and were made in much larger numbers. Whilst I do not own a Farley proofing press, I do use them regularly and they are a joy to use. They have a number of slight tweaks and improvements on more basic models that you find, making printing just that little bit easier. Their basic operation is really the same as other proofing presses, so I will not bore you with over-detailing the same printing process.

The big extras that Farley offers are a built-in gripper bar and an easy and fast way to adjust the pressure of the press. The gripper bar lives under the roller, when the roller is pushed back to the starting end of the press. There are a series of flat metal teeth that are opened when the roller assembly handle is pushed back, allowing

Inking type, opened teeth on gripper bar, inserting paper.

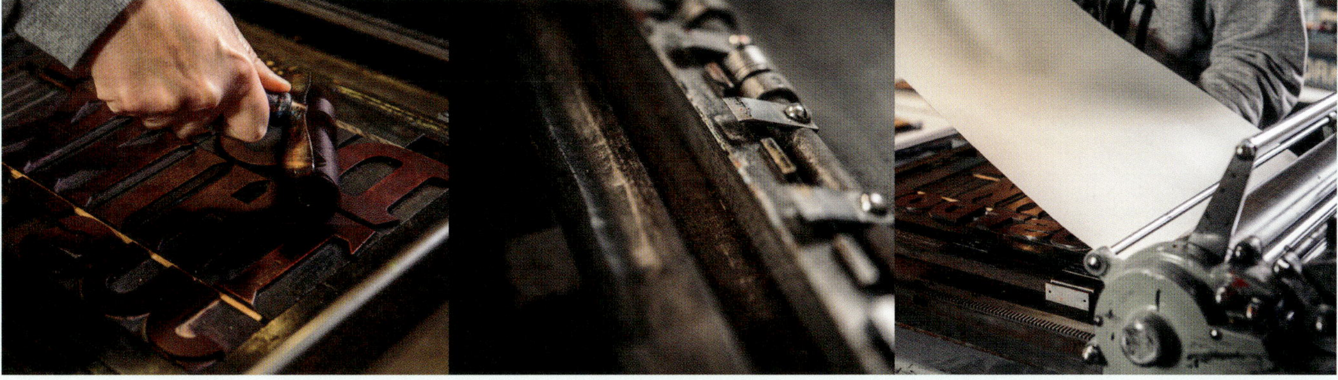

you to feed your sheet of paper in, and when the handle is rotated forwards, the teeth close to grip it. This great addition holds your sheet in place when printing, which greatly reduces the risk of paper slip and makes alignment of paper easier for designs that require multiple prints.

Some Farleys have a pressure adjuster that is amazingly well engineered and very simple to use. On the side of the roller assembly there is a rotatable part, on which you simply loosen the top pin, turn the assembly using the handle, and align to the desired type height – all of which is clearly marked. This simple-to-adjust height setter is a great development and really puts the Farley presses in a different league. Farleys are a pleasure to print on but do command a high price when they (regularly) come up for sale on-line. Keep an eye out for them, a good-condition Farley is a good press to own.

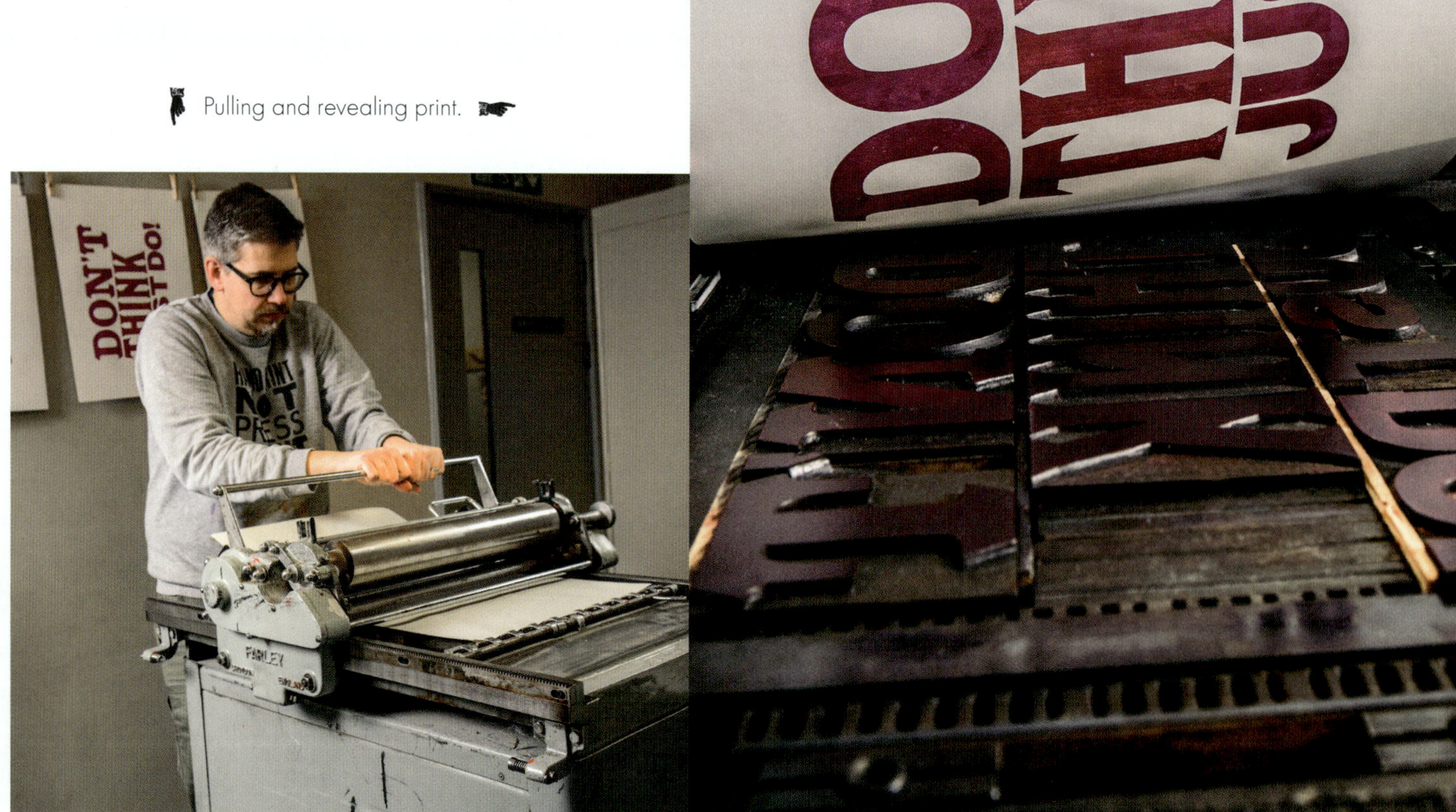

Pulling and revealing print.

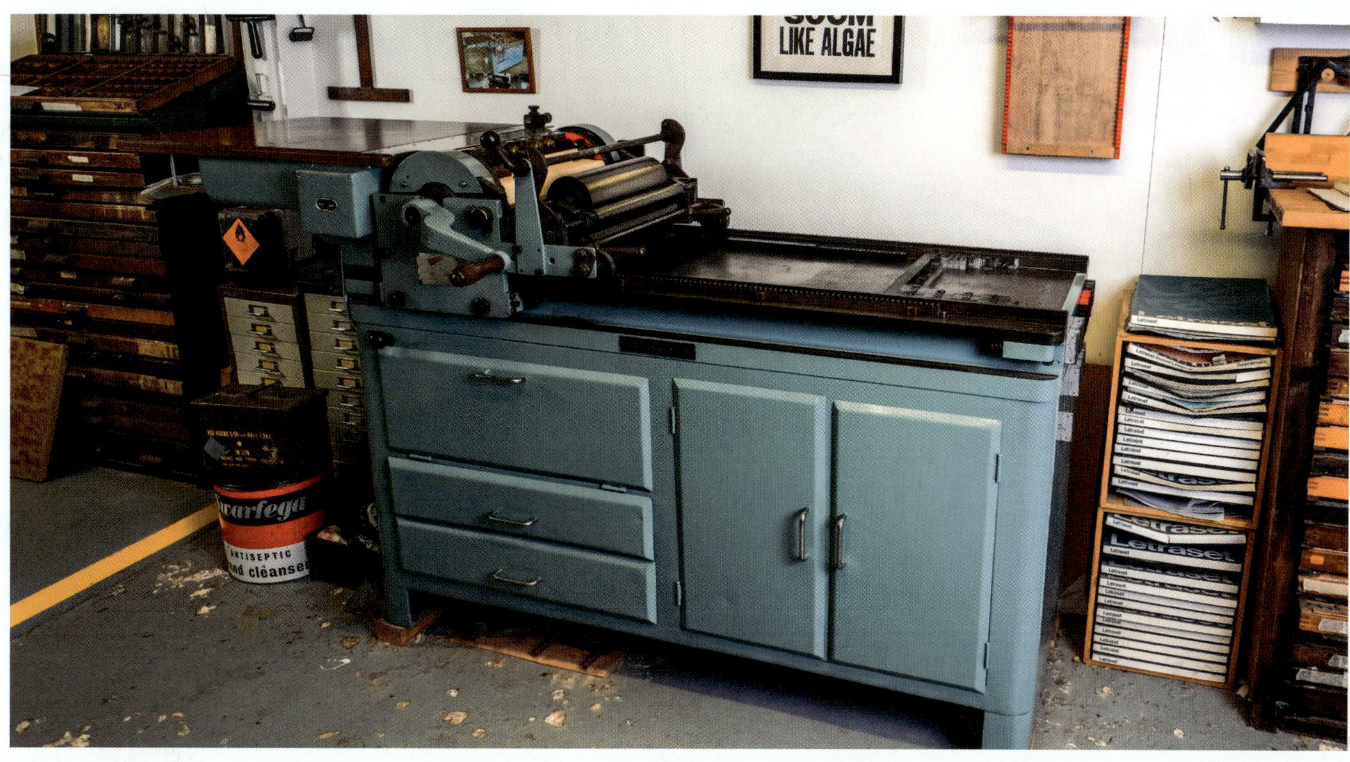

 Vandercook 4c at TypeTom workshop restored and original condition. 

Vandercook 4C

Moving on to my Vandercook 4C. This is not a basic press and is more an industrial-sized machine. Weighing in at around one tonne with its length around 8ft, it has a lot more refinements than a basic proofing press. As with most of the presses I own, it needed some level of restoration.

Restoration

The Vandercook was the biggest project I have undertaken in terms of restoration; the press had been housed in a barn for around ten years before I got it, and had been outside for a period of time, too. It was rusted solid, and a rat had even made home in the motor and gearbox! There is a tendency for presses in bad condition to be broken down and sold as spare parts, but if you have the time and the inclination fix one and use it, you will never regret it and always find joy in it.

Some basic tips on restoration: make lots of notes about anything that grabs your attention, also, you can never have too many photos of every part. This is essential, as when you start to strip everything down and clean the rust, you'll need to know how to put it back together

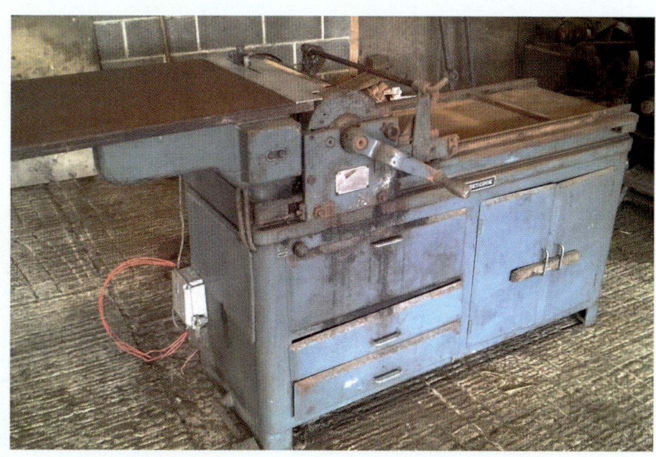

again. Group things together and get lots of grip seal bags to keep everything safe. It is very easy to lose a small nut or bolt, and things do just seem to go missing in workshops! Label everything and don't be scared to have a go. I didn't know about all the mechanisms on the Vandercook when I got it, so I learnt by doing. Rust is a real problem, you can buy some chemicals that get rid of rust and you can get things sand blasted, but I don't.

I have always gone the old-fashioned way of salt and vinegar; some parts can be soaked in sealable pots (this helps with the smell) or for the large areas of the Vandercook, I used kitchen towel soaked in a vinegar and salt solution, and covered in cling film to stop it from drying out. This was left overnight then scrubbed till clean, repeatedly rubbed with white spirit, and given a final coat of WD40 which too was then wiped clean.

The Vandercook was in a very bad state and sometimes there is long-term damage that you cannot repair. It will never be 100 per cent perfect, but for me the important thing is that everything works and prints well, and it shows its own history.

Restoring a printing press like this in the modern world, we are very lucky, as our access to information is so high. When I restore anything, I always spend some time researching online.

This can uncover scanned copies of old manuals, forums featuring past discussions about restorations or just some pictures. You can learn a surprising amount from looking at a picture of other people's presses – a godsend when you are restoring a press that was not all in one piece to begin with. After all, a jigsaw puzzle is a lot easier if you know what the picture is.

Setup

Printing on the Vandercook is always a joy. The setting up of the type is really the same as with a basic proofing press like my George Pallister & Sons press. You have the bed area of the press to lay your type out on, and with most Vandercooks you have a lockup bar or dead bar. My Vandercook 4C has a very basic drop-in-place dead bar, and using this gives you a space which is basically the same as a chase, giving you four solid sides to lock out type to.

With time and experience of using a Vandercook, you will become good at working out where the print will come out on your paper.

Drop in dead bar on Vandercook.

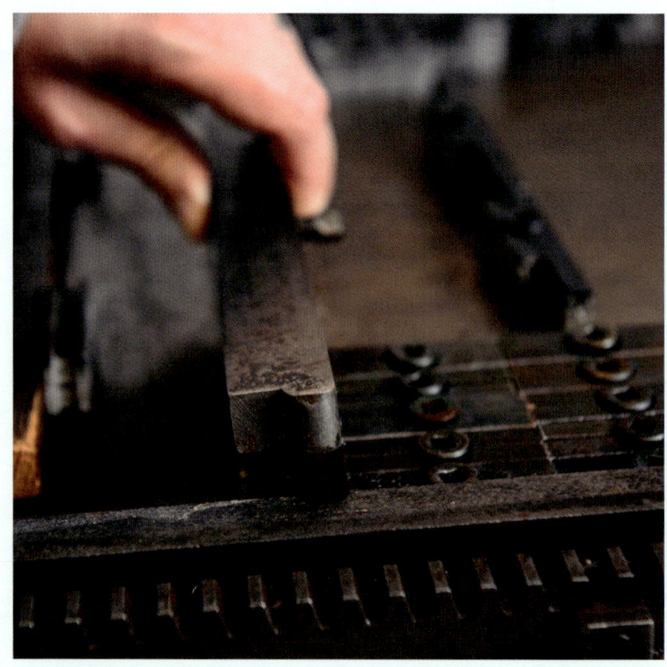

To start with, always work with a maximum size sheet of paper and set your type in the middle of the press – the oversized sheet can be cut to size after the print is dry. If you set your type too high up in the bed, for example, right at the top where the cylinder starts from, you could clash the paper guide parts on the cylinder onto your type. If you go too low on the paper as it is pulled around, the printing cylinder has a tendency to flick the paper as it comes to the end of the sheet, which can cause smudging on the lowest lines of letters.

The tympan backing on my press is made from some tough manila card, I cut a template when I first got the press by carefully removing the very old paper backing that was in the press. Always cut spare tympans when you are making them, as it's great to have a spare rolled up in an art tube.

Inking

When printing with my Vandercook I primarily like to ink by hand with a roller, which allows for quick changing of colours, more options and opportunity for experimenting with the ink. Whilst the inking system on these presses is very good, they do require a lot of ink, which means more cleaning. For printing long runs or split fountains (continue reading to find out what this is) I use the inking unit.

Vandercooks all have inking units, on mine it's powered by a motor that lives in its own space under the cylinder, where a chain runs from a sprocket to the inking cylinder, which then spins. This turning, large metal roller then makes contact with the rubber type inking rollers, causing them to rotate when set in the correct position for printing.

Replaced motor & gearbox on Vandercook.

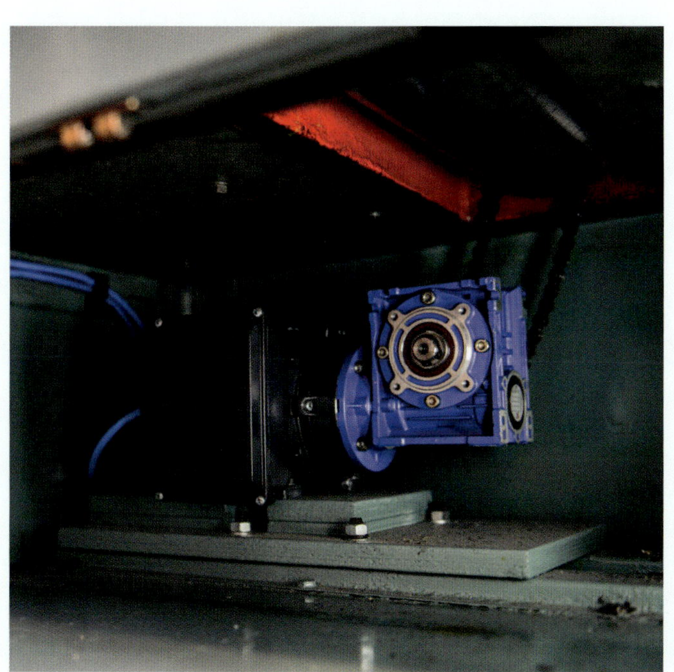

Inking cylinder on Vandercook.

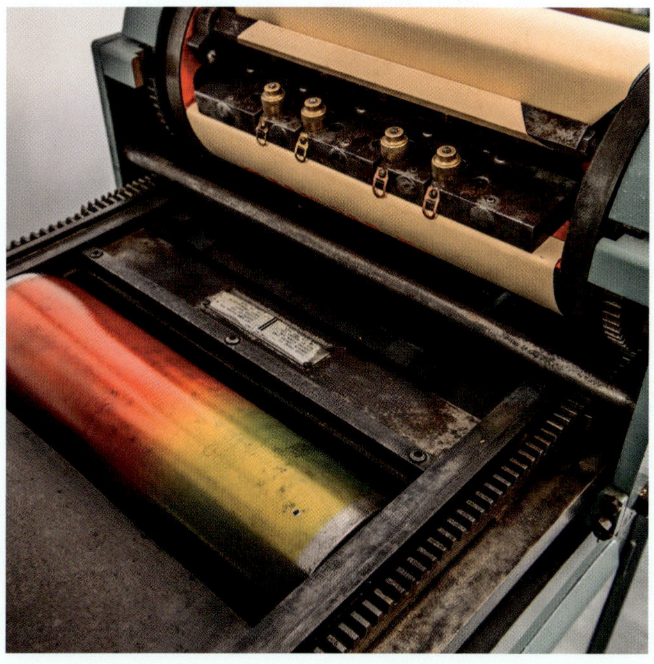

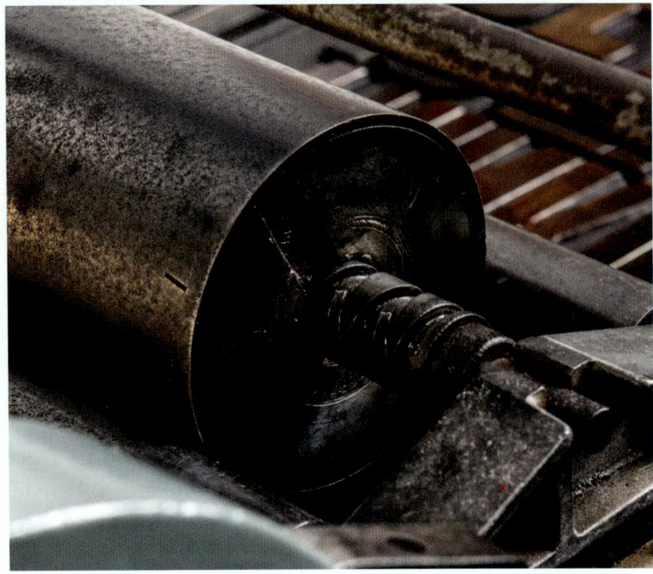

Oscillating inking cylinder.

These two rubber rollers have one large and two small metal rollers mounted above them that are lowered into place for printing. This large metal cylinder above the rubber rollers oscillates left and right as it turns on a worm thread.

This oscillation of the metal cylinder allows you to create blends of colours, by putting one colour on one side of the oscillating cylinder and another on the other end, the back-and-forth movement causes the two colours to delicately blend at the point where they meet. It's called a split fountain because you are literally splitting the inking fountain into multiple colours. Once you get good at this, you can also use it in combination with spacing in your type layout to give the appearance that you have printed 2 or 3 different colours in stages, while actually only pulling one print. This is done by precise setup of the ink and the type effectively missing the parts of the inking rollers that have the blended colours. For example, if you print smart and put yellow on one side of the cylinder and red on the other, the rollers will develop the third colour of orange, if the type is spread out far enough apart then one letter will print red and one yellow.

Let's get printing

The process of printing on a Vandercook is heavily refined compared to a hand-pull proofing press. Once you have your type locked out and inked ready to print, you need to add your paper with the gripper bar. If you go from using a basic proofing press to this, it can be quite a revelation. The gripper bar has a few parts to it that you will use a lot.

One big part is the foot pedal; pressing down causes the grippers to open (rise up) and when you release the pedal the grippers return back to their closed positions. To assist you there are paper guides, which are small pieces of brass that are screwed in place and bend slightly so the paper has an easy entrance to the grippers. The guides are screwed in place and have a turning adjuster, which ensures that your paper pulls through the press straight. I would recommend that once these are set, you don't need to tweak them too much – just make sure you do a good job cutting paper with good square edges. If the paper does not have a nicely cut square edge, then it is not the printing press's fault if it does not pull through cleanly. The paper guides do need replacing from time to time and are difficult to find (particularly in the UK). Out of desperation, in the past, I have cut and drilled some from thin sheet brass using a jeweller's saw which worked very well.

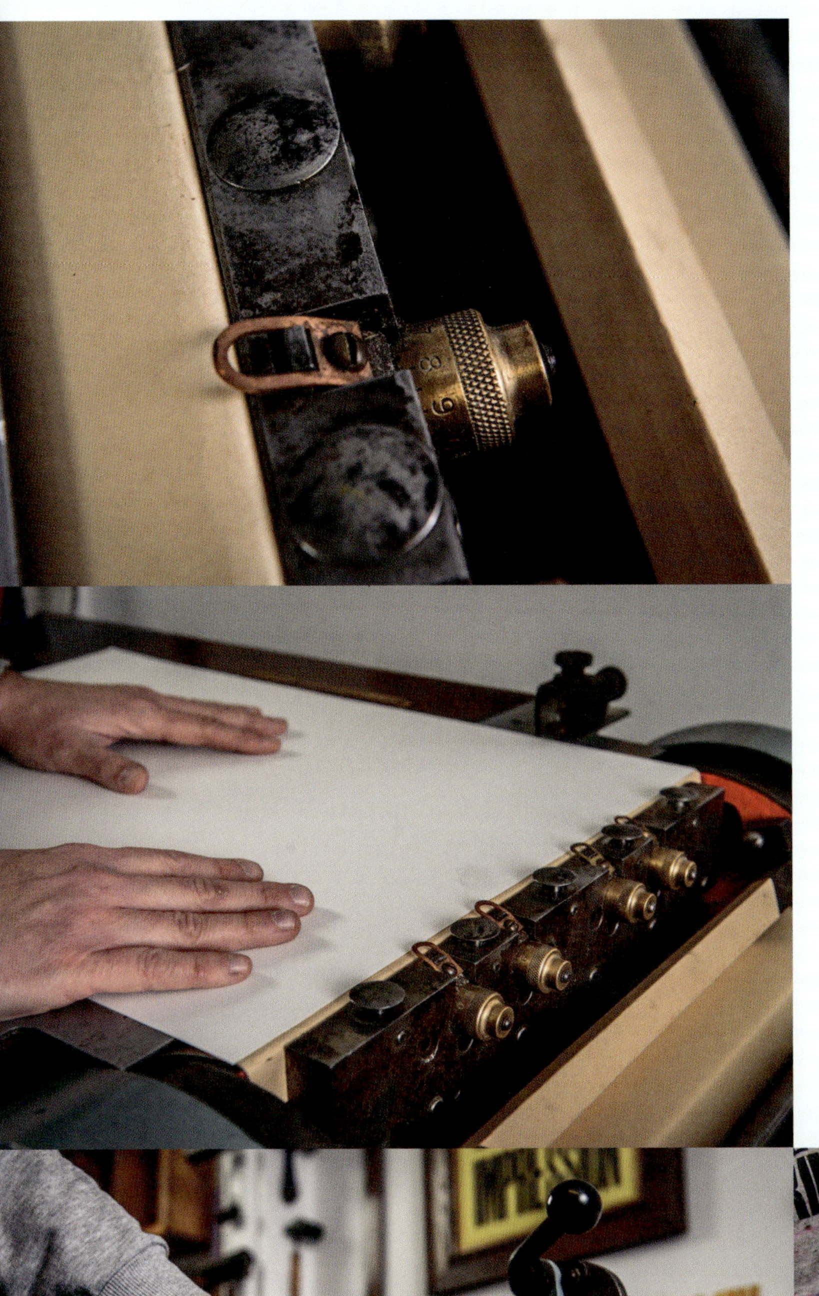

You also have a side guide, an adjustable guide that's tightened in the desired location across the feed bed, which has a ruler attached to it to make setting up easy. It also has a secondary adjuster that allows for very small alterations to its position. These mechanisms allow you to simply place a sheet of paper on the feed board, and slide it up against the side guide. Push the pedal down to raise the grippers, slide the paper under the paper guides into position, then release the pedal to let the press grip the paper. I like to make a small alteration at this point – I take a small piece of furniture and butt it up against the long edge of the paper on the feed table and double-side tape it in place, this give you a little more support to the long edge of the paper as it starts to go through the press and makes it easier to load. As with other proofing presses, you can add a sheet or two of packing paper to fine-tune the exact pressure for each print.

☛ Inserting paper, turning handle and pulling print on Vandercook.

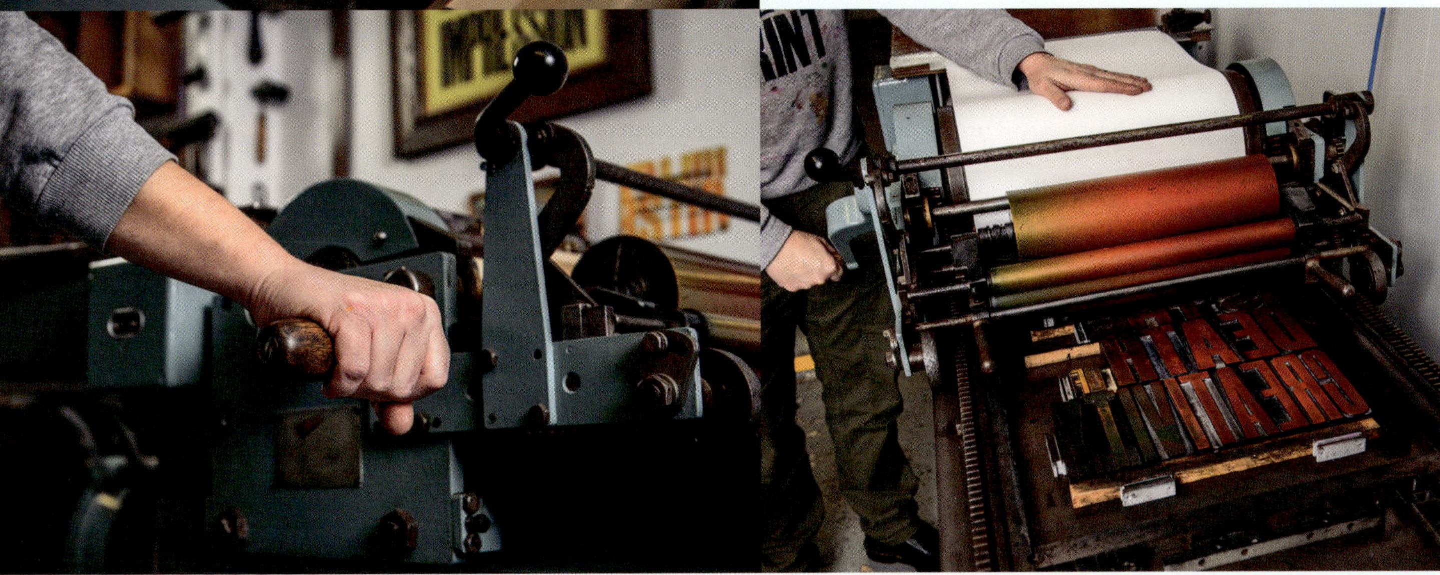

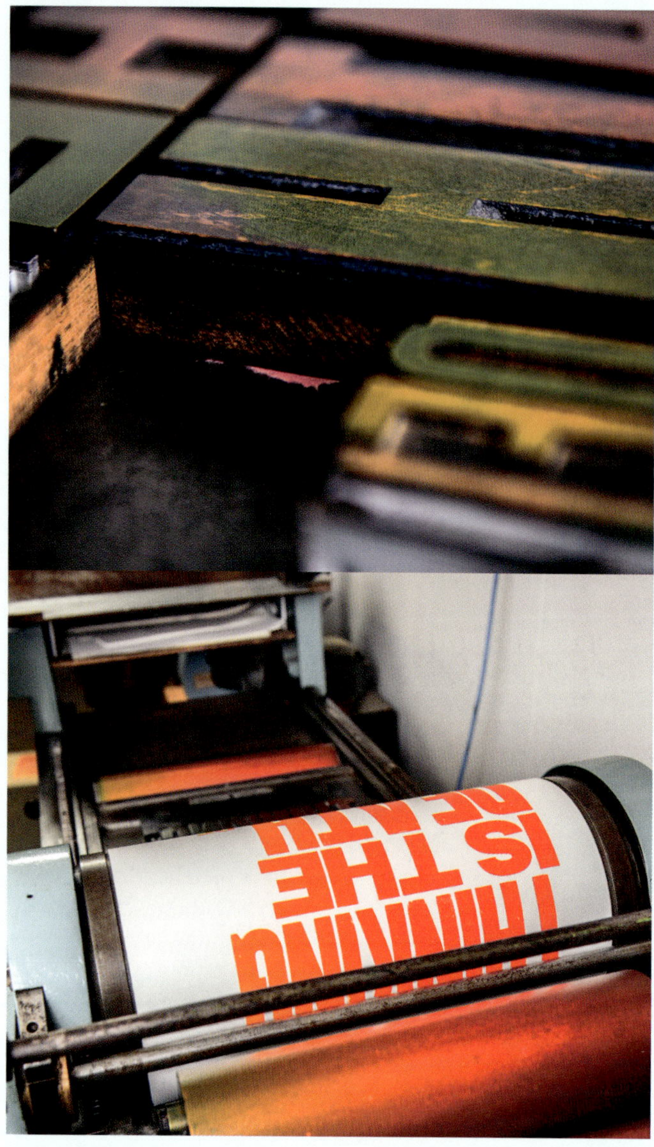

Inked type and print coming to rest to be removed.

Pulling prints

When the print is being pulled by turning the handle on the side of the press, the rubber rollers roll in front of the printing cylinder, inking your type and allowing the cylinder to follow and create your print. As the press finishes applying pressure to print, the cylinder moves to the end of the press, raising in height. You will hear a click as the paper is released from the paper grippers, and the printing head unit will come to rest on the Vandercook spring stops. You can now remove your print to see how it has come out. Place your print on your feed board where you started, then rotate the handle to return the cylinder back towards the starting position. As the cylinder's height changed, it shouldn't roll over your type on its way back. If this does happen, you did not roll the cylinder far enough when you were printing – make sure that the press touches the end spring. You should hear a click to indicate the changes to the mechanism.

On Vandercooks there's a 'print/trip' leaver near where the turning handle is, if you push it down to trip mode this means that the press will run at a height where it will not print. With these machines, setting up the pressure is quite technical – I would always recommend regular maintenance and servicing, ideally by an experienced individual. If you are struggling to find someone in your area, have a search around on social media, direct message other owners and ask them for advice or anyone that they would recommend – there is a community of specialist craftspeople that wants people to excel and continue the skills of the past.

When printing longer runs on a Vandercook the prints really do fly out and you need to know where you will be putting all these large prints, so get organised. After finishing printing make sure you clean all your type and rollers well, putting everything back in its correct place.

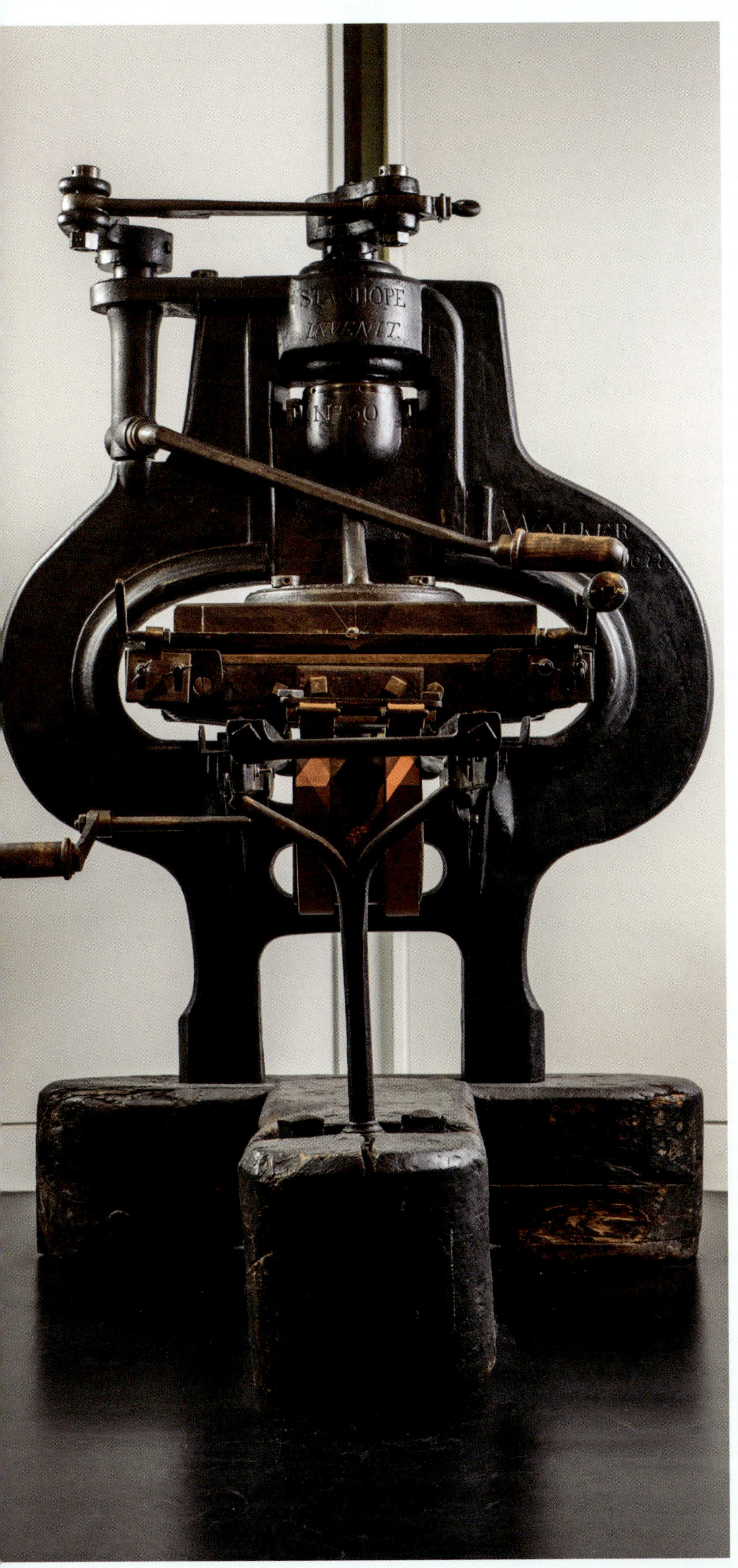

Printing on an Albion, Columbian or Stanhope

Now we are looking at the presses that put you most in touch with the industrial beginnings and history of letterpress. To print with any of the big three (as I like to refer to them) is to pull a print at the cutting edge of the technological development, and be transported to the beginning of the letterpress printing industry.

I love all these presses but sadly I do not own one, my experience of printing with these comes from using presses owned by others. This is as an example of the fact that you cannot own everything that you want, and that all printers, whether hobbyist or professional, will have an ongoing collection. Some items are just not practical and for me, owning one of them would be vanity not sanity. I have always felt that I am meant to own a broken-down Albion that I can restore, and I wait for the day when I find it.

Getting started

Printing with these presses is relatively simple in terms of operation, and depending on exactly what you are printing they'll be used in slightly different ways. When they were first built they'd have been predominantly used to print pages of books working with movable type. In the modern world these presses are more commonly used to print posters and large-scale prints, using both vintage and historic letterpress wood type but also hand-carved wood blocks and large-scale lino prints.

☛ Stanhope press at Ditchling Museum of Art + Craft.

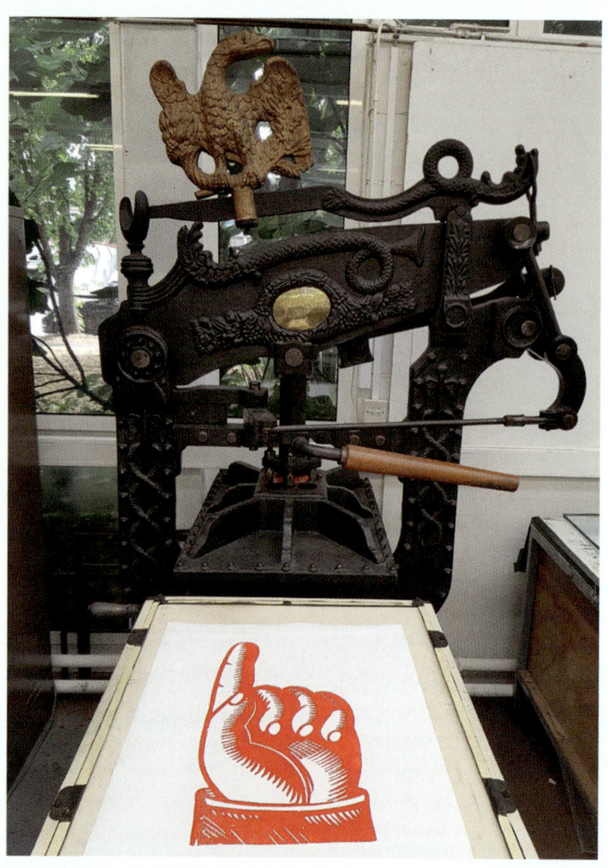

Columbian press at Ochre Print Studio.

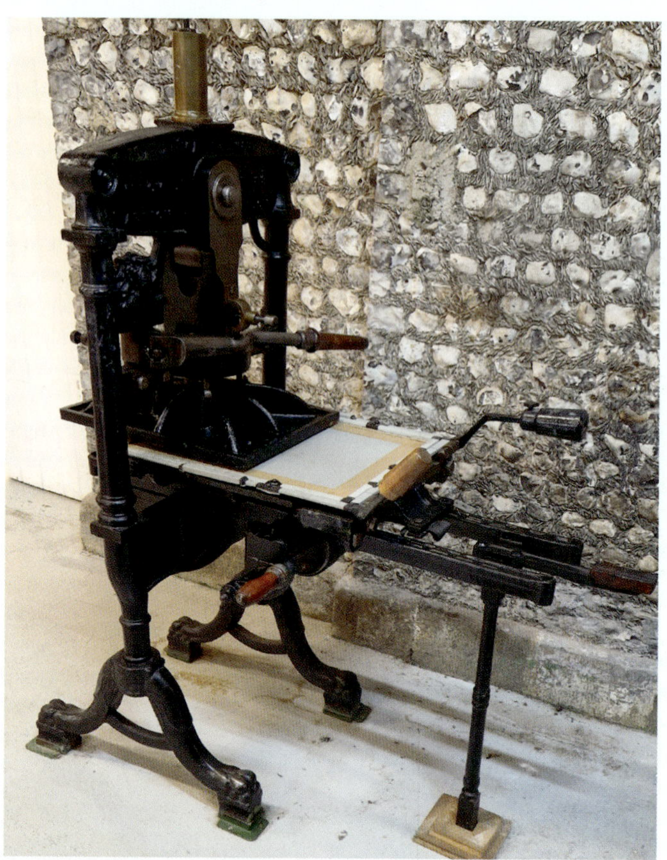

Albion printing press at West Dean College.

Each of these different materials and disciplines holds the same basic principle of operation that the press will work to. Through use you will notice the tiny variations that each requires to improve your print. This is a very personal thing that's hard to explain; when you are using these presses you get physical feedback almost like a musical reverb, it is important to understand what the press is doing and how the different printing materials interact at the point of printing.

The basic process of printing with one of these presses is quite simple and shouldn't be overwhelming. You have a press bed, and type can be secured with a very large chase or galley magnets, as with other machines. I have seen people printing without securing individual printing blocks in place, I would advise against this as you risk movement of the block and smudging of your prints. Whatever you are printing with, you want to locate it in the middle of the press bed, as this is where the pressure is the most even – even pressure will help result in an even print. If your print location is always aimed at the centre of the bed then it is easier to problem solve issues like bad inking or under-inking, as pressure can be eliminated as a cause. Importantly, putting uneven work through the press causes stress and unnecessary pressure on the printing press. When you are working with machines that are over 200 years old, it's best to treat them with full respect and care.

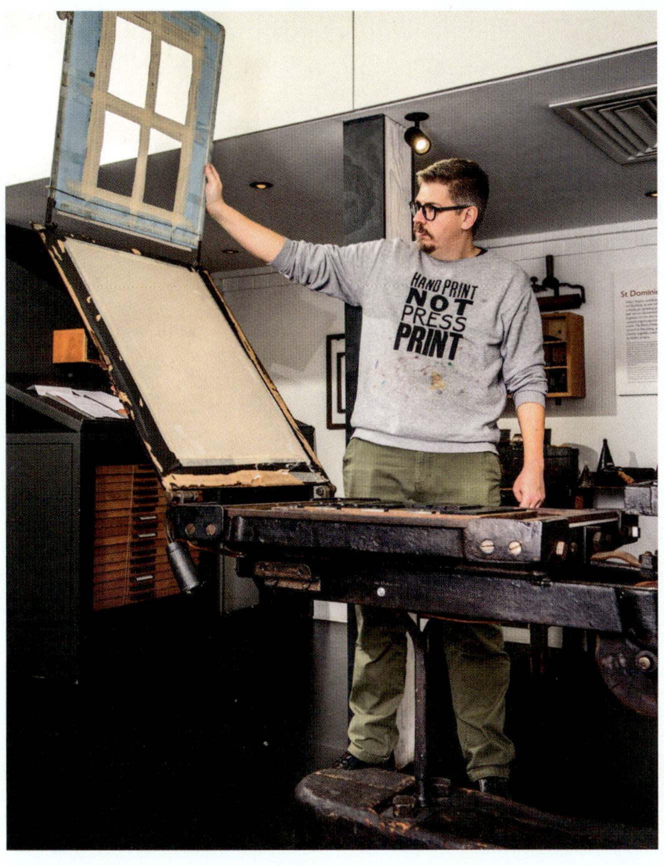

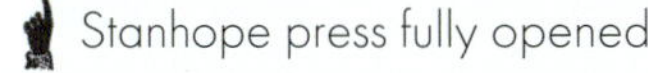
Stanhope press fully opened.

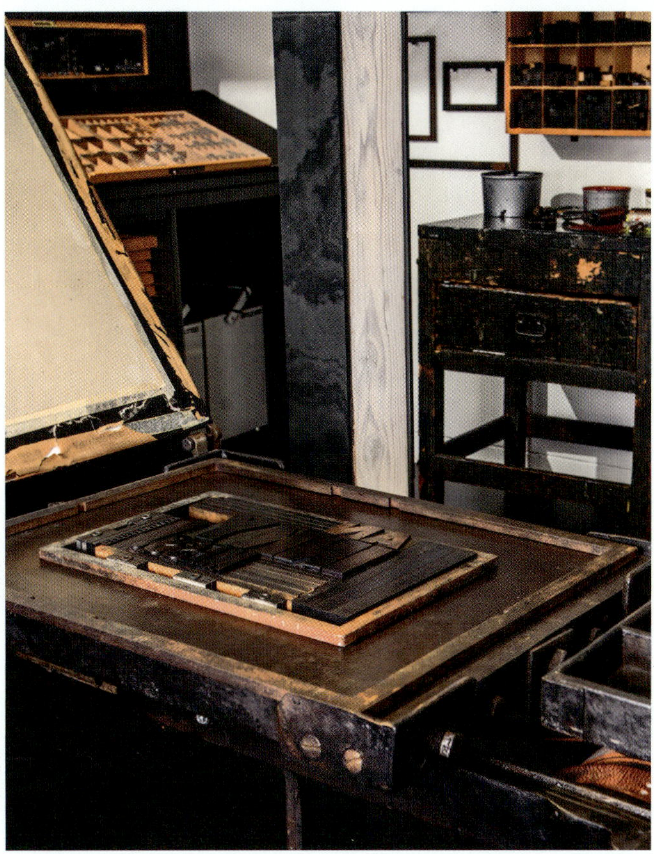

Wood type locked out in case on bed of Stanhope.

Getting printing

Once everything is in place and secured, you'll ink as per other presses with a hand roller. At the end of the press bed on Albions, Stanhopes and Columbians you have a tympan and a frisket, parts which lift up one above the other and stand proud at the end of the press. For printing book pages, the frisket in combination with the tympan would be used to place your paper in an exact alignment for printing. The printer would create locators so the paper would be held in place, then the frisket, which lowers onto the tympan, securely holds everything in perfect location. This was how books were printed in a slow and laborious way, through the developing technology of letterpress. Often with presses now, you'll find that the frisket and tympan have been removed, as art is more commonly printed than books.

If you are printing in the more modern way, loading your paper by hand, it's fiddly but satisfying when you manage to gently roll, drop, place and flop your paper perfectly centrally. The easiest way to do this is to gently grip the short edges of your sheet of paper moving your hands towards each other to allow the paper to arch down in the middle, then slowly and gently lower the paper onto the type and release the edges of the paper after making contact. Softly pat around the type to ensure the paper has contacted nicely with the printed surface, this helps avoid smudging prints when you add any packing sheets. Then return the frisket and tympan on top if they are in place.

Pulling your print

The press bed is mounted on a carriage that allows it to slide under the platen, and to make the press bed slide you turn the large handle on the side of the press that is about thigh-high. This can be heavy and it's best to do it slowly and steadily, you want to advance the press bed so it stops in the centre of the platen. This is quite easy to achieve as the framework around the edge of the tympan or the sides of the bed is very visible, so you just want everything looking nice and even around the edges. Don't drive your bed too hard at the platen end of the press as there should be stops – it is a really bad idea to crash into the stops; when working with a 200-year-old press it is best to be nice to it.

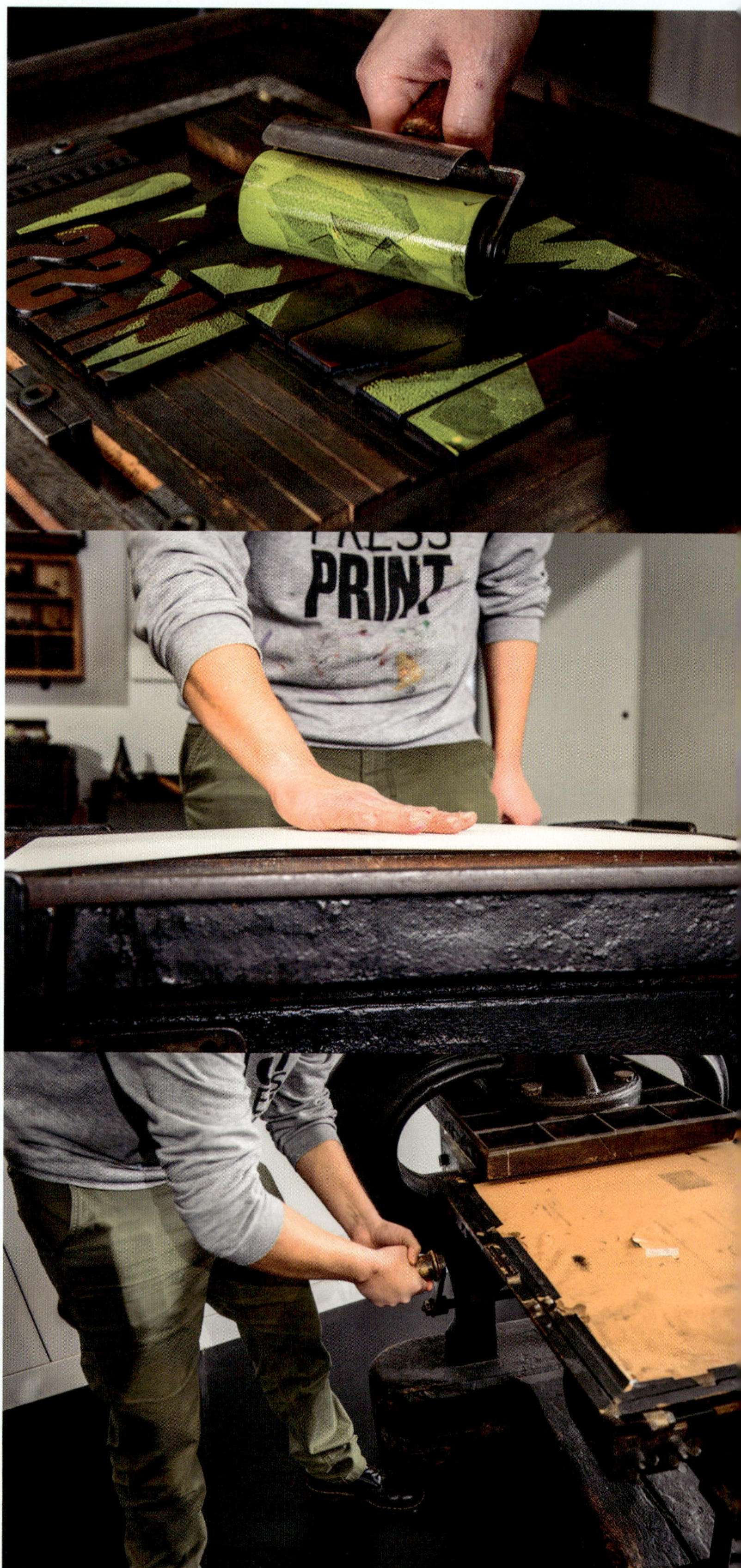

Now to print, lean forward over the press, firmly grip the large wooden handle and pull towards you. This is where you get a lot of feedback through the machine, as the pressure is delivered from your body into the mechanism of the press, increasing the pressure and pushing power that you are providing. The platen is now pushing down onto your paper and squeezing everything together. At this point it is tempting to pull for dear life, but you really don't need to.

Some printers have the bad habit of putting their boot on printing presses to get extra leverage. These signs of wear can clearly be seen – like on the Stanhope at Ditchling Museum of Art + Craft. When these machines were operated all day, every day, it makes sense that a tired printer would make his life a bit easier by using his weight. Nowadays these machines aren't used in the same way, and there's

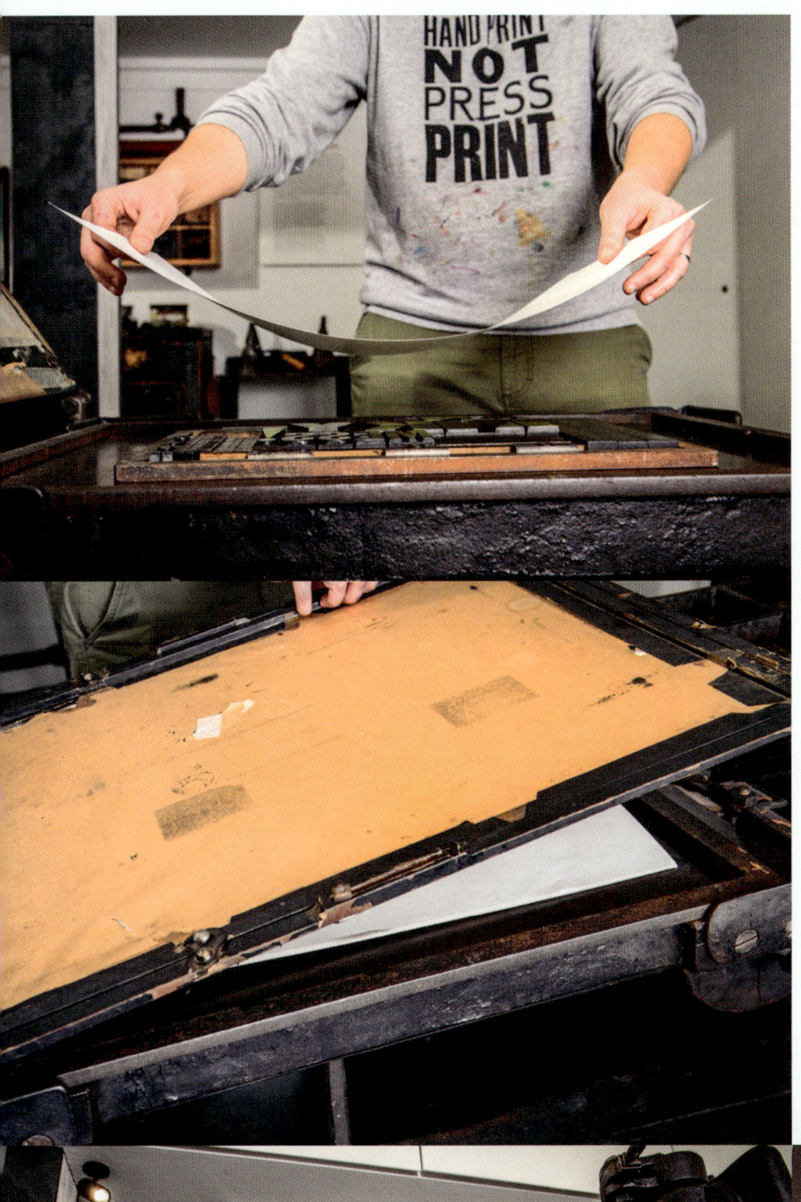

really no need. If you work using your arms, pull the handle towards your chest and lean back gently – you can feel and assess the pressure. This for me is one of the most joyous moments of printing and the ability to repeat with consistent pressure on print runs is incredibly satisfying.

What you are printing with will affect how hard and how deep you will pull; you have to visualise the object that you are printing and the material it is made from. Metal is hard, wood is softer and lino is soft. When printing with wood or lead type, you know the material is solid so you feel and know when you are pulling hard. Lino or equivalent materials are soft, so the point of true impact is harder to gauge – it is easier to pull much harder, to squeeze everything together.

☛ Inking type, applying paper, loving pat, adding packing sheet, closing press, turning handle to carry bed into the press, pull print, return bed...

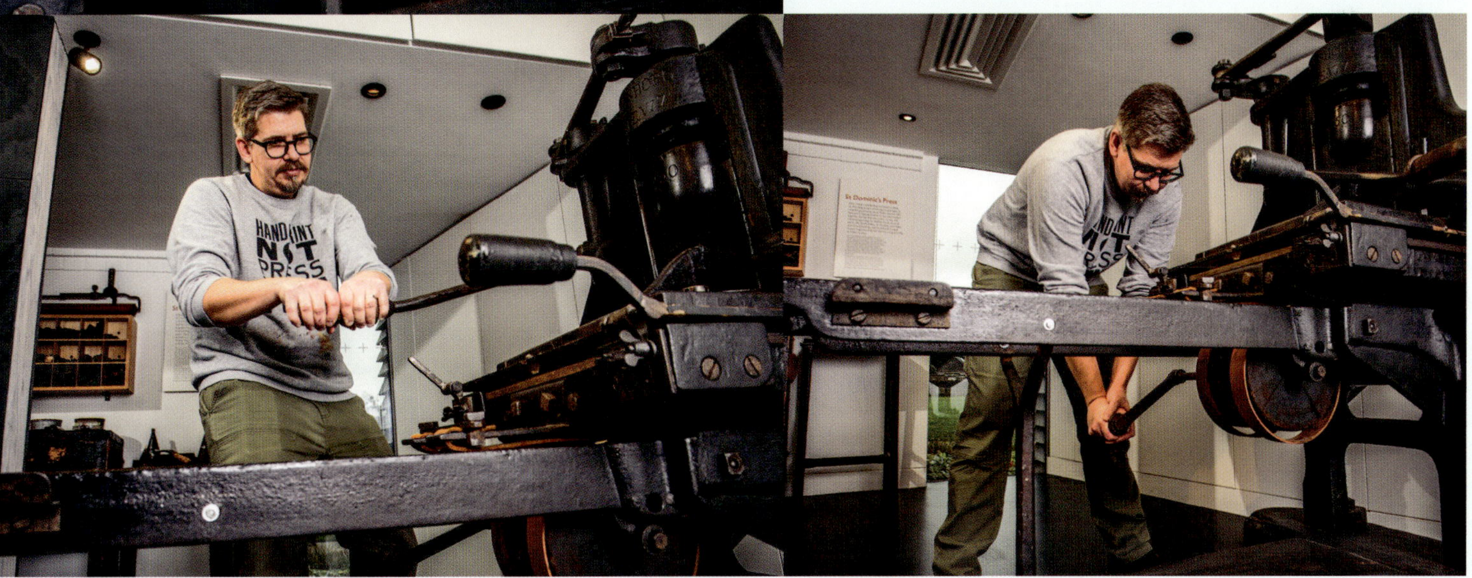

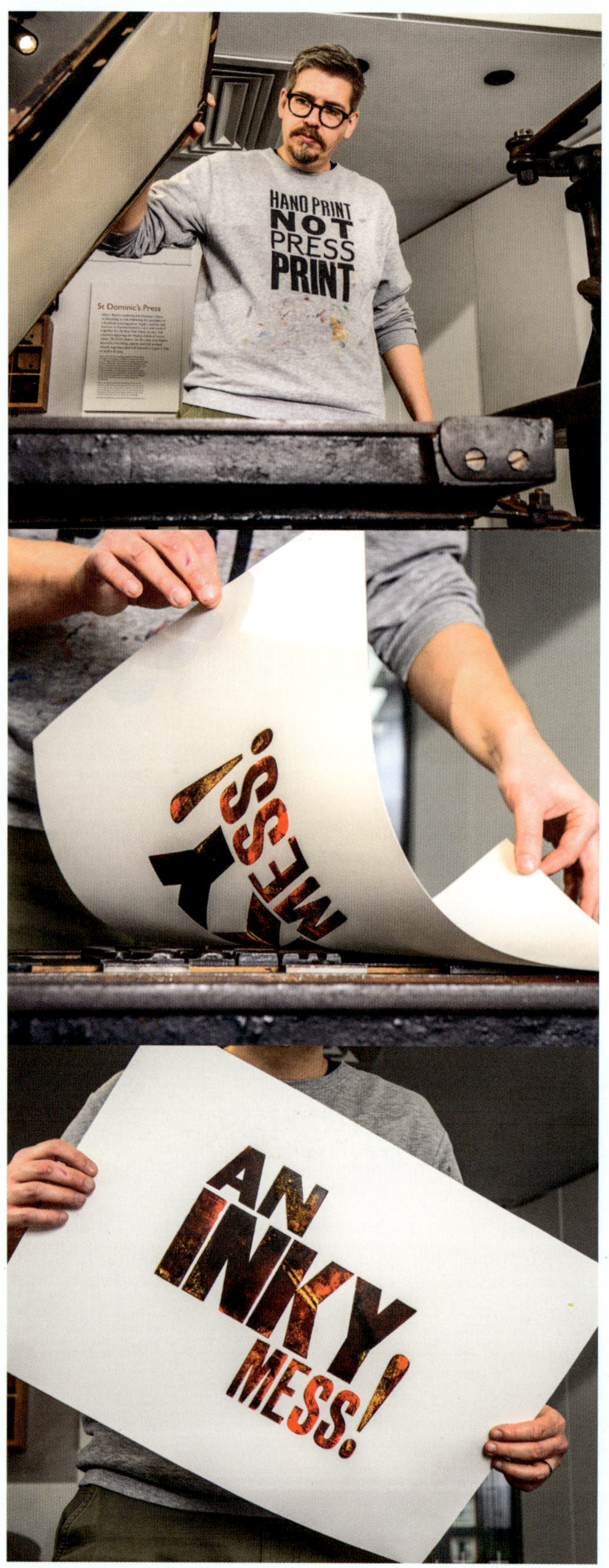

Take your time and don't pull too hard, use packing sheets to allow for more moulding around your type or blocks, do test prints and get yourself into a position where you have a really solid setup, then print.

Slowly return the pulling handle to the press, do not just let go, push or throw the handle towards the machine, as this could cause damage. Turn the handle in the opposite way to return the bed to the other end of the carriage, open the tympan and frisket (if attached), remove any packing sheets and carefully reveal your print. Two hundred years ago, this print would have been passed to an assistant and the process started again.

On presses like these the pressure is adjusted in different ways, some like the Stanhope using counterweights at the rear of the press. The Columbian had a cast iron eagle at the top of the press. Whichever unique solution was found, the platen is still set using the bolts that attach it to the press, using similar logic as to how Adanas and jobbing presses were set even and flat. With important historical presses like these, it's worth befriending a press engineer, and having your press serviced regularly – watch, learn and get some tips from them. It is worth the investment to care for all these machines, as they really are part of the history of print, not just letterpress. Whenever you are lucky enough to get to print with machines like these, fully clean down and leave them as you found them, hopefully in perfect working condition.

☛ Opening the tympan, removing and revealing the final print.

Printing without a press

If you don't have a press, it can be tricky, but also great fun to print. Let's get back to basics. You will still need something to print, in this case we will work on the principle that you have found some old type at a boot fair and want to give it a go. You will need ink and a roller, then there are a few options.

A great option is a baren – a smooth disc that usually has some sort of handle that you hold it with. Inking your type and placing your paper on top, simply rub the baren on the back of your paper to squeeze the paper onto the inked type. Barens come in different sizes and are made from different materials, you can buy plastic, glass, 3D printed, metal, and my personal favourite, bamboo barens. Bamboo barens have a belt-shaped piece of fibre pulled over the top to make a sort of handle that you slide your hand under. With bamboo barens you can feel the pressure nicely, so you feel like you have quite a lot of control. Being made of bamboo they are not going to last forever, but they are cheap, at about £4. I have found that you can get nice prints using a bamboo baren if you use a little more ink than you would with standard presses and one sheet of paper packing. This is a technique that will be one to find your own way with. It's good fun to do with kids, and you don't need to be worried about the safety issue of using a press.

If you cannot get your hands on a baren then plenty of people have printed using wooden spoons. Usually that's done with lino printing, but it does work with wood type – you just need to press quite hard and use more packing than you would with a baren. With either of these options, paper choice will massively inform the end result – smooth paper is strongly recommended over textured. It's nice from time to time to get back to basics and experiment, as you'll often find a new effect or idea. I would definitely recommend that everyone has a go just for fun, and remember, it should be fun.

Selection of barens, plastic, 3D printed ball bearing (red) and traditional bamboo.

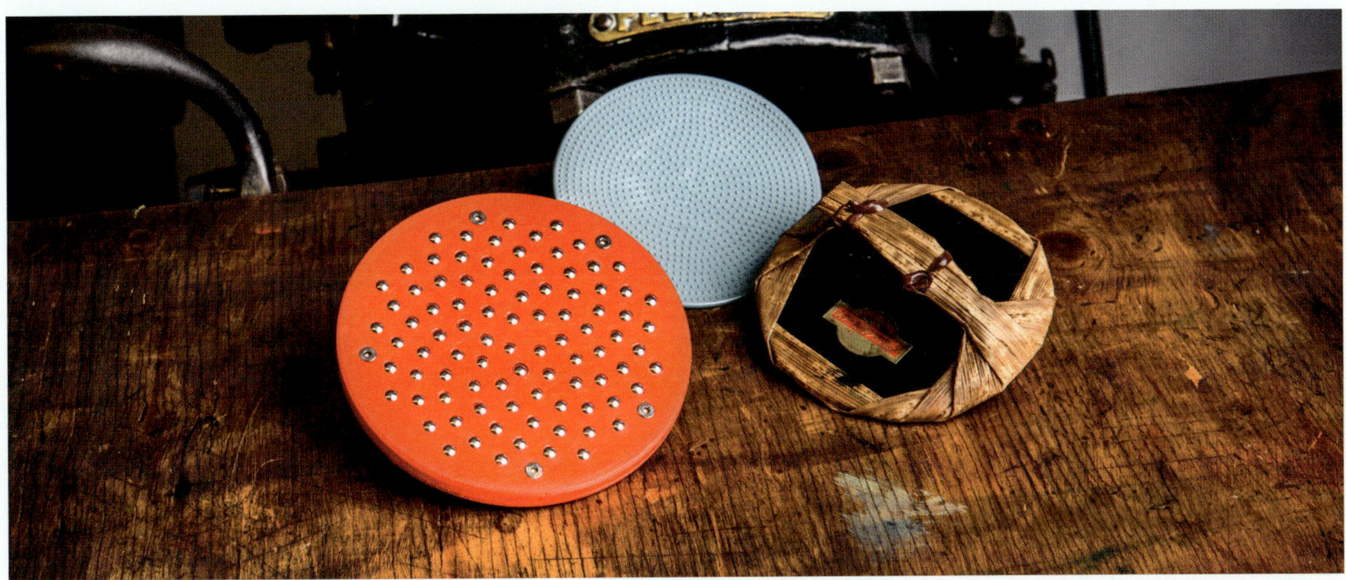

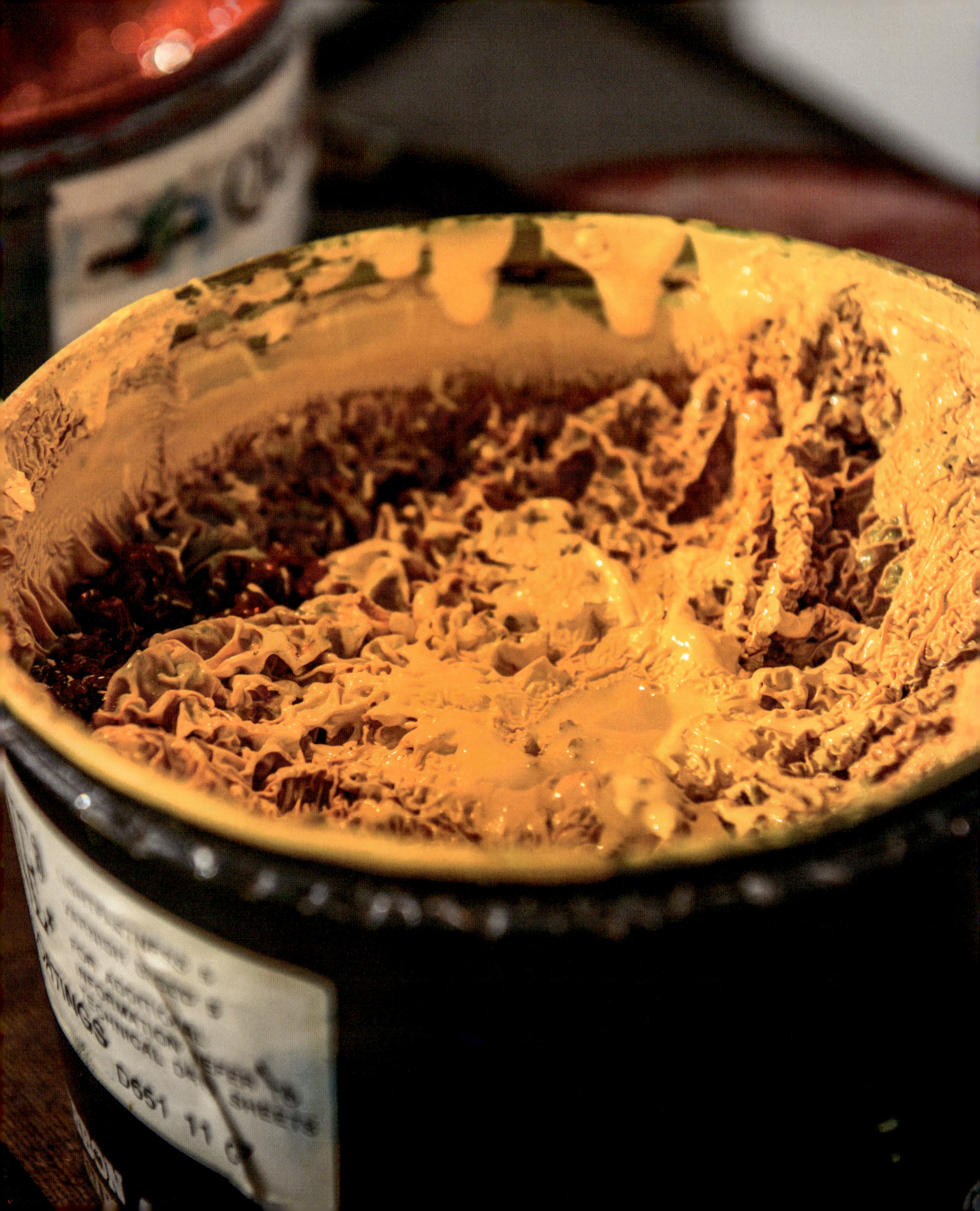

7

Inking & printing

Letterpress is seen as a traditional form of printing, and with that comes the stereotype of how a print should look and be created. In reality, letterpress can be more freely creative. Colour is a big part of a design; when the colours are printed just right, they can lift the print to a new level, make the print jump and allow the viewer to really engage with both the design and the process that went into creating it.

As you become more experienced, you'll become able to look at a print and see how it was produced. You'll be able to tell which order colours were printed in, if the printer was inking lightly with some colours and heavily with others, if some of the colours had more pressure applied when printing and how this had a knock-on effect. When you start playing with colours you begin to really create your own style.

Letterpress is sometimes a funny discipline to work with; people often comment during workshops that they are surprised by the brightness and range of colours I have. I think this comes from people seeing faded old prints on age-yellowed paper, which has created this concept that colours are muted.

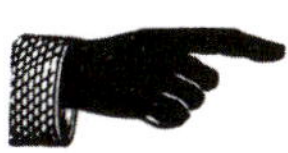

I openly admit to usually wanting to just print with red and black as I love the hard contrast. I often have to push myself to experiment with the use of colours, and whilst I do not always find that a natural process, the best results I get are when I play with new colour combinations. In this chapter I will try to break down some of the basics of printing, getting you going on your own path.

One-colour printing

One colour really is the starting point. Sometimes the boldness of one colour really makes a design. Particularly when printing with small lead type, for example, when one colour, usually black, is all you need for clear readability. To start with the basics let's look at ink. Ink is made from a pigment, or a mixture of pigments, depending on what colour it is. Traditionally these pigments were made from natural materials, things like minerals, rocks, soot, insects and more. Today pigments are mass produced and man-made, meeting modern demands for consistency from one tin of ink to another. Traditionally oil-based ink would have been made by mixing these pigments with usually a linseed-based oil, producing a sticky liquid form ready to print. Nowadays many different pigments and liquid bases are used, including water and natural oils, to meet demands for eco-based alternatives.

With one-colour printing you can really focus on getting your ink levels just right – if you are hand-inking, rolling the ink out on the glass,

Don't think just do print.

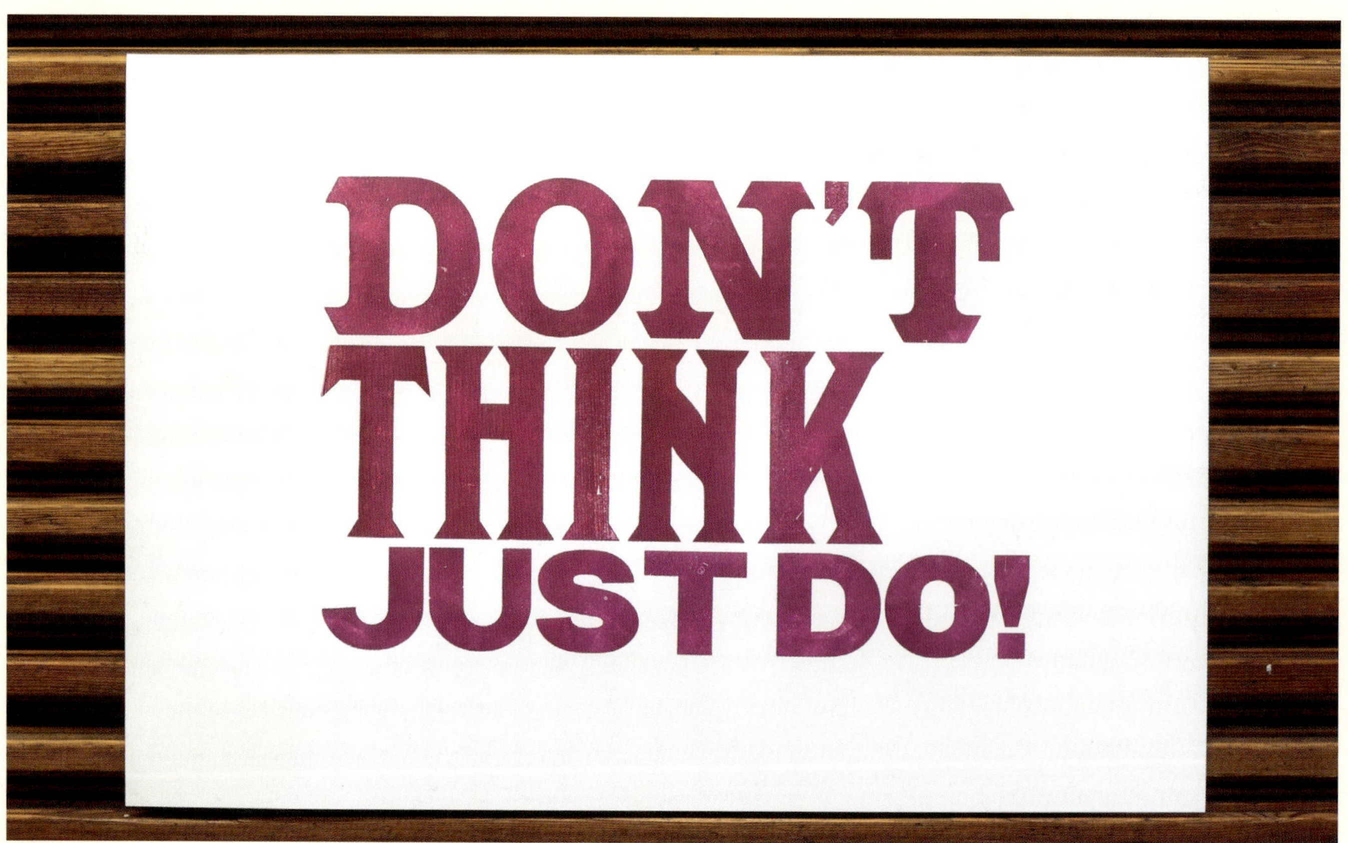

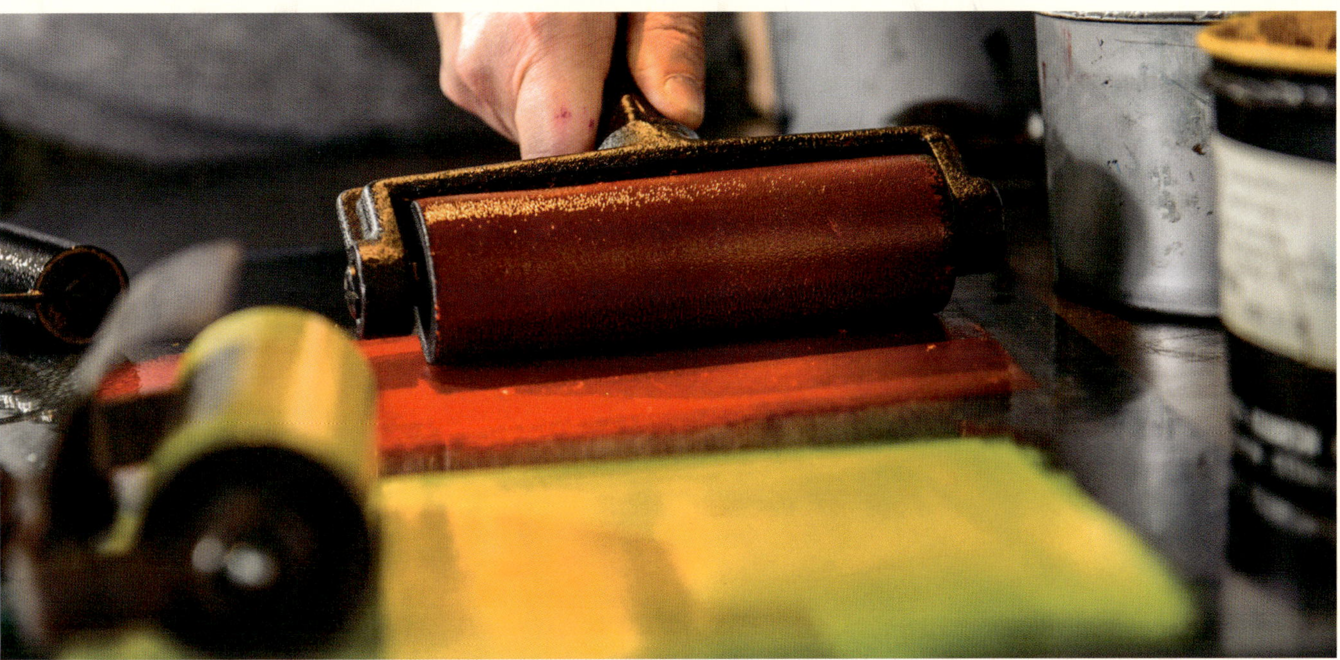

Inking rollers.

you can hear and see it. Roll out the ink evenly, listen for a nice static noise; when the noise is even and not going up and down in volume the ink is evenly spread out. Look closely at your inking roller, you should be able to see a very slightly dimpled texture across the ink. If you have applied too much the dimples will appear larger and gloopy. You can increase the rolling area on your board to use up excess ink, but it's better to under-ink than over-ink. You can apply this approach to machines with inking units like the Adana – listen to the noise and look at the rollers. On an Adana, though, if you have too much ink then you'll need to remove some. This can be easily done by putting a piece of paper on the inking plate then slowly raising the inking rollers up onto it, rolling over the paper sheet and depositing excess there. Time spent practising one-colour printing and basic alignment of your sheet is fundamental and will really make printing easier and more fun.

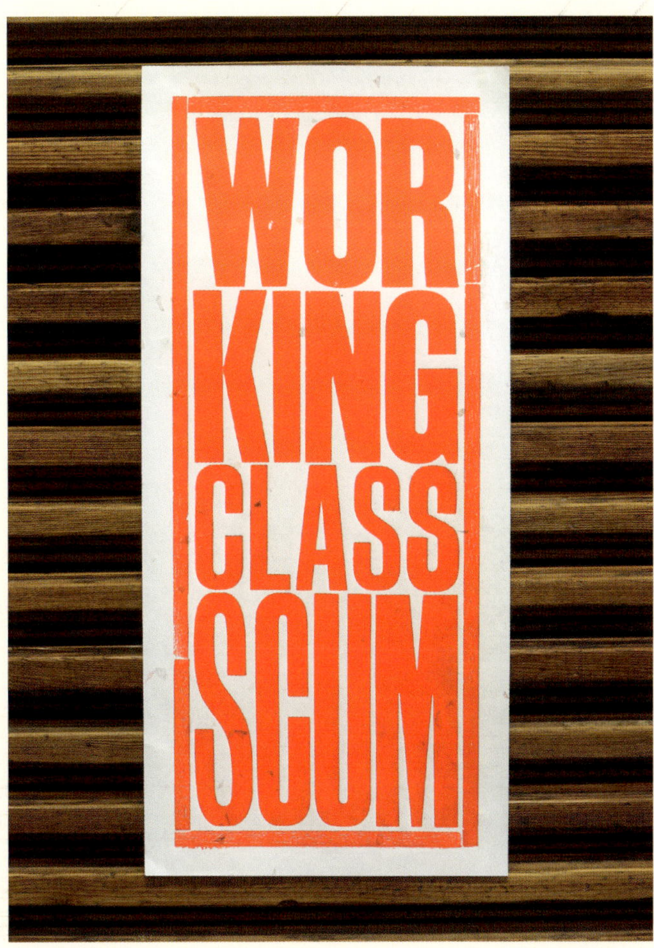

Working class scum print.

Multi-colour printing, registration and alignment techniques

Alignment, setup, good technique and logic become very important when you start doing multiple-colour prints. Let's say that we are doing a two-colour print, and that the prints have to sit in set locations and line up with each other (not touching perfectly, just lining up). You really need to think about what you are doing before you start printing, as if you rush ahead and print the first colour in the wrong location then your second print may not align, and you may need to start again.

After many years of enjoying printing, I have adopted different techniques from different processes to help with things like alignment. For instance, for printing two colours, and often even for one colour printing, I will take a piece of acetate or thin tracing paper and draw out the grid of my design on it. Then if I am printing, on say, an Adana or one of my jobbing presses, I will get the ink and pressure on the press set up, add a scrap piece of paper to the platen, securing it in place with masking tape, and pull a rough first print onto this, leaving the print on the platen. Then you can simply put your acetate or tracing paper grid over the top of the rough print, and align the print with the drawn grid lines and masking tape in place. From here it is very simple to set your gauge pins, a lay bar (if using an Adana), magnetic strips or even pieces of card in place to make sure that your paper is always printing in the same place every time.

You can also go one step further and pull a print onto your tracing paper, then when you come to pull your second colour, you can follow this process again and see exactly what the print will look like when aligned. When it comes to pulling the second print, pull a print onto the acetate or tracing paper and keep it

2 Colour printed card, with tight registration, overlapping 3rd colour created from design, printed with photopolymer plates.

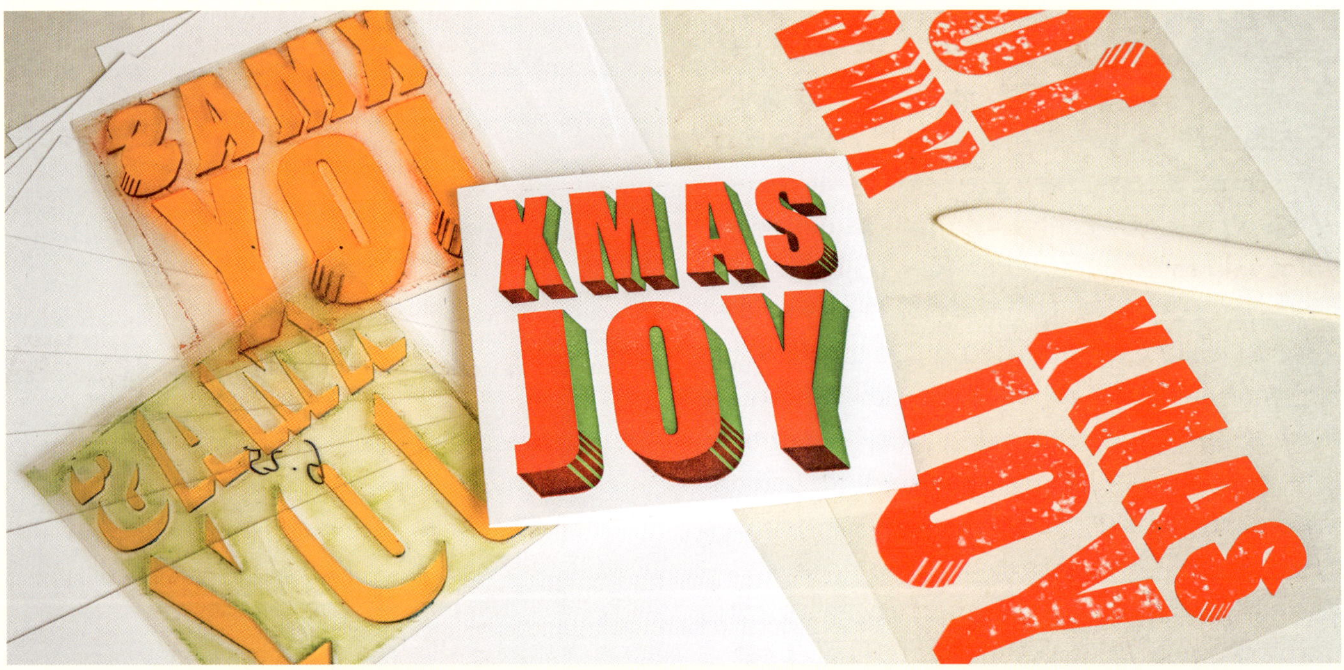

somewhere safe in case you need to print this again – then you always have a perfect registration reference for future prints.

Drying times

Letterpress is not a quick printing option; being organised and planning what and how you are printing is very important. Drying times vary depending on what sort of ink you are using and the environmental condition – whether it's hot or cold. As a general rule, oil-based ink will need about 24 hours to dry, with water-based you'll need to experiment based on the specific ink that you are using.

You can buy additives to speed up the process of drying, personally I haven't played around too much with these, as if you add too much or too little you can either create no effect at all or in the worst case, adding too much may mean the print never fully dries. I just accept and embrace letterpress' unique ways, and plan for drying times accordingly.

How and where you dry your prints can become an issue, ideally you will have some form of drying rack. I am lucky and have an A2 screen printer's drying rack that flips up to allow a large number of prints to dry in a relatively small area. When this has not been enough space, I have added washing lines and used cheap wooden clothes pegs to clip prints up to dry. If you are using this method, I would recommend folding a small piece of card and placing it over the end of your printed paper, to protect your prints' paper from getting a small dent from the peg. These options work well for larger prints, but when you are printing larger runs of smaller items, say 200 post card-sized prints, you can look to interleave your prints. This means to stack prints with a piece of scrap paper in between so that any contact that occurs from the pressure of the weight of the paper does not cause a transfer print onto the rear side of your print. When interleaving I usually only stack about 10 to 15 prints if they are on a heavyweight card, to minimise the transfer and to not extend the drying time too much. When printing on paper I will increase the stack quantity as the weight of the paper is less. These interleaved wads or bundles of prints can be placed out to dry.

Drying rack.

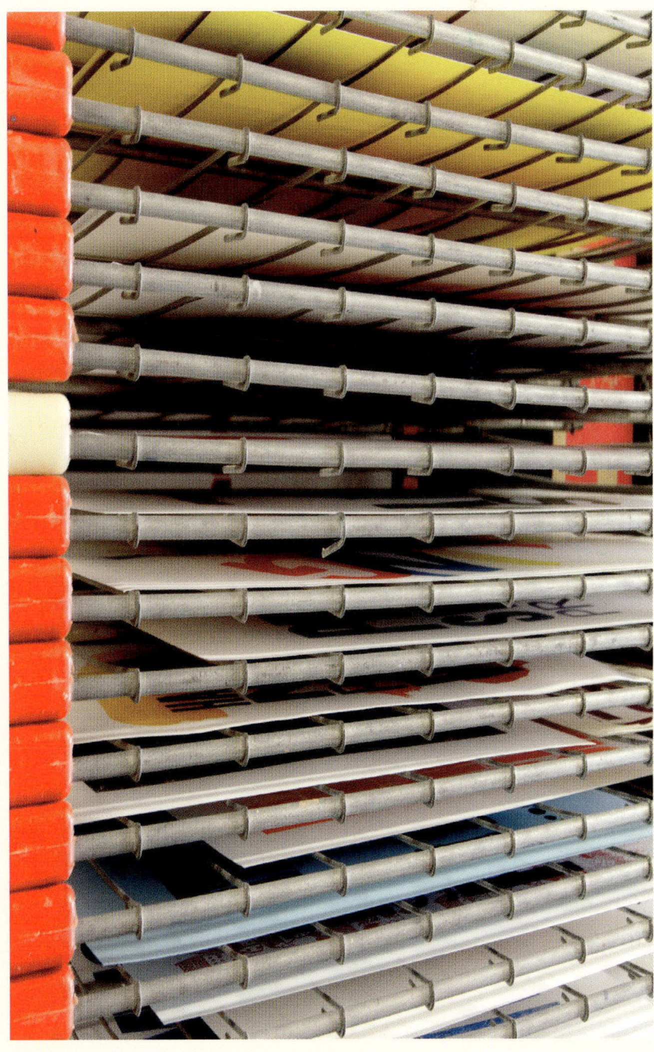

Wet-on-wet printing

Drying times are a pain, it can be annoying when you just want to get on and finish a print run. The restrictiveness of letterpress does usually mean that you should really only print a second colour once the first one is dry, but sometimes you really have to get it done by any means necessary. If you are going gung-ho, printing with wet ink, then there are some things to consider.

The first thing is very obvious: when you have lots of wet ink on paper it's very easy to place your finger in the wrong place, smudge your print, and then transfer to other pages and not notice until after you've finished printing! Work out what is the best order to print your chosen colours in. The simple rule is lightest colour first, darkest colour last; this rule is good for days when you're doing lots of printing on any press that has built-in inking rollers, as darker colours are less prone to being tainted by lighter ones.

If you have been printing yellow on an Adana for example, you would clean down, and apply your black. If there is any residue of yellow ink on the rollers, the black ink will easily absorb it without you being able to tell. If using yellow after black, it would quickly change colour, which would require cleaning down again before resuming printing. This principle also applies to the printed surface of your type, as if you have areas that overlay, the two inks that are being printed will lift off a tiny amount of the first printed colour as you print, this in turn will work its way back, onto your roller. Depending on the colours that you are using, this can mean a very slow, initially imperceptible change of colour. When you compare prints at the end of a run the colour change can look significant.

I always keep my first print out so that I have a constant reference to check against. Due to the issues that can happen with wet-on-wet printing, I tend to do an extra 10 per cent number of prints to a run, to counter any finishing issue that I may face. To summarise, printing wet-on-wet is very problematic, and really should only be for those emergency times.

Mixing ink

Getting the perfect colour combo can be difficult. Collecting a vast number of ink colours is great, but it's also nice to mix the perfect colour. Mixing ink can seem very complicated, but it is actually quite simple if you have a sample that you are looking to create. With a visual reference you can look at your existing collection of ink and start to work out what colours you are going to need.

Ideally start with a base ink that you add to, to alter that colour. This makes the task simpler and less intense than trying to mix three colours at once. Don't put too much ink out onto your inking plate to start with, add small amounts of the different colours that you think you need. Leave plenty of room for working and moving the ink around. Mix in thoroughly as you go, I always like to have plenty of scraps of white card lying around when I am mixing ink. Periodically I will lightly touch the ink onto the card to test the colour. Inking heavily or lightly alters your colour quite a lot; my finger-smearing method gives you a quick visual of a thick inky bit and a thin under-inked area to see if you like the colour.

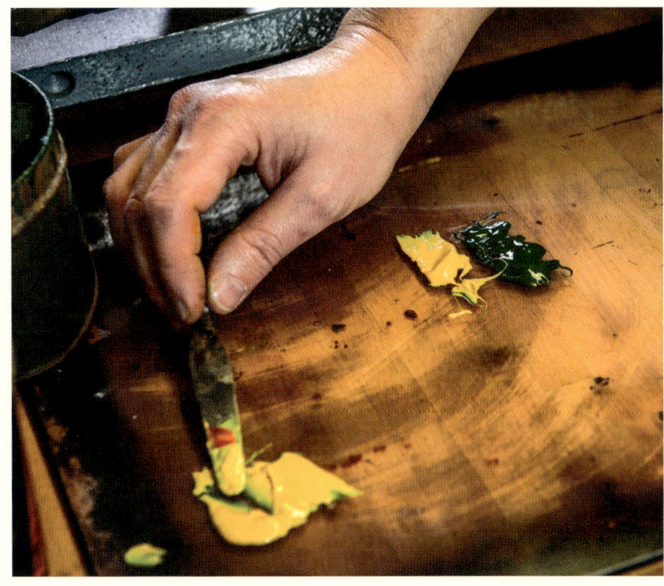

Adding and mixing ink with pallet knife.

There is lots of information online about colour theory and what colours mix with each other to make different colours, yellow and blue equals green, for example. Playing around and working out what works for you is sometimes the best way. Take notes as you mix small amounts, it's then much easier to mix a larger quantity. Collect small jam jars – I always keep the tiny single-portion ones you get at hotels for saving leftover custom-mixed inks. Plastic pots also work well, the small mango chutney pots always end up in the workshop after having a takeaway curry.

A word on Pantone references. Pantone is great, but it can be slightly difficult for letterpress, because as mentioned earlier, the thickness of your ink and the pressure used will change the intensity of your colour. I find Pantone works if you use it to mix a close colour using their mixing guide (assuming you have the colour's references for mixing ink). Then, test print and tweak the colour according to individual print needs. When I am mixing ink for my own work that is not for a customer, I create some very unique shades that I would never purchase.

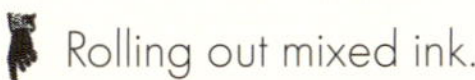

Rolling out mixed ink.

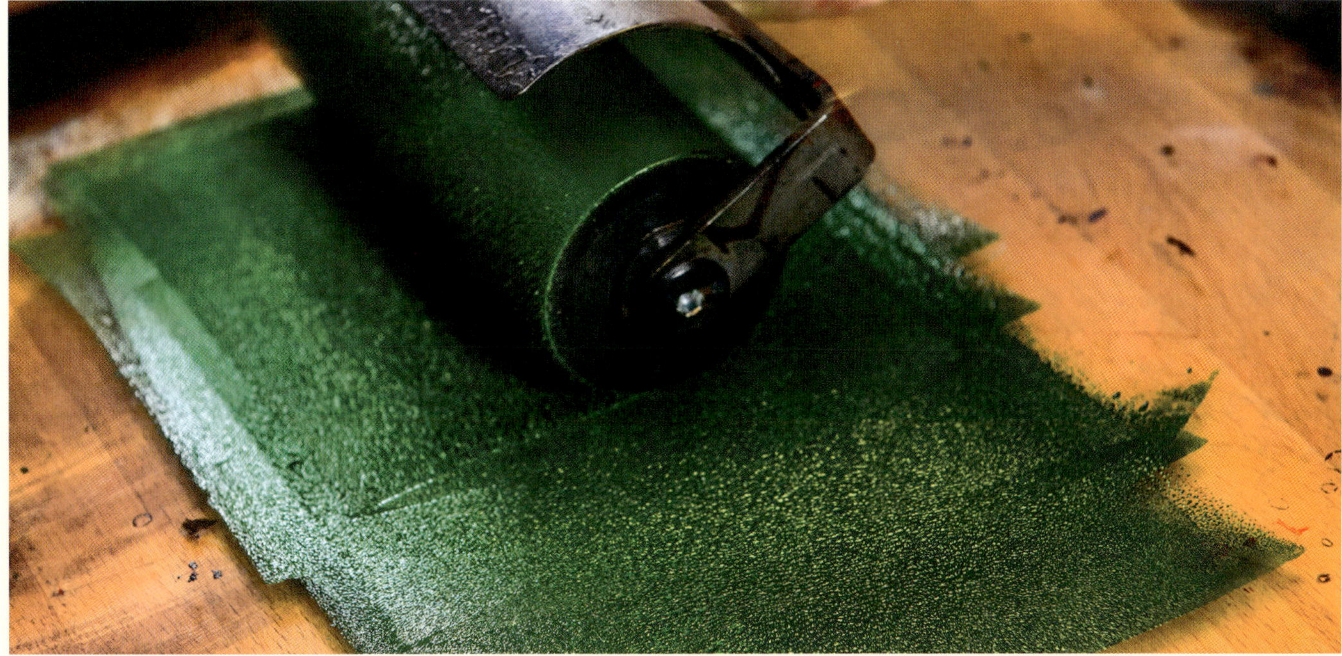

Old ink/new ink

There are advantages to both new and old ink. As a letterpress collector, I have acquired a lot of tins of ink when buying presses and parts, and so I do not really buy ink. I usually have something I can use, or that I can make work for my purpose. Old ink is what it is, old, and probably already opened and part-used. When I acquire tins of ink, I open them and see what condition they are in. Old ink will have formed a skin or crust – if you are careful you can open up a small area so you're able to get your pallet knife or screwdriver into the fresh sticky ink below. Look to see if the ink is still workable, I have found that (very rarely) the ink is dried solid or generally beyond use.

New ink doesn't have these problems; you will be buying exactly what you want, and what works for your environment. For instance, if you are printing at home, please use an ink that is a suitable – water-based inks are often less strong-smelling. We are lucky that letterpress has had a real resurgence, as it is much more known about than it was 20-odd years ago when I started on my journey. These days if you go into any good-quality art supply shop that sells printing inks, you'll find someone who knows what letterpress is and will be able to point you in the right direction. It's tempting to buy big straightaway, but buy small tubes to start testing them out.

Vintage orange ink.

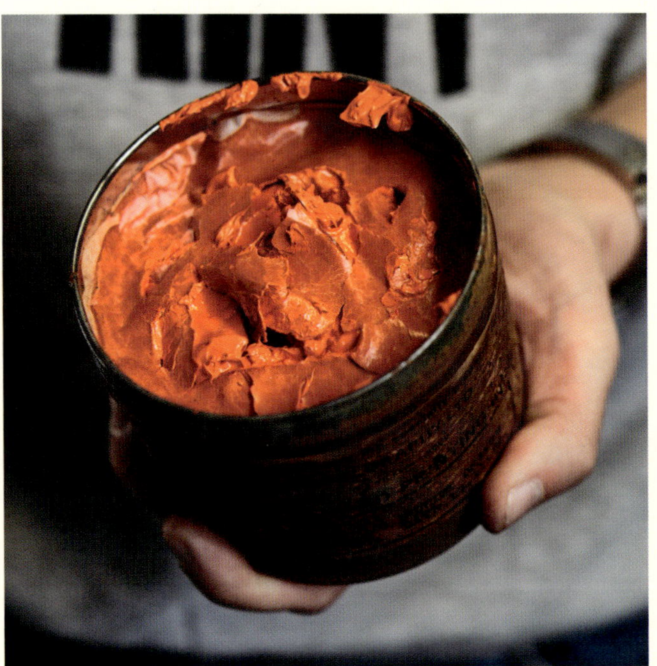

Warming ink

If you've created a working area in a shed, garage or a workshop, then the cold can cause problems. In cold weather oil-based ink gets stiffer and harder to roll out. You can warm your ink, and indeed warm your printing press – if it has a removable inking plate disc like an Adana or a jobbing press, then these can be placed near a heater. Your tins or tubes can also be placed near a heater to warm, just don't be silly and put things on heaters, as that is taking obvious risks. Warming an inking plate and ink slowly to normal room temperature will help make the ink flow better and keep inking and prints consistent.

Overheating ink can cause issues that you would never think of. I didn't initially realise that I had overheated a tin of brown ink once to such a level that the oils in the ink had changed its appearance. The brown ink on the print looked normal until natural light shone on it, showing a greenish sheen on the surface. Try to keep your printing space at a sensible average temperature.

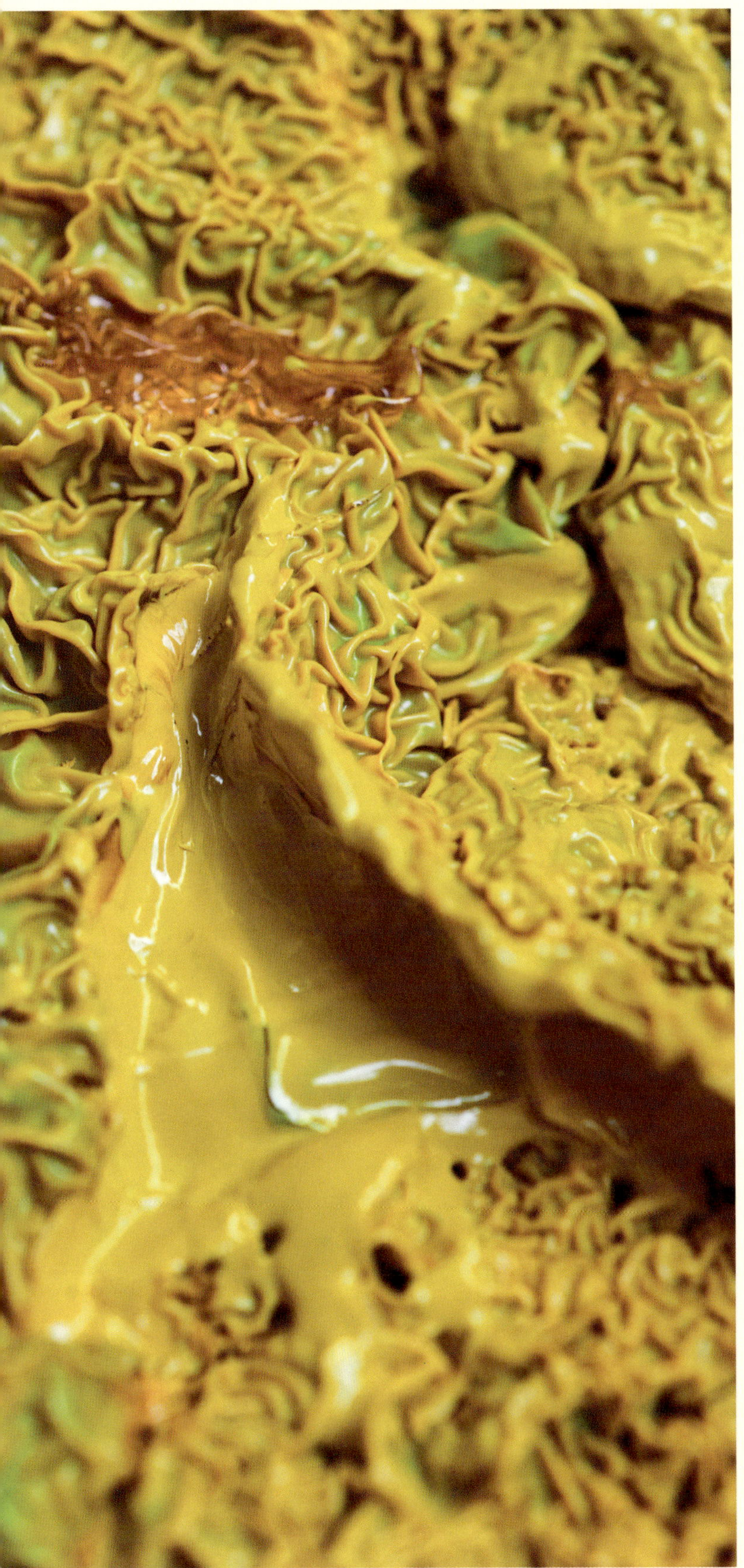

Testing colours and paper

The way colours look can be affected by the density of the ink that you are printing, not only in the thickness and stickiness of the ink, but the thickness of the layer that you apply. This change can be small and at other times, depending on the specific nature and make-up of the ink, can be much greater. Reds and greens for instance tend to have quite a lot of change from heavy to light inking. Sometimes it depends on what you are printing, with small lead type you will have to lightly ink the type's surface, otherwise heavy inking can result in bleed in the fine areas of type.

This can be compounded by the surface of the paper you are printing on. Using fine type on a highly textured paper surface, it is hard to achieve the perfect balance of ink and type pressure. Then you have large wood type with its beautiful grain that can be pressed into the paper to show its delicate nature with light inking, or the bold and punchy graphic nature of its design by heavy inking. This again is affected by the paper stock choices, as texture means more pressure to print, and when you start using highly textured papers, you can get to the point where the paper stock is dictating the printing effect more than you can. This is something that I do not like, I tend to always use light wove, uncoated paper and card stocks, then as a designer, artist and printer, I am in charge.

Close up of yellow ink showing skin/crust on ink.

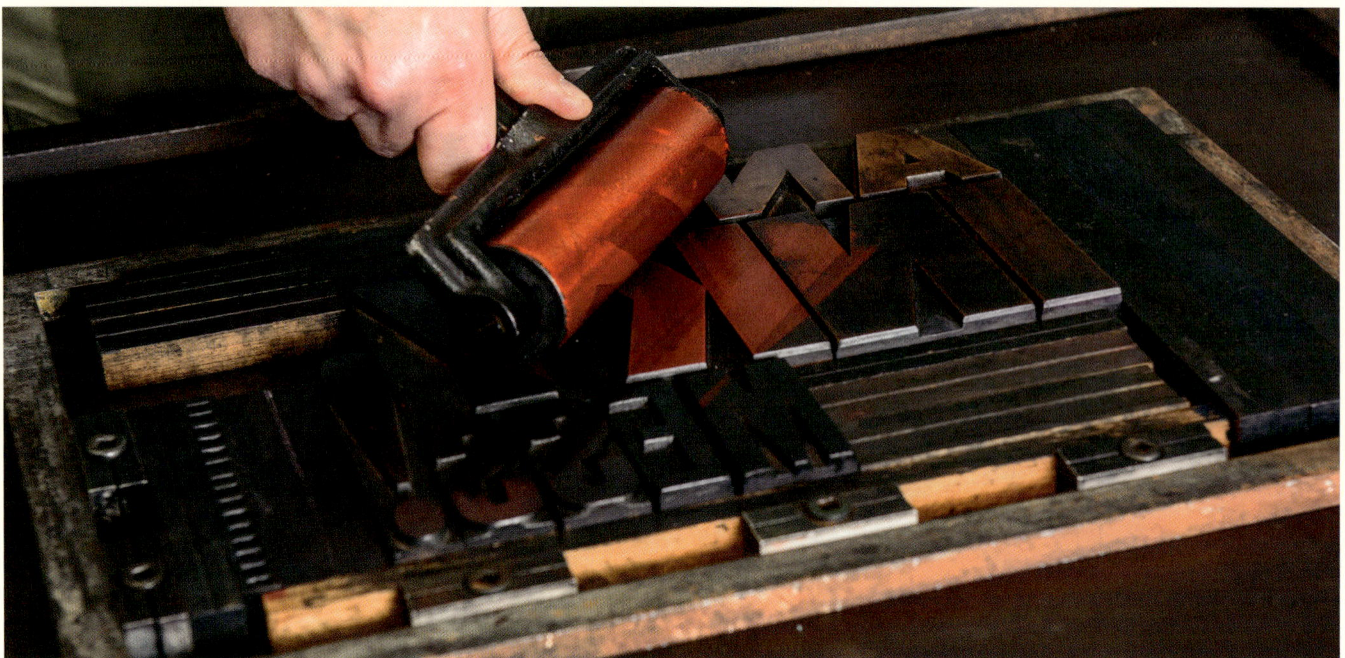

 Hand inking wood type.

Hand-inking

Hand-inking is something I love to do. Machine-inking is easier and quicker, and a must for longer print runs, but there is something special about rolling out ink onto your inking plate then transferring it to your printing surface as cleanly, evenly and smoothly as possible. You can always see the slight beauty and difference of a hand-inked print. It also gives you more control when you are working with type that may be a little battered, showing its age and the hard life it's had. With hand-inking you can focus on certain areas, to make sure that, for example, a damaged area of type gets a little ink applied at just the right spot so that it prints. These are the small details that automatic or machine-inking misses. I love to have the final say on all the small details on a print, and hand-inking gives me that.

Overlapping colours

Printing over the top of another colour in letterpress can be a complete joy when done correctly; with a little technique and expertise you can get the magic of the overlapping third colour, giving you the appearance of three colours when you only printed two. This can be a little hit or miss, and you need to think before you start printing. Work out which order is best to print the colours you are working with, to get the best effect. As with everything in life practice makes perfect, you will get used to what will and won't work.

To really get a good overlapping colour you need to follow the basic rule that light goes over dark, so your first print is always the darkest colour. To achieve a good and consistent overlapping colour, you will need to make sure that the first dark print is absolutely dry and the rollers and plate perfectly clean.

If not, you'll very quickly taint your light ink and ruin the process. To get a very clear and bright overlap of colour and to maximise the effect I mix transparent white into the chosen base colour. Transparent white is what it says it is, transparent; it will make your ink colour slightly lighter but not like when you mix opaque white into a colour, which weakens the strength. It's very different; you're effectively bulking out the ink and its pigments. This bulking out of the ink allows for the underneath colour to really pop and combine when you print over the top.

Colour theory is very important for this, and the common process colour combinations work well (cyan, magenta, yellow and black CMYK). When you start experimenting more you will find that some effects will be very pleasing, and some not so much. Everyone's own style and taste for design will direct the colour choices, it is great to just experiment with these sorts of techniques. Keep a collection of old misprints, as when you have an idea and you're not 100 per cent sure how the overlapping third colour will work, maybe you can find an old print in a similar first dark colour and do a quick second light ink test print over the top, saving drying time for a colour test. Of course, you are not restricted to just two colour overlaps – you can experiment with as many as you like!

Overlapping colours creating secondary colours.

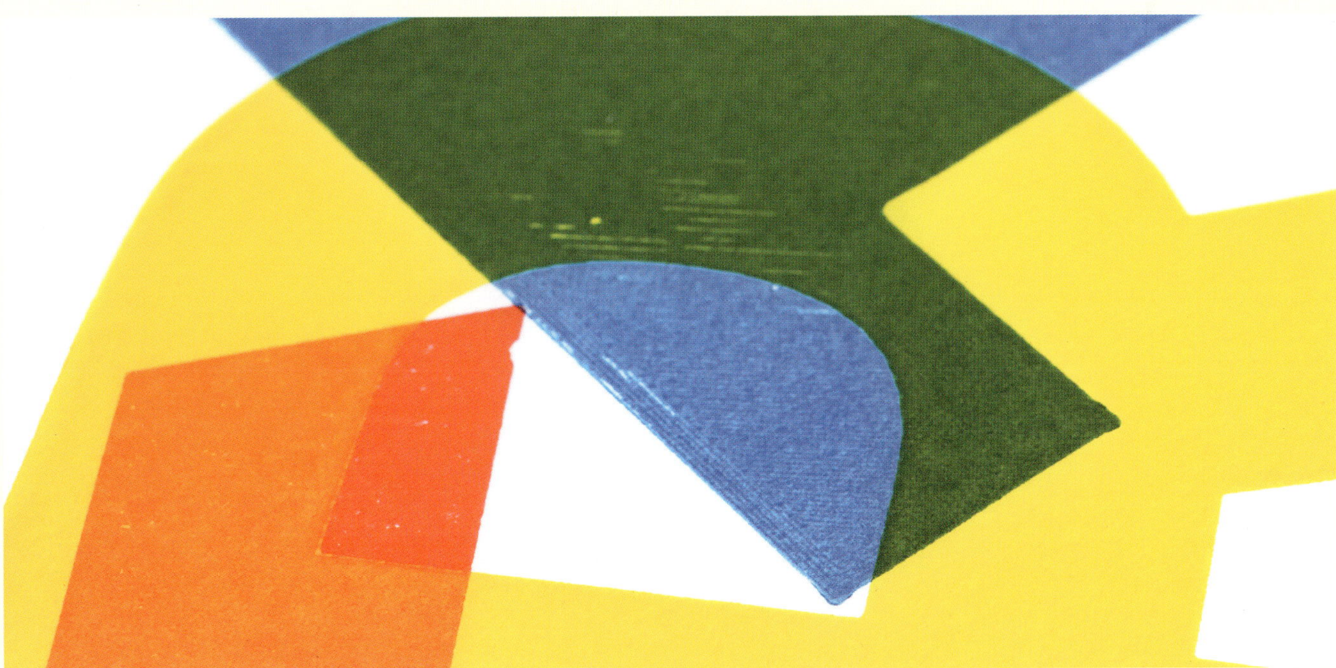

Split fountain

Gradient, split fountain and rainbow roll are a few of the common names for rolling out two or more colours on the same roller, causing a blend of the colours where they meet. Think of colours that go together separately, which when they mix, will form another colour well. My favourite colour combos include red to purple and yellow to red; both allow a pleasing middle colour that can fade smoothly between one and the other.

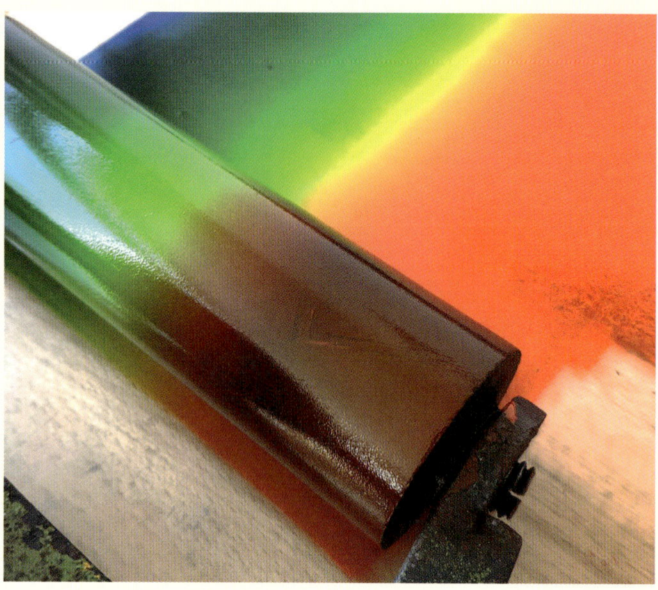

Hand roller creating multi colour blend.

The size of your roller will contribute towards how many colours you want to use. For instance, if you are printing on a Vandercook using the inking unit, you have a large roller area, but the inking unit and main inking roller is an oscillating roller, so the width of the blends is set by the press. Personally I only really do two-colour fades but I have achieved good three-colour fades using the Vandercook, and I have seen people online doing more colours. With the distance of the fade being dictated by the press, the issue is how long you can keep the gradient fade looking good, as over time the blending area extends, eventually so far that the colours are undefinable.

 Vandercook split fountain yellow to red.

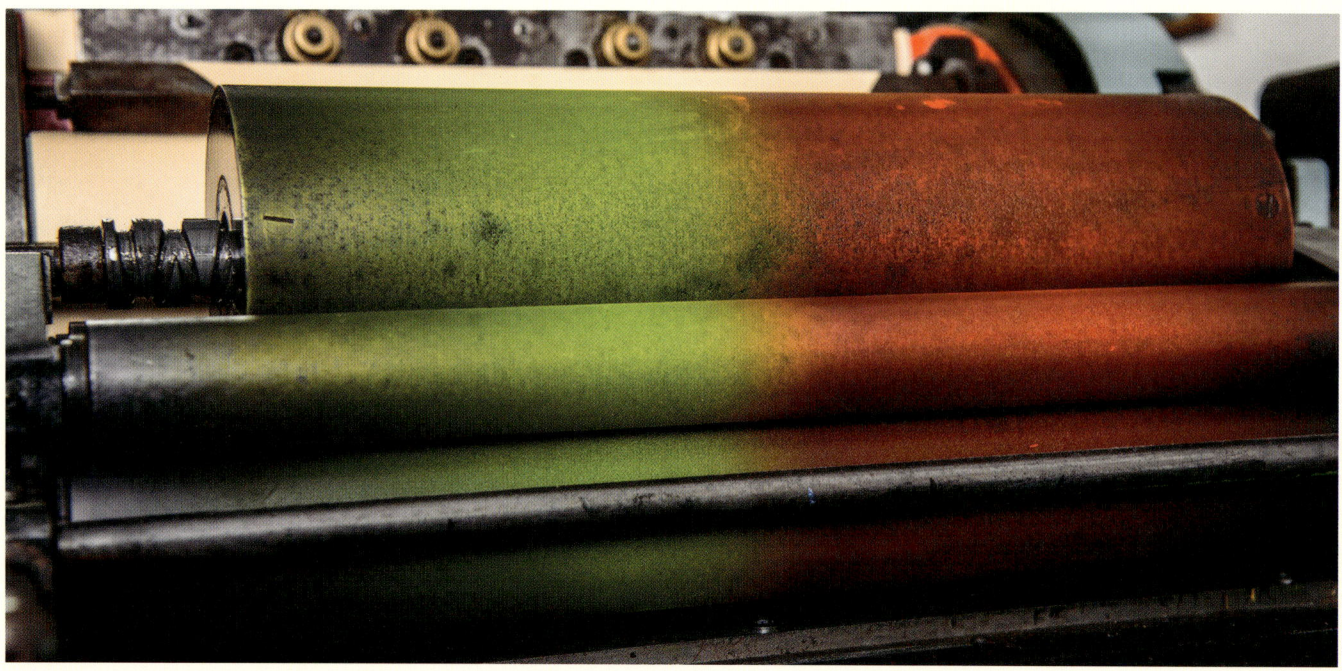

If you are doing smaller quantities of prints, then using a large hand roller is an option. If you don't have a large hand roller, you can do this with two separate rollers and make great prints, it just takes more time. To do a large colour fade, sit the two rollers you want to use on your inking plate, this is merely to give you a gauge of size of the rollers and where you will be putting ink. Take a moment, work out the overall size and spacing distance between the inks you are using, if it makes it easier, put a line of masking tape along the edge of the ink plate and draw lines where you want to put each of the original colours and how much blended area you want. Then, place equal quantities of each ink in a line, take the pallet knife, and slide the ink over to create lines of ink. You really want to get the two colours close to each other, as it will help give you a nice tight blend, and then you don't have to try over-rolling your ink to get the two colours to meet. Take your first roller and start to roll out one half of the ink, just go back and forth to start with to get the ink nicely rolled out. Repeat this process with the second roller, you should now have a rolled-out section over two rollers. Now for the fun part, using your first roller, roll the ink out again but this time shifting the roller slightly left and right, then repeat again with the second roller. You'll then reach the point where the two rollers cross over. Note that when hand-rolling you can dictate the blend thickness with the roller.

Now you need to carefully transfer the ink to the printed surface. Make sure that you have the right spacing for your inking and simply transfer the ink in a straight line thus keeping the blend intact and repeat with the second roller. With this technique you cannot change the direction of inking, so if one side's not inking enough, collect and apply more. Play around with this technique, it's good fun and can offer up some inking treats.

Vandercook printing a slit fountain effect red to yellow.

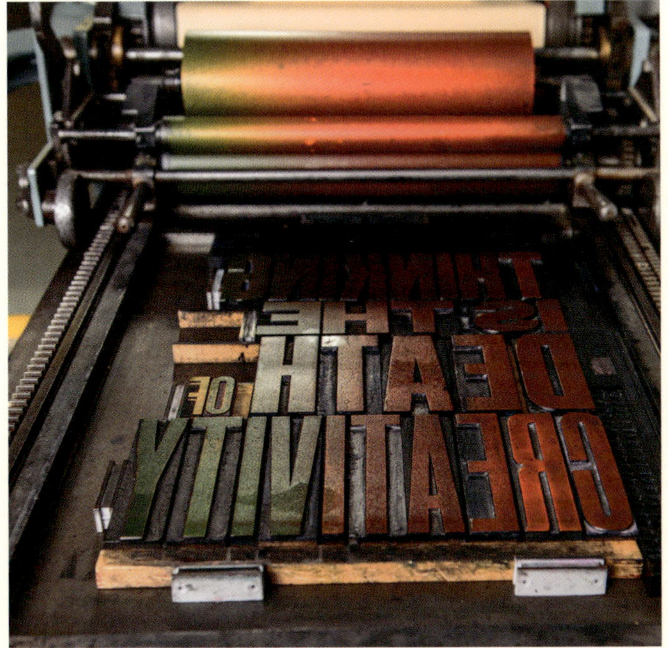

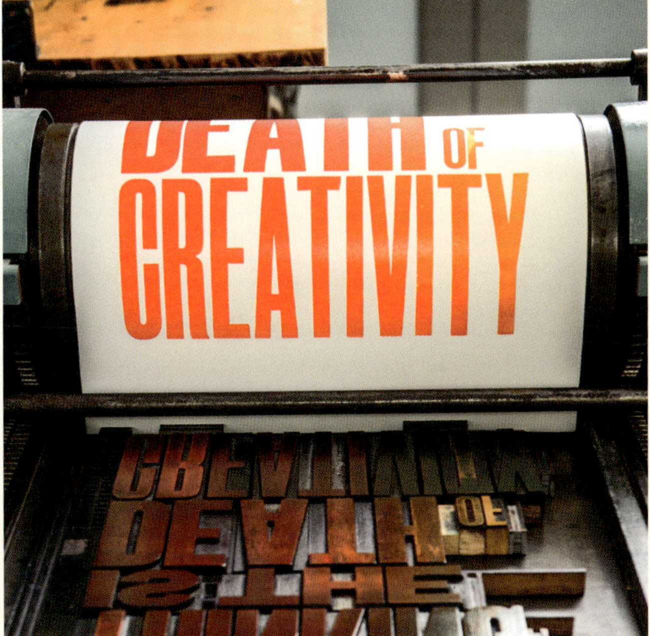

Print runs

It's worth spending some time looking at the difference between pulling one or two prints, and printing larger consistent print runs. There are some basic things you can do to prepare for doing a long run that will pay dividends.

Materials

Make sure the size of the material you are printing with is as consistent as possible. Take your wad of printing paper or card and bang it against a surface on one edge to see if all the sheet sizes are exactly the same size. If they're not and you have significant inconsistency, you'll need to consider recutting. If that's not an option due to not having a guillotine, or if the difference is quite slight (1 mm or less), then make sure you print all your sheets of paper by loading them into the press the same way around, as then the base line of any type or design printed is always in the same spot.

The problems that you can encounter can be quite simple, like the paper or card being cut slightly on the angle, which can make quick changeover of sheets of paper difficult. If you're printing multi-coloured prints with tight alignment, then the paper size difference can cause all sorts of problems with alignment. It's very easy to suddenly have a lot of misprints due to misalignment. By paying attention to all the small details you really refine your process, reducing the opportunity for problems to arise.

Fanning your paper/card

Picking paper up can be surprisingly fiddly, particularly if you are doing it very repetitively and quickly. To fan your paper means to take your paper in a wad, bang it lightly on your work surface so all the sheets are lined up, then grip and hold one side of your paper and with your other hand move the other side of the paper to form a U shape, the edge of the paper on the loosely held side will form a triangle. Grip the triangle-edged side of the block of paper and then let go with the first gripping hand, now put your paper in the ideal location for printing on your work surface. Your paper is now stacked and stepped very slightly, making it much easier to pick up individual sheets. Card is much easier to pick up than paper, thin paper can be particularly difficult and slow to pick up and put in the press, so this simple technique is a good time saver.

Fanned stack of printing paper.

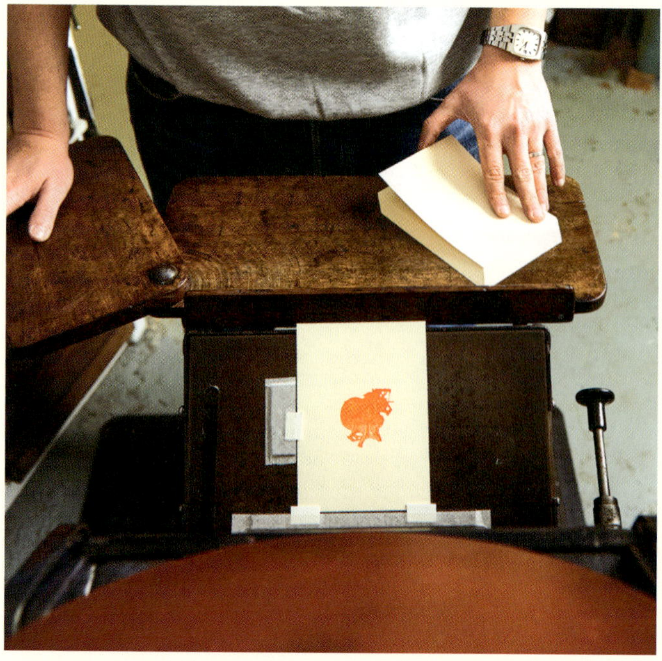

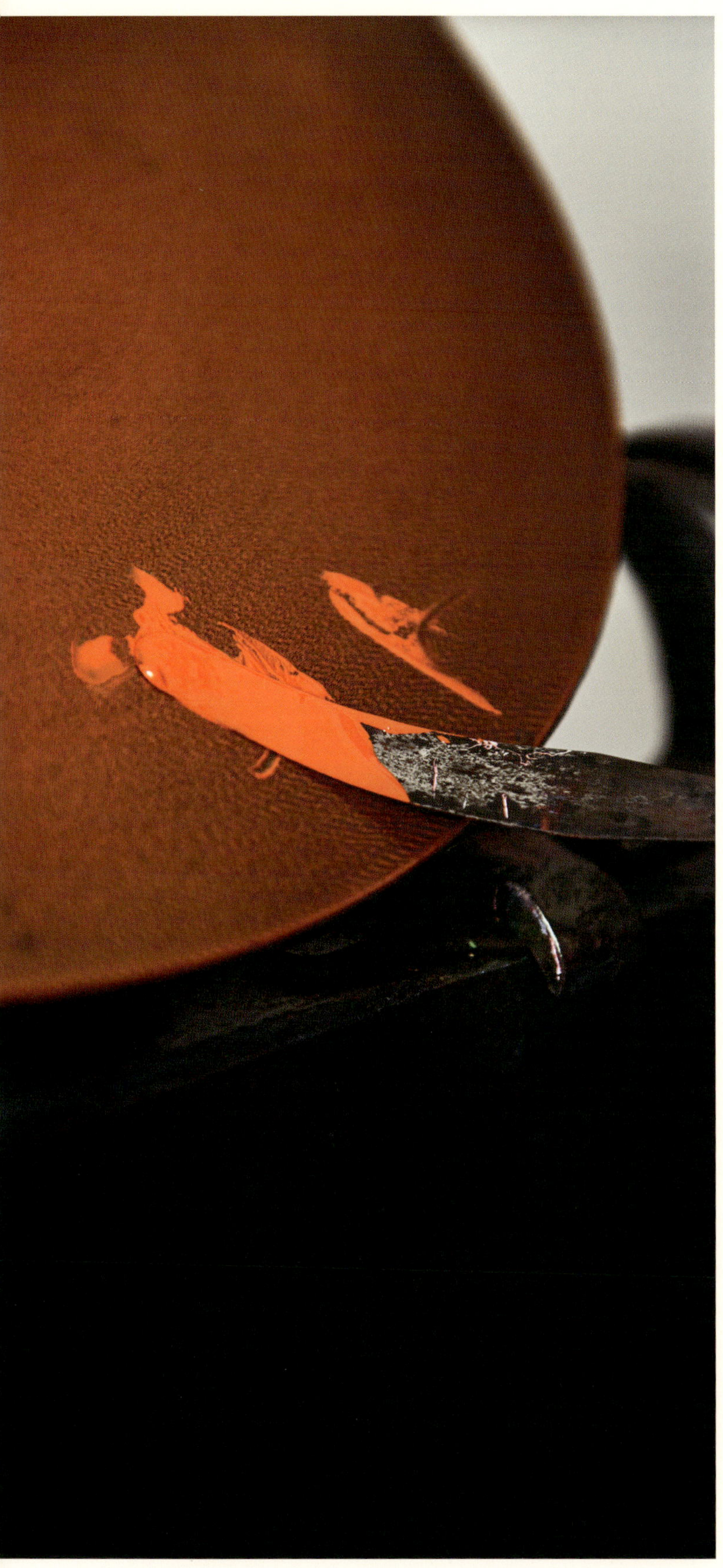

Inking

Ink levels are sometimes hard to keep static and even; constant checking is required and a keen eye for detail is key. There are some basic tips and tricks that you can follow. Always keep the first good print you pull, this is your reference print, then print in batches of 10s or 25s, whatever works for you. Take the last print from each batch and quickly compare with the reference print to check the colour hasn't changed, and the print is correctly located on the page.

As you print and consume ink, the colour will start to lighten. Depending on the colour that you're printing with, this may or may not make a big difference. Black ink is generally unaffected by the thickness of the ink, but you will get a slight textural change. Whereas green is a colour that seems to change quickly, and the difference can be quite dramatic. Keep checking prints; if the light is not great in your workspace, move and try other light sources. You want to aim to always be ahead of the print, so you need to try to predict when the ink is going to start to run low. This becomes very important when using a printing press that has machine inking, as it takes time to add more ink.

Adding more ink to a printing press like an Adana or a jobbing press can be done in a couple of simple ways, and the choice of how really comes down to what you are printing. If you are only printing something that is small and relatively lightly inked, then you can add a touch of ink directly to the circular ink plate, putting the ink on the outer-most right edge of the inking plate.

Adding ink to inking disc.

You need to make sure that you place the ink on the very edge of the inking disc, as this doesn't align with any type you are printing. This then will feed round onto the inking plate slowly as you print, and the fresh ink will not spread out unevenly.

If you are printing something larger, then you'll need to stop printing, remove your chase, add more ink to your inking plate, evenly re-inking your rollers, then re-insert your chase and get printing again. Be careful and sensible with how much ink you apply, as it can be tempting to add more in an attempt to cut down on stopping and starting – this can give you a bigger problem of over-inking, leaving you with prints looking smudged, undefined, and lacking quality. The prints will also take longer to dry, and the colour will then be a bit darker. Take your time with your inking, it will show in your prints.

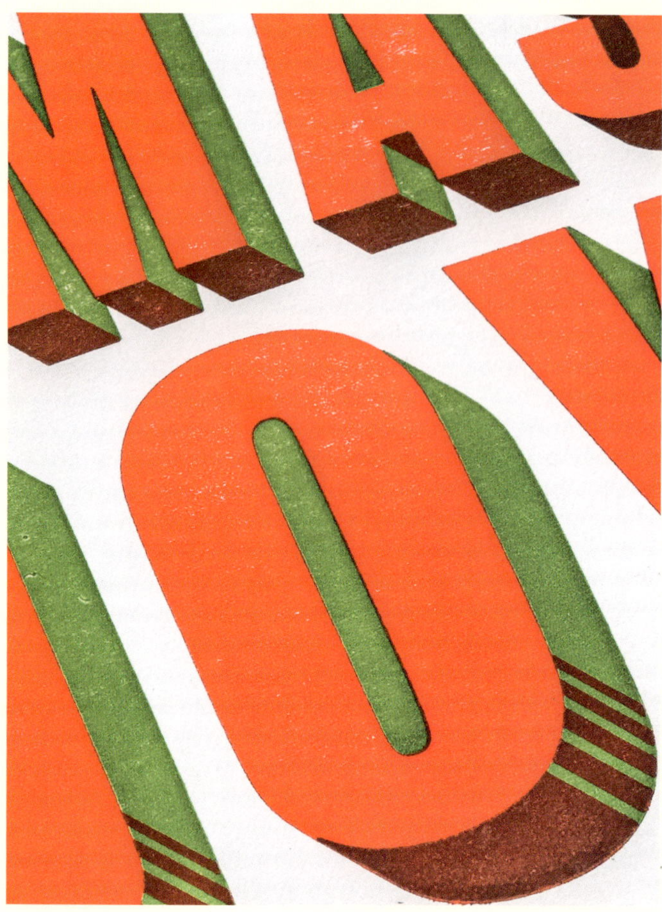

Tight registration/alignment when printing.

Alignment

Keeping consistently aligned prints in longer print runs is not as simple as you would think, you really need high-quality control. Even a fraction of a millimetre's misalignment will be noticeable – tiny differences can cause problems. Make sure all the paper or card that you are printing with is cut nicely and is in good condition. Dampness and moisture in your paper can cause rippling, particularly to thinner paper stocks, making feeding paper into your press harder. If you do not get the paper onto its registration points perfectly, then this will show on multi-coloured prints. If your card is not cut well and if you don't place your paper in the same direction each time you print, the size difference can knock your following prints out of position.

Poster prints

Pulling larger format prints requires more ink so hand-inking is simpler – you can add more ink to your inking plate as you go. Machine-inking larger runs on machines like Vandercooks does speed up the process, with the use of the inking unit.

To add ink to a Vandercook, simply turn the handle on the top side of the inking roller unit to raise the rollers from making contact with the bottom inking drum. With the top metal drum roller not spinning, smear small dollops of ink in a line across the metal drum with a pallet knife. Lower the rollers back down to make contact with the powered roller in the printing press. You will be able to see that the top large metal roller is oscillating back and forth to allow the ink to become even and smooth. It's worth watching this process as you will become familiar with the size of the oscillation of the roller, which is good to remember for when you want to do split fountains or two-colour gradients.

At this point you have fresh ink on your rollers and you are ready to go. This is quicker, but you'll need to periodically apply more ink to the top metal roller. Being more productive and printing faster is great, but think before you start how and where you will be putting your prints to dry, otherwise you can end up stopping a lot just to find places to dry prints.

Hand-inking poster prints is a lot quicker for cleaning down, and does offer you some more options when it comes to style and finish. For instance, if you have a nice collection of inking rollers both large and small, then you can ink certain areas of the print with specific colours, which is not an option when printing using the inking unit. With larger prints, don't get tempted towards the end of a longer run to try to run the ink out and not apply more for the last few prints. You'll only be disappointed with their quality.

Poster prints using wood type, lines printed using wood furniture and lino cut for coloured patches.

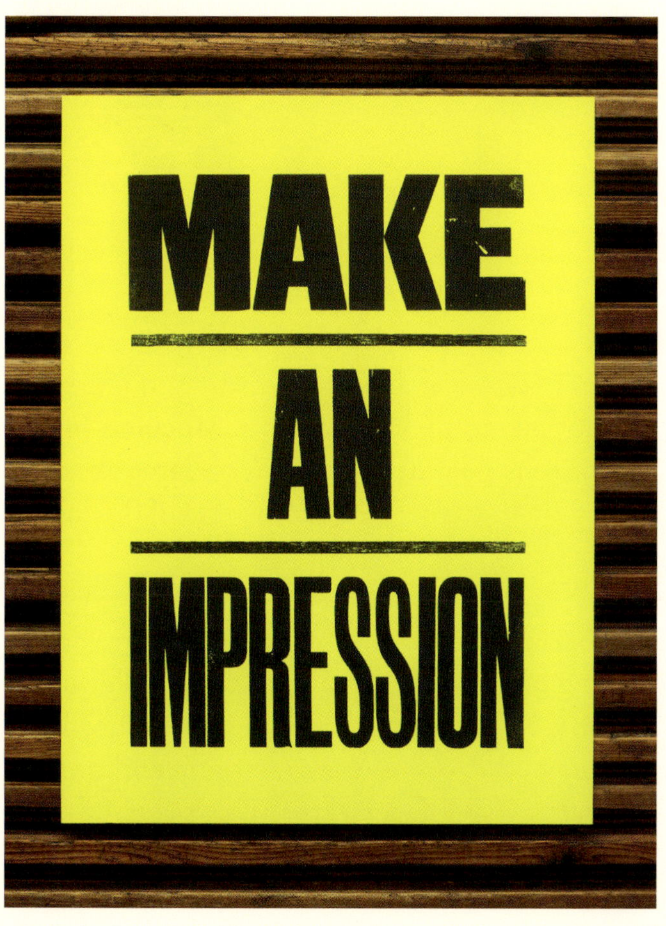

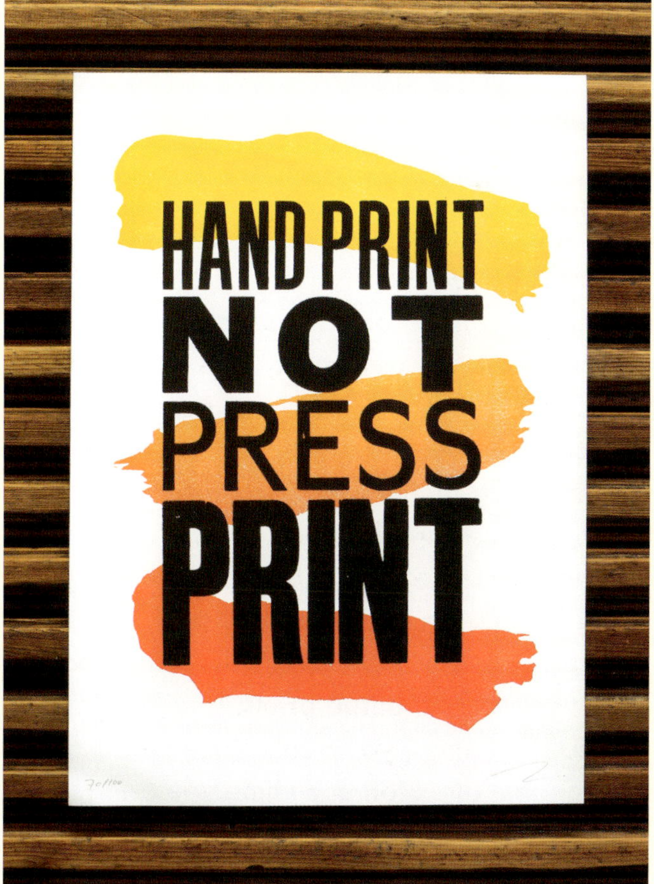

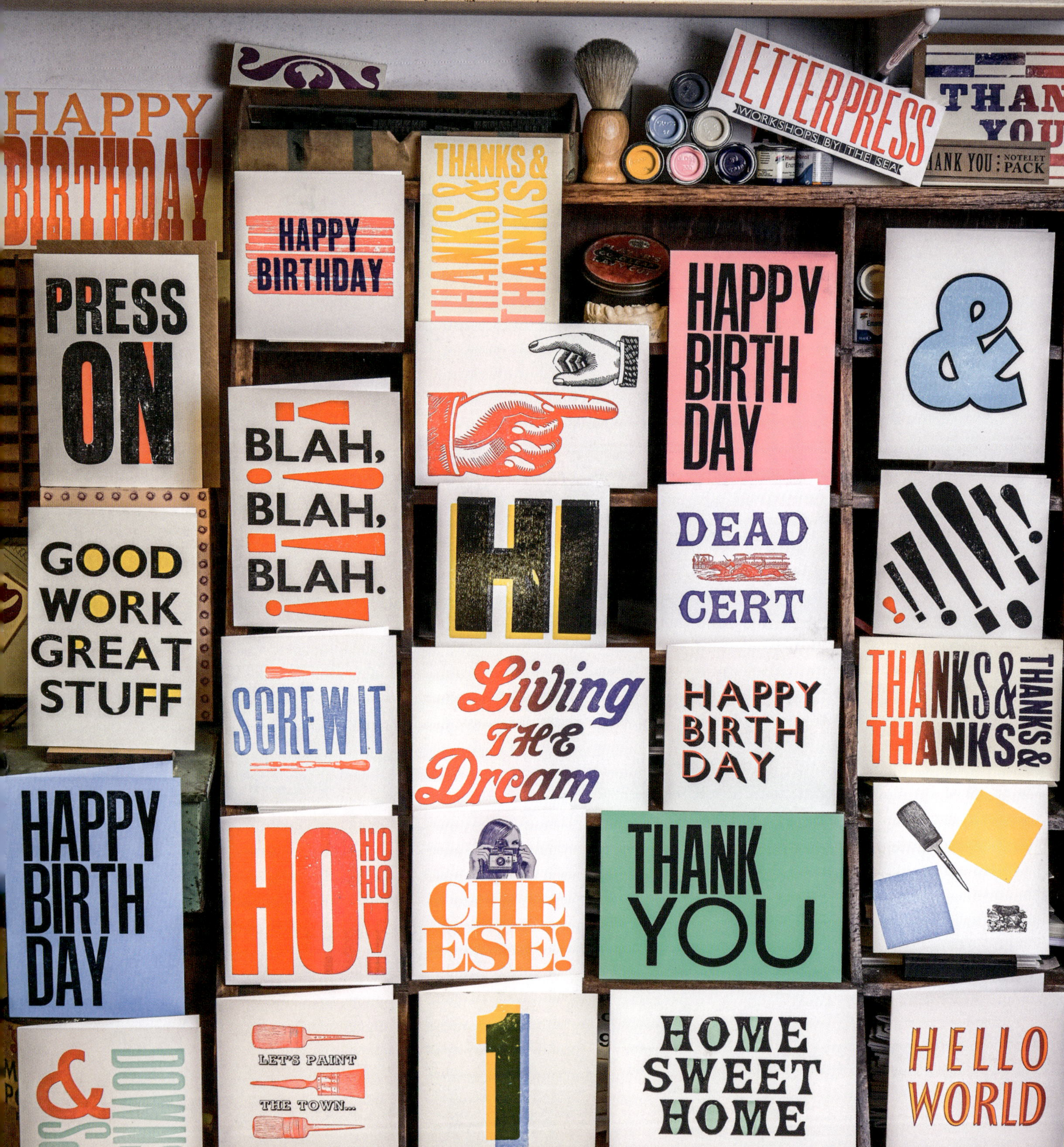
HAPPY BIRTHDAY
LETTERPRESS
WORKSHOPS BY THE SEA
THANK YOU
NOTELET PACK
HAPPY BIRTHDAY
THANKS & THANKS
PRESS ON
HAPPY BIRTH DAY
&
BLAH, BLAH, BLAH.
HI
DEAD CERT
GOOD WORK GREAT STUFF
SCREW IT
Living THE Dream
HAPPY BIRTH DAY
THANKS & THANKS & THANKS &
HAPPY BIRTH DAY
HO HO HO!
CHEESE!
THANK YOU
LET'S PAINT THE TOWN...
1
HOME SWEET HOME
HELLO WORLD
UPS & DOWNS

8

Let's get experimental

Traditional processes offer up a lot of creative options and plenty of fun. As you develop your way through printing with letterpress, you'll get to know that even with the restrictions on fonts, colours and printing area size, you're able to make unique prints and products using this age-old craft. In this chapter we are going to look at some of the different options you have to let creativity shine, showing that this craft is only limited by the imagination of the printer using it.

There are some simple but useful techniques you can learn; adjusting different type heights, printing with unusual objects, mixing and matching traditional type with picture blocks or other objects, and printing them all at the same time! There are some tips and tricks, offering great and inspiring results that can be used for your next print. Towards the end of the chapter, I will also give you some simple hands-on activities that will get you printing and making. Including, one of my favourite things to make, a stab-bound notebook.

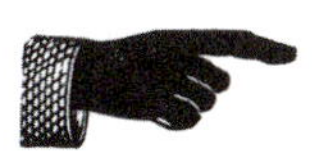

Type height, and getting there

A note on international type heights. Type height in this book is referred to as 0.918in or 23.32mm, which is the standard used and available in the UK (where I am based) and America. Other countries in Europe use slightly different height systems, with their type mostly being 23.56mm high. To compound this discrepancy, you then find that some countries like Holland have their own local type heights. This is worth bearing in mind if you are not reading this book in the UK or America, and if you're looking at purchasing type internationally. Mixing different heights of type can cause issues.

Type height is important in letterpress, and perfecting type height can be tricky. As previously mentioned, adding a small piece of tape or paper to the back of type or a printing block can completely change the quality and impression both physically and visually.

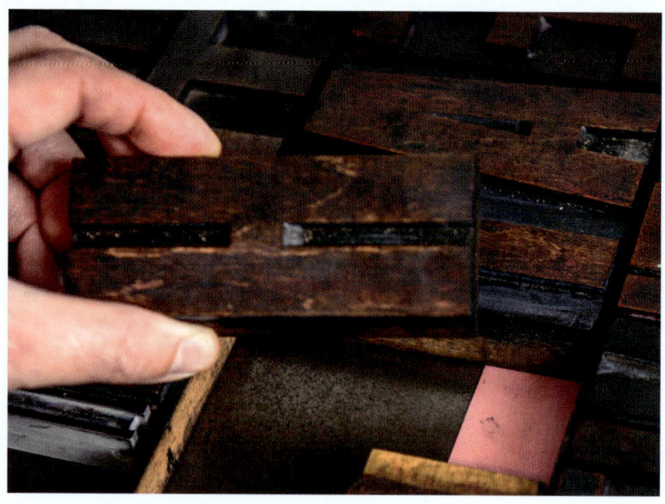

Piece of thin card added under type to raise individual letter.

Personally, I like to add images, illustrations and sometimes just areas of colour to a print, to make it my own. For this I often use hand-cut lino blocks or printing plates (photopolymers that I make in-house), which need to be raised up to type height for printing. Photopolymer printing plates are possible to make, if you have the time, experience, knowledge and

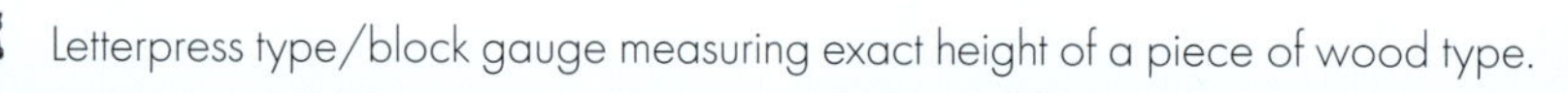

Letterpress type/block gauge measuring exact height of a piece of wood type.

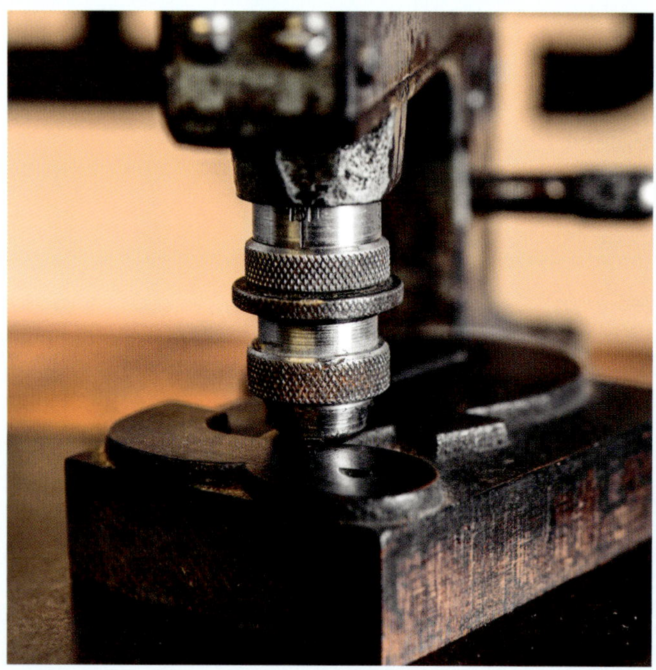

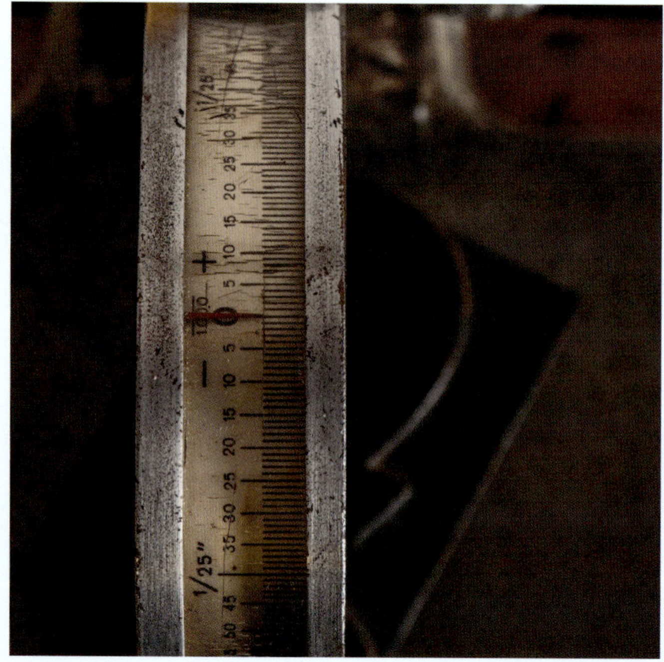

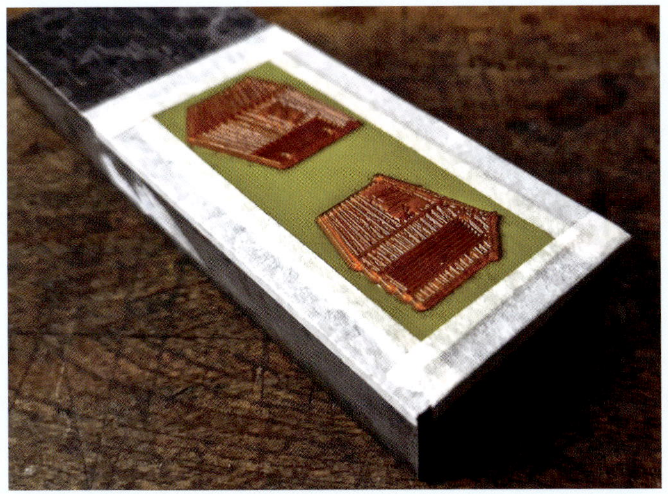

Photopolymer plate mounted to a mounting block.

equipment. The alternative is creating your design on your computer to order online and have your plates delivered to you.

If you scour eBay, you may get lucky and find old metal blocks that were designed to have printing plates mounted to them, giving you the perfect type height. With these you can simply take your printing plate, trim down any excess backing material that is on the plate, and secure in place on your mounting block with a line of tape. When using the correct polymer plates with a mounting block, you shouldn't need any packing to fine tune it for printing. If it does not print well, treat it like any piece of wood type and simply add a thin piece of paper or masking tape to the reverse side of the mounting block to raise the height a tiny amount.

If you are printing with very large printing plates incorporating smaller blocks into a larger print and need to fit the printing plate into a small space, the issue is that you won't have the correct-size mounting block. It's good to develop the skills and knowledge of making your own base or mounting block, which isn't difficult. Start by working out how thick your printing material is, for instance if you are printing with lino, you can use a ruler or a pair

Enlarged version of original wood block printer's fist cut in lino, includes tools and print.

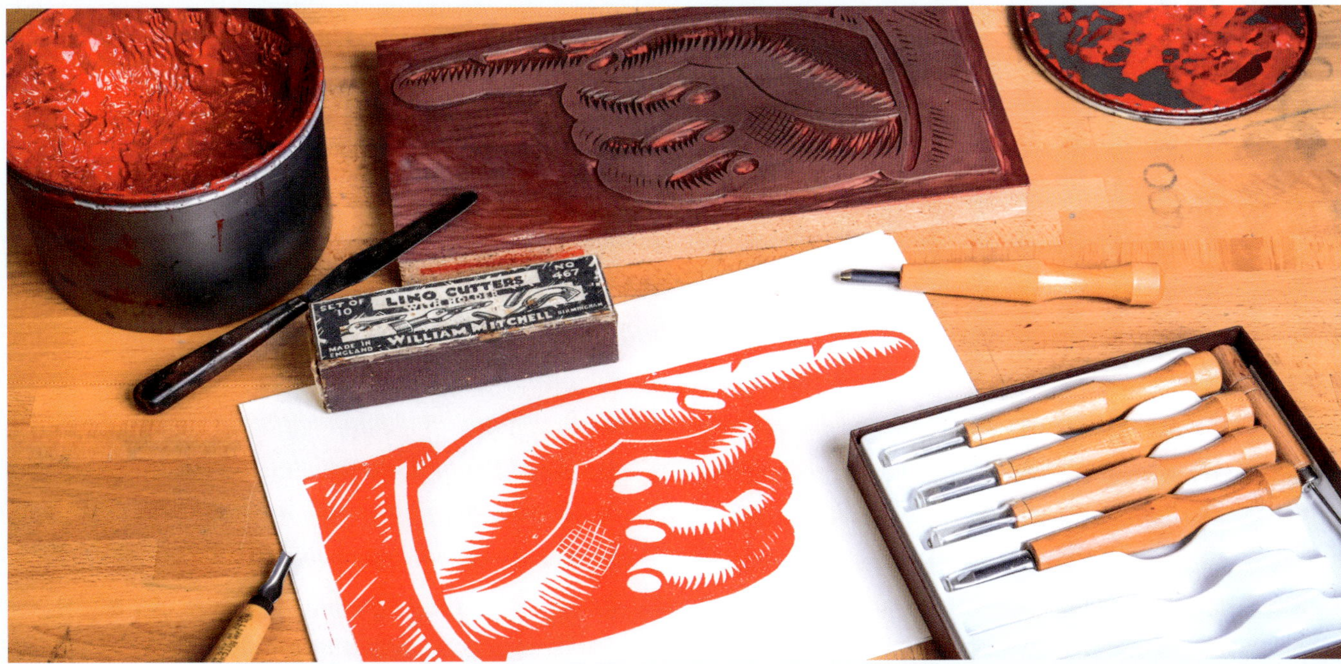

of callipers to check precisely. It probably says on any packaging sheet, but it is always good to double-check. You can then subtract this number from UK type height which is 23.32mm or 0.918in to get the correct thickness of backing material that you will need. You need to find a piece of timber that is as close to this thickness as possible.

A lot of sheet wood and timber materials come in 18mm and some in 21mm, however the thickness measurements that are given on timber are often not very accurate. When I purchase material to use for backing, I go to local suppliers with a pair of callipers in my pocket so I can search through sheets of timber until I find a piece that is the exact thickness that I require. From there you can cut the wood into whatever size you wish.

Remember to try to cut and sand all the edges as square as possible, as wonky edges will cause you problems while locking out. It's also worth thinking outside the box when considering what to use for a mounting block, and look around with an open mind, I once used free samples of oak floorboards that were exactly the right thickness. If you can't find something just right, then go for something that's lower than the ideal height, and pack out the mounting block to bring it up to height. When you have larger areas of packing out to do, then it's worth using something like thick grey board and then thinner card under a sheet of ply to achieve the increased height. This gives you the basic principle of bringing an item up to type height.

Unusual printing objects

You can pretty much print with whatever you want as long as it's flat – you just need to focus on creating a type-high surface. You need to think three-dimensionally about the process. When I am printing with unusual objects that are not traditional letterpress, I tend to start with a very basic wooden 18mm board, from there you can work out how much the height difference is between your item, your 18mm board and the type height you need (0.918in). Then using the same technique as described for lino, mount your item using double-sided carpet tape (stronger and often cheaper than standard double-sided tape). In the past I've enjoyed making different textures, backgrounds and generally experimenting to see what I enjoy printing. I particularly enjoy fast intuitive printing – the act of just going with it, working in the moment.

I always have rolls of tape lying around my workshop. For one print I simply took a basic 18mm block that was roughly the right

What day is it print.

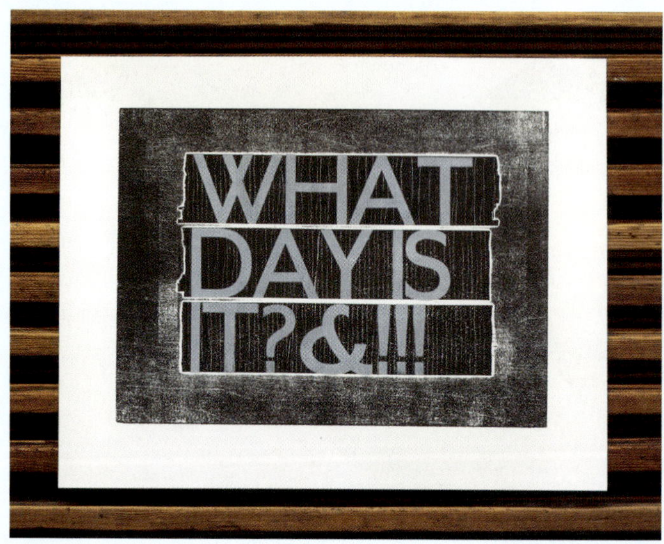

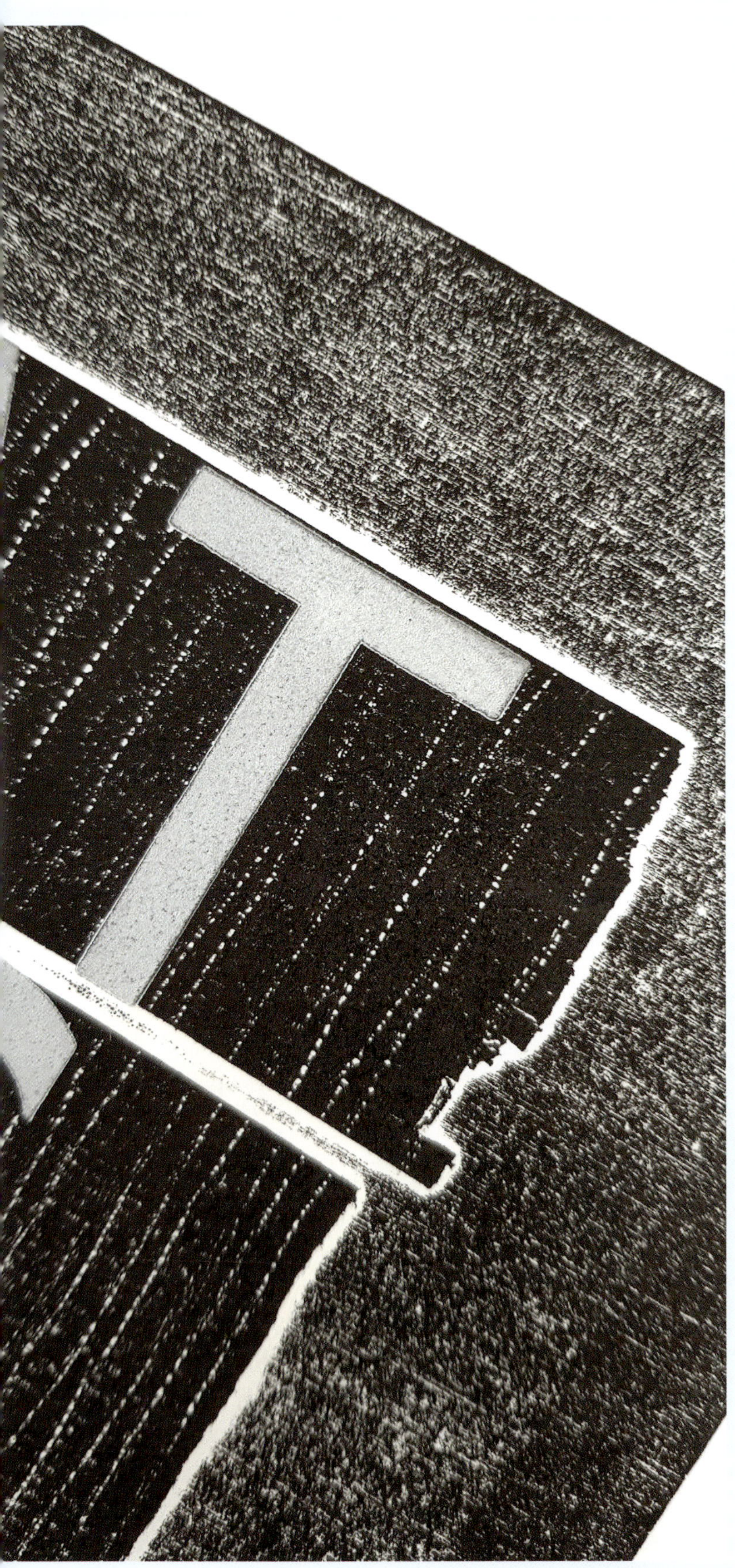

dimensions for the print I was working on, but it was just not yet working for me. I took a roll of gaffer tape, tore three pieces off, stuck them onto the board and printed both the board and the tape to create a background for my type. The tape produced an interesting texture and unprinted halo of white around it.

I played around a little with the pressure of the printing press (using packing sheets) and found I could lighten or darken the overall background by increasing the pressure. I also found that I could print just the tape if I applied a few lines of tape on top of each other. Ultimately, I decided to stick with my first prints with the tape and the background printed.

You can use this approach to print simple things like leaves, using double-sided tape to secure in place – just be aware that depending on their condition, they may start to deteriorate. It is worth thinking about how your paper is applied and secured when printing like this, as, if you are using a press like a Vandercook with gripper bars, it removes the paper directly after printing, which isn't necessarily delicate enough. If using a press with such mechanisms, try applying the paper manually and then just using the press for the pressure. Or go back to basics and use a baren and rub the print, this often gives its own effects and can add a different dimension to your print if it's multi-layered.

☚ Close up of print, printed using gaffer tape, wooden board and traditional wood type.

Mixing and matching

Part of the joy of creating with traditional and manual processes is that you are working with your hands to produce whatever you can imagine. You should not feel restricted to work with only one form at a time – mix things up, you can print with wood type, metal type, a hand-cut lino block and all at the same time. All you really need to worry about is how you are locking your type out; if you are using a flat-bed press this process is much easier, as gravity is your friend and any small movement has minimal impact.

Think about changing things up a bit with what you are printing onto. I have worked with students who've taken sheets of paper, glued brightly coloured torn pieces of very thin paper on top of their original sheets then printed, which gave really nice effects. If the thickness of the paper is not a great difference, then the impact on the overall print is minimal. If your inking is good then this creates an interesting effect. You can also block off areas that you are printing with torn paper to create negative areas of the print. If you pull multiple layers of the print over the top of each other, removing different sections at a time then it gives different effects, sometimes it can give a military camo effect, other times very clean and graphical. Also think about printing onto other sources of paper, this could be a terribly damaged old book from a car boot fair, a newspaper, an old map or just printing over the top of old test prints. Really just allow yourself to play around and find what works for you.

Fun inking

The way you ink a print is often seen as a very static thing, with just one colour being used. You can use secondary colours to pick out specific areas of a print to highlight a word, to pull the viewer's eye in a certain direction. Again, this is quite a static use of inking and printing with the effect being clean and often quite formal in its intent and design.

Letterpress can be bold and exciting, and this can be represented by the use of dynamic inking techniques. Using ink in a more dynamic and fluid way does have is positives and negatives. Experimenting is fun, and through experimenting you discover new effects. Often you'll have something in your mind for an ink colour that just works, but sometimes after printing you find that you didn't get the results that you were expecting. This is when I start to play around with different inking options.

For example, I had a nice composition for a design and I was sure it would work as a one-colour print. It read 'the will to do will see us through'. I visualised it in a bold, plain red ink, but when printed it looked boring, and I didn't like the layout or colour! I decided to add in a second colour with a rough, choppy and jarring intersection between the two inked colours, using my favourite red and black combination. For me this completely changed the read and feel of the design. I refer to this style of inking as a directional, interruptive inking, or creating a visual noise to a print. If you use high-contrasting colours you can make designs feel very different, forcing the viewer to stop and start reading because of the changes in the ink.

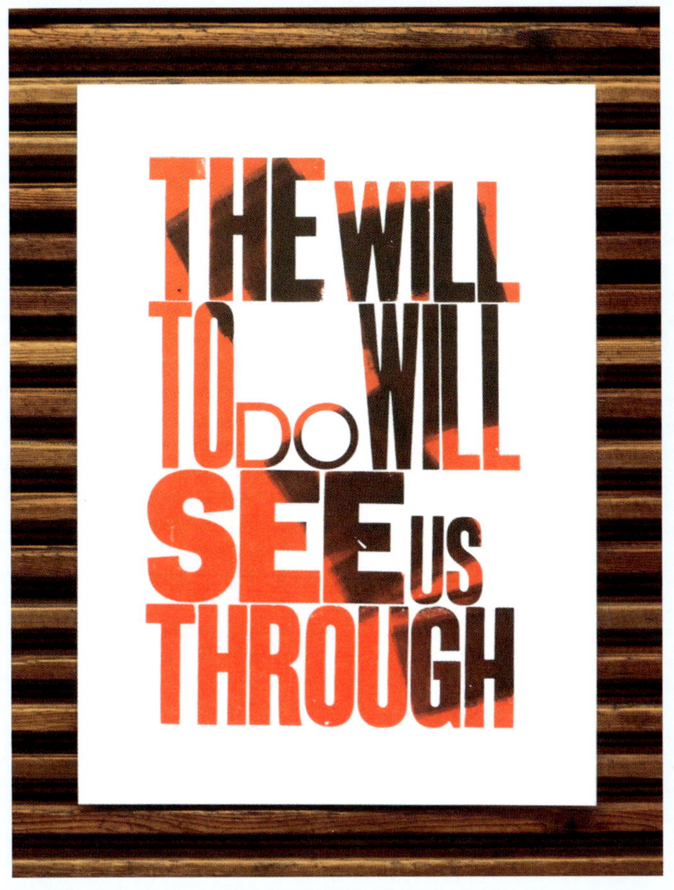

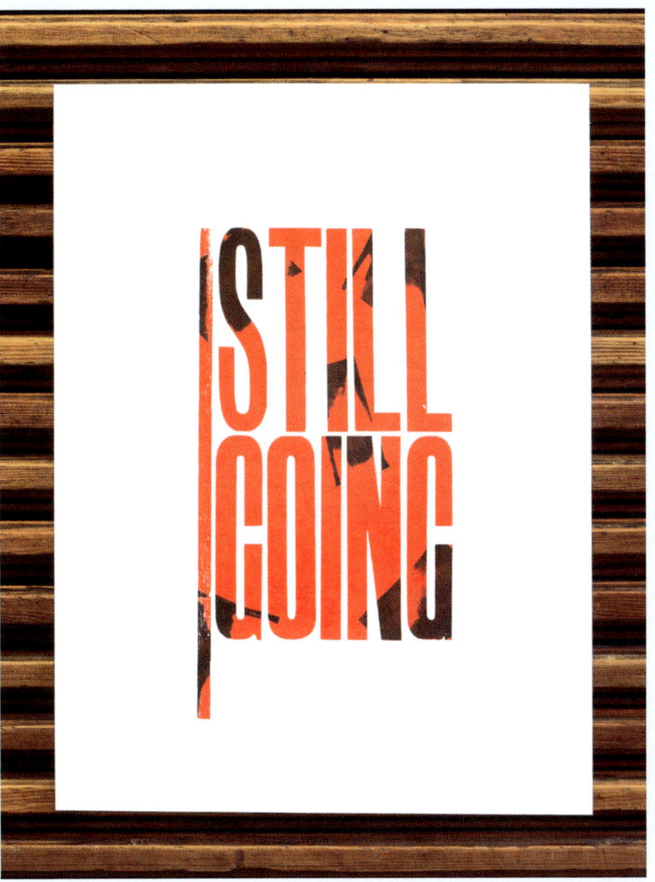

Inking to add visual noise/more interest/direction and flow to a print. 

To achieve this, it is really as simple as it looks, though with some planning you can make your life a little easier.

I started by cleaning off the plain red ink that was originally on the type, then I inked most of the type in red on the sort of angle that I thought would work. Then with the black roller, I inked all the type that had not already been inked, ignoring any overlapping of the red, just with the aim of getting two sections of type inked. I then reloaded my roller with black ink and without thinking added the inky overlap.

Prints like these are great for one-offs but pulling multiples is tricky. In the case of this print I found that I could very carefully re-ink the red, making sure that I did not come in contact with any of the black, as this would taint the brilliant bright red. For each subsequent print in the run, I overlapped the black a little more into the red, the black slowly getting larger and the red area smaller, pulling seven or eight prints before the effect starts to change and the red area looked too small. When this happens, the only option is to clean the wood type, wait a few minutes to make sure there was no residue from the cleaning chemicals and then start over again.

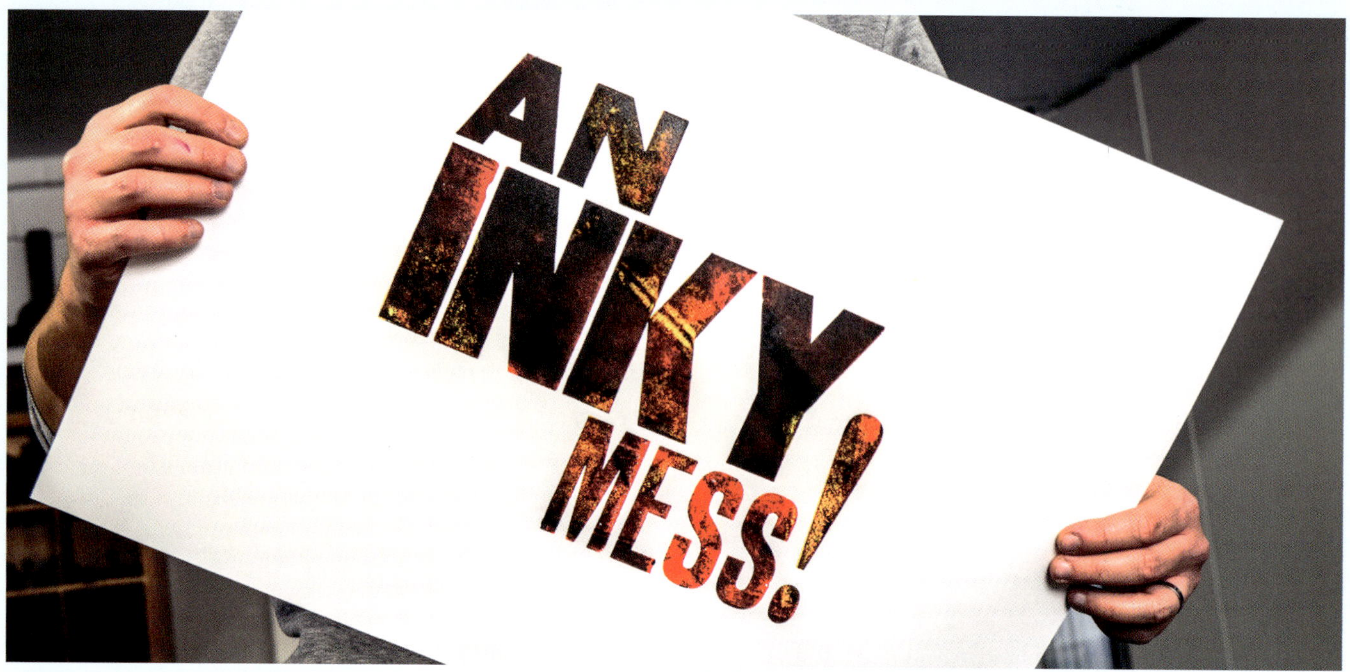

Multiple colours of inks overlayed to give unique inking effect.

This technique of rolling colours over the top of one another can be used in many different ways, in some cases if you accept the one-off nature of this way of inking, then you can pull some amazing prints. It is really a technique that requires playing with, on some days, you will create something truly beautiful and on other days, more of an inky mess.

Using smaller rollers helps to give you a better level of control over the inking, and what is overlapping. If you use the basic logic of trying not to mix the darker colours into your ink through roller transfer then the impact on the original colour will not be so impacted, and it is less likely to cause serious change to its colour. For example, if you get a small transfer of yellow ink into red ink on your inking plate then it will make next to no change, but if you get a tiny amount of transfer of red into yellow then the colour change is dramatic. So, think before you ink, and plan the order in which you roll out your ink.

Activities

Printing and binding your own notebook

If you are into letterpress then you probably are going to be into stationery, so what's better than a great handmade custom notebook? Working with simple size formats to start with is easiest, so we will be making an A5 notebook. As you get more confident in printing and binding, you can start playing around with mixed paper stocks and changing size formats. For an A5 notebook the paper sheet size needed is A4, which is readily available in accurately pre-cut reams.

It's always worth making a basic mock-up of what you plan to make, in this case fold a sheet of A4 in half (into A5) then write 'front' and 'back' on the correct sides as a visual reference to avoid printing in the wrong position. Once you've worked out your design, write it down on the front of your mock-up, refer back to it as you set up and lock out your type. If you are not sure how the size of the type or the layout will work as a cover design, simply lay your type out on top of your mock-up, step back, and see how you feel about it.

I usually only print notebook covers in one colour as they tend not to need any more for the way I design, as I like to use coloured card. If you print too many colours onto coloured card, it can look messy. Once your design is printed in the perfect spot, leave it to dry properly overnight. Sometimes you will want to quickly make a notebook to check the finished design, which means working with a smudgeable print. For this you can use my cheat's way of working, which is to use Post-it notes to cover the wet print. Post-it notes are great as the glue is so low-tack that it doesn't damage the card, plus they're very cheap.

With your cover print either dry or covered in Post-it notes, let's think about binding. I use 120gsm paper, though inexpensive 100gsm printer paper is fine if you're making yourself a notebook. The thickness of your paper will affect how many sheets you want to use – the thinner the paper the more sheets you may want to add to make the finished notebook feel substantial for its intended purpose. I use nine sheets of A4 paper per notebook, with a bright yellow sheet of paper as a central sheet to help to divide up the notebook for when I am working in it, and to make it a bit more interesting.

Selection of hand printed and hand bound notebooks.

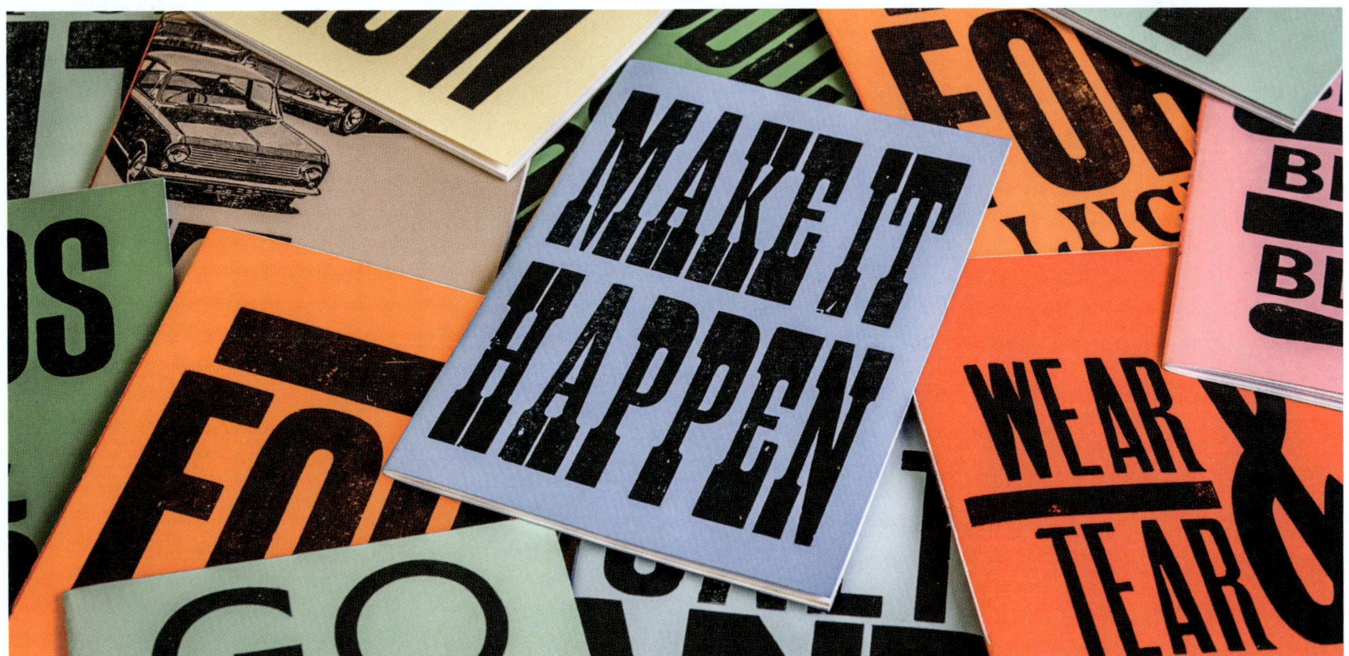

Creasing your pages and cover

The first thing you will want to do is crease and fold your sheets of paper and card. There are several ways to do this.

(A) If you have an Adana and you are making a slightly smaller notebook, you can use a type-high length of flat brass to crease on your press. Start by removing your inking rollers, put the length of brass into the chase just like it was type, surround with furniture and lock in place with quoins. Now when you tweak and set up the Adana's pressure, you are setting up a creasing form. Use a couple of pieces of backing card and you don't need to go too hard on the impression to create a workable crease. Set up the location of the crease as if you were printing.

(B) If you have a hand guillotine, on the flat part of the guillotine where the paper rests, you may see some lines cut out into the plastic. These are for creasing paper, using a 'bone' (a creasing stick). Simply put the paper in the correct location so it lines up exactly with where you want the crease to be, then hold the paper or card in place and run the point of the 'bone' folder into the creasing groove, this will give you a nice crease into your paper that you can then simply fold over.

(C) You can make a very cheap and easy alternative, with some grey board or other thick card to act as a backing sheet. Cut two other pieces of slightly thinner card (ideally 1mm thick) and double-sided tape them to the backing sheet of card with a 1.5/2mm gap between them in the middle. This creates your creasing line; you can then draw the exact point where your sheet needs to sit for the perfect crease. It is surprising how well this works, I do this when I am working on projects that require odd creasing for a small number of prints.

If all of these options seem too much, there is the simple solution of just folding over the paper or card on your worktop and flattening out. This option can leave a poorer-quality crease, particularly on card, as it is thicker and harder to force over without damaging the fibres that make it. I'd always recommend using a 'bone' folder.

Contrasting stitching thread colours on notebooks.

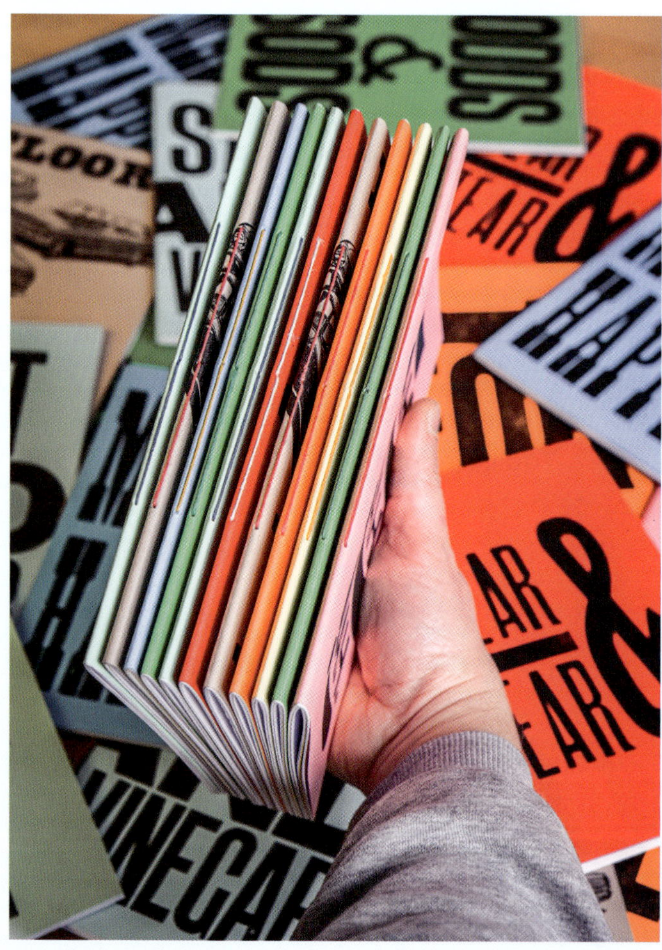

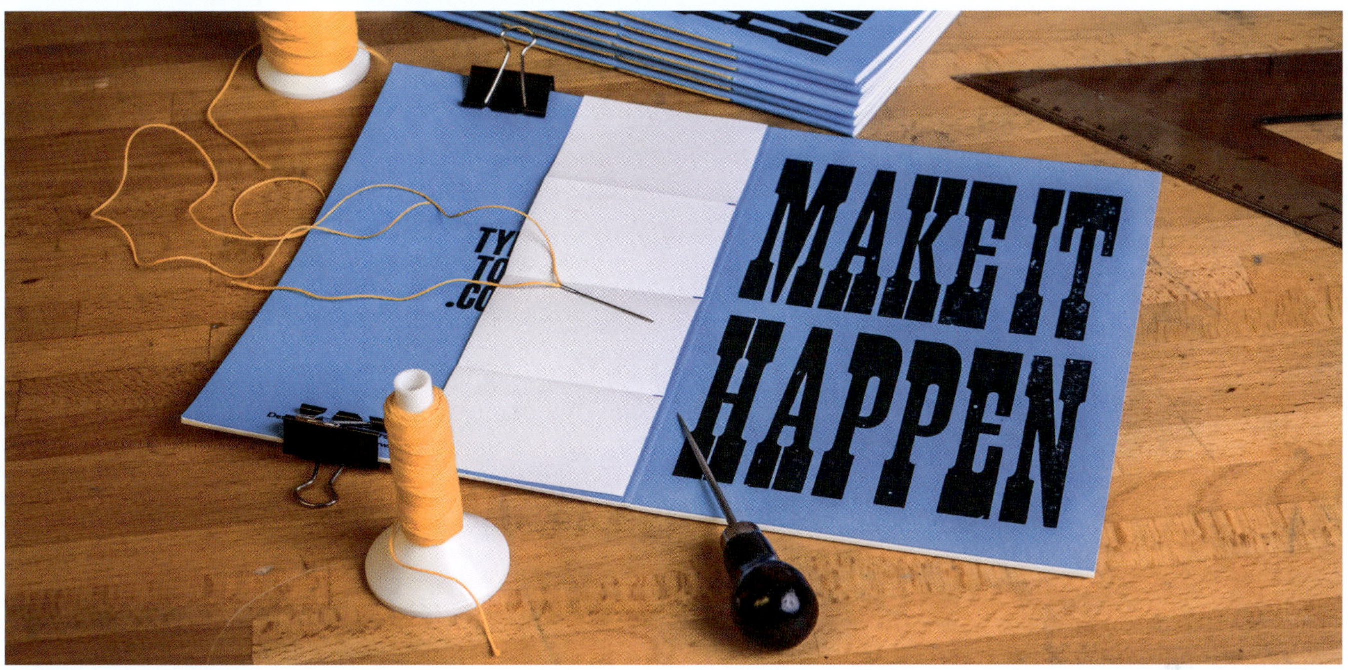

 Tools and materials for binding notebooks.

Tools and materials

To bind your notebook, you'll need the following: bookbinding thread, a bookbinder's needle, an awl (a hole-piercing tool) and two bulldog clips. Bookbinding thread is made from linen and comes waxed or unwaxed. The wax helps the thread run smoothly when you are pulling it through your sewing hole, and keeps the knot you will tie at the end grip tighter. You can buy thread pre-waxed, or you can use a stick of beeswax and lightly run the thread over it before you bind. You can also bind without waxing the thread if you want to cut down on processes, or you do not have wax or waxed thread.

I like to use a heavy gauge thread 18/3, as with this binding technique the thread is exposed, and I like to use a bright thread that really shows on the edge. You can use thinner gauge binding thread or at a push any thread you have, but bookbinding thread is a lot stronger than standard thread. If you are binding with a more common thread, be aware not to pull as tightly, as you can snap the thread.

For the sewing needle I use a standard straight bookbinding needle. If you have a quick search for bookbinding needles online you'll see there are quite a lot of different types, which is why I went for a very basic one when I started and just stuck with that. I recommend buying a mixed size pack of needles, you usually get around five different needles for a couple of pounds, so it's not a big investment. The awl is what you will be pushing the holes into your paper and card with. You can buy them at art or binding suppliers but also at DIY shops; again, you do not have to spend a fortune. The bulldog clips are for holding everything together when you are binding.

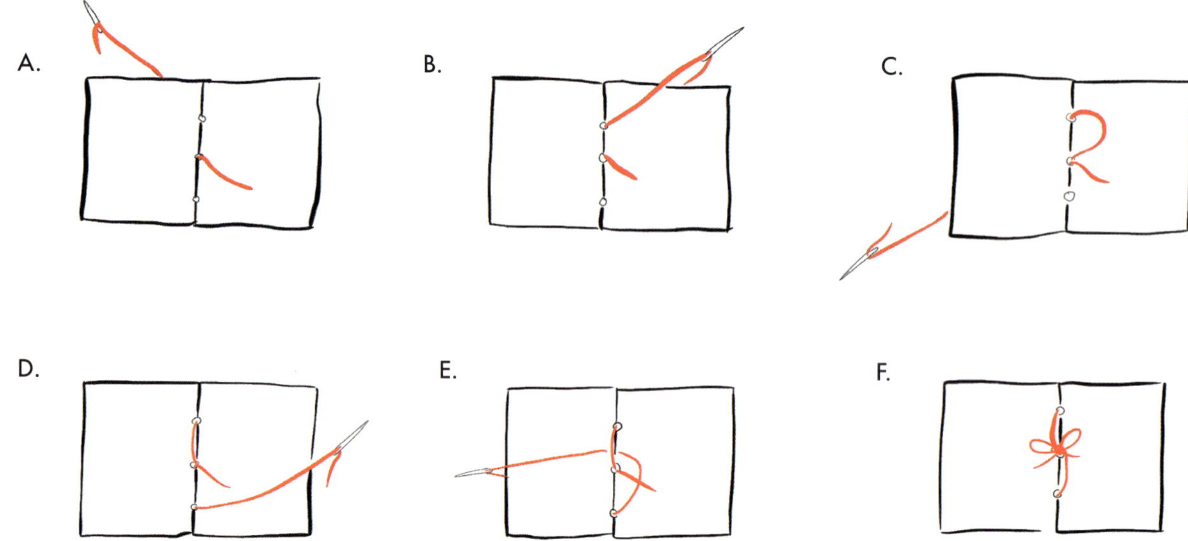

Stich from the middle out, from top into centre of notebook, back out through middle, in through the bottom, loop under, tie off and trim thread.

Binding your notebook

So, you have printed your design, gathered your pages and got all tools and materials ready, now it is time to bind up your notebook. The first thing to do is to take all your notebook pages and put your cover design facing up on top of the pages. Then apply your bulldog clips, one on each long edge of the back cover area around a quarter of the way into the sheet. This means all your pages are secured, but the clips are not in your way. Now you need to work out where your binding holes for stitching are going to be, for this notebook I use a very simple but nice-looking figure of 8 that only requires three holes to be pushed in using the awl. This is a simple binding method, but as with most simple things in craft and design, when they are done well, they look great.

The easiest way to work out the perfect location for the holes is to take a sheet of paper the same size as the finished notebook, in this case A5, and fold in half from top to bottom, then half again the same way. When you unfold, you'll be left with three horizontal folds on your portrait A5 sheet. These folds are perfectly spaced for your binding holes – line this sheet of paper up to your cover sheet and push the awl into the card in the middle of your crease lines.

Please be sure to have some waste card, a cutting mat and/or a piece of old wood under where you're pushing your awl down, to avoid damage to your worktop. Using the awl is a bit of a skill as it is tempting to open up the holes at this point to make binding easier, you can do this just a little bit, but if you make the holes too large then your binding will be a little loose, as you want to pull the thread snugly through the notebook's paper and card.

Next, pull out the thread to around three times the length of the notebook's binding edge (around 60cm). This gives you a bit more than you need but not too much waste. Thread your needle, and starting at the middle hole, push from the inside of the notebook out, then go up to the top hole and push from the outside in. Ensure you don't pull it all the way through. Now comes the tricky part – you need to push the thread back through the middle hole and you really want to push the thread alongside the previous thread not through it.

A tip for this is to hold the thread in the middle of the book, lightly pull and hold towards the top of the book then try your best to run the needle back through the hole next to the existing thread. Now you just need to pull the thread through, go to the bottom hole and push from the outside to the inside. Loop your needle and loose thread under the secured middle thread, remove your needle (so you won't be able to stab yourself), pull tight and tie off. You will notice that the book binding thread grips and holds tightly by itself, which makes this process quite easy.

Cut off any loose ends of thread, remove your bulldog clips, fold your notebook over and fold along the crease line using your 'bone' folder. You now have a bound notebook. I make batches of notebooks, so I take 12 notebooks and put them in a bookbinder nipping press to compress the fold, then cut clean the staggered page sides on my guillotine, to make everything look nice and tidy. You can do this at home by placing your notebook under a weight overnight, then cutting the edge with a metal safety ruler and a craft knife. Now you have your very own notebook to record your future ideas in.

Stack of finished notebooks.

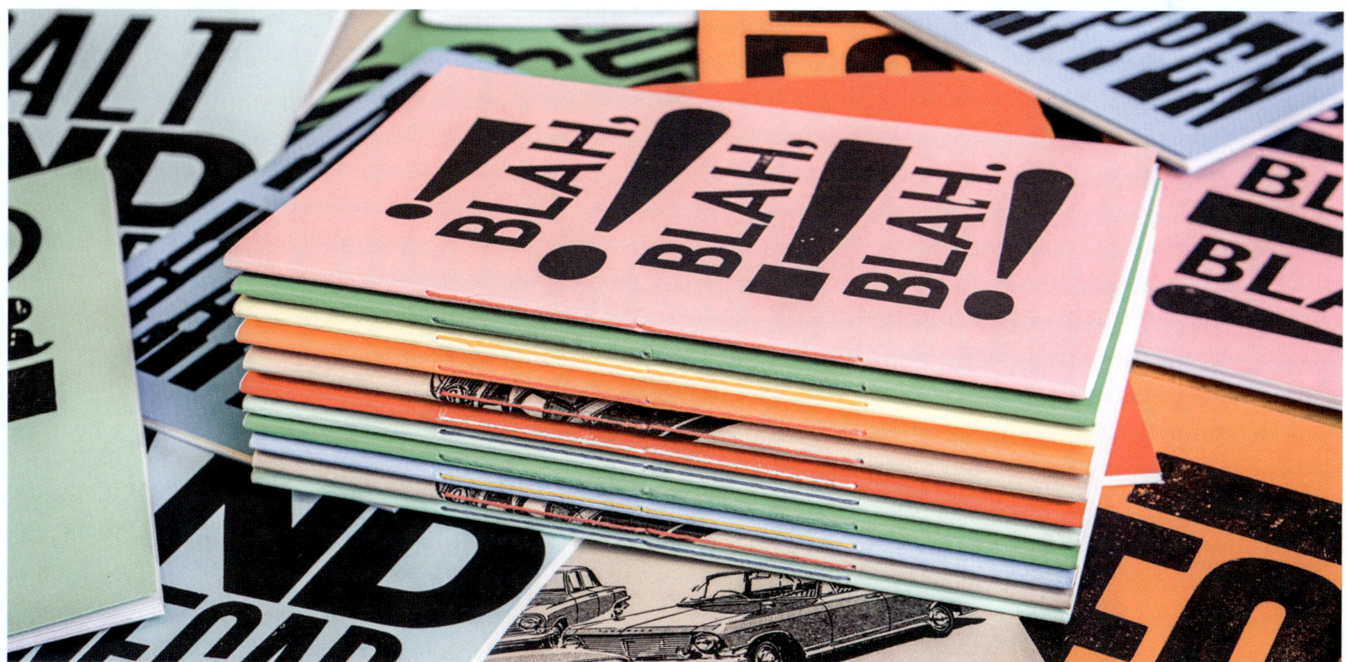

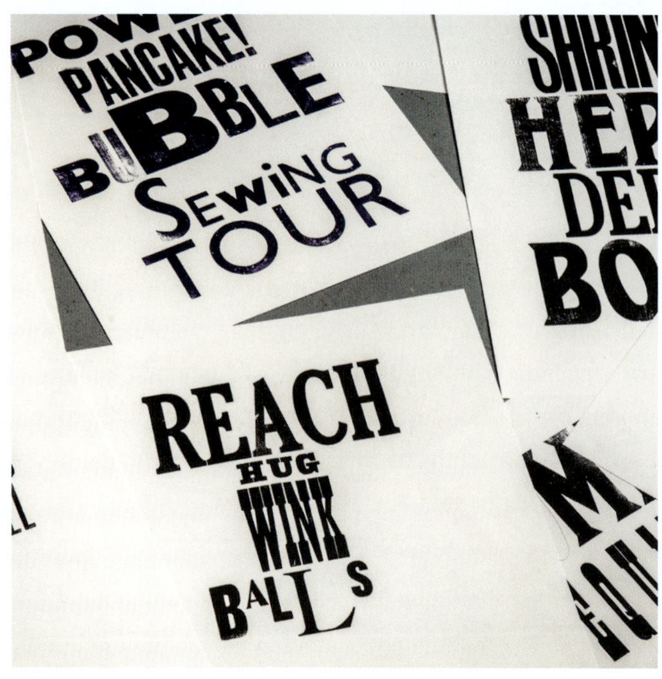

 Random word poster prints.

Random word poster print

For me this is where I really practiced printing with wood type, using random words that ultimately mean nothing, have no emotional connection or baggage connected to them. It just leaves you as the creative printmaker in a position to just work with what takes your fancy. Try not to think too much, just choose and put your type down on the bed of your press. Lock out your type in whatever composition feels right and go ahead and pull prints.

This process means you learn and practice to print, tweak designs and do all the small adjustments that turn a basic and lifeless print into a fully-fledged letterpress print, showing all the history and character that your type has to offer. I genuinely think this helped me both as a designer and as a printer, it's made me very quick to just do and not overthink. This aids the natural element of designing and the artistry of contemporary crafts. It's about being in the moment and working with what you have, purely on instinct, allowing that experience and practice to work for you when you are designing and printing something you really care about. You can of course use these random word prints to experiment with different colours and effects. I do this often at the end of day when I have had a few different inks out, using up any leftover to just play around with before I clean up.

Print some ephemera

Print something just for the sake of it, play around with strange and wonderful formats. I like printing notelets (basically a postcard-sized print that can be used for many purposes). I can never have enough, they're great to have to hand, and I like to send them out with a product order. A good notelet is passable as a greetings card, and they are perfect as a thank you card. Use a size of card that's easy to find an inexpensive envelope for, 6 × 4 inch is a good old-fashioned postcard-ish size, this seems to always work well with letterpress type (not too square and not too wide). Notelets are a great use of waste material and it's nice to develop a collection of different card stocks to work with. Ideally the card should be around 300gsm to feel quite solid – anything thinner does feel a little flimsy.

If you don't fancy printing yourself some notelets try making up a fun business card for a fictional person, maybe they have a dynamic job that you always fancied and a great name... say Little Jimmy Two Feet – the back-flipping tightrope walker of old London town! It's always good just to have some extra practice, it's a bit silly but makes for improving your skills while having fun.

Once you have enjoyed printing some crazy cards, you'll feel ready to move on to printing yourself some truly amazing hand-printed business cards. There is no greater sin, in my opinion, than the letterpress printer that does not have handprinted cards! If not a business card, print a calling card; these are quite a nice way of leaving both your details but also an introduction when trying to make new contacts or doing some direct selling. They contain a little bit more information about what you do than a standard business card, and you can have some real fun with it and go a little wild. Bookmarks are also another nice thing to print and also a good excuse to use picture blocks, as an old found picture block often seems to be about the perfect size for a bookmark.

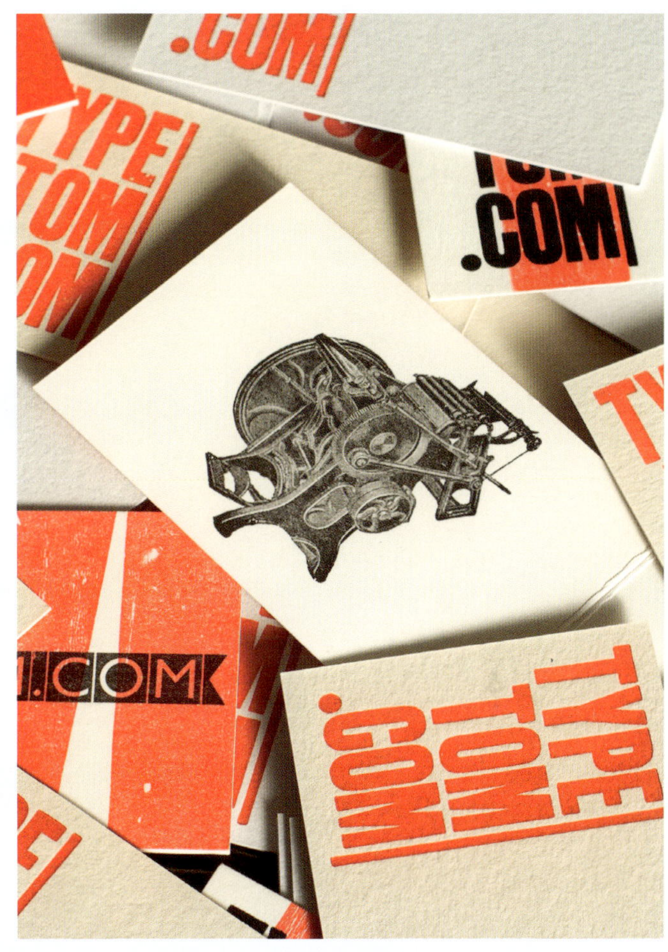

Typetom business cards various designs.

Notelet card design.

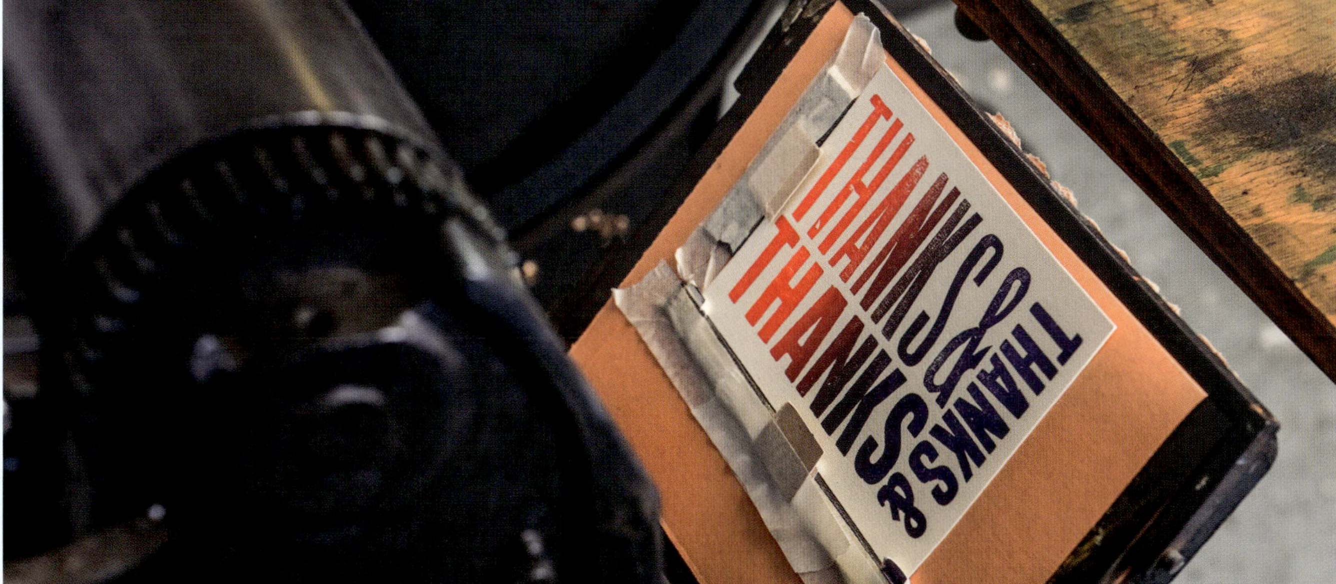

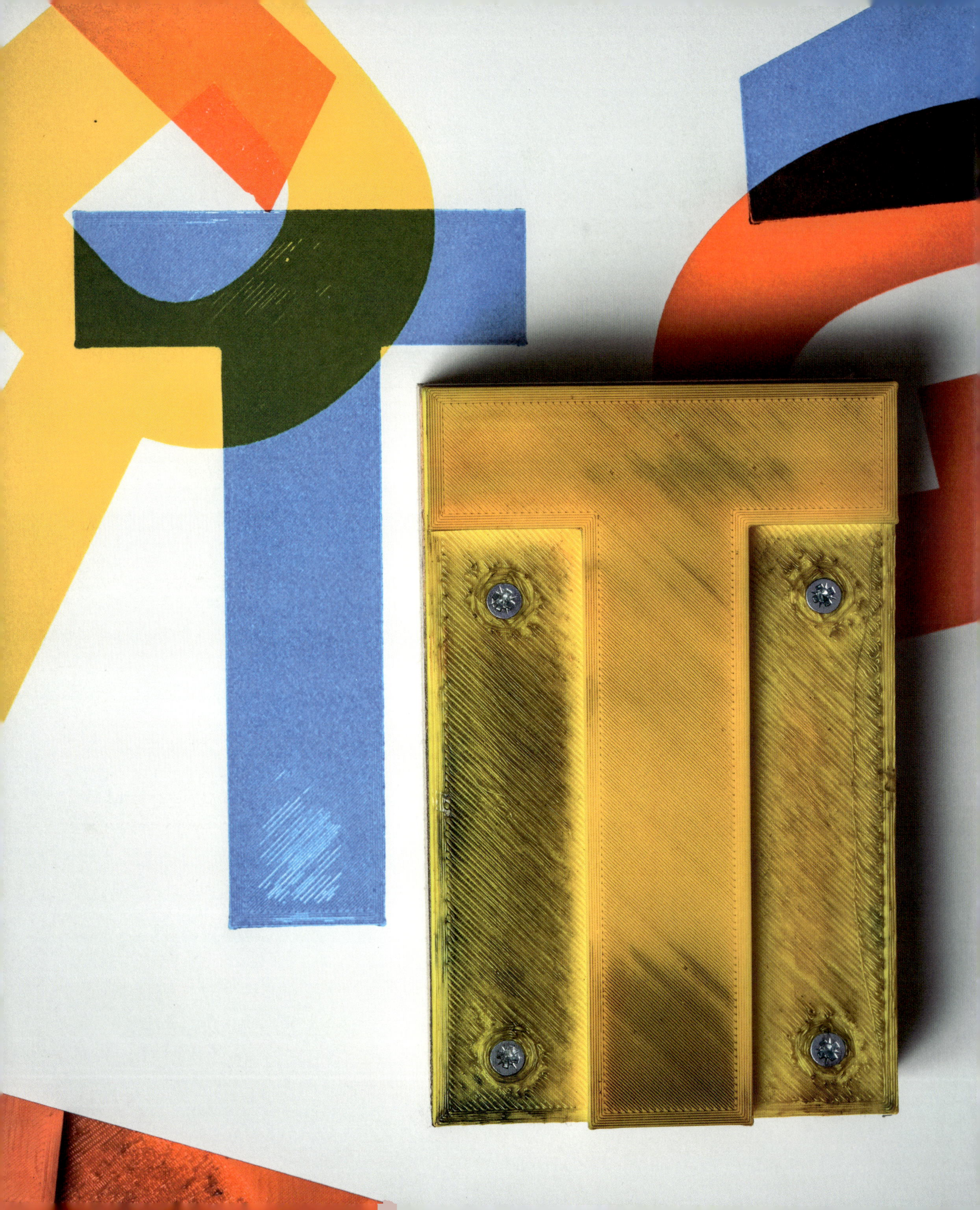

9

Futureproofing letterpress

When you start working with any traditional craft you start to really feel its history. With letterpress it's the enormous amount of highly skilled labour, from an industry that played a massive part in shaping the social climate, and the developing world industries. It always impresses me how well things were made and how much work went into making them.

The idea of a highly skilled craftsperson working 200 years ago to make something that has passed the test of time, still working for its purpose today, fascinates me.In our modern throw-away society this is the opposite of not only what and how we currently make things, but how we feel about things.

The longer I've worked with letterpress, the more I feel how important it is that we don't lose skills and knowledge, but develop and grow from them, work out new ways to share them, and grow into the future.

I find it reassuring to know that all the machines that I have collected in various states of disrepair are now in the best condition that they can be, and hopefully they, if given the chance, will long outlive my short existence.

We need to use modern technology to its fullest, to understand how it can help preserve what we already have, and to create exciting new options for others; to not be stuck in the past, but to work in the present and plan for the future. For a while I have been experimenting with what's possible using modern technology, integrating it into my creative practice and being happily surprised by what I've discovered. I've often found myself down the rabbit hole of what is possible, spending extensive amounts of time playing around with my 3D printers and CNC machine to see what one man in a workshop can do. In this chapter I'll break this down into some of the processes I use and where I have used them.

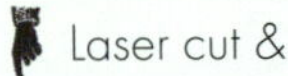
Laser cut &

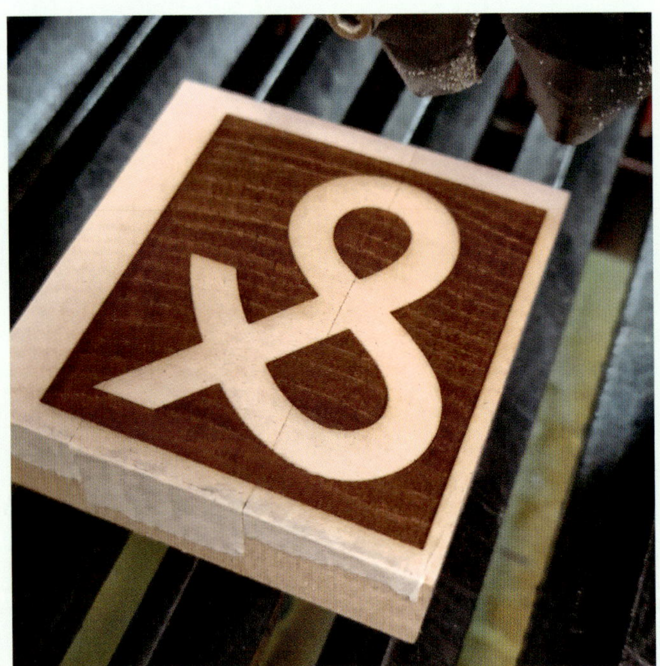

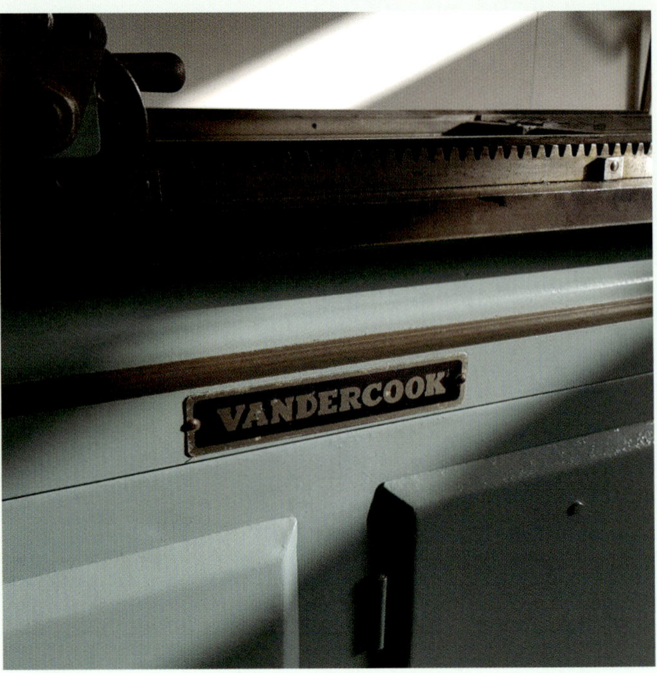

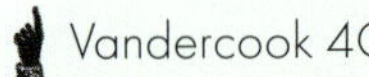
Vandercook 4C.

3D printing

3D printing has a bad reputation for low-quality and weak parts. The truth is that it's like many other processes, it can be as good as you want it to be. I work with quite standard 3D printers that use rolls of filament. There are other types of 3D printing which involve resin and they work differently, but these processes have issues with fumes, so I stay away from them. On my machine, layers of filament are printed from a spool (roll), building layer upon layer to create a design. Melted hot filament is pushed out through a tiny nozzle so individual lines of hot PLA (plastic) stick at first to the bed of the 3D printer, where layers are formed on top of each other, bonding as they go. These outside layers are then infilled with filament in different patterns and percentage of density that you can set in the slicing software. With 3D printing you design on computer software. For those dipping their toe into the world of 3D

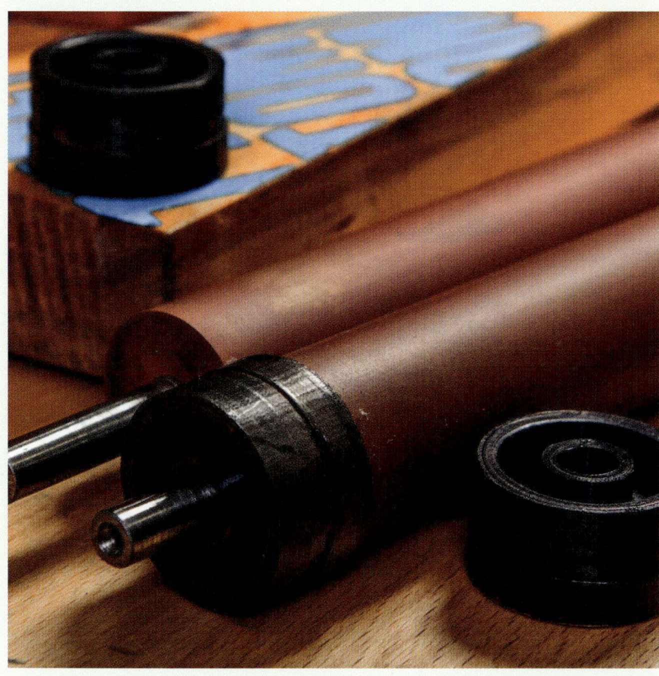

3D Printed Adana roller trucks.

designing, I would recommend starting with the web app Tinkercad, as it is user-friendly and free to set up an account.

You quickly learn with 3D printing that accuracy is everything. The joy of designing in software is that you can make shapes that are set to very fine tolerances. For instance, on one of my Adanas, the roller truck (used to carry the rollers over the type at the correct height for inking) had broken, and I was trying to source original sets but was struggling with delays in shipping, and finding both original used sets and new stock was very expensive. Using a pair of callipers I carefully measured out all of the different parts of an existing Adana truck that I had, and recreated it as a digital design in Tinkercad.

Taking this file into slicing software (software that takes a 3D design file, changing it to G-code, coding that controls a 3D printer), I then tweaked the settings and set the percentage infill to be high around 75 per cent density and printed them. With the first printed pair, some tweaking to the design was required. I have always found a small discrepancy between design and printed sizes – this is only very small in real world terms, being fractions of millimetres, but when you are making something like a roller truck, these small differences are important.

After tweaking the design files, the second print was done, and I had perfectly working roller trucks – they also looked the same as the originals. The important thing I have learnt from 3D printing is that how you set up the print dictates the quality of the print, so I set a high infill percentage and high-quality print settings, making strong and accurate printed parts. I was surprised by how strong the prints were – I tested them in a very old-fashioned way, clamping them in a vice and hitting them with a hammer. It proved that in the hands of people who take care in what they are making, technology can be utilised to make perfectly strong parts. 3D printing is a slow process, and it does take a lot of time to build larger parts, but while the machine is working you can be spending time on something else.

Parts are not the only thing that 3D is useful for, I have worked on printing new type. Even with the tiny nozzles on the 3D printer, small type is very difficult, and for me there's not enough detail. So, I went big and tried making equivalents to wood type. After experimenting, I found my own way to make working type. Using a PEI build plate (this is a smooth metal sheet that I swapped for the textured surface plate bed that came with the machine),

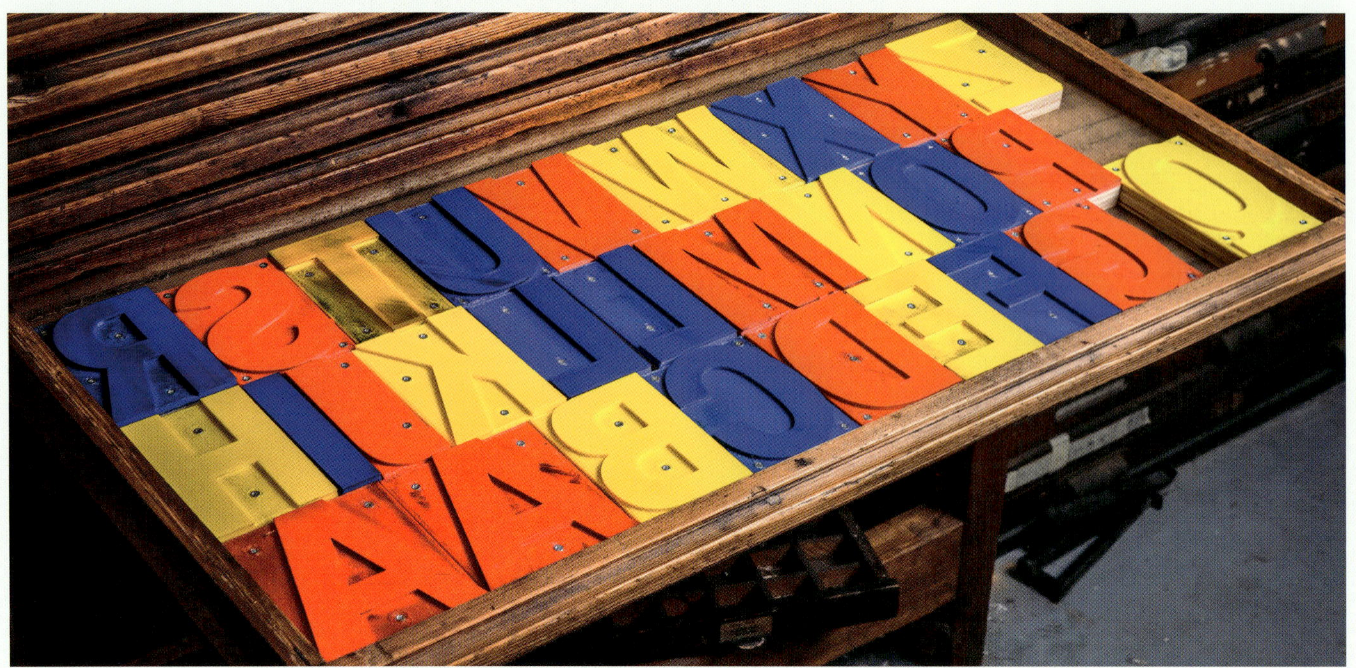

3D Printed full font and closeup on letter T.

I print the large letters upside down so that the end printing surface is the first layer that prints on the 3D printer, giving me a very smooth top surface when removed and turned over. I also only print the letter part to be around 5mm thick overall, then mount to 18mm ply.

I measure the thickness of the plywood very accurately and counter the thickness of the 3D part to get to type height. This is the joy of 3D printing; you can quickly alter files to counter tolerances in materials that you are using. The end result is large moveable type – sure, it's not 100 years old and it's not wood, but it can be set in the same way as setting traditional wood type. Interestingly, the 3D printed type, when lightly inked, in some spots shows a slight imprint of the process, the printing tracks. I really like this; I think the juxtaposition between old and new is very interesting and something that the unknowledgeable would probably not even notice.

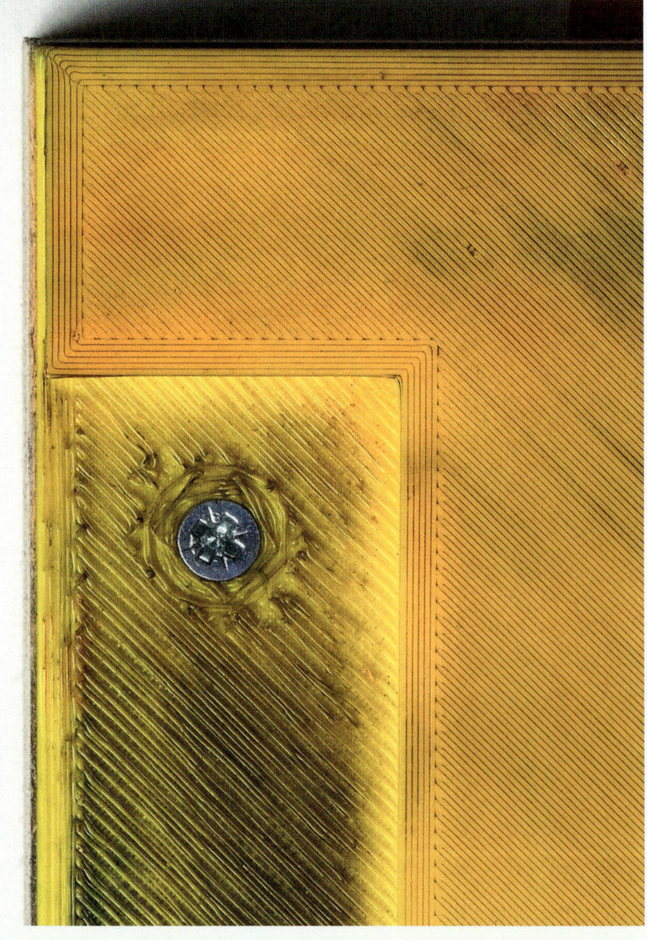

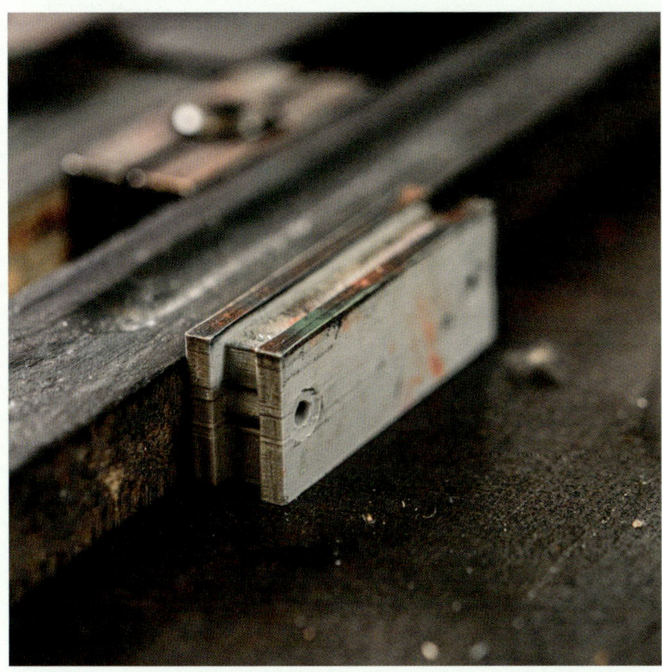

3D printed galley magnets.

The most daily-used items that I've printed are galley magnets. I didn't have a large number of original ones in my collection, as they are expensive to purchase. Taking an original galley magnet, I digitally re-designed it, adding three holes in the bottom of the design for high-strength cube magnets to be forced into. I tweaked the design to ensure the magnets were very tight, and I put a single drip of super glue in each hole before driving the magnets in using my bench vice. The end result is a very usable and traditional-looking galley magnet. I also found that with the surround of the magnets being PLA, plastic based, if you rotate the galley magnet on the bed of your press it doesn't scratch it, which was a bit of an issue with original ones where everything was made out of metal. My problem of lacking galley magnets is no more.

CNC machines

CNC stands for computer numerical control, which in layman's terms means a computer-controlled drill bit. Earlier in the book we looked at how wood type was originally made with a pantograph, and as we look at what a CNC machines does, we'll see a clear crossover in technology. I own a CNC machine, which I purchased as a kit from Inventables. It was a challenge to build but it has been very reliable to date.

I always felt that CNC was the way forward when it comes to making new wood type, as you're not changing the materials that you are working with, nor the process of how the type is made as you're using a drill bit that cuts the wood. What you're changing is the machine and how that process is controlled. This really interests me, as the end product is not different to the original, so there's no reason why new

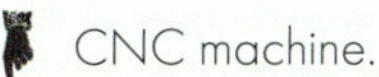

CNC machine.

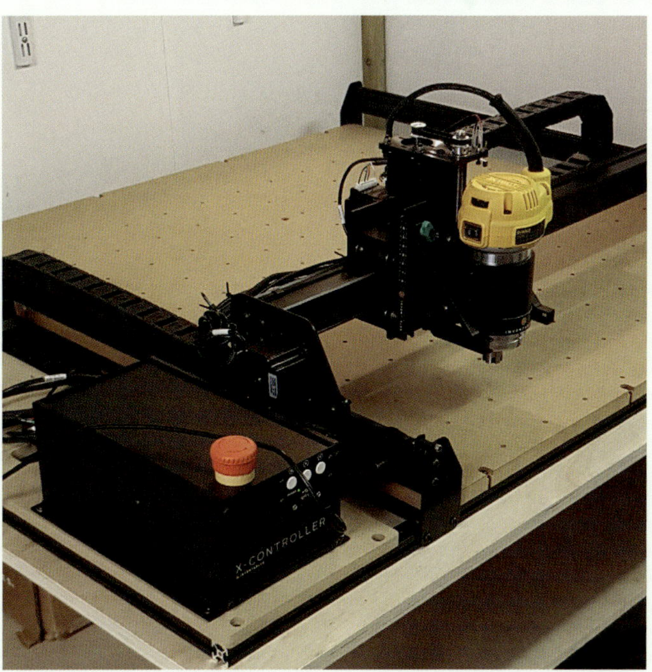

wood type cannot last just as long as original wood type when made with the same level of care and consideration.

I have tested and found that my CNC machine is very capable of making new wood type, but as with original wood type, there is a level of craftmanship that needs to be applied, it is the small touches that really make the difference. The major issue is getting the timber to type height. This sounds easy enough, as with a CNC machine you can use large one-inch router bits to plane the surface of the timber, however this is very time consuming, and whilst they are very accurate machines, hitting that perfect type height is not as easy as you would first think.

I have moved to using a 'planer thicknesser' to carefully and slowly plane down the timber to get the thickness as close as possible, then sanding with a power sander. Finally, I switch to hand-sanding with a block and different grades of sandpaper. This gives good accuracy and an excellent finish to the top surface of the timber. The timber then has layers of shellac applied by hand in a traditional French polish style (I apply around five layers of shellac) to have the wood finished and ready to cut. A lot of work goes into the process of prepping the materials before cutting the type happens.

Learning and developing new processes takes time, and I realised that I would need additional machines to be able to start to make myself new wood type. This involved sourcing and buying a traditional letterpress type saw (a powered circular saw which clamps the timber when cutting, designed for the purpose of cutting out the blocks after cutting the letter's shape) and a better-quality type block gauge. Finding these objects is part of the collecting process and it was not easy, quick or cheap to source them.

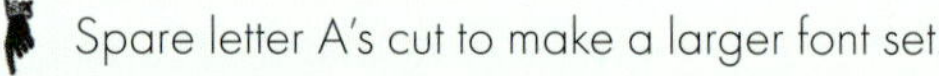
Spare letter A's cut to make a larger font set.

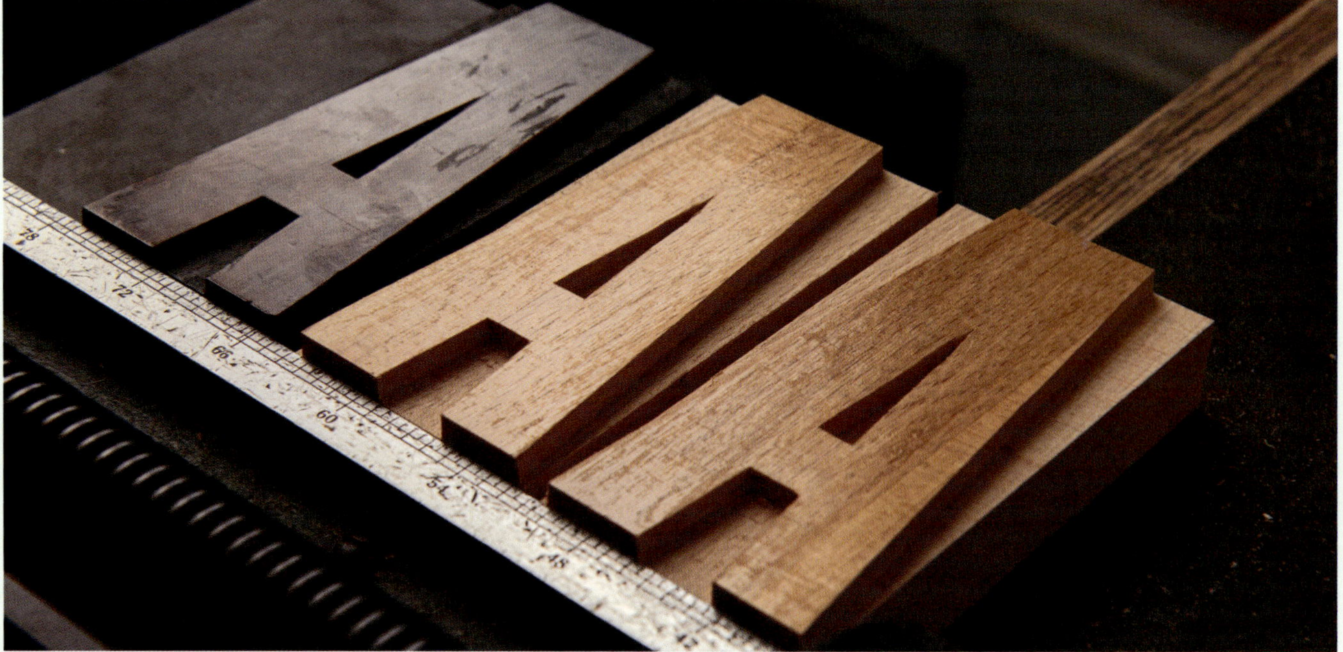

After experimenting, I focused on fonts in my collection that were missing letters. I took specimen sheet prints of the existing font, then in Adobe Illustrator retrospectively re-designed the missing letters. For this process a bit of investigation is good, if you have a collection of old type catalogues, often you can find the font, then be able to see exactly how the missing letters were designed, making the design process easier. If not, you use the existing letters from the font that you do have, as your guide, to unpick how it would have been designed. Once you have this design created digitally, you run it through the CNC software, cutting out the desired letter or letters.

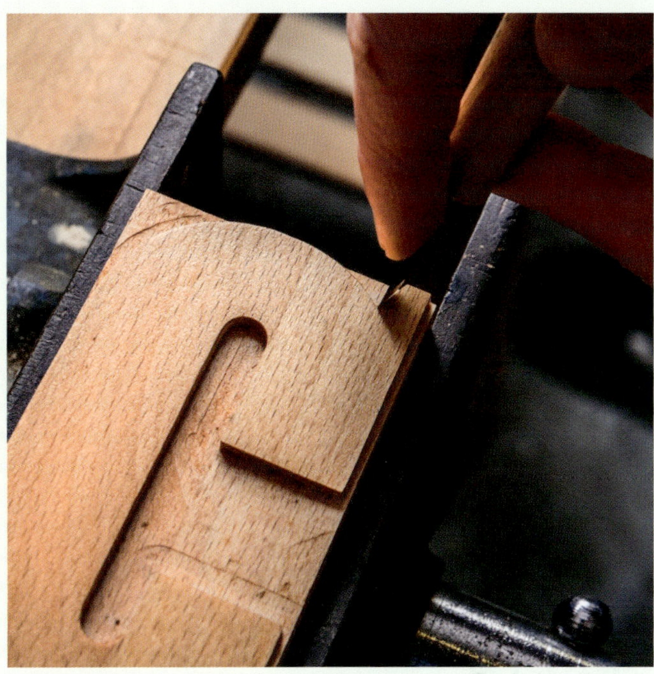

Hand finishing internal corners of letters.

As with traditional type making, after the letters have been cut out with the router bit, they all have to be hand-finished with the tight internal angles of the type needing to be trimmed with a hand blade. Cutting into these corners to get a sharp point that the CNC's round router bit would never be able to cut, this is nerve-racking and awkward, but very rewarding. The type then has to be cut out on the type saw to give you your finished moveable wood type.

Final cuts to letters on a printer type saw.

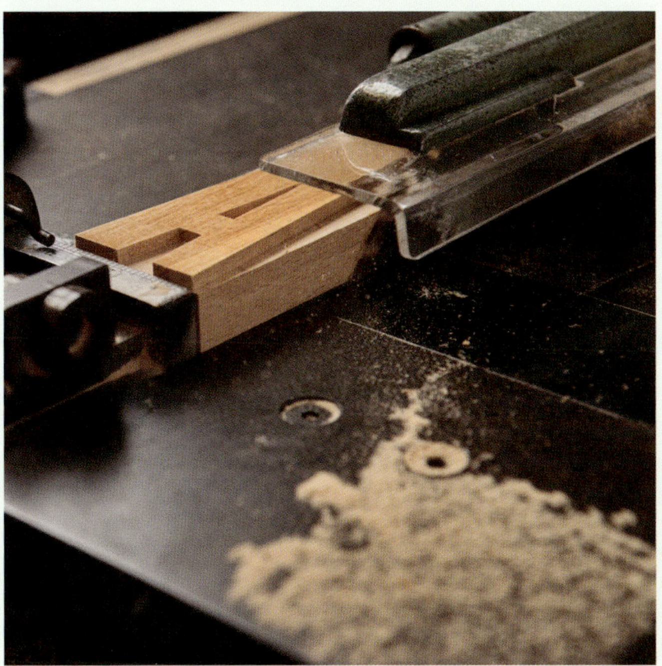

Whilst CNC does offer the ability to create new wood type, there are a lot of processes that go in to making this possible that can't be overlooked. Another application that is possible with more industrial CNC machines, is to cut out machine parts in metal. You see people online reporting common breaks to parts that would be possible to cut with CNC. For example, when people are moving a proofing press and they drop it and the side end plate cracks, it always cracks across the plate where the rods are bolted to. These parts are notoriously hard to have welded and often re-break due to the large forces put upon them when used. Breaks like these can make a machine a write-off.

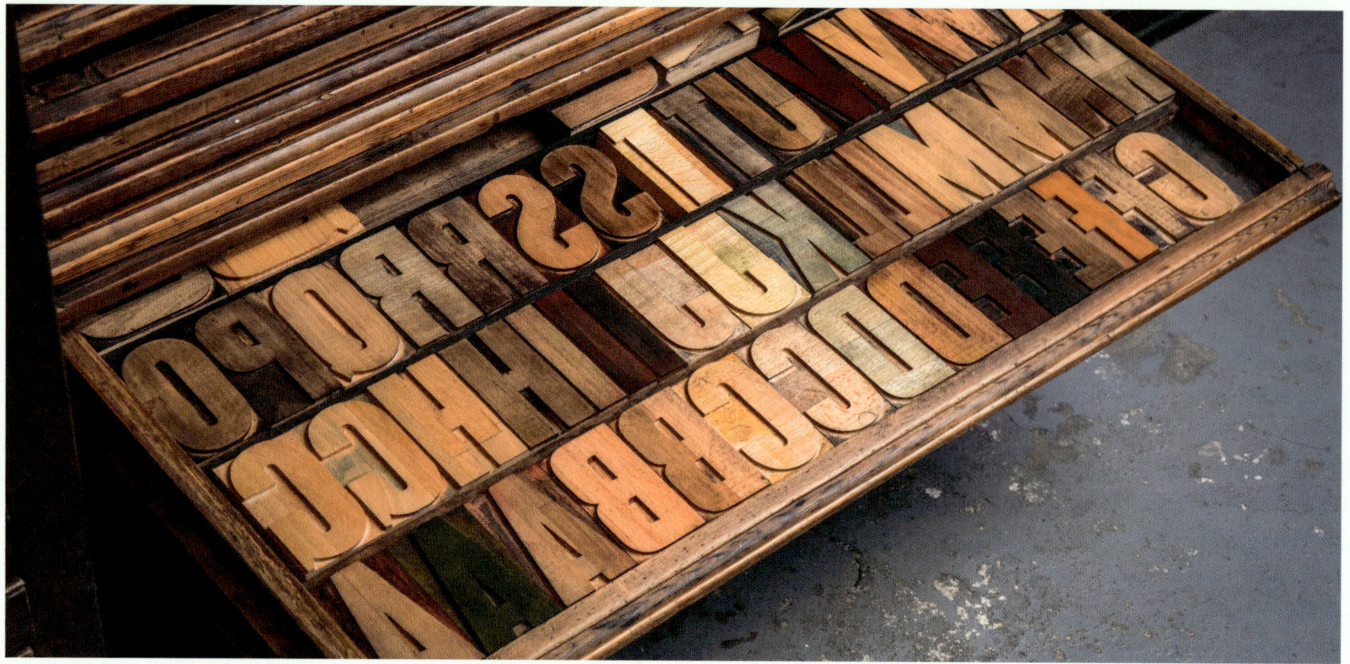

Full font cut with CNC, starting with a handful of original letters.

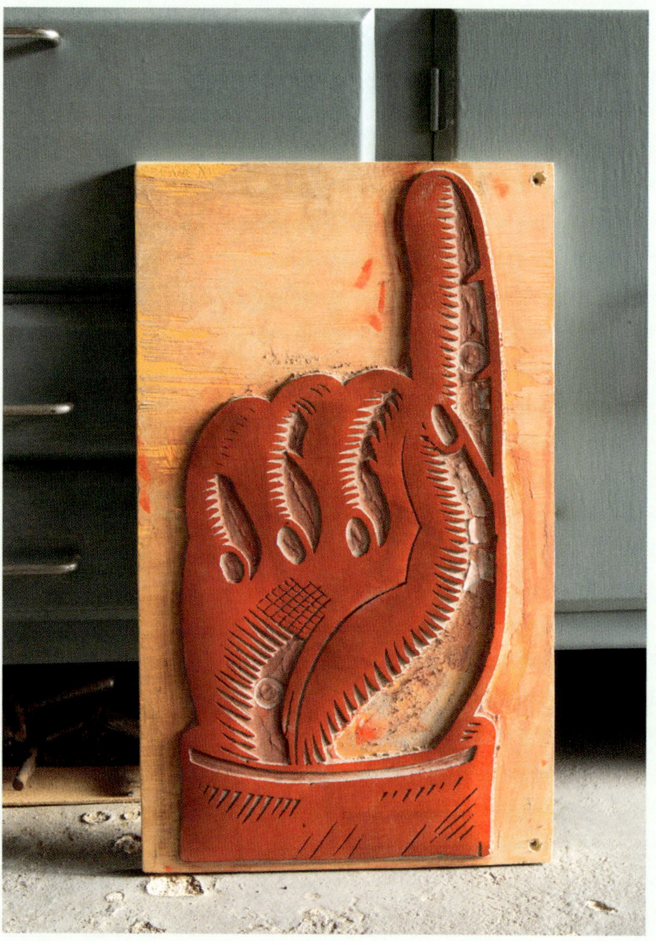

Higher-end technology would be able to cut suitable steel parts that would be more than adequate replacements, though financial costs would be high.

Another fun thing I tried out with my CNC machine was to try cutting lino. It is messy and you do need to use a spiral router bit, running the machine a little slower than normal. I took a print from an ancient printer's manicure (pointy finger), scanned it into my computer spending very little time altering it digitally, and just cut it out to see what was possible – I was impressed. I then cut a massive version and printed it on a suitably large Columbian press, all of which worked really well.

CNC cut giant printer's fist.

Laser cutters

Laser cutters are perhaps my least favourite of new technology, they are expensive to buy and you need to be very aware of what you're doing, as there are some real health and safety issues to consider. I don't own a laser cutter as my needs didn't justify the large expense. Laser cutters are great at cutting thin materials like laser plywood and acrylic but when it comes to thicker materials, then really, they're not the right tool.

I've played around with lasers to cut acrylic letters and then mount them to blocks of timber to make them type-high. These can then be printed and do print well, but gluing down the shaped pieces is fiddly, and they don't look particularly appealing. I have also taken blocks of timber that I have planed and sanded to type-high, then used the laser to burn out replacement letters for incomplete sets.

This does work, but it is very slow as the laser has to run back and forth burning out large areas of wood to create a wood type letter. When you work with timber you're very aware that it is a natural material, which often has knots and flaws. When you are burning out areas with a laser you'll find sections that are physically tougher, where the laser does not cut as well.

For me, lasers are not the answer to my problem of how to make new wood type, although I have seen others online getting great results. I do think the process of laser cutting is fascinating, and the technology, as with all modern production methods, does have crossover uses, but not really in my practice. For example, I have seen people engrave lino to create lino printing blocks with halftone in them, which look really interesting.

Laser cut replacement/missing letters for wood type.

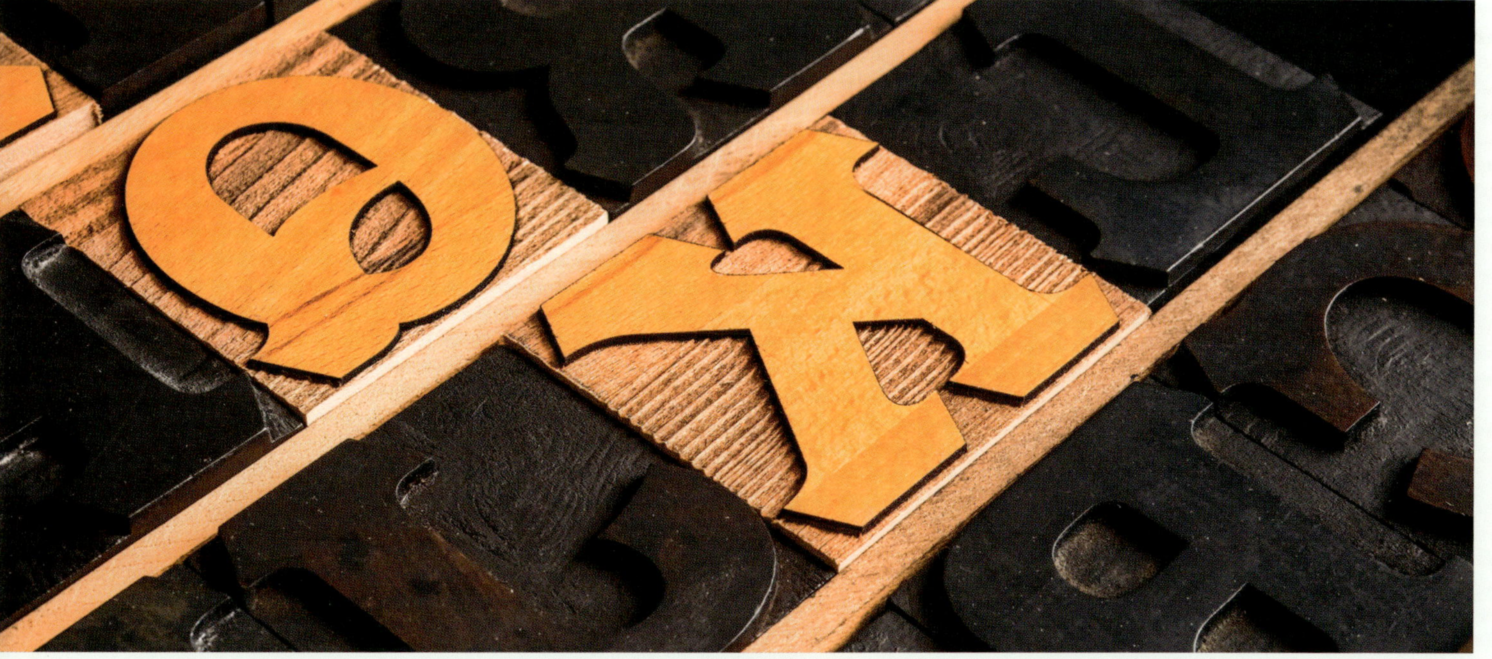

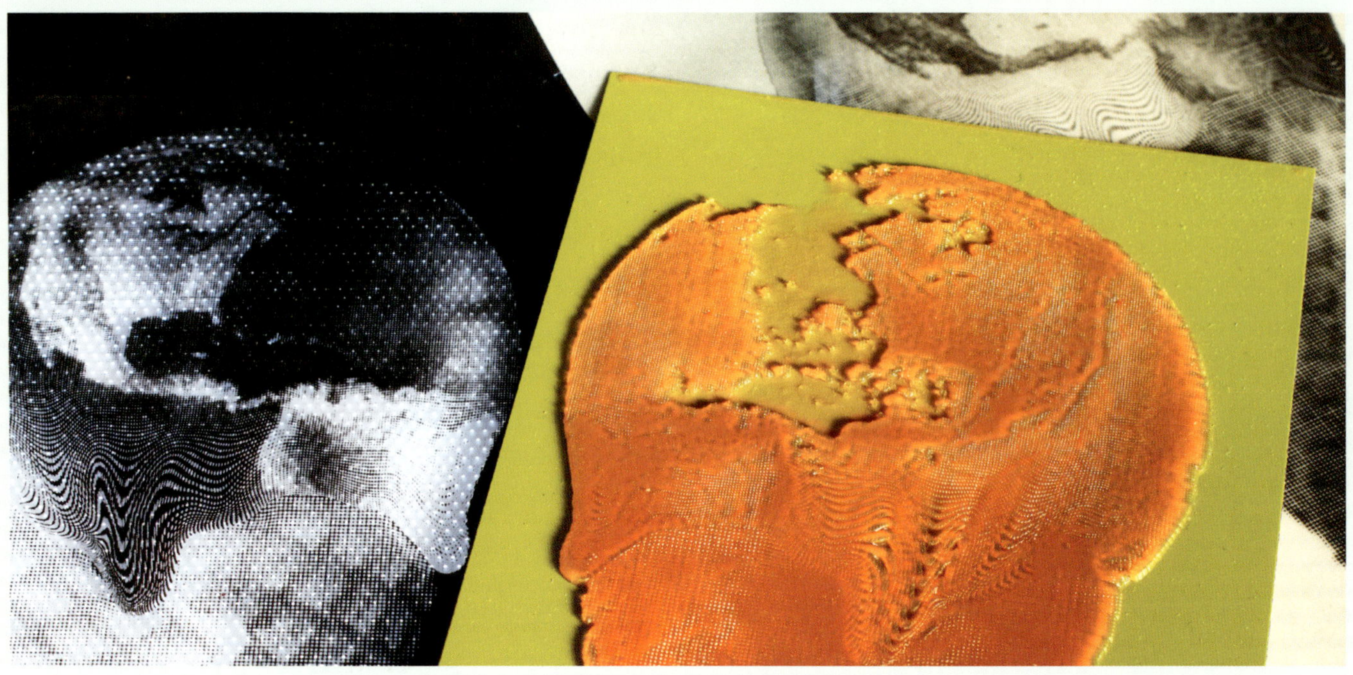

Photopolymer printing plate, negative and computer printed film and corresponding print.

Photopolymer printing plates

Printing plates are very useful in the modern era of letterpress printing, sometimes you really have no choice but to use them – when a client wants their company logo printed, you can't easily refuse. Letterpress does need to work in the modern world, to not just be seen as a craft of the past that holds no place in the present and future. I have no problem using photopolymer printing plates in my workshop when the need is there. In fact, I decided a while ago to teach myself how to make them in a very low tech and low investment DIY way. The process is not as difficult as you may think, but there is a knack to making them and they can be tricky for some designs.

The basic process is that you need to get your design printed onto acetate, film or at a push, some good quality tracing paper. From there you need to produce a negative film, then make your negative using a UV light to expose the printout onto the film. Exposing UV sounds very complicated, but it really isn't. You can buy exposure units online that are usually aimed at screen printers, but there are some smaller UV units out there for photopolymer plate making. I ended up making my own exposure unit out of a face tanning lamp I found at a boot fair. When I moved into my current workshop there was a very old and broken light box, I removed all the lights and mounted the UV tanning lamp inside. A vacuum bed is ideal for holding the plates and film together when exposing; for this I made a very simple wooden frame out of some timber I had lying around, then purchased a vacuum bag that is intended for storing clothes. I opened it up, glued it to the frame, applied a line of foam tape to the underside of the wooden frame to help form a vacuum, then the frame was hinged and clamped down.

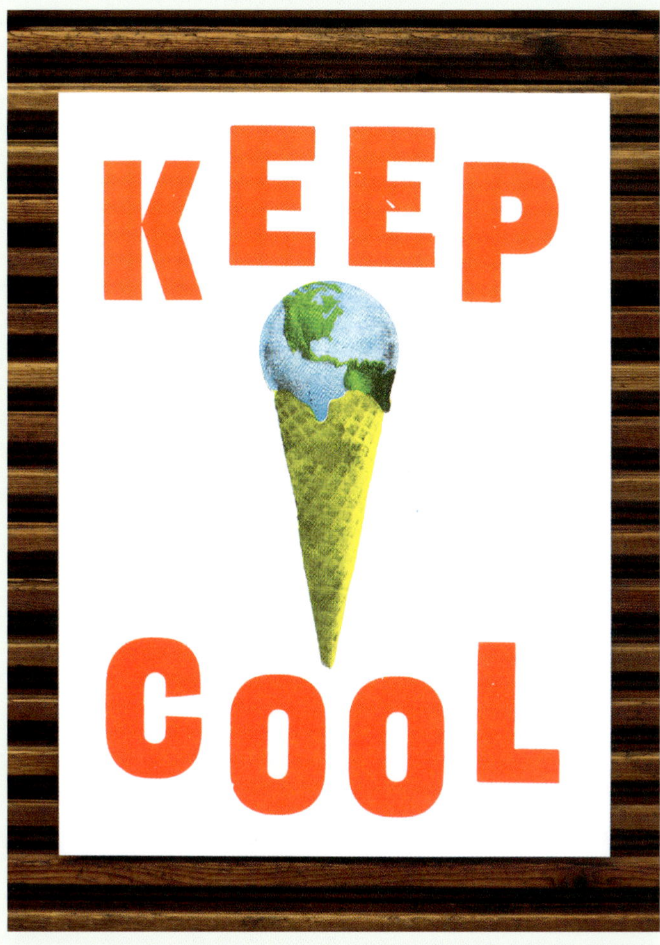

DIY exposure unit.

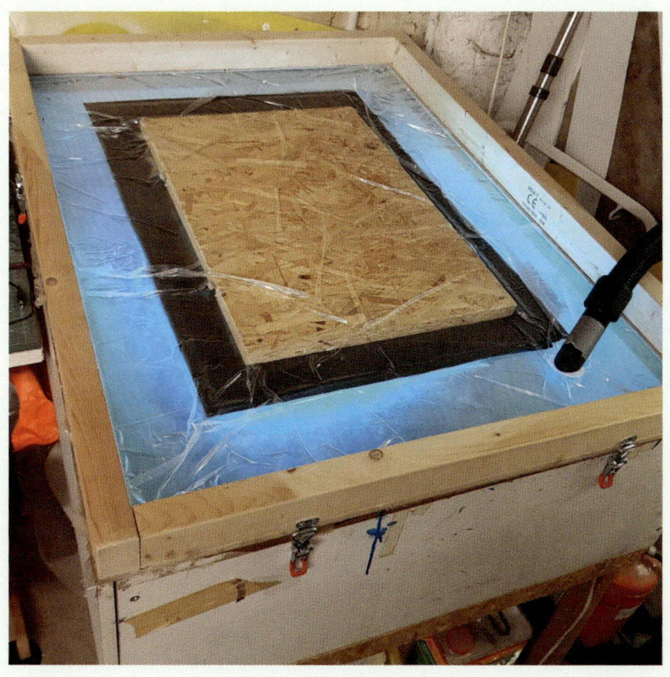

The power for the vacuum part of my UV unit is obviously my workshop vacuum cleaner! It all works a treat. Originally, I made it just to test out the idea of making my own plates, but seeing as it works well, it seemed pointless in purchasing a new machine when my DIY bodge does the job.

You'll need to take a piece of unexposed negative film and your printed acetate, placing them together with the printed sheet on the bottom of the exposure unit, and shine UV light on them. The light passes through the printed acetate sheet transferring the black printed design onto the negative film. Remove the negative film, placing it on a sheet of glass, spray it with a developer chemical and leave for a short period of time, then wipe gently with a cloth to remove the unexposed areas, once all of your print is revealed you then rinse this sheet and leave to dry. This process of exposing the negative to UV is what you then repeat with the unexposed photopolymer printing plate.

Exposure times are important: depending on the exact materials you have purchased, they will vary. Once you have exposed your photopolymer plate you need to wash away the areas that have not been exposed wearing gloves, using warm water, a litho sponge and a brush. You can buy expensive brushes but I use a boot-cleaning brush that is not too hard-bristled and a litho sponge that cost around £3. You simply submerge your plate and slowly and gently in circular movements rub away the layers of polymer that have not been set by UV. This is tricky and does take a bit of practice, you need to be careful as it can be easy to push off small text, and things like full stops are very easy to lose!

Once you have finished, leave to dry. When this is fully dry you should give it a second exposure in the UV unit or leave out on a windowsill with direct sunlight, if you're not using it straight away. The second pass just makes sure that everything is fully exposed and hardened.

Making my own plates has changed my way of designing, and on occasion, it has made designs that I want to print possible. I have always loved half-tone printing in old magazines, where the misalignment of plates caused an almost 3D effect. Half-tone plates were not something my plate maker would do, due to failure rates, so that route wasn't an option. When making my own plates I am not limited by what others won't make, for instance I designed 'the earth', which was a melty ice cream using halftone photos and some dodgy Photoshopping. I then produced the photopolymer halftone plate, making other layers for a multi colour and multi print effect. I really enjoyed the difficult alignment of the layers to get the effect I wanted. Sometimes it's worth taking the extra time to learn new skills like this, so you can get a greater understanding of the process and improve your practice.

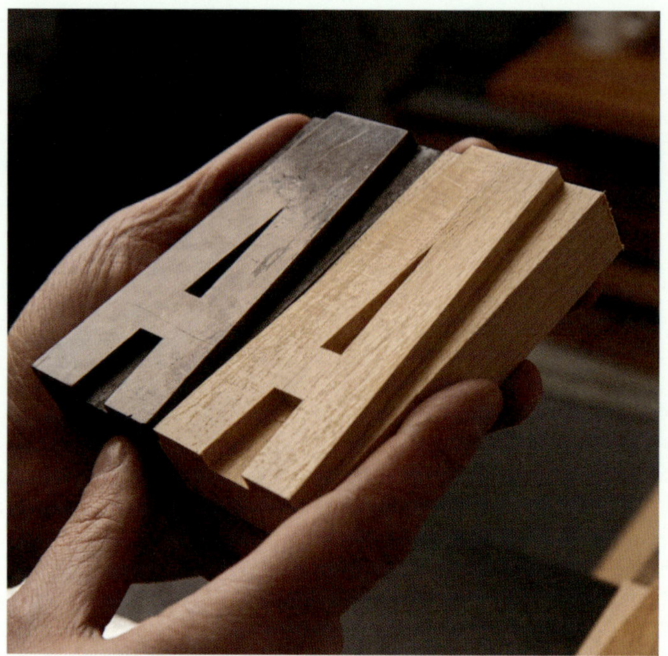

Checking letters for quality.

Traditional skill

Having spent a number of years playing around with new technology, I have found that with all machines, they are only as good as their operator. It takes intelligence and planning to use them to their full potential. Knowledge, hand skills and traditional crafts like wood working, designing, engineering, mathematics and learnt experience is paramount. Working with modern technology has driven me to learn new practical skills, so I can new concepts. Traditional skills should not be overlooked when thinking about how we all can take part in futureproofing crafts for future generations. Just the act of learning and passing on knowledge is a way of futureproofing; we should all share knowledge and learn from each other's experience. Whilst I have learnt a lot from using modern affordable technology, I have also learnt more about hand craft skills and how they work together.

The crossover and in summary

After my foray into the world of 3D printing, CNC and laser cutting, I started to look at how they could all work together and what could be created. During the Covid pandemic I had to shut down my normal business activities and work from home. I took this time to work on some ideas.

One of those ideas was to make a small light-weight printing press, a new press, designed for the modern world. I also had a self-serving motivation, as I often have to lug around heavy printing presses to teach in different locations. So, I looked at my Vandercook, my proofing press, and what I do, and just started seeing what I could simplify. I asked myself which parts could be made with a 3D printer, what could be cut out with my CNC machine. I ended up designing and building my F-Press, which has a thick aluminium roller with a steel shaft that mounts into high-quality bearings, held in place with 3D-printed parts that squeeze into CNC-machined parts cut in 18mm plywood. I took every part of what I loved about my presses and redesigned them to look modern.

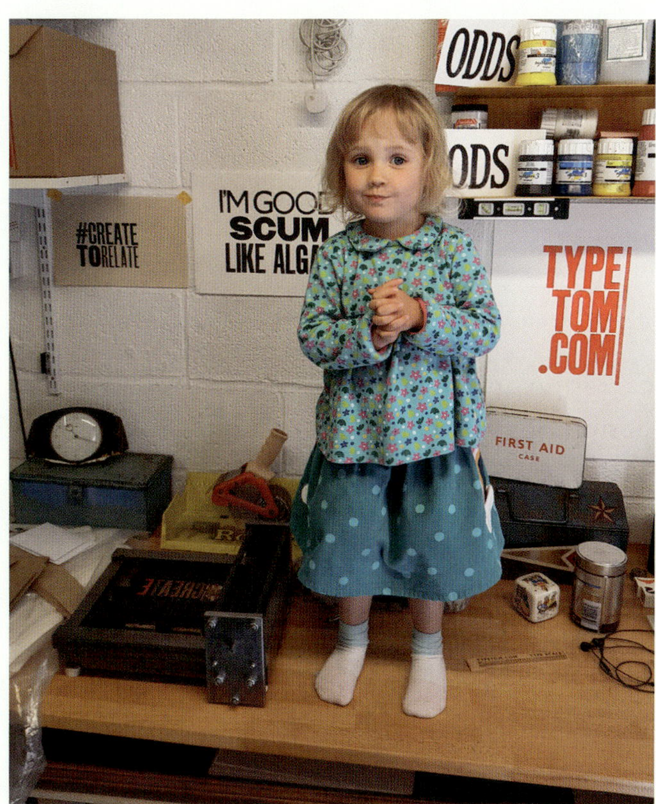

Edie research and development session with mk1 F-Press.

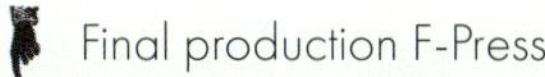

Final production F-Press.

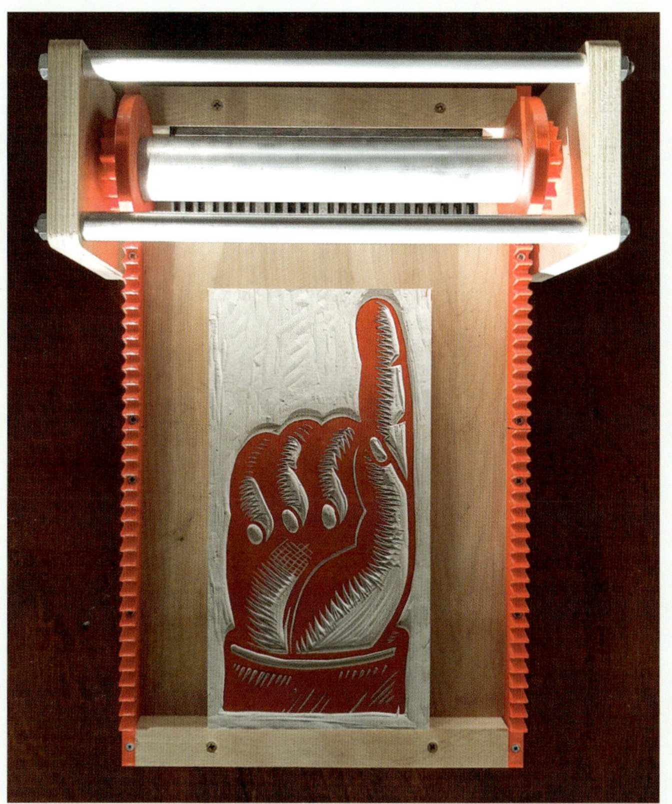

I asked my then four-year-old daughter Edie for feedback, which is always a unique experience. The F-Press ended up being brightly coloured and fun, but still a nicely working press for small prints, taking a standard A4 paper size. It will always be the moment when I looked beyond the individual processes towards the bigger picture, to see how letterpress can have a future and how new generations of artists, designers, printers and enthusiasts can take their first steps in printing. Interest in crafts is on the rise, and I've seen this particularly with letterpress over the last 20 years. I sincerely hope this continues, and that the true values of creative output are embraced, that future generations have the opportunity to learn about the enriching value of art, design and crafts.

Index

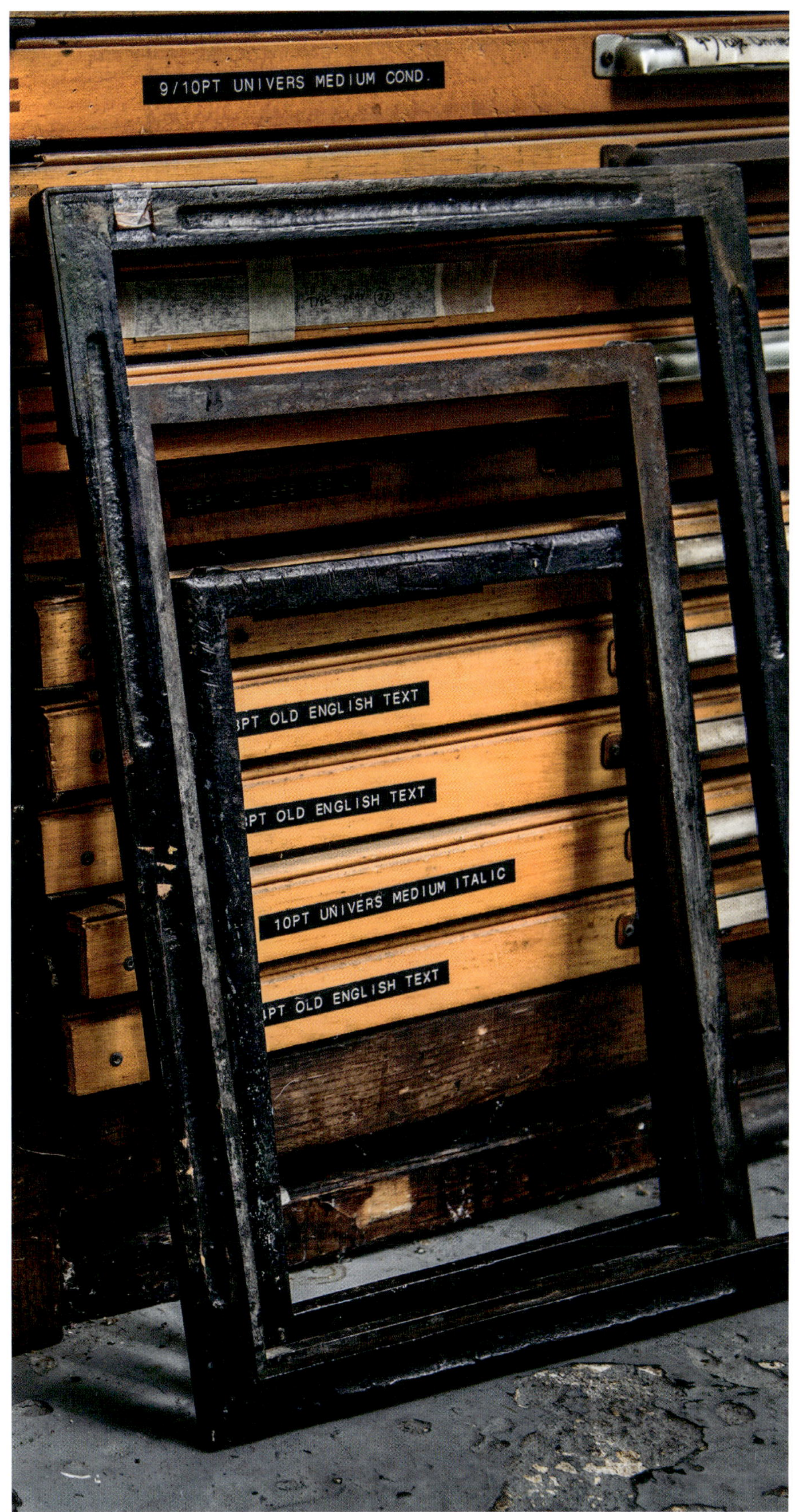
9/10PT UNIVERS MEDIUM COND.
PT OLD ENGLISH TEXT
PT OLD ENGLISH TEXT
10PT UNIVERS MEDIUM ITALIC
PT OLD ENGLISH TEXT

First published in 2025 by
The Crowood Press Ltd
Ramsbury, Marlborough
Wiltshire SN8 2HR

enquiries@crowood.com
www.crowood.com

British Library Cataloguing-in-Publication Data. A catalogue record for this book is available from the British Library.

For product safety-related questions, contact: productsafety@crowood.com

ISBN 978 0 7198 4553 6

Cover design & typeset by Tom Boulton
TYPETOM.COM

Photography by Rob Luckins

Printed & bound in India by Parksons Graphics

Acknowledgements

Writing a book is something that I never thought about doing, I would like to thank all at The Crowood Press for asking me to, and for making it possible. A massive thanks to all my family for their time, talking over ideas, proof-reading, and generally putting up with me for years spent printing and talking about print, and to my wife Catherine and daughter Edie for their constant encouragement and boundless patience. The great pictures in this book were taken by the talented eye of photographer Rob Luckins (robluckins.com), thanks for far too many photoshoots! Finally, to anyone I have met, interacted with and those who have come to take part in a workshop with me, getting hands on and inky. The hands-on element of what I do is everything, the years of doing and creating are not possible without these small moments of encouragement that you all bring.

Thanks.

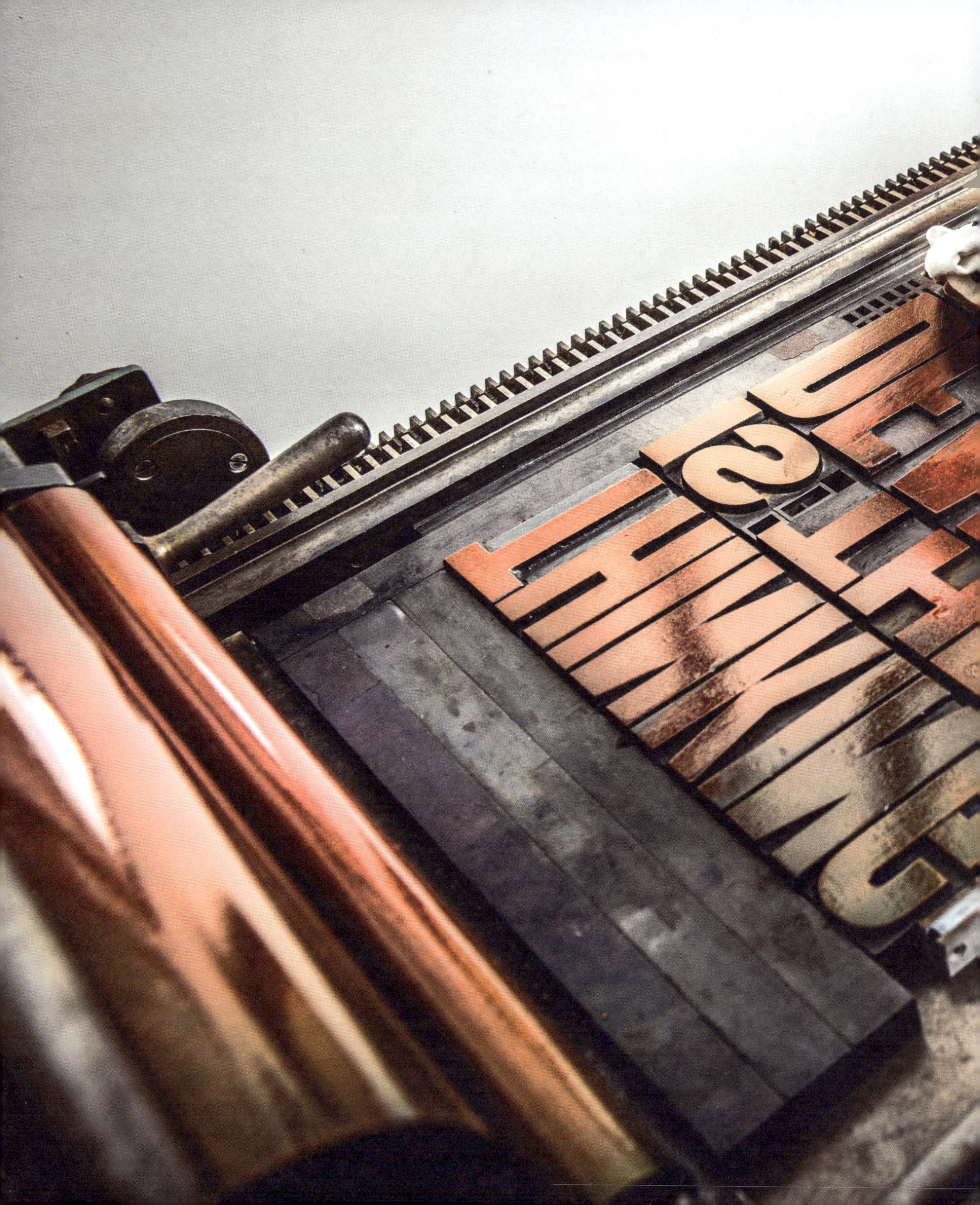